# COMMIT SOCIOLOGY

## Volume 2

Introduction to Sociology | University of Toronto

First Custom Edition

Christian O. Caron & Robert Brym

NELSON / EDUCATION

# NELSON / EDUCATION

ISBN-13: 978-0-17-656324-0
ISBN-10: 0-17-656324-5

**Consists of Selections from:**

*New Society, 7th Edition*
Robert J. Brym
ISBN 10: 0-17-650999-2, © 2013

*Seeing Sociology: Core Modules, 1st Edition*
Joan Ferrante
ISBN 10: 1-133-96316-1, © 2014

*Sociological Odyssey: Contemporary Readings in Introductory Sociology, 4th Edition*
Patricia A. Adler, Peter Adler
ISBN 10: 1-111-82955-1, © 2013

*Sociological Footprints: Introductory Readings in Sociology, 11th Edition*
Leonard Cargan,
Jeanne H. Ballantine
ISBN 10: 0-495-60128-4, © 2010

*Images of Society: Readings That Inspire and Inform Sociology, 3rd Edition*
Jerry P. White, Michael Carroll
ISBN 10: 0-17-651416-3, © 2013

*Society in Question, 7th Edition*
Robert J. Brym
ISBN 10: 0-17-650998-4, © 2014

*Sociology in Our Times, Sixth Canadian Edition*
Jane Lothian Murray, Rick Linden, Diana Kendall
ISBN 10: 0-17-651000-1, © 2014

*Sociology: Your Compass for a New World, 4th Canadian Edition*
Robert J. Brym, Lance W. Roberts, John Lie, Steven Rytina
ISBN 10: 0-17-650386-2, © 2013

**Cover Credit:**

©Ted Soqui/Corbis

# Table of Contents

# Globalization

# CHAPTER 19

# GLOBALIZATION

**Josée Johnston**
UNIVERSITY OF TORONTO

- Globalization is a term used to describe how the world "shrinks" as capital, ideas, corporations, commodities, and workers rapidly cross vast distances. You will learn about the complexities of globalization, a term much used and abused, and acquire a working definition of it.

- Globalization is not a distant force but a real-world phenomenon that affects you daily as you eat, drink, work, and go shopping. By the end of the chapter, you will better understand how globalization relates to you as a consumer, a worker, and a citizen.

- Globalization is dynamic because it is contested by different social forces promoting different kinds of capitalist development and social organization. This chapter will give you a conceptual framework that will allow you to appreciate the "top-down" forces of globalization that promote the expansion of global markets and the "bottom-up" forces demanding greater democracy, social justice, and sustainability in the global system.

# INTRODUCTION

## THE BURGER AND FRIES GO GLOBAL

Think about your average fast-food meal: a burger, fries, and a pop. This is the food of North America—simple, greasy, fast, and familiar. Maybe fast food has something to do with the sociology of health or the sociology of food, but what does it have to do with the sociology of globalization?

It turns out that globalization has a lot to do with everyday events like eating fast food. The average North American meal travels more than 1600 kilometres to reach your dinner table, so there is a good chance that your burger and fries have been *globalized*.

Let's start with the burger. Although Canadian ranchers pride themselves on their cattle exports, at least 30 percent of the beef eaten in Canada is imported from the United States, Australia, New Zealand, and Uruguay. Even if the beef in your burger did originate in Canada, the process of transforming a cow into your hamburger was deeply affected by globalization processes. Because of global market pressures, the meatpacking industry in Canada was restructured in the 1980s and 1990s; the goal was to cut costs by centralizing production and finding cheaper labour supplies.

SOURCE: © Dwight Cendrowski/Alamy.

Today, just two slaughterhouse companies, Cargill Foods and XL Packers, account for more than 80 percent of Canada's beef-slaughtering capacity. The small town of Brooks, Alberta, is home to Lakeside Packers (XL Packers bought Lakeside in 2009, and controls 47 percent of meat packing capacity in Canada) (National Farmers Union 2009). Global restructuring in the meatpacking industry has also meant a shift in the global labour force. Thousands of people immigrated to work at Lakeside, and many languages are spoken inside the factory walls including Arabic, French, Spanish, Tagalog, Chinese, and Cambodian.

Even a vegetarian's fast-food choices are affected by globalization. In 2001, six vegetarians from British Columbia working with an American lawyer moved to sue McDonald's after it was revealed that McDonald's French fries use beef fat for "flavouring." After hearing the announcement, vegetarian activists in India held demonstrations and attacked a McDonald's in Bombay, demanding that McDonald's leave the country ("McDonald's Apologizes," 2001). McDonald's settled the lawsuit in 2002 by agreeing to donate $10 million dollars to Hindu and other consumer groups.

If our fast food is influenced by global forces, North American fast food also influences global eating. North American markets became relatively saturated with fast-food outlets in the 1980s, so McDonald's made a push in the 1990s for international expansion. The number of countries with a McDonald's went from 59 in 1991 to 119 in 2011 (McDonald's, 2011). Today, McDonald's operates more than 33 000 restaurants, and more than half of these are outside the United States (McDonald's, 2011). McDonald's opens a new restaurant every 17 hours and is the world's largest user of beef. Ronald McDonald himself is the second most recognized figure in the world, next to Santa Claus (Brownell and Horgen, 2004: 58), and by 2005, sales in the United States accounted for only 34 percent of McDonald's revenue (Workman, 2006). For these reasons, scholars now believe we should be studying not only the globalization of fast food but also the globalization of obesity (Sobal, 2001). The World Health Organization (WHO) estimates that 1.5 billion adults over the age of 20 are overweight; a third of them are obese (WHO, 2011).

It turns out, then, that everyday activities—like eating a hamburger and fries—have a lot do to with globalization. In an obvious way, the resources and labour that make up a fast-food meal originate from locations all around the globe. But even when the ingredients come from close to home, the food itself can be affected by global events, such as international trade agreements, European social movements, international labour migration, and faraway protests against McDonald's.

## GLOBALIZATION OR "GLOBALONEY"?

But before going any further, let's raise perhaps our most difficult question in this chapter: What do we mean by *globalization*? It is a frequently heard buzzword, yet there is no consensus on its meaning. The term was coined in the late 1970s, and today there are thousands of globalization books, conferences, university courses, and references in newspapers and magazines, many of which contradict each other. This confusion has led some academics to dismiss the term altogether as a confused mixture of globalization and baloney—what some crankily refer to as "globaloney."

While it is hard to find agreement on a definition of globalization, you don't have to look hard to find controversy about whether globalization is good or bad. A common tendency on both the left and the right of the political spectrum is to depict globalization in simplistic terms. For right-wing free-marketers, globalization represents the welcome spread of capitalism throughout the world. For many left-wing social activists and politicians, globalization is more like a Death Star. In the words of Barry Lynn, former executive director of *Global Business* magazine,

> Globalization is many things, and much has been written about it and said. But throw all the tomes and studies and placards into a giant try-works, and you'll render two simple arguments:
>
> 1. Globalization is good because it spreads what is good in America, such as a liberal approach to business, and McDonald's.
> 2. Globalization is bad because it spreads what is worst about America, such as a liberal approach to business, and McDonald's. (Lynn, 2002: 34)

A primary objective of this chapter is to get beyond this kind of simplistic thinking and gain a more sophisticated sense of what exactly is meant by globalization. The objective is not to provide the ultimate definition of globalization that will ring true for all people until the end of time, but to understand how different political and economic interests struggle to promote their own brand of globalization.

# DEFINING GLOBALIZATION

While figuring out exactly what we mean by globalization is a primary objective of the chapter, we need a neutral definition to get us started: **Globalization** is a social, economic, and political process that makes it easier for people, goods, ideas, and capital to travel around the world at an unprecedented pace (Waters, 1995: 3). Globalization makes the world look and feel smaller.

Of course, the world is not shrinking literally. What is instead occurring is that people, money, corporations, and ideas are travelling across the globe more quickly and efficiently than ever before. Distance no longer seems as relevant, and time lags that used to characterize our social relations are diminished. We no longer think it's crazy to have a romantic relationship with somebody across the country or even across the world. We can now communicate instantly through telephone, email, instant messenger, or a web-camera connection. If we want to see our girlfriend or boyfriend in person, we can take a relatively inexpensive plane trip rather than waiting for an ocean-going vessel to take us for a week-long journey across the seas. If our beloved is broke and needs money, we can transfer money instantly through electronic banking networks. And if you are single, you can systematically search the world for love through the thousands of online dating sites, some of which are devoted just to vegetarians, tattoo artists, and cat lovers.

One term for this shrinking world phenomenon is **time–space compression,** which suggests that we are no longer slowed down by long distances and time differences (Harvey, 1990: 284). Not only do we feel less constrained by time and distance, but some global phenomena also seem to transcend the idea of physical space altogether. The Internet has facilitated the creation of **virtual communities,** in which people can meet, share ideas, play games, and build relationships across borders without ever meeting face-to-face. Use of the Internet has not only increased dramatically but has also changed the patterns of our daily lives and interactions. In a survey of college graduates in 14 countries, including Canada, 40 percent felt that the Internet is more important to daily life than is music, dating, or spending time with friends (Cisco, 2011). While the Internet may seem indispensible to many readers of this textbook, it is important to note that the just 30 percent of the world's population is connected to the Internet (see Table 19.1).

There are many examples of time–space compression but there are also many instances in which time still passes slowly, and the limits of geography are still relevant. People may be more "wired" in

---

**TABLE 19.1**   WORLD INTERNET USERS AND POPULATION

| WORLD REGIONS | POPULATION (2011 EST.) | POPULATION % OF WORLD | INTERNET USERS | USAGE GROWTH (2000–11) | INTERNET USERS AS % OF POPULATION | PERCENTAGE OF WORLD USERS | FACEBOOK USERS |
|---|---|---|---|---|---|---|---|
| Africa | 1 037 524 058 | 15.0% | 118 848 060 | 2 527.4% | 11.4% | 5.7% | 30 665 460 |
| Asia | 3 879 740 877 | 56.0% | 922 329 554 | 706.9% | 23.8% | 44.0% | 152 957 480 |
| Europe | 816 426 346 | 11.8% | 476 213 935 | 353.1% | 58.3% | 22.7% | 208 907 040 |
| Middle East | 216 258 843 | 3.1% | 68 553 666 | 1 987.0% | 31.7% | 3.3% | 16 125 180 |
| North America | 347 394 870 | 5.0% | 272 066 000 | 151.7% | 78.3% | 13.0% | 167 999 540 |
| Latin America/ Caribbean | 597 283 165 | 8.6% | 215 939 400 | 1 037.4% | 36.2% | 10.3% | 121 192 460 |
| Oceania/ Australia | 35 426 995 | 0.5% | 21 293 830 | 480.4% | 60.1% | 1.0% | 12 881 560 |
| WORLD TOTAL | 6 930 055 154 | 100% | 2 095 006 005 | 480.4% | 30.2% | 100.0% | 710 728 720 |

the global age, but they are often connecting with friends and family in their city—not necessarily making new friends around the world (Ghemawat, 2007). In fact, fewer than 2 percent of phone calls and less than 20 percent of data transmitted over the Internet cross national borders (Ghemawat, 2011). In addition, not all people and ideas have access to channels of globalization, such as the Internet or even the telephone. Inequality of access to means of communication is commonly called the **digital divide** (see Table 19.2).

There is a lot of academic debate about how recent globalization is. We won't venture far into this hotly contested territory, but it is important to note that the world has been shrinking for a long time. Time–space compression can be traced back at least to the sixteenth century with the beginning of trans-oceanic European exploration. The world became smaller with the invention of the steamship and the locomotive—two technologies that connected distant populations at a rate unimagined by previous generations. Colonial relationships in the eighteenth

**TABLE 19.2**    GLOBALIZATION AND TIME–SPACE COMPRESSION

| EXAMPLE | HOW IT COMPRESSES SPACE AND TIME | LIMITS TO GLOBALIZATION |
| --- | --- | --- |
| The telephone | Person-to-person communication is made possible across oceans and most national boundaries. | Many of the world's inhabitants do not have access to a telephone. In Africa, there are only 1.4 fixed telephone lines per 100 inhabitants, far below the world average of 16.6 telephone lines per 100 inhabitants (International Telecommunication Union, 2011a). Mobile telephony has greatly increased, but there are still significant differences around the globe: European consumers enjoy 119.5 mobile lines per 100 inhabitants, but Africa has only 53 mobile lines per 100 inhabitants (International Telecommunication Union, 2011b). |
| The Internet | Ideas, images, articles, videos, music, and text forms can be transmitted almost instantly across vast geographic distances. | On a global scale, access to the Internet is even more limited than access to the telephone. (See Table 19.1.) |
| Satellite television | Television is no longer restricted to local television stations; satellites allow transmission of programming from multiple points of production around the world. | Television ownership is concentrated in wealthy countries, television production is controlled by a small number of media monopolies centred in the industrialized North, and television content globally is fairly homogeneous and closely linked to consumer capitalism (McKibben, 1993). The top five media corporations in the world are concentrated in North America, and include Walt Disney Company, Time Warner, and Rupert Murdoch's News Corporation. Together, these conglomerates control hundreds of broadcasting, publishing, Internet, television and film companies ("Media Giants," 2011). |
| Electronic money markets | Capital can flow across national borders almost instantly. | The World Bank estimates that 2.7 billion people around the world do not have access to formal financial services, including bank accounts—let alone access to electronic financial markets (World Bank, 2011a). |

and nineteenth centuries moved millions of people and shiploads of wealth around the world.

The current phase of time–space compression is not radically different in form, but its pace has grown especially quickly since the 1980s. A jet is much faster than a steamship. Email is less cumbersome than mail travelling by truck or ship. Ships moving silver, spices, and opium across the ocean can transfer wealth globally but not as quickly as the enormous and instantaneous flows of capital that move in and out of the stock market in seconds.

## THE GLOBAL AND THE ETHICAL

Understanding globalization as a series of processes connecting people, resources, and capital across the globe gets us away from seeing it as either a blessing or an evil. Globalization is inherently neither good nor bad, but the consequences of globalization processes do affect human lives and the environment. These consequences generate strong opinions and ethical positions, particularly as they relate to economic processes and the role of the United States on the global stage.

Ethical debates surrounding global capitalism, and the global spread of insurrection, have become particularly pronounced in recent years. In December 2010, an incident in Tunisia sent shockwaves across this tiny country and the world. Mohamed Bouazizi, a young university graduate, could not find a job, so he began selling fruit and vegetables to make ends meet. When the authorities confiscated his produce because he did not have a licence, Bouazizi set himself on fire out of desperation and anger. In the days and weeks that followed, protests escalated across the country as Tunisians decried the bleak future they faced. In mid-January 2011, after a month of unrest, the Tunisian president, Zine al-Abidine Ben Ali, was overthrown. By late January, similar rumblings were occurring in nearby Egypt. Thousands began to gather in Tahrir ("Liberation") Square to protest the regime of President Hosni Mubarak. Egyptians rallied against difficult living conditions, increasing unemployment, corruption, and stagnation. Mubarak's 30-year rule ended in February. In the months that followed, similar uprisings took place in several Arab countries, including Libya, Bahrain, and Syria, as these countries' populations spoke out against the economic adversity they faced ("Egypt Protests," 2011; "Egypt Uprising," 2011; "Tahrir Square's Place," 2011; Whitaker, 2010).

Reclaiming public space and challenging inequality was also a common theme for the Occupy Wall Street movement that began in September 2011 in the United States. "Occupy" protests soon spread to many cities in Canada and around the world, including Toronto, Montreal, Tokyo, Tel Aviv, and Paris (see Figure 19.1). Like dissidents in the Middle East, the members of the Occupy movement criticized the inequalities generated by capitalism. However, unlike demonstrators in Tunisia, Egypt, and Syria, tent protesters did not seek to overthrow their leaders. They focused instead on glaring contrasts in the global economy: CEOs earn millions of dollars a year while middle-class families struggle to keep their homes. The movement resonated even among people who didn't protest. Former Canadian prime minister Paul Martin noted that he "[had] yet to talk to anyone who says [the protesters] aren't reflecting a disquiet that they themselves feel," and added, "the powerful thing is that Occupy Wall Street has hit a chord that really is touching the middle class—the middle class in Canada, the middle class in the United States, the middle class right around the world—and I think that makes it ... very, very powerful" (Freeland, 2011).

## TOP-DOWN VERSUS BOTTOM-UP GLOBALIZATION

Questions of equality, security, and social justice are critical in the ongoing debate about globalization and will be explored in the rest of this chapter. These debates can be understood as part of the tension between top-down and bottom-up globalization. **Top-down globalization** involves the actions of groups promoting globalized capitalism and free trade. The term *globalization* was first widely used by the American Express credit card company, which boasted in the 1970s that its card was accepted worldwide (Harvey, 1990: 13). The term was then taken up in financial and business circles, where it came to represent hope for a world where capital could flow freely, uninhibited by national boundaries or governments insisting on national regulations and taxation.

Top-down globalization has been dominated by neoliberal economic policies, which have become prevalent in both rich and poor countries since the 1980s. **Neoliberalism** is associated with a retreat from state spending and regulation, a focus on individual responsibility for one's own welfare, less protection for labour and the environment, privatization of state resources, and faith in the power of the market and the profit motive to create wealth (see Chapter 9,

**FIGURE 19.1** OCCUPY PROTESTS AROUND THE WORLD OCTOBER 2011

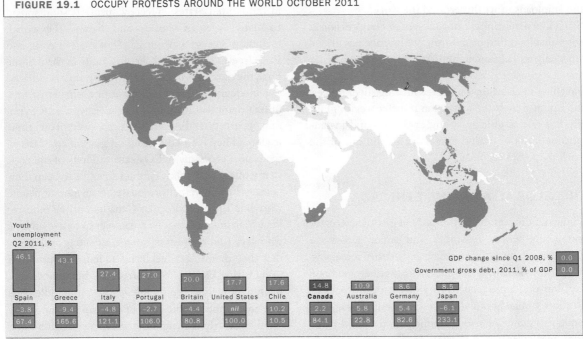

SOURCE: From http://www.economist.com/blogs/dailychart/2011/10/occupy-protests © The Economist Newspaper Limited, London (November 2, 2011).

Development and Underdevelopment). Top-down globalization is also strongly associated with the United States because of its role in promoting neoliberal policies globally through such institutions as the International Monetary Fund (IMF) and the World Bank, headquartered in Washington, D.C. For this reason, top-down globalization has also been referred to as the "Washington consensus." In addition, the United States is often perceived as an exemplar of neoliberal policy domestically, even though it seems to deviate on such key matters as a balanced budget (in part because of high levels of U.S. military spending).

**Globalization from below** describes the actions of groups that criticize the injustices that result from globalization processes, and in particular, the expansion of global markets. The mass media frequently describe these groups as being opposed to globalization. That is inaccurate. Many groups that criticize the injustices resulting from globalization actually support particular types of globalization, such as the spread of international human rights and global labour standards. Moreover, they use technologies, like the Internet, to help them organize and communicate internationally. In general, groups that support globalization from below advocate more democracy, environmental protection, and social

justice in the global system. Bottom-up globalizers are against the neoliberal forms of globalization that put capital mobility, markets, and profits before people's basic needs, and they criticize the powerful economic, political, and military influence of transnational corporations and the United States government.

Top-down globalization has been targeted by environmentalists, peasant organizations, and farmers' unions, but it has also been criticized by capitalist insiders, such as world-famous economist and policy adviser Jeffrey Sachs, international financier George Soros, and Joseph Stiglitz, Nobel Prize winner and former chief economist and vice-president of the World Bank (Sachs, 2005; Soros, 1998; Stiglitz, 2003).

While everyone from rock stars to prime ministers demands greater justice in the global system, how to achieve it is not clear. There is no consensus on whether moderate capitalist reforms are sufficient, whether trade liberalization will help the poor, or whether the answer lies in partial or total withdrawal from global markets. Because of these differences, globalization from below should be understood less as a cohesive movement and more as a broad framework that encompasses multiple perspectives, including moderate critiques of neoliberalism, radical anti-capitalist positions, various forms of anarchism, armed peasant uprisings, and fair-trade coffee projects.

How then do the forces of globalization operate in our daily lives? People are involved with globalization processes as capitalists, consumer, workers, and citizen (Robbins, 2005: 2–4). In the remainder of this chapter, we explore the profound influence of time–space compression in each of these realms.

## CAPITALISTS GO GLOBAL

### THE RISE OF FINANCIAL CAPITAL

In economic terms, money used for investment, currency trading, and so forth is "financial capital." In the globalized economy, financial capital has grown much faster than production and trade. More than US$1.5 trillion flow through electronic financial channels every day, and an estimated 98 percent of these flows are purely speculative, meaning they are unrelated to the buying and selling of physical goods but involve short-term trading of such things as foreign currencies. Global trade in goods and services equalled $15.2 trillion in 2010. While this seems an impressive number, it is equal to only three days' worth of trade on foreign exchange markets (Bedell, 2010; United Nations Conference on Trade and Development, 2010). Using a fully computerized global financial system, traders can move around billions of dollars to profit from minuscule changes in currency rates.

The rise of financial capital has been labelled "casino capitalism" since financial speculators, like casino gamblers, stand to make or lose millions of dollars in short periods (Strange, 1986). The rise of casino capitalism has been facilitated by the financial deregulation that has occurred under neoliberal regimes since the 1980s as governments gave up regulatory powers. The danger with casino capitalism is that investor speculation (a process akin to placing a bet) makes financial systems unstable. Money floods into markets during periods of optimism, creating a financial "bubble" that drives markets up. The bubble bursts when investors realize that the market is overpriced relative to the value of real assets. This causes a period of panic involving an outflow of capital and, in due course, economic recession.

A snowball of financial panic is precisely what the world witnessed during the 1997 Asian financial crisis, which started in Thailand and went on to affect the currencies, stock markets, and asset prices of a host of Asian countries, including Indonesia, South Korea, and Hong Kong as well as the financial systems of Brazil and Russia. In 2008–09, a similar crisis occurred when the real estate market collapsed in the United States. Initially, inexpensive mortgages lured millions of Americans into the housing market. All was well while house prices rose. People felt richer, and they borrowed more and more money against the value of their homes. When people had to renew their mortgages at higher interest rates, many of them could not afford it. Foreclosures increased. With more houses on the market, house prices began to fall. The spiral of falling house prices and skyrocketing foreclosures soon put some large financial institutions in a position of not having enough cash on hand to continue operations. Some of them went bankrupt while others sought government assistance to stay in business. Because financial institutions around the world had invested heavily in U.S. debt, the financial crisis was global, not simply American. Some institutions, such as Iceland's three biggest private banks and Lehman Brothers, the fourth largest investment bank in the United States, went bankrupt, while governments had to lend money to keep other financial institutions afloat. Among other things, the crisis demonstrated how porous global financial borders are. In the words of the chief European economist at Deutsche Bank, "In this day and age, a bank run spreads around the world, not around the block" (Landler, 2008).

### OVERCAPACITY AND CENTRALIZATION

The growth of casino capitalism is also linked to declining profits and overcapacity in the economy of goods and services. Put simply, global corporations can produce more things than the world's consumers can afford to purchase. Justin Lin, chief economist at the World Bank, noted in 2009 that, "unless we deal with excess capacity, it will wreak havoc on all countries," thus acknowledging the connection between recent economic downturns and the tendency towards overproduction (Evans-Pritchard 2009). In 2008, the car industry made about 94 million vehicles, over capacity by about 34 million cars (Welch, 2008). While financial markets boomed throughout the early 2000s, and wealth appeared to be growing exponentially for some people, a number of economists worried that excess capacity in the productive economy—accompanied by growing inequality and global poverty, which erode the worldwide consumption base—meant that a global recession was in the works (Bello, 2002). The 2008–09 U.S. financial crisis demonstrated both the overcapacity problem and the interpenetration of global financial markets. Global investors worried about the bankruptcy even of giants of the productive economy, such as General Motors and Chrysler, and the U.S. slowdown spread around the world. In 2008, the Indian high-tech and outsourcing industries, which rely heavily on business from the U.S. financial sector, began to freeze wages and announce layoffs for software programmers and workers in call centres (Kahn, 2008). Even China, whose rapid growth has been powered by exports, experienced a drop in exports at the end of 2008, leaving Communist Party officials worrying about employing the millions of workers in the export sector, which in turn depends heavily on American consumers (Jacobs and Barboza, 2008).

Besides creating complex webs of interdependence among national economies, the creation of a global economy has changed the way corporations look and operate. In short, these conditions have made corporations leaner, meaner, bigger, more diverse in terms of the goods they produce, and more involved in complex financial dealings and investments throughout the world.

To survive problems of overcapacity and economic slowdown, corporations have merged to trim operating costs. The Chinese automaker Geely bought Volvo from Ford (Nicholson, 2010). Renault took over Nissan, and Chrysler teamed up with Daimler-Benz (briefly) and then with Fiat. Chasing the high profits found in the financial sector, traditional corporations have gotten into the money-lending business, while banks have become involved in new kinds of businesses, such as securities trading. Today, transnational corporations find it hard to survive without diversifying into multiple goods in many countries, and this explains why the last decades have witnessed the greatest rate of mergers and consolidation in history (International Forum on Globalization, 2001: 6; see Figure 19.2). It also helps explain why the same handful of corporations can be found almost everywhere, offering a similar range of products in the world's shopping malls and airports (Box 19.1). These giant corporations trade with one another, but they also trade goods and services internally. Economists estimate that a third of all global trade involves transfers among different branches of the same corporation (Ellwood, 2001: 54).

## GROWTH OF THE CORPORATE GIANTS

Corporations have become bigger and more powerful than many national governments (May, 2006). Consider just these two facts (White 2009):

- Of the largest 175 economic entities in the world, 109 (62.3 percent) are corporations (measured by sales), and 66 are countries (measured by gross domestic product).
- The world's biggest corporation, Wal-Mart earns annual revenue that is 2.24 times the size of the gross domestic product of Singapore (52nd on the list).

It will perhaps surprise you to learn that big corporations do not necessarily pay big taxes. In fact, corporations are paying less in taxes today than in the 1990s. Companies regularly play nation-states against one another, pressuring governments to lower taxes rates by threatening to move production to a more favourable location. The resulting decline in corporate taxes can be observed across all developed countries in the last two decades, as mobile individuals and corporations increasingly take advantage of global tax shelters, forcing governments to rely on taxes paid by less mobile individuals and small businesses (Figure 19.3). Recent trends in several countries show that tax rates for corporations are being maintained, and even lowered. In the midst of the economic crash in 2008, Ireland actually hiked tax rates to individuals, but maintained its corporate tax rate—one of the lowest among the wealthy countries at 12 percent. In Germany, corporate taxes were cut from 39 to 30 percent the same year ("Corporate Tax," 2009). In 2005, the U.S. Government Accountability Office reported that between 1998 and 2005, more than two-thirds of all corporations did not pay taxes every year (Borosage, 2008). These corporate tax breaks have taken place in spite of relatively high government debt.

Canadian corporations have also enjoyed big tax breaks, which they justify by their need to compete with the United States. Reductions in corporate taxes between 2000 and 2010 decreased the Canadian government's federal revenues by $12.5 billion a year (Jackson, 2005). Canada's own corporate tax rate was reduced from 50 percent in the early 1980s to just 29.5 percent in 2010 ("Canada's Corporate Income Tax," 2011). These corporate tax breaks have significant implications for income inequality. A recent report

**FIGURE 19.2**    FOREIGN DIRECT INVESTMENT AND ANNOUNCED MERGERS AND ACQUISITIONS, WORLDWIDE

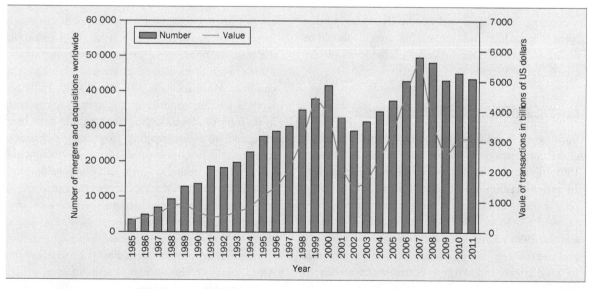

NOTE: "Net direct investment position" is the difference between foreign direct investment in Canada and Canadian direct investment abroad.

SOURCE: Statistics Canada (2011).

SOURCE: Institute of Mergers, Acquisitions, and Alliances. (2011). "Announced Mergers and Acquisitions, Worldwide 1991–2010." Thomson Financial, Institute of Mergers, Acquisitions and Alliances. On the World Wide Web at http://www.imaa-institute.org/statistics-mergers-acquisitions.html (retrieved 15 August 2012).

found that "taxes and benefits reduce inequality less in Canada than in most OECD countries" (Grant, 2011a). Before the mid-1990s, Canada's tax-benefit system used to be able to offset 70 percent of income inequality, with a redistributive effect similar to that of some Scandinavian countries. Today, this number has fallen

to less than 40 percent (Grant, 2011a). The problems caused by tax imbalances because of corporate tax cuts and growing inequality in the redistribution of wealth have not gone unnoticed, even by Warren Buffett, one of the richest businessmen in the world. In an interview for ABC in November 2010, Buffett denounced the

BOX 19.1    KRAFT: YOUR FRIENDLY NEIGHBORHOOD MULTINATIONAL CHEESE CORPORATION
(THAT ALSO SELLS BEER, SMOKES, AND CHOCOLATE)

The Kraft food brand demonstrates the complexity and expansiveness of a diversified transnational corporation. Today, it is difficult to go grocery shopping without buying a Kraft product, even if you are a vegan and don't eat cheese. Kraft Foods is the largest food producer in the United States and the second largest in the world, sells in 145 countries, has more than 200 production facilities, and has a global work force of more than 103 000. Even though Kraft is both large and omnipresent, it can be difficult to keep track of the many corporate structures linked to Kraft products. Kraft's story began simply enough, when it was founded as a wholesale cheese company in Chicago in 1903. Kraft's corporate genealogy quickly became very complicated as it acquired new products, took over other firms, and was in turn acquired by another corporation.

In 1988, Philip Morris—a multinational tobacco company—purchased Kraft Foods for US$12.9 billion. Some analysts speculated that Kraft's family-friendly image might offset the negative associations of Philip Morris being the world's biggest tobacco company. Philip Morris combined Kraft with General Foods a year later to form Kraft General Foods. Like other corporations in the early 1990s, Kraft General Foods experienced merger mania; Kraft gobbled up multiple companies around the world that sold coffee, candy, cheese, chocolate (including Toblerone), and cereals (including Shreddies and Shredded Wheat). In 1995, Kraft General Foods was reorganized and renamed Kraft Foods, while Kraft General Foods International became Kraft Foods International. In 2000, Philip Morris purchased Nabisco Holdings (a giant cracker and snack company), which it also merged into the Philip-Morris Kraft empire. In 2003, after negative publicity about a tobacco giant making food, as well as rising concern about the company's liability in tobacco and obesity class action suits, a company with the vague name of Altria became the parent company to the Kraft and Philip Morris family of food, cigarettes, and beer. In 2010, Kraft took over Cadbury, making it the largest confectionary company in the world (Jones and Dorfman, 2010).

overtaxing of the lower and middle classes, saying that "people at the high end—people like myself—should be paying a lot more in taxes. We have it better than we've ever had it" ("Warren Buffett," 2010).

## CRITICS OF CORPORATE POWER

Bottom-up globalizers have reacted to the growth of global corporations in various ways (Bello, 2002; Starr, 1999). For example, the 1990s saw the emergence of an anti-sweatshop movement in North America after poor working conditions in the garment industry were exposed (A. Ross, 1997). Of particular importance was the 1996 Kathie Lee Gifford controversy, which revealed that her Wal-Mart clothing line was produced by child labour and involved human rights abuses. In 2000, Naomi Klein's *No Logo* became an international best-seller. She argued that large corporate brands are vulnerable to a backlash against corporate power. "Today," she wrote, "more and more campaigners are treating multinationals, and the policies that give them free reign, as the root cause of political injustices around the globe" (Klein, 2000: 338). AdBusters, a rabble-rousing media organization headquartered in Vancouver, launched multiple campaigns to "un-cool" famous brand names associated with sweatshop labour and environmental degradation (Adbusters, 2005).

Corporate Accountability International (formerly Infact) launched a Kraft boycott in 1994 to expose the business practices of its parent company, Philip Morris, such as its alleged promotion of tobacco to children. More recently, the Sierra Club criticized Kraft for using genetically engineered ingredients in its food products. Other corporations have been criticized on issues ranging from labour practices (particularly in coffee production), environmental sustainability, animal welfare, and relationships with the military-industrial complex operating in Iraq.

Corporations responded to this wave of anti-corporate criticism in various ways. For example, some have changed their names, diverting attention from their infamous brand. Philip Morris became Altria, much to the dismay of anti-smoking groups who argued this was an underhanded public relations move to obscure the company's roots in the tobacco industry. After receiving bad publicity about its genetic engineering, Monsanto became Pharmacia for most of its communications after merging with pharmaceutical giants Pharmacia and UpJohn.

Another way that global corporations are attempting to stem the tide of bad press is through a growing movement for corporate social responsibility, in which corporations voluntarily try to introduce best practices for labour and the environment.

**FIGURE 19.3**    CORPORATE TAX RATES WORLDWIDE

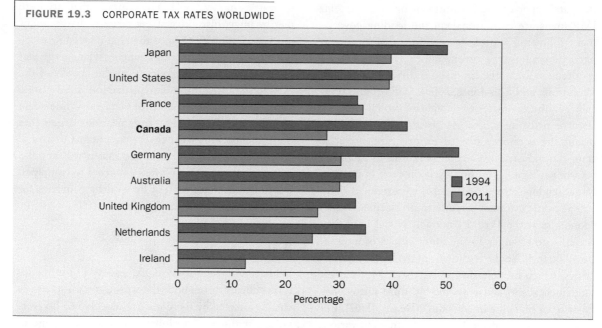

SOURCE: Organisations for Economic Co-operation and Development. (n.d.). OECD Tax database. On the World Wide Web at http://www.oecd.org/ctp /taxdatabase and http//www.oecd.org/dataoecd/26/56/33717459.xls (retrieved 15 August 2012).

The Gap, for example, released a report in 2004 that openly admitted a host of wage, health, and safety violations by its production subcontractors and promised to do better. Controversy exists over what is certified as responsible corporate behaviour and who is in control of the certification process. Philip Knight, CEO of Nike, withdrew a $30 million donation to the University of Oregon in May 2000 after the university endorsed a student-run regulatory organization (the Workers' Right Consortium) instead of the Fair Labor Association, a labour-rights group backed by the White House with corporate executives on its board of directors. Unfortunately, more than 15 years after the Gifford scandal, the institute for Global Labour and Human Rights reports that little has changed in terms of sweatshop labour. Such corporations as Wal-Mart, Target, J.C. Penney, and Macy's continue to sell goods from factories in which workers earn abysmally low wages, under-age labour is common, and supervisors routinely engage in physical and sexual abuse (Institute for Global Labour and Human Rights 2011).

The growing power of corporations has not emerged in a political vacuum. As corporations have grown in strength, some governments have lost ground, both to corporate power and to international institutions, such as the World Trade Organization. This change has led many analysts to wonder if the age of globalization means the end of the state system.

## ARE STATES RELEVANT IN THE GLOBAL WORLD?

Critics of neoliberal policies have wondered about the extent to which states continue to be the main instrument of democratic governance. Has the state been replaced by a kind of "global governance?" Does real power rests in the hands of unelected officials in the world's three biggest international financial institutions: the International Monetary Fund (IMF), the World Bank, and World Trade Organization (WTO), sometimes called "the three sisters"? Because of pressure to meet the demands of these three very powerful international financial institutions, some critics argue that states have become less oriented toward meeting the demands of citizens. The result is a **democratic deficit** in which ordinary citizens are disenfranchised from the process of governance. Let's look briefly at how the three sisters challenge the capacity of states to make democratic decisions for average citizens.

### THE THREE SISTERS

The IMF was established after World War II. Its official role was to maintain the stability of the international monetary system. Since the 1980s, the IMF has come to serve a different yet important role as the gatekeeper of the institutional financial system. IMF loans are conditional on the lending government following a package of reforms of known as "structural adjustment programmes" (renamed "poverty reduction strategies" in 1999; Brym et al., 2005; Woodroffe and Ellis-Jones, 2000). IMF reforms typically require countries to deregulate capital markets, remove price subsidies, decrease social spending, orient the economy toward exports, and privatize state-run industries. If a country refuses to adopt the reform package, it can find itself shut out of international lending circles and unable to service its debt. Joseph Stiglitz, former senior vice-president and chief economist at the World Bank and Nobel Prize laureate, is no stranger to the inner circles of international finance. Yet he is also one of the IMF's harshest critics, which he describes as imprisoned in "market fundamentalism" and as staffed by "third-rate economists from first-rate universities" (Denny, 2002). For Stiglitz, decisions made by the IMF to solve various financial crises show that "the IMF is not particularly interested in hearing the thoughts of its 'client countries' on such topics as development strategy or fiscal austerity," and that "[all] too often, the Fund's approach to developing countries has the feel of a colonial ruler" (Stiglitz, 2003: 40). Many poor countries have witnessed massive protests against the IMF.

Like the IMF, the World Bank was also established after World War II, and its job was to make loans to help postwar reconstruction. Most World Bank loans were made to poor countries and were often tied to large development projects, such as hydroelectric dams. As a condition of receiving loans, the World Bank required that certain structural adjustment criteria be met. Like the IMF, the World Bank has had its share of critics, both external and internal (Chapter 9, Development and Underdevelopment). In response, the World Bank increased its collaboration with local nongovernmental organizations (NGOs). While some observers applaud these efforts as part of the Bank's self-help approach to social problems, others argue that the Bank's NGO collaborations do not change its fundamentally undemocratic nature or the severity of its structural adjustment reforms.

The WTO emerged in 1995 out of the postwar trade treaty the Global Agreement on Tariffs and Trade (GATT). The WTO's job is to lower trade barriers, thereby increasing international trade and, presumably, prosperity. The WTO became known to many North Americans with the famous "Battle of Seattle" in 1999. WTO meetings in that city were met by huge, disruptive street protests. Every major meeting of the WTO since then has elicited protests, often from citizens of poor countries who charge that international trade works only to the benefit of the rich and ignores the unfair protection of corporate agribusiness at the expense of farmers. While some globalization-from-below organizations argue that trade liberalization will help the poor (e.g., Oxfam and Live 8 organizers), others argue that it will not and that entry to the WTO forces countries to comply to a set of trade rules written by wealthy countries for their own benefit (Bivens and Hersh, 2003).

## A U.S. EMPIRE?

While the IMF, World Bank, and WTO influence state policies throughout the world, not all states are equally affected by these institutions. Some observers note that the age of globalization is also an age of more power for some states and relative powerlessness for states at the bottom of the global hierarchy. Critics of the United States sometimes accuse it of acting like an empire. Neoconservative thinkers in Washington acknowledge that the United States acts like an empire, although they argue that it uses its power benevolently to promote peace and democracy throughout the world.

Analysts debate whether the United States is a modern empire or a fading superpower (Ferguson, 2004; Wallerstein, 2002). The United States still enjoys enough political, economic, and military power to make unilateral foreign policy decisions (such as invading Iraq, which it did without United Nations endorsement), maintain a substantial global military presence (see Figure 19.4), and adopt unorthodox economic policies (like running huge fiscal deficits). Do these policies indicate the *decline* of U.S. hegemony? The United States is the world's biggest debtor, with a deficit of $16 trillion dollars in 2013. Especially after the 2008–09 financial crisis hit, some analysts argued that the power of the United States was waning relative to that of the countries that own its debt holdings, notably China (Fallows, 2008).

## GLOBAL INEQUALITY AND THE "FOURTH WORLD"

Another feature of the global state system is a widening power gap between and within states. In the 1970s, analysts often divided the world into three

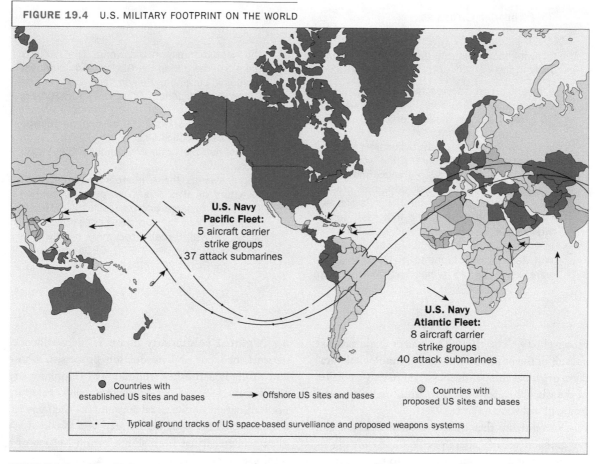

**FIGURE 19.4**   U.S. MILITARY FOOTPRINT ON THE WORLD

**U.S. Navy Pacific Fleet:**
5 aircraft carrier strike groups
37 attack submarines

**U.S. Navy Atlantic Fleet:**
8 aircraft carrier strike groups
40 attack submarines

● Countries with established US sites and bases

⟶ Offshore US sites and bases

○ Countries with proposed US sites and bases

— · — Typical ground tracks of US space-based survelliance and proposed weapons systems

SOURCE: U.S. Department of Defense. *Base Structure Report, 2008*. On the World Wide Web at http://combatingglobalization.com/articles/combating_globalization4.html (retrieved 12 August 2012).

parts. The "first world" comprised the wealthy capitalist countries. The "second world" comprised the countries of the communist bloc. The "third world" comprised all the rest. This division is now inaccurate. The old third world now comprises a disparate assortment of nations that don't necessarily share common traits, the communist second world has for the most part collapsed, and it has become evident that widespread poverty exists even in the rich first world.

To meaningfully capture asymmetries among the world's countries today, analysts sometimes refer to the division between the "global north" and the "global south" or between developed and developing countries. Another useful terminological distinction is between the "majority world," which is generally poor and lacks basic social goods like housing, food, employment, and education, and the "minority world," which is generally well educated and has access to good jobs and public goods like healthcare.

People from the privileged minority world may live in wealthy countries like Canada, but they can also live in Mexico City or Hong Kong. Similarly, people from the majority world can be homeless and searching for adequate food and shelter in downtown Toronto. The majority world–minority world distinction serves as a valuable reminder that state borders do not always indicate who benefits and suffers in a globalized economic system and that the high living standard of the Canadian middle class is a global anomaly (Milanovic, 2005; see Box 19.2).

While the global economy has made a portion of the world's population wealthy, a large proportion of the world's people (at least 50 percent) are considered poor. The global economy operates independently of large populations and geographical areas, which are seen as irrelevant for its functioning. These marginalized populations and regions are sometimes called the **fourth world** (Cardoso, 1993; Castells, 1998;

Hoogvelt, 1997: 66, 162). The fourth world exists as a result of the new economic and technological paradigm of global competitiveness, where only a portion of the world's states and inhabitants are competitive in the global economy.

Recognizing that time–space compression and the global economy affect people differently allows our understanding of globalization to become more nuanced. Globalization does involve a number of intense connections within the core of the global system, as people in the minority world travel more, hold global investments, and integrate the Internet into their daily lives. At the same time, globalization also involves a process of *peripheralization* that marginalizes certain groups. Some people in rich countries like Canada—Aboriginal peoples, homeless populations, unemployed workers—are subject to exclusionary processes like those that affect people in parts of Africa, Asia, and Latin America (Hoogvelt, 1997: 129).

## THE GLOBAL CONSUMER

Maybe you have yet to be convinced that globalization has anything to do with you. But have you gone shopping lately? If you consume commodities—meaning goods purchased in the marketplace rather than made from your own labour—then you are inevitably part of globalization. The tags on your clothing are more likely to read "Made in China" or "Made in Bangladesh" than "Made in Canada."

A **global commodity chain** is "a [worldwide] network of labor and production processes, whose end result is a finished commodity" (Hopkins and Wallerstein, 1986: 159). Global commodity chains are not transparent to the casual consumer. When you eat a tomato on a fast-food hamburger, you usually don't know whether it has been shipped from Mexico or a local greenhouse. When you buy a pair of running shoes, the price tag doesn't tell you much about the workers who made the shoes or the company's environmental track record. In this section, we will learn about the critical role consumption plays in the global economy, as well as some of the social and environmental critiques of globalized consumerism.

## A GLOBAL GLUT

While consumers don't always understand the complexity of global commodity chains, consumption plays a critical role in driving growth in the global economy. High consumer spending increases economic growth, while a lack of consumer confidence is associated with economic slowdown and recession. Because North American and European markets are relatively saturated consumer markets, many corporations see expansion into global markets as essential for growth. **Consumerism**—a way of life in which a person's identity and purpose is oriented primarily to the purchase and consumption of material goods—is currently being exported to the world's middle and working classes.

As noted above, the global economy suffers from a problem of overcapacity that makes finding new consumer markets essential. In particular, many corporations are looking to expand sales to China, the world's most populous country, to solve the problem. So far, Chinese production has been focused mainly on export markets, thereby worsening the problem of global overproduction (Bello, 2002). This situation is beginning to change. In 2010, China was the third largest consumer market behind the United States and Japan, and by 2015, it is expected to be the second largest (Liao et al., 2010).

## CULTURE AS COMMODITY?

Another characteristic of globalized consumerism is the tendency to treat culture like any other commodity. The United States has been instrumental in advancing this viewpoint—not surprisingly, given the tremendous size and power of the culture/entertainment industry in the United States. The biggest U.S. export consists of mass-produced products of popular culture (Barlow, 2001). While many countries have a tradition of protecting cultural products, the United States has used the WTO to prohibit states from using subsidies and quotas to protect domestic cultural products, like films, music, magazines, books, and music. For example, in 1997, the WTO supported a U.S. complaint and ruled that the Canadian government's usage of preferential tax and postal rates to protect the domestic magazine industry was unlawful. (U.S. magazines make up 85 percent of the magazines found on Canadian newsstands.)

A growing movement to resist the interpretation of culture as a commodity is centred around a 2005 UN treaty: the United Nations Educational, Scientific, and Cultural Organization's (UNESCO) Convention on Cultural Diversity (CCD). The UNESCO Convention was vehemently opposed by the United States, since the treaty will allow states to exclude cultural policies from free trade deals. As with most treaties, the devil will ultimately lie in the legal details, yet the CCD opens up the possibility for states legally to protect domestic cultural industries from the rules of trade.

## CULTURAL IMPERIALISM?

The global spread of consumerism has been criticized as form of **cultural imperialism** (Barlow, 2001). From this viewpoint, global corporations, bolstered by sophisticated advertising tools, media monopolies, and declining trade barriers, are exporting a Western way of life throughout the world (Tomlinson, 1991). Cultural imperialism is often associated with liberal values around sexuality, feminism, and secularism.

Of course, people are not passive recipients of Western cultural products, which can be taken up in unique ways. A Japanese game show like *The Iron Chef*, for instance, represents a unique cultural hybrid that combines an American game-show format with Japanese cultural and culinary mores. When it was first shown in the United States, it was unlike any show made by American television producers, yet it was a huge hit on the American-based Food Network and inspired *Iron Chef America*, a highly successful English-language spinoff of the original Japanese show.

Western cultural products are transformed as they are consumed by different global cultures. However, this does not mean that the world's cultural products compete as equals. Free trade favours large economies and big economic actors. Canadians are more likely to eat in a McDonald's than they are to eat in a Jollibee, the leading fast-food restaurant in the Philippines. Because of the tremendous economic power of Hollywood, filmgoers in Canada are more likely to watch a movie made in Hollywood than we are to watch a film made in Denmark or even a film made in Canada (see Table 19.3). French political figures, such as former president Jacques Chirac, have been particularly vocal in criticizing the cultural power of Hollywood. He used the French state to protect and promote the French film industry. Chirac warned of a "catastrophe" for global diversity if U.S. cultural dominance goes unchallenged (Agence France-Presse, 2004).

Although tremendous economic and cultural power is centred in the corporate culture of the United States and Europe, there are important exceptions. The al-Jazeera television network counters the global prevalence of CNN, offering an Arab alternative to U.S.-produced news. An English-language channel of al-Jazeera went on air in 2006, making al-Jazeera's presence felt even more widely. The largest producer of movies in the world is not Hollywood, but Bollywood—the film industry based in Mumbai (formerly Bombay), India, which produces more than a thousand films a year and attracts more than 10 million Indians to the cinema every day. Bollywood films are seen in Russia, the Middle East, Africa, and Indian immigrant communities around the world. The cultural pervasiveness of

**TABLE 19.3**   U.S. MARKET SHARE OF FILM INDUSTRY FOR SELECTED COUNTRIES, 2008

| COUNTRY OR REGION | PERCENTAGE OF FILM INDUSTRY BELONGING TO U.S. MOVIES |
|---|---|
| United States | 91.5 |
| Canada | 88.5 |
| United Kingdom | 65 |
| Australia | 84.2 |
| Spain | 71.5 |
| European Union | 63.2 |
| Poland | 56.1 |
| France | 44 |
| South Korea | 48.8 |

SOURCES: Marché du film. European Audiovisual Observatory. *Focus 2009: World Film Market Trends.* On the World Wide Web at http://www.obs .coe.int/online_publication/reports/focus2009.pdf (retrieved 14 December 2011).

Bollywood films is so great that smaller Asian countries, like Bangladesh, have reacted against the perceived domination of Indian movies, which crowd out Bangladeshi films. In addition to Bollywood, a film industry arising out of Nigeria, called Nollywood, produces films with actors and themes that are wildly popular with African viewers, and which some Nigerians believe have "eliminated the cultural stranglehold of Hollywood" (Kennedy, 2004).

## GLOBAL BRAND BACKLASH

While the term *cultural imperialism* may drown out the subtlety of global cultural exchange, visible signs of antagonism toward Western-style consumerism remain. One way that global consumerism is being contested is through a backlash against corporate brand names. Branded goods, like Coke, Barbie, and Nike, have a particular political, social, and cultural importance because of their connections to global corporations (Klein, 2000: 5). Just as transnational corporations have spread globally, so have their brands, and now McDonald's, the Gap, and Starbucks are all frequent targets of street protests around the world.

McDonald's has been the target of protests in more than 50 countries, and Hindu activists have demanded that the prime minister shut down all McDonald's because it offends traditional Indian vegetarian food culture (Brownell and Horgen, 2004: 61). Tens of thousands of Indians protested the opening of the first Kentucky Fried Chicken outlet in 1995, bringing together environmentalists, farmers, health officials, and anti-globalization activists (Wall, 2000). A global-brand backlash has also inspired greater attention to Coca-Cola's corporate practices throughout the world (see http:// killercoke.org; Nestle, 2011). In some instances, consumption of Coke has dropped off in favour of domestic soft drinks, leading Coke to retool its sales strategy by focusing on specialized local drinks (Hays, 2000).

The idea that corporate globalization can be effectively fought by protesting against branded products is controversial. Many people argue that global corporations are geniuses at using social dissent to sell new consumer products (Frank, 1997; Heath and Potter, 2004). Just as 1960s radicals wore tie-dyed T-shirts and drove around in Boogie Vans, people today can purchase consumer products that express their disgust with the global capitalist system. You can wear a Che Guevara T-shirt while reading *Adbusters* and listening to K'Naan on your iPod. The extent to which countercultural consumption disrupts global flows of wealth is unclear. Marketing gurus are well aware of such consumer tendencies and advise global corporations to advance their brand by using

The Church of Stop Shopping, led by "Reverend Billy," promotes "retail interventions" into corporations like Starbucks. To see material on the Reverend's anti-consumer campaign and its intervention scripts, visit www.revbilly.com.

SOURCE: Reprinted by permission of Reverend Billy.

anti-establishment messages to sell products to young people around the world (Lindstrom, 2003: 132).

## CONSUMER ALTERNATIVES: FAIR TRADE

Subverting corporate logos is not the only tactic used to disrupt global commodity chains. Bottom-up globalizers also focus on developing consumer products that are environmentally sustainable and produced by relatively well-paid workers. The fair-trade movement is one of the main proponents of this approach, arguing that producers should be paid a fair price rather than the free market price (Figure 19.5).

The fair-trade movement has paid special attention to coffee. Around the turn of the twenty-first century, the market for coffee plummeted to a 30-year low, leaving coffee prices below the cost of production for many farmers and causing heightened levels of poverty and debt for 25 million coffee-producing families worldwide (Oxfam, 2002). According to its proponents, fair-trade coffee is an important solution to the "sweatshops in the field" that characterize contemporary coffee production. Fair-trade coffee allows producers to earn a living wage and offer a guaranteed price that protects farmers against wild

price fluctuations (see Figure 19.5). Fair trade also promises to protect the environment since most fair-trade coffee is "shade-grown" (that is, grown alongside trees that support wildlife and biodiversity).

While the market for fair-trade coffee is growing, it represents only a small fraction of the total coffee market. An estimated 6 percent of the coffee sold at Starbucks is fair-trade, and about 4 percent of all the coffee sold in the United States is fair-trade certified (Hickman 2008; Haight 2011). Fair-trade coffee organizations must convince consumers to pay more for their coffee—a choice that goes against the socialization of most consumers to shop for the best deal.

## ECOLOGICAL CONSEQUENCES OF CONSUMERISM

Global consumerism has also been criticized for being based on a Western high-consumption lifestyle that is ecologically unsustainable, particularly if it is adopted by more people around the world. Twenty percent of the world's population (1.2 billion people) living in the industrialized developed world currently consume two-thirds of the world's resources and create 75 percent of all waste and pollution

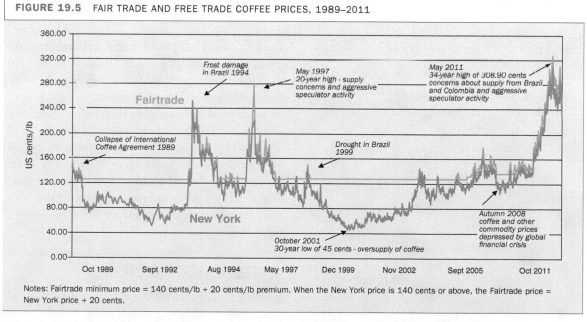

**FIGURE 19.5**  FAIR TRADE AND FREE TRADE COFFEE PRICES, 1989–2011

Notes: Fairtrade minimum price = 140 cents/lb + 20 cents/lb premium. When the New York price is 140 cents or above, the Fairtrade price = New York price + 20 cents.

This graph shows a comparison of minimum Fairtrade price and the world market price for coffee, as measured on the New York Stock Exchange.
SOURCE: Fairtrade Foundation. (2011). *The Arabica Coffee Market, 1989–2011: Comparison of Fairtrade and New York Exchange Prices.* London, UK: Author. Reprinted with permission from the UK Fair Trade Foundation. http://www.fairtrade.org.uk/resources/reports_and_briefing_papers.aspx.

(Speidel, 2003: 5). What would be the implications if even a quarter of the remaining 80 percent of the world's people began to consume at the rate of wealthy Europeans and North Americans?

The size of China's economy has increased dramatically since it introduced free-market reforms in 1978, and it currently consumes more grain, meat, fertilizer, steel, and coal than the United States does (Speidel, 2003: 5). If China consumed as much oil per capita as the United States, China's total oil demand would be 80 million barrels a day—and currently the world produces only 60 million barrels a day (Speidel, 2003: 5). While some analysts say the solution to this problem is to find more oil, most experts believe that the world does not have enough reserves to sustain this level of consumption for long. Moreover, the current level of fossil fuel consumption is linked to global climate change. Sustainable consumption probably lies somewhere between the world's two extremes of overconsumers and underconsumers—at levels maintained by the roughly 3.3 billion people who eat moderate amounts of food (especially meat), rely primarily on sustainable modes of transportation, such as walking and public transportation, and consume minimal amounts of raw materials in their daily lives (Durning, 1992; see Figure 19.6).

While proponents of top-down globalization hope to turn the global middle-income stratum

Some observers think that a Western, high-consumption lifestyle is ecologically unsustainable if it is adopted by people around the world. For example, each passenger taking a round trip from Toronto to Vancouver on Air Canada (economy class) is responsible for putting nearly 533 kilograms of carbon dioxide into the atmosphere. What happens when hundreds of millions of additional people take to the skies?
SOURCE: © iStockphoto.com/EGDigital.

into overconsumers, the ecological challenge is to extend middle-income consumption habits to the world's poor underconsumers and the world's elite overconsumers. This will not be an easy political feat given the push to expand global consumption to address the problem of overcapacity in global production. The global economic system is currently organized around, and requires, high levels of consumption. In addition, it seems that members of the world's consumer class are often more interested in maximizing their individual consumption possibilities than they are in voluntarily curbing their consumption habits. Surveys show that totally committed ethical shoppers constitute only a small percentage of the shopping population (Bird and Hughes, 1997: 160) and two-thirds of Americans in the US$75 000+ income bracket believe they need 50 to 100 percent more income to satisfy their consumption desires (Schor, 1998). It is unclear how to build a more sustainable economy that also provides economic opportunities and good jobs—a topic to which I now turn.

## GLOBAL WORKERS

Karl Marx and Friedrich Engels (1972 [1848]) ended the *Manifesto of the Communist Party* with the now famous phrase, "Proletarians [workers] of all countries, unite." The political unification of working people across national borders is, however, relatively rare. Capitalists, in contrast, have proven adept at

**FIGURE 19.6**   SHARE OF WORLD'S PRIVATE CONSUMPTION, 2005

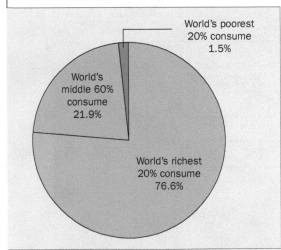

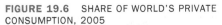

SOURCE: World Bank. (2008). "World Bank Development Indicators." © World Bank. On the World Wide Web at http://www.rrojasdatabank.info/wdi2008toc.htm (retrieved 19 August 2009). License: Creative Commons Attributiuon CC BY 3.0.

global planning and organization. Global capitalists have used numerous organizations and venues to formulate economic policy and interact with government policymakers, like the World Economic Forum held annually in Davos, Switzerland.

Global workers are relatively immobile and politically fragmented. Some of them cross international borders, but working abroad is constrained by international travel restrictions, work permits, and passports. When workers do move abroad to work, they are not always able to take their families with them and may be separated from loved ones for years at a time. Labour unions are struggling to protect workers in the competitive, footloose business environment of neoliberalism. While capital can move across borders with relative ease, unions are organized primarily within rather than across states. There have been attempts to increase the level of transnational union organization and solidarity, but most unions are oriented mainly to protecting domestic workers and wages against competition from foreign workers. In addition, many workers who travel abroad work in sectors that are relatively nonunionized and underregulated (e.g., nannying, the sex trade, agricultural workers), leaving them vulnerable to exploitation. While serious obstacles to organizing global workers remain, globalization processes have increased public awareness of sweatshop exploitation in factories around the world, leading some companies to ban the use of sweatshop labour. This section details some of the opportunities and challenges that globalization presents for global workers.

## WAGE LABOUR AND WAGE INEQUALITY

The world of global labour might seem relatively mundane compared with the branded world of transnational corporations and global consumer goods. Yet without a global labour force there would be no goods for consumers to consume and no profits for capitalists. Most people exchange their labour for a wage, which they then use to pay their rent, buy groceries, and so forth.

Throughout the world, however, there is still a sizable section of the population for which the concept of wage labour is new. These people gain access to food, water, and shelter directly through their own work rather than receiving a wage and purchasing needed commodities. Many of the world's people still make a living off the land and subsist mainly on

what they produce themselves; a little less than half the world's population lives in rural areas (World Bank, 2011b).

As urbanization increases and the use of wage labour spreads across the globe, so does the *segmentation* of labour markets. Women, people of colour, rural workers, and the people from the developing world in general are overrepresented at the bottom of the wage hierarchy. There is a tremendous disparity in global wages, particularly when we compare lower-level employees' salaries to CEO earnings (see Figure 19.7).

While income inequality in the United States is the most extreme among the world's rich countries, income and wealth inequality is a problem that worsened in Canada in the late 1990s (Picot and Myles, 2005). A 2007 study found the income gap between the richest 10 percent and poorest 10 percent of the population to be at a 30-year high (Yalnizyan, 2007). The average Canadian worker earned around $42 988 in 2009, while the average CEO earned $6.6 million (Grant, 2011b). Disparities in the Canadian labour market are based on class, as well as on race and country of birth. While many Canadians try to avoid minimum-wage work, thousands of migrants from Mexico and the Caribbean travel to Canada each year to work at agricultural jobs for minimum wages seven days a week with no overtime pay or statutory holidays (Basok, 2002).

While Mexicans working in Canada are denied labour rights granted Canadian citizens, minimum-wage jobs in Mexico are worse in terms of remuneration. Wages in Mexico remain stubbornly low despite the 1994 North American Free Trade Agreement (NAFTA) that Mexico signed with Canada and the United States. NAFTA was sold as a "rising tide" that would "lift the boats" of workers in the three countries. Yet the Mexican Labour Ministry reported that in 2003 workers earned an average of $360 a month, 16 percent less than they earned a decade earlier (Peters, 2004: 4; Jordan, 2003). Because per capita income is about one third that of the United States, the incentive to migrate (legally or illegally) remains higher than ever before, and cross-border migration remains a serious economic and political issue in both Mexico and the United States (CIA World Factbook, 2011).

Are low wages an age-old problem, or are they a unique result of globalization? The historical record shows that the search for cheap labour has been going on for hundreds of years. Indentured workers were

**FIGURE 19.7**    CEO'S AVERAGE PAY, 1990–2005

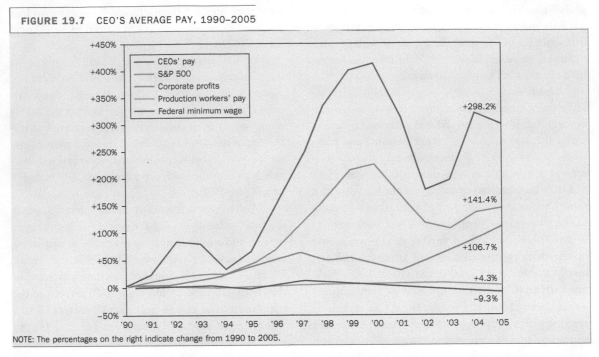

NOTE: The percentages on the right indicate change from 1990 to 2005.

SOURCE: Institute for Policy Studies and United for a Fair Economy. (2006). "Executive Excess 2006." On the World Wide Web at http://www.ips-dc.org /getfile.php?id=155 (retrieved 19 August 2009). Reprinted with permission.

brought from China to construct the North American railway system, while impoverished Irish immigrants competed with freed African American slaves for unskilled work in nineteenth-century North America. Globalization has heightened corporate competition for cheap labour. Firms use the threat of relocation as a way of keeping wages low. In effect, workers from different parts of the world compete against one another to attract foreign investment, driving wages down.

Given growing corporate competitiveness to find cheap labour, employment in a solid blue-collar job can no longer be taken for granted. Millions of North American workers in the manufacturing sector were laid off in the 1980s and 1990s (Beder, 2000: 132) and organized labour suffered serious setbacks, especially in the United States (Nissen, 2000: 3). Factory employment hit a 35-year low in Canada in 2011; while manufacturing was the number one sector of Canadian employment between 1976 and 1990, by 2011 it was only the third largest (Grant and Keenan 2011). Not only have North American manufacturing jobs declined since the 1980s, but corporations have also thinned out their management tiers, eliminating white-collar positions, **outsourcing** service jobs (e.g., call-centre jobs and

computer programming) to South Asia, and making it unclear whether a university degree guarantees middle-class economic status (Anderson, Cavanagh, Lee, and the Institute for Policy Studies, 2005: 33; Ehrenreich, 2005). The solid blue-collar manufacturing job or white-collar office job that allowed men to support a stay-at-home wife and two children in a middle-class lifestyle is now relatively rare, and about two-thirds of Canadian mothers work outside the home. Economists report that a third of Canada's economic growth between 1997 and 2005 was due to the proliferation of two-income households ("Canadians Made Little," 2005).

Although manufacturing jobs were lost to lower-wage settings in the globalization period, service sectors jobs have mushroomed in the world's rich countries. Certain well-paying job sectors have expanded their ranks (e.g., teachers and nurses), but most new jobs are created in low-wage, temporary sectors of the service sector with median wages that fall near or below the poverty line (e.g., retail salespersons, cashiers, food preparers and servers, janitors, home care workers, and waiters; Anderson et al., 2005: 43–44). Economic analysts have identified the problem of "sub-employment" and the "working poor," terms that describe a situation in which workers have work but it is poorly paid, unstable, nonunionized, and fails to lift workers above the poverty line (Ehrenreich, 2001; "Paid to Be Poor," 2004; Sheak and Morris, 2002; Shipler, 2004). The number of such workers increased substantially in the 2007–09 recession, which drove the unemployment rate up to 9.7 percent in the United States and 8.6 percent in Canada by July 2009 (Statistics Canada, 2009; U.S. Bureau of Labor Statistics, 2009).

The growth in service jobs has been partially met by a rising number of migrant labourers who moved from developing countries to Europe and North America. Labour migration has increased the ethnic diversity of the labour force in the world's rich countries and, in turn, fuelled a racist, anti-immigrant backlash in some countries, raising questions about the meaning and practice of multicultural ideals. Despite these political conflicts, international migration is likely to continue to Europe and North America given that the baby-boom generation of workers is aging, birth rates are low, and a potential shortage of skilled workers looms in the future for most advanced industrialized countries. Together, these trends have increased competition among Canadian provinces and among highly industrialized countries to attract highly educated immigrants (Howlett, 2005: A7). The trend of south-to-north labour migration has raised questions in countries like Canada about how to recognize foreign credentials and integrate new immigrants into the economy, particularly since new immigrants experience a disproportionate degree of poverty and lower levels of unionization (Milkman, 2000; Picot and Myles, 2005: 20). Meanwhile, voices from less developed countries speak of a "global brain drain" in which skilled professionals leave their homeland to seek better opportunities in developed countries, a trend thought to cost India alone US$2 billion a year (United Nations, 2001).

## SEARCHING FOR CHEAP LABOUR: "THE RACE TO THE BOTTOM"

Governments have reacted in different ways to the global competition to create jobs and attract corporate investment. In the less developed countries, some states have set up **export processing zones (EPZs)** where special financial deals—tax holidays, preferential rates for electricity and telecommunications, special exemptions from national labour laws, and the like—are used to lure corporations to set up shop and provide jobs. The most famous EPZ in

North America is the *maquiladora* region in northern Mexico. *Maquiladoras* are factories that allow companies to assemble goods for export by using low-cost Mexican labour and imported high-tech machinery and parts.

*Maquiladoras* employ low-cost labour compared with the United States and Canada, but since 2001 hundreds of thousands of *maquiladora* workers have been laid off, threatened with layoffs, paid lower wages, and compelled to work in worse conditions. Why? Mexican labour is cheap, but not cheap enough in a global marketplace where transnational firms try to find the world's least expensive, least regulated, and least unionized labour supply. Although Mexican wages are a bargain by Canadian standards, low-cost manufacturing has increasingly moved to Indonesia, Vietnam, and China, where labour is even cheaper; the Chinese legal monthly minimum wage is around US$176 ("Seven Countries," 2011). Wage competition pits workers against one another in a "race to the bottom." Globalization has placed Mexico in a difficult position: wages are too low to alleviate poverty rates yet too high to continue to attract low-cost manufacturing.

Although working conditions in the factories of the developing countries are often wretched, some members of the world's labour force suffer in conditions that resemble slavery in the literal sense of the word. An estimated 27 million people worldwide are enslaved—more than at any other time in our history—and slavery generated $91.2 billion in profit in 2007 (Bales, 1999; Kara, 2008). We are connected to this extreme form of labour exploitation through global commodity chains. In the words of Kevin Bales, a sociologist and expert in global slavery,

> Slaves in Pakistan may have made the shoes you are wearing and the carpet you stand on. Slaves in the Caribbean may have put sugar in your kitchen and toys in the hands of your children. In India they may have sewn the shirt on your back and polished the ring on your finger. They are paid nothing. ... Your investment portfolio and your mutual fund pension own stock in companies using labor in the developing world. Slaves keep your costs low and returns on your investments high. (1999: 3–4)

The injustices of the global labour system have not gone unnoticed or uncontested, even though serious obstacles lie ahead for unions and workers.

In Canada, unionized workers as a percentage of nonagricultural workers fell from a high point of 38 percent in 1981 to 31.5 percent in 2010 (Human Resources and Skills Development Canada, 2011), while the American unionization rate fell to just 11.9 percent in 2010 (Bureau of Labor Statistics, 2011). Historically, unionism arose in large capitalist factories, yet globalized firms often decentralize and subcontract work to small, independent firms, making unionization and labour regulation more difficult. Unions have responded by developing new strategies that include cross-border organization, transnational solidarity campaigns, emphasizing the importance of good wages for all working people (not just union members), and drives to organize service-sector workers, such as janitors, hotel workers, and security guards (Babson, 2000; Frundt, 2000; Milkman, 2000; Nissen, 2000).

The anti-sweatshop movement of the 1990s also raised awareness of labour exploitation by transnational firms (A. Ross, 1997; R. Ross, 2004). Today, prominent retail corporations like Nike and the Gap must at least appear to take global labour issues seriously (reports suggest that working conditions are still abysmal in Nike's subcontracted operations; R. Ross, 2004: 42). Although it was unimaginable to promote a "sweatshop-free" clothing line in the early 1990s, the popular label American Apparel has proven that it is possible (albeit difficult) to run a successful business without the use of sweatshop labour. Although American Apparel rejects unions and does not consider itself an "altruistic company," it produces all of its garments and shoes in Los Angeles and pays its workers more than California's minimum wage (R. Ross, 2004: 1). Recently, American Apparel has become vocal about the fight to legalize undocumented workers in Los Angeles, launching the "Legalize LA" campaign. In a letter that introduced this campaign, Dov Charney, founder and CEO of American Apparel, says that "[American Apparel's] dream for Los Angeles is that the over 1 million undocumented migrant workers who live here, and contribute to the city economically, culturally, and socially will have the opportunity to become legal residents of the city, and the United States" (American Apparel, n.d.). Other clothing lines, such as No Sweat, use unionized labour in North America *and* developing countries. According to the No Sweat website, "We believe that the only viable response to globalization is a global labor movement" (No Sweat, 2005).

# GLOBAL ECOLOGY

Consumers, workers, citizens, and nations all play critical roles in the globalization processes we have outlined. In turn, all these actors fit together in a larger global ecology that connects people, resources, and commodities. To better understand these ecological connections, I now examine the globalized food system.

## GLOBAL FOOD

Global trade in agriculture allows relatively prosperous people to consume a wide variety of exotic fruits, imported bottled water, and distant marine life, such as shrimp and fresh tuna. Although the global trade in food products is a boon for discriminating eaters, critics of industrialized global agriculture question its environmental costs. Trade experts and environmental groups warn that agriculture is the largest contributor of greenhouse gas when food production and distribution chains are taken into account, and suggest that the global food system represents the biggest environmental challenge facing humanity (Clay, 2004; Shrybman, 2000).

One of the major environmental problems with the world's agricultural system is the immense amount of fossil fuel required to produce, package, and transport food. Fossil fuel consumption generates greenhouse gases, such as carbon dioxide, which is linked to global climate change. But why is food so closely linked with carbon dioxide emissions? The first and simplest answer is transportation. Today, most Europeans and North Americans eat foods that have travelled a long distance to get to their plate. Food's travel time is captured in the concept of "food miles," a measure of the distance food travels from production to consumption and an indicator of the amount of fossil fuels burned in the process. A Toronto study compared the distance travelled by conventional agricultural products purchased at a discount supermarket with the distance travelled by the same basket of goods purchased at a nearby farmers' market (Bentley, 2004). While the supermarket food travelled 5734 kilometres on average, the same farmers' market produce travelled an average of only 101 kilometres to get to the consumer (Bentley, 2004: 7).

Food transported from far away might add variety to our diet, but it frequently involves an unsustainable and irrational energy tradeoff. For a head of iceberg lettuce transported from California to the United Kingdom, 127 calories of nonrenewable fossil fuel energy are required to produce 1 calorie of food energy (Sustain/Elm Farm Research Centre, 2001: 1). The way that most of our foods are produced and packaged also relies heavily on fossil fuels. The food processing industry uses 10 calories of fossil fuel energy to produce 1 calorie of food energy. Intensive livestock operations are even more wasteful: 1 calorie of beef requires 35 calories of fossil fuel, and 1 calorie of pork requires 68 calories of fossil fuel. Because of these energy-intensive production techniques, food scholars estimate that if the entire world adopted North American food habits, fossil fuel reserves would be gone in just seven years (Manning, 2004: 42, 44).

Just as consumers in India and China move toward a meat-intensive diet, increasing demand for both animal feed and oil calls into question the stability of global food supplies. Despite short-term fluctuations, demand for oil is increasing while supply is just about stagnant. As a result, the price of oil increases, and agricultural crops, such as corn, are increasingly turned into biofuel to offset oil supply problems. However, the diversion of food crops into biofuel production causes food prices to rise. In 2007–08,

news headlines reported food riots by poor people in many developing countries, ignited by sharply rising food prices (Walt, 2008).

## Soil, Water, and Genetic Engineering

Besides relying heavily on fossil fuel, industrial methods of food production are associated with global environmental problems like deforestation, soil erosion, and declining water tables. In the past 40 years, soil degradation has caused farmers around the world to abandon about 430 million hectares of arable land. This area amounts to one-third of all cropland (Kindall and Pimentel, 1994; see Figure 19.8). Every year, 130 000 square kilometres of forest, an area four times the size of Switzerland, are destroyed to make way for agriculture. By 2020, an estimated 22 million hectares of savannah and forest, an area as large as the United Kingdom, will be cut down in South America to meet global demand for soya, a crop that is used largely for livestock feed and vegetable oil (World Wildlife Fund, 2004).

Even when adequate land can be found to grow crops, water is also needed. Seventy percent of world water usage is for irrigation, and food analysts worry about an emerging "world water deficit"

---

**FIGURE 19.8**   GLOBAL SOIL DEGRADATION

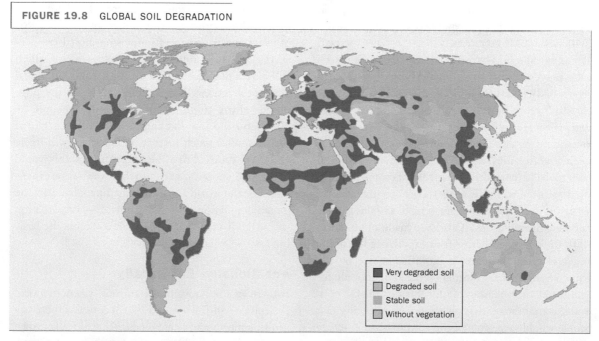

Very degraded soil
Degraded soil
Stable soil
Without vegetation

SOURCE: UNEP, International Soil Reference and Information Center (ISRIC), *World Atlas of Desertification, 1997*. In Philippe Rekacewicz. (2002). "Degraded Soils." UNEP/GRID-Arendal Maps and Graphics Library. Retrieved 17 May 2009. http://maps.grida.no/go/graphic/degraded.soils.

(Brown, 2005: 10). Underground aquifers refill slowly and are currently being pumped at rates that are unsustainable. In Northern China, for instance, groundwater levels are falling by at least one metre a year, while aquifers in the United States are being pumped at a pace that vastly exceeds replacement rates (Pimentel and Wilson, 2004).

Some scientists believe that global agriculture problems can be addressed by switching to genetically modified (GM) crops that have been designed to be drought- and pest-resistant by reengineering the plant's genetic structure. This technological solution is opposed by many environmentalists who worry about the long-term health and ecological impact of GE crops, particularly the negative impact on biodiversity, since GE crops tend to out-compete and contaminate related species. GE canola has already infected organic canola in Western Canada to such an extent that it is impossible for organic farmers to grow and market uncontaminated (GE-free) organic canola. Saskatchewan farmer Percy Schmeiser launched a lawsuit against seed giant Monsanto, suing for damages, and was awarded an out-of-court settlement. Activists in less developed countries are concerned that GE crops will permit large corporations to consolidate their control over agriculture and erode traditions of seed saving and innovation by farmers.

Although much of the world's (GM) crops have been grown in North America, their usage in the Global South has expanded considerably—by 2010, developing countries were growing 48 percent of the world's GM crops (ISAAA, 2010). One estimate suggested that by 2010, GM crops were being grown in 29 countries by 15.4 million farmers, many of whom ran relatively small, resource-poor operations (Federoff, 2011). Because of the huge capital investment in these technologies, multinational bioscience companies would like to expand adoption rates globally (currently 10 percent of crop land globally is planted with GE crops). One way this may be occurring is through food aid, which contains genetically engineered crops. This issue made headlines in 2001–02, when southern Africa experienced a famine and was given genetically modified maize by the United States. African leaders protested, not only for health and safety reasons but for fear that the GE corn would contaminate their own supplies (assuming that people would save some of the corn to plant in future harvests), and endanger export markets in Europe, where GE foods have faced bans and stiff consumer resistance (African Centre for Biosafety, 2005).

In 2005, scientists discovered that grain donated by the United States Agency for International Development (USAID) through the World Food Program (WFP) to Central American and Caribbean countries was heavily contaminated with genetically modified corn. Eighty percent of the samples tested included GE corn, including "StarLink," corn that is not authorized for human consumption in the United States (Organic Consumers Association, 2005). The UN Cartagena Protocol on Biosafety stipulates that genetically engineered crops can enter countries only with prior informed consent, but the WFP's heavy reliance on USAID grain supplies means that this right is currently not being enforced and that genetic contamination of the world's global grain supplies is likely to continue.

## Global Hunger amid Plenty

The world grows enough grain to provide nearly three thousand calories per person per day (Lappé, 2005: 13), yet the number of undernourished people in the world has risen since the early 1980s, totalling at least 842 million people (Wheeler and Thompson, 2004: 212). World grain production is a general measure of global food security. Per capita grain production has been falling since 1984, while overall grain production was flat between 1996 and 2003 (Brown, 2005: 4).

It is especially troubling to consider these numbers in the context of widespread soil erosion, loss of crop land to urbanization, rising global temperatures, and shrinking water supplies—all of which will have a negative impact on the capacity of global grain production (Brown, 2005: 7). With the population rising to an estimated 9 billion people by 2050, and the low likelihood of expanding global grain supplies much further, grain prices will likely rise in the future. For affluent consumers, this would make food supplies, particularly meat, more expensive. For the world's malnourished people—half the global population by some estimates—this situation will make it increasingly difficult to access the basic food staples needed for survival.

## Act Globally, Eat Locally

Is there an alternative to the current system of global agriculture? In Europe and North America there is a growing movement to eat foods that are locally grown and produced with organic farming techniques. Researchers in Britain estimate that if all farms in there became organic, an estimated $1.1 billion in environmental costs would be saved (Lang and Pretty, 2005; Lappé and Lappé, 2002).

The move to promote organic, locally grown food is not confined to the affluent minority world. The Nadvanya movement in India, for instance, aims to promote indigenous agricultural techniques to counter the presence of multinational agribusiness in ways that improve the environment and increase people's food security (Navdanya, 2005). Many organic farmers and food activists believe that organic farming techniques, not genetic engineering or food aid, are the answer to famines and food shortages (Hall, 2005), although not all food experts agree (Paarlberg, 2010).

The tension between local and global food represents the challenge and the paradox of bottom-up globalization. It is a challenge because most small-scale activists and food producers, like most of the world's workers, are rooted where they grow food and are not nearly as globalized as corporate agribusiness and its CEOs. It is a paradox because peasant and small farmer movements want to encourage *local* food consumption, defend *local* agricultural ecosystems, and, at the same time, use *global* networks to fight these battles. Their motto could be "act globally, eat locally."

## Cuba: An Island's Isolation and Innovation

What would happen if globalization processes were reversed, and a country suddenly found itself isolated, without the ability to trade for food in global markets? Cuba provides a real-life answer to that question. It is literally an island, but is also a metaphorical island in that it is largely isolated from the major ebbs and flows of global food trade. The United States has refused to trade with Cuba since 1960, a year after the Cuban revolution in 1959. After the collapse of the Soviet Union, Cuba lost access to an extremely important source of food supplies and fossil fuels.

Suddenly, the nation was hungry. Calorie consumption per person per day fell from 3000 in 1989 (the year the Soviet Union collapsed) to 1600 four years later.

Without fossil fuels or cheap grain supplies, Cuba's agriculture had to change, and change it did. Cuban agronomists began experimenting with more sustainable, low-input agriculture that used crop rotation to provide natural fertilization. They developed large urban gardens to feed and employ thousands of Cubans. Farmers began using oxen instead of tractors, saving fossil fuel. Today, almost completely cut off from global agricultural trade, Havana feeds itself from gardens within city limits. There are still problems ensuring adequate supplies of milk and meat, yet Cuban agriculture is remarkably successful, leading some analysts to suggest that the Cuban model is a possible future scenario for what agriculture could look like when fossil fuel supplies become scarce and the environmental consequences of globalized industrial agriculture become too onerous to ignore (McKibben, 2005: 69).

In an article profiling the costs and benefits of the Cuban agricultural experiment, environmental journalist Bill McKibben concludes with a provocative and difficult question that we would do well to ponder—a question that applies not only to Cuban agriculture, but to globalization more generally:

> Is it also possible ... that there's something inherently destructive about a globalized free-market society—that the eternal race for efficiency, when raised to a planetary scale, damages the environment, and perhaps the community, and perhaps even the taste of a carrot? Is it possible that markets, at least for food, may work better when they're smaller and more isolated? The next few decades may be about answering that question. (McKibben, 2005: 69)

# SUMMARY

1. Globalization effectively shrinks the world; workers, commodities, ideas, and capital cross distances more quickly. Sociologists use the term "time–space compression" to describe this process.

2. Globalization processes have generated contradictory outcomes that benefit some groups but have also been linked to poverty, economic marginalization, democratic deficits, and the digital divide.

3. Developments in information technology have facilitated the economic integration of financial markets. Consequently, global flows of financial capital are much bigger than global flows of tangible goods and productive capital.

4. Corporations in the global era have become much bigger and are under pressure to become more competitive in the global marketplace. Local and even national competitiveness is no longer seen as sufficient for economic survival.

5. Politically, the globalization era has witnessed the creation of new international institutions of governance like the IMF, World Bank, and WTO, which have diminished the power and sovereignty of some states.

6. Globalization processes have allowed communities around the world to gain knowledge of the injustice and suffering inflicted by the global economy. Such awareness has inspired efforts to increase social justice in the global system. These efforts are known as "globalization from below."

7. Most of the goods Canadians consume connect them to workers and production processes thousands of kilometres away. The globalization process is almost impossible to escape given the extent of global commodity chains.

8. The period of globalization is associated with a shift in manufacturing employment out of the more developed countries. Competitive pressure is driving corporations to seek the lowest wages possible in the less developed countries (the so-called race to the bottom).

9. Global ecology is not something that exists separately from globalization processes. It is connected to the actions of citizens, consumers, workers, and states.

# QUESTIONS TO CONSIDER

1. How do you benefit from globalization processes? What are the negative consequences of these processes? Consider your role as a worker, consumer, and citizen.

2. Do you think globalization has caused the Canadian state to lose sovereignty? Do you think Canadians suffer from a democratic deficit?

3. Do you think that consumer activism and social movement campaigns like the anti-sweatshop campaign are an effective way of making global commodity chains more equitable? Do you think that the corporate movement for social responsibility offers a more promising avenue for change? Is voluntary corporate action sufficient or are governments needed to make legislation and enforce corporate responsibility?

# GLOSSARY

**Consumerism** (p. 476) is a way of life focusing on the purchase and acquisition of commodities. While traditionally thought of as a problem for North America and Europe, consumerism is also a cultural and ecological issue among affluent populations in the less developed countries.

**Cultural imperialism** (p. 477) is a controversial theory of cultural domination according to which powerful economic and political actors (primarily Euro-American) are thought to impose their values, norms, and lifestyles on other populations. Cultural imperialism often refers to the export of certain Euro-American cultural practices, such as materialism, consumerism, and sexual liberalism through the media of television, music, and film.

A **democratic deficit** (p. 473) involves the disenfranchisement of ordinary citizens from the decisions and process of governments. Democratic deficits are often attributed to the influence of corporate actors and international financial institutions on governments and the transfer of governance to institutions such as the IMF and WTO, which do not permit average citizens to vote or influence decisions.

The **digital divide** (p. 466) is the gap between people who are easily able to access communication technologies, such as the Internet and cellular phones, and people who lack the material resources, education, or infrastructure to access these technologies.

**Export processing zones (EPZs)** (p. 483) are manufacturing areas in which government programs provide special incentives to help promote export-oriented manufacturing. Sometimes EPZs are actual territorial zones demarcated by fences and borders, while in other cases they indicate programs that apply to all industries in a country. For instance, in 1991 Sri Lanka declared the entire country an EPZ.

The **fourth world** (p. 475) comprises marginalized populations and regions that are not competitive in the global economy.

A **global commodity chain** (p. 476) is a worldwide network of labour and production processes, the end result of which is a finished commodity.

**Globalization** (p. 465) is a social, economic, and political process that facilitates the movement of people, goods, ideas, and capital around the globe. With globalization processes, the world appears to shrink, although the ability to cross borders varies tremendously depending on one's position in the global economy.

**Globalization from below** (p. 468) is a short-hand way of describing a diverse range of projects seeking greater democracy, equality, and sustainability in globalization processes. These projects are generally opposed to neoliberal policies and U.S. hegemony in the global system and are also referred to as alternative globalization, the global social justice movement, and anti-globalization.

**Neoliberalism** (p. 467) refers to economic policies that became prominent in the late 1970s in both developed and developing countries. Neoliberalism is associated with a retreat from state intervention and regulation, greater focus on individual responsibility, less protection for labour and the environment, privatization of state resources, and faith in the power of the market and the profit motive to provide the greatest good for the greatest number.

**Outsourcing** (p. 482) occurs when firms contract production and services to smaller, independent firms. When outsourcing occurs on a global level, multinational corporations contract production and services to firms in less developed countries.

**Time–space compression** (p. 465) refers to the diminished importance of geography and time lags because of globalization.

**Top-down globalization** (p. 467) refers to the extension of capitalism globally, particularly as a result of the neoliberal policies and programs authorized by international financial authorities, such as the IMF and World Bank, and implemented by national governments. Top-down globalization is organized by elites in governments, corporations, and international institutions with little democratic input.

A **virtual community** (p. 465) is a group whose members share interests and meet primarily on the Internet.

## SUGGESTED READING

Ehrenreich, Barbara and Arlie Russell Hoschschild, eds. (2002). *Global Woman: Nannies, Maids, and Sex Workers in the New Economy.* New York: Metropolitan Books. This captivating account offers personal and insightful analyses of how globalization affects women around the world. The economics of globalization come to life through the stories told in these chapters.

Sachs, Jeffrey. (2005). *The End of Poverty: Economic Possibilities for Our Time.* New York: Penguin. You may not agree with Sachs's hopeful analysis, but this is an undeniably influential account written by one of the world's most important economists (and endorsed by none other than Bono, who wrote the Foreword). The book is highly readable and combines economic analysis with personal stories from the author's travels in the world's poverty-stricken areas.

Smith, Jackie, ed. (2007). *Global Democracy and the World Social Forums.* Boulder, CO: Paradigm Publishers. This book provides a nonspecialist's account of the World Social Forum (WSF), one of the most exciting and important global activist events in recent decades. Each chapter is written by a scholar who has participated in the WSF, and together they show how the WSF is a critical part of the transnational movement for global peace, justice, and democracy.

# Multinational and Global Corporations

## Objective

You will learn a way to think about the size and power of the world's largest corporations.

What does it mean to be the largest corporation in the world and have $421.8 billion in annual revenue?

Chris Caldeira

Walmart's annual revenue of $421.8 billion in 2011 made it the 36th largest economy in the world, after South Africa, which has a $422 billion GDP.

## Multinational Corporations

A **multinational corporation** is an enterprise that owns, controls, or licenses facilities in countries other than the one in which it is headquartered. It is difficult to estimate the number of multinationals in the world, because digital technologies allow as few as two people in different countries to form a corporation. The last estimate made by the United Nations was 65,000 multinationals, with 820,000 foreign affiliates (Chanda 2003). A multinational corporation can range in size from fewer than 10 to millions of employees. In fact, most multinationals employ 250 or fewer people (Gabel and Bruner 2003). Regardless of size, multinationals compete, plan, produce, sell, recruit, acquire resources, and do other activities on a multi-country scale.

Multinationals establish operations in foreign countries for many reasons, including to obtain raw materials (such as oil and diamonds), to avoid paying taxes, to employ a low-wage labor force, and to manufacture goods for consumers in a host country (as does Toyota Motor North America, Inc.). Multinationals are headquartered disproportionately in the United States, Japan, and Western Europe. These global enterprises make "the key decisions—about what people eat and drink, what they read and hear, what sort of air they breathe and the water they drink, and ultimately what societies will flourish and which city blocks will decay" (Barnet 1990, 59).

The world's largest multinational corporations are often referred to as global corporations (see Table 5.9a). Theoretically, a truly global corporation should have some kind of presence in every country in the world. Probably no corporation is yet global in that sense. Still, many corporations such as McDonald's, with a presence in 119 countries, and UPS, with a presence in 200-plus countries, are called global because of their size and reach (McDonald's 2012; UPS 2010).

▼ **Table 5.9a: The World's Largest Global Corporations, 2011**

Notice that 6 of the 10 largest corporations in the world extract or refine oil. In what ways might petroleum industries slow down national efforts to use less oil?

| Rank | Global Corporation | Industry | Revenues (in billions) | Profits (in billions) | Headquarters |
|------|-------------------|----------|------------------------|-----------------------|--------------|
| 1 | Walmart | General merchandisers | $421.3 | $16.4 | United States |
| 2 | Royal Dutch Shell | Petroleum | $378.2 | $20.2 | Netherlands |
| 3 | ExxonMobil | Petroleum | $354.7 | $30.5 | United States |
| 4 | BP | Petroleum | $308.9 | –$3.7 | UK |
| 5 | SINOPEC | Petroleum | $273.4 | $7.6 | China |
| 6 | China National Petroleum | Petroleum | $240.2 | $14.4 | China |
| 7 | State Grid | Electricity (power) | $226.3 | –$4.6 | China |
| 8 | Toyota Motors | Automobile | $221.8 | $4.8 | Japan |
| 9 | Japan Post Holdings | Banking, insurance, mail delivery, and over-the-counter services | $204.0 | $4.9 | Japan |
| 10 | Chevron | Petroleum | $196.3 | $19.0 | United States |

Source: Fortune Magazine (2012)

When you read the names of the world's largest global corporations, 10 of which are listed in Table 5.9a, it is difficult to imagine their size and power of influence without some basis for comparison. We can get some idea of their size by comparing the annual revenues of a corporation to a country's GDP. A corporation's annual revenue is the total amount of money it receives for goods sold or services provided over the course of a given year. Taken together, the annual revenue of the top 10 global corporations is $2.825 trillion. GDP is the total value of all goods and services produced *within* the country over a year's time. Only four countries in the world—the United States, China, Japan, and Germany—have a GDP that exceeds $2.825 trillion. The annual revenue of the world's largest corporation, Walmart, is $421.8 billion. Only 35 countries have a GDP larger than that amount; those countries include Australia, Brazil, Canada, China, India, Iran, Italy, Japan, Mexico, and the United States.

In 2008 the global economic crisis alerted us to the possibility that many of the world's largest corporations were "too big to fail." That is, if these corporations failed, the economy as a whole might fail, too. So the United States and other governments intervened to prevent key financial and automobile institutions from failing. At that time, the combined annual revenues of just four troubled financial institutions—Citigroup, Bank of America, JPMorgan, and AIG—was $504 billion (Fortune Magazine 2009).

# Criticism and Support for Multinationals

Critics of multinational corporations maintain that they are engines of destruction. That is, they exploit people and natural resources to generate profits. They take advantage of desperately poor labor forces, lenient environmental regulations, and sometimes almost nonexistent worker safety standards. As a case in point, in the decade leading up to the Great Recession that started in 2008, financial institutions set terms and loaned money to people and businesses who could never hope to meet payments (e.g., subprime loans) and then passed that risk on to others.

Supporters of multinational corporations, by contrast, maintain that these companies are agents of progress. Most obviously, multinationals employ millions and distribute goods, services, technology, and capital across the globe. In addition, they praise the multinationals' ability to raise standards of living, increase employment opportunities, transcend political hostilities, transfer technology, and promote cultural understanding. As one measure of their positive contributions, consider that Royal Dutch Shell and other oil producers make it possible for billions of people to drive cars, warm their homes, and so on.

On another level, however, multinationals' operations can aggravate problems related to obesity, poverty, mass unemployment, and overall inequality. Still, one can also argue that multinationals are not responsible for creating or solving social problems, such as obesity. After all, nobody forces people to eat fast foods or choose Walmart over a locally owned store (Weiser 2003).

◄ McDonald's and other fast-food establishments sell healthy items such as real fruit smoothies. As one former McDonald's CEO pointed out, "You can get a balanced diet at McDonald's. It's a question of how you use McDonald's" (Greenberg 2001).

Moreover, corporations claim that they merely respond to consumer demand. For example, virtually all the major fast-food companies have introduced healthy items on their menus, and most have proven unpopular with consumers. The typical McDonald's restaurant, for example, sells 50 to 60 salads per day versus 300 to 400 double cheeseburgers (Warner 2006). Nevertheless, critics question whether corporations should have the right to ignore the long-term effects of their products and practices on people and the environment, even if they are responding to consumer demand. Profitable products may benefit a corporation's bottom line and shareholders, but they can also be costly for a society due to **externality costs**—hidden costs of using, making, or disposing of a product that are not figured into the price of the product or paid for by the producer. Such costs include those associated with cleaning up the environment and with treating injured and chronically ill workers, consumers, and others. These costs must eventually be paid by someone (Lepkowski 1985).

While multinationals and other corporations are very powerful, consumer advocacy organizations have demonstrated that they can hold corporations in check. One thing is clear: when corporate executives feel real pressure from consumers, they act. However, if only a small number of consumers speak out, their claims are often dismissed. Consider comments from a McDonald's CEO after as many as 2,000 protesters trashed McDonald's restaurants and other businesses during four days of protest in Seattle against the World Trade Organization. The CEO noted that while 2,000 people protested, 17.5 million other people visited a McDonald's restaurant to eat (Greenberg 2001). The point is that there is no need to be concerned about the voices of 2,000 activists when 17.5 million consumers are voting with their feet—or mouths. McDonald's has changed some of its practices in response to pressure from other organizations, however. Greenpeace is one example of an organization dedicated to mobilizing people to hold governments and corporations responsible for crimes against the environment or for failing to protect the environment. It has recorded a number of successes, including pressuring McDonald's Corporation to agree not to use chickens that have been fed on soya, a feed that is grown in the Amazon rainforest. For a list of Greenpeace victories, see http://www.greenpeace.org/international/about/victories.

## (Write a Caption)

Write a caption that relates Coca-Cola to the concept of a multinational corporation.

### Hints: In writing this caption

- review the concept of a multinational corporation,
- find out how many countries sell Coca-Cola products, and
- identify the geographic location of its first sale.

Robert K. Wallace

## Critical Thinking

Review the most current list of the world's 500 largest corporations, which can be found online by using the search term "Global 500." Identify one that has had a positive or negative impact on your life. Explain.

## Key Terms

externality costs          multinational corporation

# Global Inequality

# CHAPTER 9

# DEVELOPMENT AND UNDERDEVELOPMENT

**Anthony Winson**
UNIVERSITY OF GUELPH

SOURCE: © Christie's Images/CORBIS.

# COMMONSENSE THEORIES OF DEVELOPMENT

Many people entertain pet theories or working hypotheses about why some parts of the world are poor and others are rich. A personal example may help illustrate this point. My parents lived for several years in countries that were poor by Canadian standards, and my mother held a theory that was popular at the time. She told me about living in a small South American jungle mining camp in what was then the British colony of British Guiana and commented that "if you had lived in that heat and humidity you would know why they are so poor." It was perhaps not surprising that a young woman who had lived through 20 Saskatchewan winters would find the tropics an obstacle to productive activity. It was just common sense to her that the climate explained why British Guiana was underdeveloped.

Decades later, my experiences and observations in Mexico and Central America challenged my mother's views. I confronted the architectural evidence of a wealthy colonial past and the archaeological wealth of complex indigenous civilizations that predated the invasion of Europeans. Excavations in Mexico City had just unearthed evidence of the rich city-state of Tenotitchlán that existed when Hernán Cortés and his Spanish soldier adventurers arrived on horseback from the Atlantic Coast in 1519. Just to the north lay the pyramids of Teotihuacán, structures that dwarf the fabled pyramids of Egypt. This city-state reached its peak between 500 and 600 CE, encompassed 21 square kilometres, and had a population 10 times larger than that of contemporary London (Waldman, 2005). To the south, I encountered the imposing ancient hilltop city of Monte Alban near present-day Oaxaca City and evidence of several other precolonial settlements of considerable size and development along the highway leading farther south into the mountains of the mist-shrouded Lacandon forest in the Mexican state of Chiapas that borders Guatemala. In the lowland regions of this zone, I came across some of the most impressive archaeological finds in the Western Hemisphere, relics of the extensive Mayan civilizations that existed from approximately 50 BCE to 1000 CE. Over time, the Mayans constructed a series of cities that boasted ornate architecture, elaborate irrigation infrastructure and palatial structures for their nobility, and massive platforms to accommodate elaborate religious rituals. Between 600 and 800 CE, this civilization reached the highest development of its arts and sciences. By then, the Mayans had invented an elaborate system of hiero-glyphic writing, a complex calendar for predicting the seasons, accurate computations of time, and detailed astronomical observations. All of this 1500 years ago in the midst of a part of the world notable for its heat and humidity. So much for my mother's climate theory of development.

Climate is not completely insignificant in under-standing the origins and development of human civili-zations. Regions with year-round permafrost or great deserts do not allow dense human settlement and the agriculture it depends on, let alone the accumulation of wealth. Or at least they did not in the past. Today, as the example of the desert kingdom of Dubai shows, oil wealth can help spur impressive development in formerly inhospitable places. The key word here is *can*; other oil-rich countries, such as Nigeria, have failed to mobilize their wealth to realize development goals. They remain mired in poverty. Why? With this question we enter ongoing debates that animate the study of development and the explanations for global inequalities that flow from these debates. One of the goals of this chapter is to introduce you to key expla-nations or theories of development and the contro-versies they have engendered.

But why study development at all, you might ask? What relevance does it have for my life? What *is* development anyway? It makes sense to address these questions before we examine key debates in the field.

## WHAT IS DEVELOPMENT?

The idea of development dates from the eighteenth century, when scholars in Scotland and France for-mulated the idea of progress. They promoted the industrialization and democratization of society based on the equal rights and freedoms of its citizens.

At first, development was just an idea. It was not until after World War II that the idea crystal-lized into a full-blown project or, more accurately, a series of projects that became part of state policy and the policy of some non-state organizations (Parpart and Veltmeyer, 2003). After World War II, devel-opment came increasingly to mean a process that generated economic growth, industrialization, and modernization in regions and countries perceived to be poor, traditional, and undeveloped. More recently, development has had a broader, more complex meaning, incorporating such notions as progress for women, empowerment of the underprivileged, and environmental sustainability.

Two main factors motivated interest in develop-ment after World War II. First, the Cold War broke out between the developed capitalist countries led by the United States and the communist countries led by the Soviet Union. Among other things, the Cold War involved intense competition between the two rival blocs to amass power by gaining influence and control over less developed countries. Second, businesses in the developed West, particularly the United States, were interested in new markets outside their tradi-tional spheres of operation. Latin America, Africa, and Asia were thus of great interest to the Western powers for geopolitical and economic reasons.

Given the context just described, it may not sur-prise you to learn that some analysts have argued that development, and the study of development, have served to support world **capitalism,** an economic system based on competitive enterprises seeking to maximize profits by using wage labour. However, as we will see, other analysts deny that that genuine develop-ment can occur within the confines of capitalism. They have promoted a non-capitalist road to development.

## THE RELEVANCE OF DEVELOPMENT AND GLOBAL INEQUALITIES: SOCIAL JUSTICE AND SECURITY

Earlier I asked why you should care about develop-ment. We can look at this question from two perspec-tives, one involving morality and social justice, the other involving self-interest and the need for security.

Development is an important issue for many people because they find it morally repugnant that more than a billion people earn a dollar or less a day (see Figure 9.1). They consider it a matter of social justice that the world's desperately poor be lifted out of a life of illiteracy, disease, and hopelessness. They regard it as unacceptable that a Canadian student buys a coffee at Starbucks for three times the average daily wage of more than a billion people, or spends more on a laptop computer than the per capita gross domestic product of the world's 51 poorest coun-tries (less than US$1000; Milanovic, 2009; United Nations, 2009).

Other people are more concerned with the practical implications of having so many people in the world with so little to sustain them. Few of us would feel comfortable living in a luxurious house with expensive furnishings and two luxury cars in the driveway if several of our immediate neighbours lived in a one-room shanty with a tin roof, owned virtually

**FIGURE 9.1**   PERCENTAGE OF GLOBAL POPULATION BY REGION LIVING BELOW $1/DAY (PPP*)

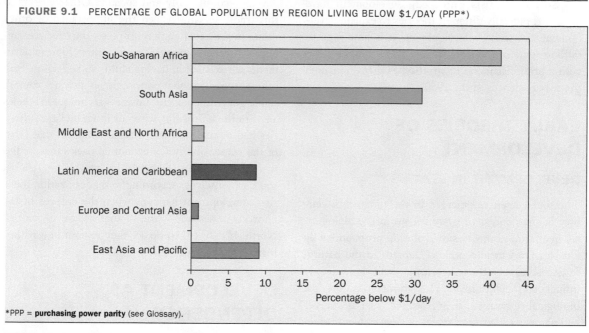

*PPP = **purchasing power parity** (see Glossary).

SOURCE: Based on data from 2005 World Development Indicators, World Bank, March 2005, page 67.

nothing, lacked regular employment, and spent much of their time staring enviously at our lifestyle and property. Eventually, our neighbours' poverty would have unpleasant implications for us.

The higher levels of violence and unrest that accompany poverty would likely wash over to our side of the street. We would have to pay higher taxes to bolster police forces to maintain order and deal with those who decide that it's not fair for us alone to have all the nice things in life. We would soon come to realize that our personal security cannot be divorced from the living conditions of our neighbours, and our failure to help raise their living standard must inevitably have serious, negative implications for us.

Life today is like the scenario painted above, but with added complications. Our poor neighbours might, for example, be living on land we own or land we took from them by using to our advantage property laws and the fact that our neighbours didn't have formal title to the land they had been living on for generations. We might allow our poor neighbours to grow crops, but they would have to give us most of their harvest for the privilege of living on our land. We might select a few of the poor neighbours to supervise the land and reward them with a disproportionate amount of the crop and some extra money under the table. We might also provide the chosen

few with firearms and training so they could protect the property and especially the production of fruits and vegetables, dealing appropriately with anyone who might want to challenge existing property rights.

Challenges would likely arise because most households enjoy only a bare subsistence and grow rapidly, making less food per person available over time. Unrest would mount. We would therefore be forced to send some of our family members to help our managers keep order, and some of them would come back with injuries from the skirmishes. Before long, it would be necessary to lock up and occasionally kill people in the poorer households to maintain the status quo, and some of our own family members would undoubtedly get killed trying to police the growing violence.

When we add these complications to our fictitious neighbourhood economy, we have a model that better mirrors the world as it has existed for some time. It is a model that not only describes huge differences in income between our neighbours and us but also points out the inequality that exists *within* poor neighbourhoods. Importantly, the model also establishes that the neighbourhood economy is maintained by a system of power relations backed up by disproportionate wealth and, ultimately, our willingness to exercise violence when all else fails.

Social scientists who study development have proposed radically different theories to explain development and lack of development. It is now time to outline some of the most important of them. I begin with a brief discussion of approaches that dominated the social sciences in the 1960s.

# EARLY THEORIES OF DEVELOPMENT

## DEVELOPMENT IN STAGES

The social sciences emerged in the nineteenth century in the context of lively debate in the biological sciences around theories of evolution propounded by Charles Darwin and others. Debates in the natural sciences, especially concerning evolution, deeply influenced social thinkers. Human societies were like biological organisms, they reasoned. Just as animals and plants pass through stages of development, so do societies; and like animals and plants, societies are susceptible to pathologies or diseases.

Such ideas were still influential in the 1960s, when W. W. Rostow argued that societal development follows several necessary **stages of development** (Rostow, 1960). According to Rostow, in the beginning, a society might be traditional, undifferentiated, and undeveloped. When it comes into contact with a developed society, however, science and technology spread, and the traditional society enters a stage of possible "takeoff." Takeoff occurs when and if an increase in market transactions, manufacturing, and trade takes place. The faster society moves along the path to development, the more quickly barriers to the spread of market relations are removed and the more efficiently scientific and technological diffusion occurs.

## DEVELOPMENT AS A STATE OF MIND

Another popular approach in the 1960s was **modernization theory,** which emphasizes the importance of values and norms as drivers of development. David McClelland (1961), for example, argued for the importance of entrepreneurship and what he called the "need for achievement," the desire for feelings of accomplishment and personal satisfaction. People who enjoy a high need for achievement are more likely to become successful entrepreneurs, McClelland argued, and societies that encourage entrepreneurial behaviour and competitiveness are the most likely to

develop economically and socially. Other writers in this tradition emphasized the importance of other values in the development process—the need for savings, investment, innovation, education, high achievement, self-control in having children, and so on. Still others recognized that poor societies also lack capital, stable governments, and business techniques (Inkeles and Smith, 1976). But what all modernization theories had in common was their assumption that most of the responsibility for economic backwardness lies with the societies of the "third world" or "global south" themselves. According to modernization theorists, development happens when the citizens of the poor countries adopt the virtues of the developed North. If they fail to do so, they remain in a pathological, undeveloped state.

# DEVELOPMENT AS DEPENDENCY

**Dependency theory** sharply challenged the notion that lack of development is due to the deficiencies of less developed countries. It did so by taking a holistic view—recognizing that each part of the world is shaped by, and helps to shape, a wider, global reality—and attending to the history and structure of relations between countries.

Dependency theorists produced abundant evidence of strong and enduring economic and social relationships between "metropolitan powers," such as Spain, Portugal, Britain, and France, and "satellite regions" of the global south. First focusing on Latin America and the Caribbean (Cardoso and Faletto, 1979; Frank, 1966), they established that it was precisely the nature of the relationship between metropolitan powers and satellite regions that blocked economic progress in the global south. Let us consider the implications of this argument in detail.

## FROM CONTACT TO CONQUEST

Evidence contradicts the notion that the societies of the global south existed in an undeveloped state, as stage and modernization theories suggest. From China through the Middle East and the Mediterranean to Central and South America, great civilizations rose and fell. For example, between 1200 and 200 BCE, Carthage flourished on the northern shores of Africa, while the later naval, military, commercial, and cultural advances of the Muslim people of the Maghreb region of northwestern Africa allowed them to invade and dominate Spain and Portugal until the twelfth century. In the area of east Africa now known as Zimbabwe, we find great stone constructions and evidence of extensive metallurgical development and trade across vast distances. Africans had developed a great deal on their own before Europe began asserting its dominance over the continent (Rodney, 1972).

Initial contact between Europe and the societies of the global south took place around 1500. For the next several hundred years, the Europeans engaged in wholesale pillage and plunder, causing massive death, migration, and economic upheaval—unpleasant facts that stage and modernization theories ignore. Before Europeans could exploit the global south for its riches, they had to conquer existing civilizations. Superior technology in the form of gunpowder and firearms helped to secure the conquest, as did diseases borne by the Europeans. Europeans had evolved resistance to smallpox, influenza, and other diseases that they introduced into the global south. In Mexico alone, the population was reduced from 20 million to 2 million in the first century of contact with Europe. A population collapse of similar magnitude occurred in North America, and among the Inca of Peru. Overall, some 95 percent of the New World's population was wiped out in a fairly short period after European contact (Diamond, 1999: 210–11).

Following their conquest of the New World, the Spanish established a feudalistic landholding system based on hierarchical relationships imported from Europe and subordinated to the power of the Spanish Crown. Its purpose was to support a local European landed elite and funnel valuable minerals, principally gold and silver, and agricultural commodities to the mother country. The Spanish monarchy appropriated much of the profit.

## THE SLAVE TRADE

Another disruptive aspect of the relationship between Europe and the global south involved the West African slave trade. It undermined traditional state structures and forms of governance in West Africa and created deep-seated ethnic animosities.

Forced labour had existed for centuries in Europe. Muslim pirates from North Africa had undertaken raids as far afield as southern England to enslave captives. However, the trans-Atlantic slave trade, initiated by Europeans after 1500, established slave economies of unprecedented size, with dire consequences for West Africa in particular.

African slaves taken on board HMS Daphne, November 1, 1868.
SOURCE: The National Archives of the UK, ref. 84/1310.

The Portuguese initiated the trans-Atlantic slave trade near the mouth of the Congo River around 1500. Taking advantage of the custom of local African chiefs to buy household slaves, the Portuguese began trading European merchandise for human lives and shipping enslaved Africans across the Atlantic to work in the vibrant Portuguese colony of Brazil, where they produced first sugar, then coffee. By 1530, five thousand slaves a year were being removed from their homelands for shipment to Brazil (Hochschild, 1999: 12).

Slavery soon became a major disruptive force in West Africa. The ruler of the Kingdom of the Congo, Nzinga Mbemba Alfonso, a convert to Christianity who learned Portuguese, wrote to the King of Portugal to protest what was happening to his people:

> Each day the traders are capturing our people—children of this country, sons of our nobles and vassals, even people of our own family. ... Corruption and depravity are so widespread that our land is entirely depopulated. ... We need in this kingdom only priests and schoolteachers, and no merchandise, unless it is wine and flour for Mass. ... It is our wish that this kingdom not be a place for the trade or transport of slaves. (quoted in Hochschild, 1999: 13)

The King of Portugal was unmoved. Slave trading accelerated, and before long, Dutch merchant traders began introducing slavery to the English Caribbean, initially on the island of Barbados. Later, the English established a major Caribbean sugar colony in Jamaica and the Spanish followed suit in Cuba. Later still, American rice and cotton plantations stimulated demand for still more slave labour. By the early nineteenth century, some 12 million Africans and their descendants worked on the plantations of the Caribbean and the United States.

The societies of entire regions of Africa were thus ruined, and the foundation was set for the deep, enduring impoverishment of Africa. Matters worsened when, in the nineteenth century, England, Belgium, France, and Germany carved up much of Africa for its resource wealth. They established artificial boundaries that ignored traditional ethnic spheres of influence, thereby increasing ethnic antagonism and warfare. In some areas, such as the territory that the British named Rhodesia, the colonizers imposed heavy taxes on peasant farmers, forcing them off the best agricultural lands and into wage labour for white farmers (Arrighi, 1970). Later, some dispossessed Africans began a mass migration to South Africa for work in the expanding gold and diamond mines.

Meanwhile, across the Atlantic, the slave economies of the Caribbean and the United States flourished, generating unheard of wealth for slave traders, slave owners, and the European aristocracy and royalty. Slavery enabled capital to accumulate—capital that industrialists would later use to spur European development.

## THE STRUCTURAL ROOTS OF UNDERDEVELOPMENT

Dependency theory shows how social and economic structures established by European colonizing powers since about 1500 distorted local societies for the benefit of European traders and merchants, and later blocked the emergence of industrial capitalism in the global south. In the words of Andre Gundar Frank, a leading dependency theorist, "the historical development of the capitalist system generated **underdevelopment** in the peripheral satellites" (Frank, 1966: 3). At the same time, the extraction of resources from the global south propelled the rapid development of industry in Western Europe and, later, North America. What remains unclear is whether European *countries* or *classes* were responsible for underdevelopment in the global south.

Slave labour on a Caribbean sugar plantation in the 1830s
SOURCE: © HIP/Art Resource, NY.

## COUNTRIES VERSUS CLASSES AS CAUSES OF UNDERDEVELOPMENT

During the 1970s, debates on development and underdevelopment focused on the *mechanisms* through which metropolitan powers exploited the global south. Originally, dependency theorists conceived of underdevelopment as a process involving one area—Western Europe—extracting surplus from other areas—Latin America, Africa, and Asia. Some scholars argued that, in recent times, it was primarily through unfavourable **terms of trade** that exploitation took place. They held that prices of agricultural exports primarily from the underdeveloped south declined over time relative to prices of industrial goods made in the developed countries and imported by the poor countries. However, they still imagined that one area was exploiting another.

Robert Brenner (1977) challenged the geographical version of dependency theory and revived interest in a Marxist approach that emphasized class relationships. He argued that dependency theory ought to focus on exploitation occurring at the level of *class relationships*. In his view, by analyzing the nature of the class interests that shape underdevelopment and the types of class conflict that underdevelopment engenders, we can gain a fuller and more precise understanding of the process of underdevelopment. Following Marx, Brenner argued that the struggle among classes to achieve dominance is the prime mover of social change. Accordingly, identifiable classes in the metropolitan countries—merchants, traders, shippers, and the aristocracies and monarchies of Spain, Portugal, Holland, Belgium, France, and England—orchestrated the plunder of the global south. Moreover, these social actors counted on elites in the global south to establish mechanisms for extracting valuable commodities by using the forced labour of indigenous peoples and imported slaves. Brenner further argues that, in more recent times, the mechanisms of underdevelopment changed as England and then the rest of Western Europe began to industrialize under the direction of a new class of industrial capitalists. As industrialization occurred, so too did the nature of demands on the global south (for example, see Box 9.1).

## NOT ALL COUNTRIES ARE ALIKE: CLASS ALLIANCES AND STATE CONTROL

The global south is not homogeneous. Each country has a unique history. In particular, different class alliances came to control the states of the global south, with widely different consequences for the pattern of underdevelopment that ensued (Cardoso and Faletto, 1979). For example, in Argentina and Brazil, the large export-oriented economy that developed under the control of foreign capitalists allowed local elites and a sizable middle and industrial working class to emerge by the late nineteenth century (Murmis and Portantiero, 1969). Especially in periods when foreign influence was weakest (during global recessions, for instance), internal elites and their allies were able to establish local industrial enterprises and internal markets that deepened the process of development and strengthened local economies. In contrast, foreign capital was so dominant in small countries, such as Honduras, Costa Rica, and Guatemala, that middle and industrial working classes of much political significance failed to develop, and the economy was based almost exclusively on the exports of just a few commodities, such as bananas and coffee (Ellis, 1983; Handy, 1985; Stone, 1975; Winson, 1983, 1989).

## BEYOND DEPENDENCY: AGRARIAN CLASS STRUCTURE AND UNDERDEVELOPMENT

In the 1980s and 1990s, researchers focused increasingly on the role of class structures, class alliances, and state policies to better understand the processes of development and underdevelopment. Consider, for example, research on estates—large, privately owned agricultural enterprises employing many agricultural workers to produce export crops, such as coffee, wheat, and cotton, in societies as diverse as Chile, Brazil, and Egypt. Analysts found that, for three reasons, estate agriculture was more of an impediment to development than were agrarian structures dominated by small family farms (the North American model in the nineteenth and early twentieth centuries). First, estate owners tended to compensate their workers with small plots of land rather than substantial money wages. This greatly restricted the purchasing power of rural workers and therefore the demand for goods that small manufacturers could have produced locally. Second, with a ready supply of cheap labour at hand, estate owners had little incentive to employ advanced agricultural machinery on their estates. This limited the local market for manufacturers of agricultural machinery, who in North America were central to early industrialization. Third, estate owners exercised enormous political power. They influenced governments to maintain

## BOX 9.1    THE DESTRUCTION OF THIRD WORLD DOMINANCE IN MANUFACTURING

Before the Industrial Revolution of the late nineteenth century, many goods other than foodstuffs were produced in both Europe and the global south by traditional industry. Small workshops produced a huge variety of metal goods and wooden implements, and all manner of luxury goods made from glass, silver, gold, and so on. Grain was ground in stone grinding mills powered by water or animals. People wove textiles at home on looms from yarn or thread spun on hand-operated spinning wheels. While productivity was low, many people worked in these ways, so output was considerable. Paul Bairoch (1982) estimates that in 1830, the global south (including Japan) accounted for 63 percent of world manufacturing, compared with just 37 percent for Europe and North America. Levels of productivity differed little by region. This would soon change, however.

In England, the rising influence of modern industrialists challenged the longstanding dominance of old merchant families whose fortunes relied on trade. The old "mercantilist" system relied on protected markets and trade monopolies within them. For example, the British East India Company was allowed to block the import of European manufactured goods into India, which was good for traders but bad for industrialists. In 1813, however, the monopoly of the British East India Company was ended by the British Parliament. Now, Birmingham textile manufacturers could export cheap textiles

produced by modern machinery to India. This devastated millions of Indian domestic textile producers. Similar events took place elsewhere. As Bairoch argued, it was "in the years 1830 to 1860 that this division between the future developed world and the Third World ... began to take shape. The industrialization of the former led to the deindustrialization of the latter, and the proportional contribution of each region to the total [world] output of manufacturing production was almost exactly reversed" (Bairoch, 1982: 274).

Even relatively wealthy countries are not immune to the distortions of capitalist development. For example, the Maritime Provinces were the first locus of industrial development in Canada, with a thriving shipbuilding and steel industry (Alexander, 1978). By the 1890s, the proportion of people employed in manufacturing was about the same in Nova Scotia, New Brunswick, and Ontario (Winson, 1985: Table 1). Despite this promising early start, and in some ways reminiscent of the impact of British manufacturers on Third World industry described by Bairoch, Maritime industries were disadvantaged by federal policies and the actions of central Canadian financial institutions that control Canadian industry. Maritime industry went into decline, negatively affecting the regional farming economy and resulting in a long-term legacy of high unemployment, underemployment, and lower average income for the Maritime population (Acheson, 1972; Winson, 1985).

free trade policies so they could export agricultural products and import whatever machinery they needed, unhindered by tariffs. This made it difficult for local industry to develop. In contrast, in Canada and the United States, tariffs protected local manufacturing in the early stage of industrialization (Richards, 1976; Winson, 1989).

## DEVELOPMENT IN CANADA

Canada achieved independence in 1867. Before then, it consisted of a number of British colonies and a vast western and northern territory controlled by the Hudson's Bay Company, which was incorporated by British charter in 1670. How did Canada become a prosperous country despite its colonial past?

First, like Australia, New Zealand, and the United States, Canada was settled by large numbers of Europeans who soon overwhelmed the Aboriginal

population. The European settlers were determined to reproduce or improve the standard of living they enjoyed in the old country. Much of the wealth they produced was therefore reinvested locally. In contrast, when the European powers colonized most of Africa, they set up only small enclaves of white settlers. Their main aim was to exploit local resources and populations, sending nearly all of the wealth back to Europe.

Second, Canada's geopolitical position helped it overcome its colonial past and develop economically. Canada served as a major supplier not just of raw materials but also of manufactured goods, such as airplanes, to the Allies during World War II. Canada's favourable geopolitical position gave its industry a major boost.

Third, Canadian state policy sometimes protected and stimulated Canadian industrial growth. For example, the 1879 National Policy established a duty on imported manufactured goods. The National

Policy sheltered the growth of Canadian industry, then in its infancy, by making foreign-made manufactured goods more expensive. Similarly, the 1965 Auto Pact required that foreign automobile companies wanting to sell cars in Canada duty-free manufacture cars in Canada and use a certain proportion of Canadian-made components. The Auto Pact stimulated the growth of an industry that, directly or indirectly, is now responsible for the employment of one-sixth of Ontario's labour force (Brym, Roberts, Lie, and Rytina, 2012: 232).

# GEOGRAPHY AND BIOLOGICAL RESOURCES

A recent, provocative contribution to the study of development and underdevelopment is Jared Diamond's examination of the early history of human civilization. Diamond set out to understand why wealth and power are distributed as they now are rather than in some other way. For Diamond, the answer is complex but boils down to the following idea: "History followed different courses for different peoples because of differences among peoples' environments" (Diamond, 1999: 25).

To make his case, Diamond (1999) distinguished between proximate (or immediate) and ultimate (or fundamental) causes of development. He found that the development of firearms and modern metallurgy by Europeans, along with lack of resistance to deadly diseases in the peoples of the Americas, were the *proximate* causes of the defeat of established, complex civilizations by the marauding Spanish army in Latin America in 1520. The conquest set the stage for the emergence of commercial, administrative, military, and industrial structures over the next several hundred years—structures that helped to enrich Europe while retarding progress in the Americas, Australia, Africa, and much of Asia.

Why did the Europeans alone enjoy such early advantages as firearms, modern metallurgy, and resistance to diseases that proved deadly to the peoples they subjugated? What, in other words, were the *ultimate* causes of European development? Diamond (1999) argues that the geographical features of different continents and the biological resources available to early peoples were fundamentally important. Europe (and the adjacent Middle East) was especially rich in plants and animals that could be domesticated. Moreover, their east–west axis facilitated the intermingling and dissemination of a wide variety of species because geographical barriers were few and climate was roughly similar across the region. In contrast, relatively few animals were available for domestication in the Americas. Moreover, the Americas, Africa, and most of Asia ran along a north–south axis with physical barriers and climatic differences that made the dissemination of species difficult. Australia was isolated and had no animal species that could be domesticated. The wealth of species available for domestication in Europe and the Middle East allowed for the accumulation and storage of large food surpluses, which in turn enabled the growth of large, complex, hierarchical societies. The first cities emerged in the Middle East and so did technological advances beyond the stone tools of the pre-agricultural period, including the refinement of metal, the manufacture of implements and arms, and the construction of oceangoing vessels. These advances spread to Europe relatively easily. Dense population centres and proximity to domesticated animals also allowed germs to spread and cause the first mass epidemics. However, the survivors developed resistance to these germs. For Diamond, then, the early domestication of plants and animals made agriculture possible and was a prerequisite for the development of the guns, germs, and steel that eventually ensured the dominance of European colonizers in the Americas and later in Asia and Africa.

## CRITICISMS OF DIAMOND'S THESIS

Diamond's thesis has sparked much debate. Some critics argue that he ignores the mountain ranges and deserts that surely impeded the diffusion of domesticated plants and animals across Europe. Others point out that corn, a major staple, *was* disseminated from Central to South America (Blaut, 2000). Still others note that Diamond ignores crucial political factors. For example, the Ottoman Empire cut off Europe's trade with Asia in the fifteenth century, so European merchants were encouraged to develop marine transportation technology and navigational and cartographic knowledge to reach the East by travelling around the southern African coast. Their technological advantage later allowed them to dominate the seas, exploring and exploiting much of the rest of the globe (Pickover, 1997). Despite the criticisms of Diamond's work, the broad scope of his argument and the eloquence with which he makes it have proven attractive to a wide audience.

# THE NEOLIBERAL ERA: DEBT, STRUCTURAL ADJUSTMENT, AND UPHEAVAL IN THE SOUTH

## THE RISE OF NEOLIBERALISM

In recent years, the **neoliberal theory** of economic development has become influential in the highest policy circles. It is worth analyzing because the most important institutions affecting development policies in the global south adopted it and still apply it today. A central idea of neoliberal theory is that only in societies where markets are free of government interference can competitive entrepreneurs maximize economic growth for the benefit of themselves and the rest of society. This idea was not always popular. A "hands off" approach by governments contributed to the severity of the Great Depression of the 1930s, when the North American unemployment rate reached 30 percent. Thereafter, desperation brought a strong desire for a new approach to economic thinking. In the United States, the Democratic Party under Franklin Delano Roosevelt, inspired by the economic thinking of the British economist John Maynard Keynes, took the view that government *should* intervene in the market. Its policies, and those of likeminded governments in Canada, Britain, and elsewhere, favoured massive government spending to stimulate the economy and the establishment of public enterprises where the market had failed to provide viable alternatives.

The "Keynesian" approach to economic development worked well for four decades. Then, in the 1970s, it too began to run into difficulties—specifically, high inflation coupled with low or stagnant economic growth. This situation provided the context for American economist Milton Friedman and his allies to advocate a return to policies that would drastically restrict the role of government in the economy in favour of private market solutions.

What implications did the spread of Freidman's ideas have for the global south? In the 1970s, international banks and lending institutions had gone on a lending spree. Many governments in the global south were eager to accept low-interest loans to assist in the industrialization of their nations. The election of Republican president Ronald Reagan in 1981 brought a dramatic change in monetary policy along the lines advocated by Friedman. Among other things, the change entailed a drastic increase in interest rates to deal with inflationary tendencies in the economy.

Interest payments on loans made by the countries of the global south soared, and a debt crisis, especially acute in South America, ensued. As governments faced defaulting on their loans, international lending agencies put in place a new set of policies poor debtor countries would have to follow to be bailed out of their dilemma. These policies reflected Friedman's neoliberalism.

The new policy, often called the **Washington consensus,** united the International Monetary Fund (IMF), the World Bank, and the U.S. Treasury around Freidman's neoliberalism. The chief economist at the World Bank, Joseph Stiglitz, wrote that the three pillars of this consensus are austerity, privatization, and market liberalization (Stiglitz, 2003: 53).

In practice, **structural adjustment programs (SAPs)** became the basis of the bailout of the countries of the global south facing a debt crisis. The IMF and the World Bank offered to help the debtor countries financially if they met a set of harsh conditions: Privatize state-owned enterprises, such as telephone and oil companies and national banks; let in international corporations and goods produced in the developed countries; end tariff protection of local industry and agriculture; radically curtail social welfare programs; encourage new lines of agricultural exports—these were key aspects of SAPs. Proponents of SAPs claimed they were necessary to provide needed economic discipline and achieve economic growth. Critics argued that SAPs would cause social upheaval and misery. As we will see, the critics were right.

Neoliberals assumed that markets work perfectly if left free to do so. Demand for labour, capital, and commodities will equal supply. There will be no unemployment. The only thing that could prevent this ideal outcome is market interference. If greedy unions constrain the workings of free markets by demanding and receiving excessively high wages, or if meddling politicians encourage the growth of social policies (employment insurance, welfare, universal health insurance, and so on), then the market will not be able to work its magic. By implication, if economic problems exist, markets must be unleashed. By this logic, the solution to unemployment, for example, is a reduction in wages.

## NEOLIBERALISM AND SAPS AS SOLUTIONS TO POVERTY

Proponents of neoliberal reforms in developing countries argue that they have raised incomes in poor countries and lifted millions of people out of poverty

(Neilsen, 2007). Critics have argued that neoliberalism has produced a dramatic increase in global **income inequality,** widespread misery, and social dislocation. Who is right? Let us consider the conflicting evidence.

Clearly, there have been winners in the neoliberal global economy. For example, after Mexico opened its economy to foreign capital and free trade, and privatized publically owned companies, a new class of billionaires emerged. Some benefited from the sale of public sector enterprises at low prices. Others managed to monopolize lucrative new markets. Notably, Carlos Slim Helu became the richest man in the world in 2007—richer than Bill Gates. Large commercial agricultural producers also benefited from the development of new agro-export industries oriented to the U.S. market.

India and China also opened their economies to foreign corporations and trade, helping them realize exceptional rates of economic growth. New industries have rapidly expanded to serve overseas and domestic markets. New entrepreneurial and professional middle classes have arisen in these countries, while masses of rural poor flood into cities to take up work in new factories that provide incomes considerably higher than those available in rural areas.

Do these examples not prove the success of the neoliberal economic model? The answer depends partly on how we define success. In narrow economic terms, policies associated with neoliberalism have succeeded in some places. The wealth of some countries has increased, as has the standard of living. New infrastructure, including hydroelectric stations, rail networks, highway systems, and air transportation facilities, has been built. These facts suggest development is indeed taking place.

Nevertheless, even among the success stories, glaring problems have emerged. And then there are the many countries that have benefited little or not at all from neoliberalism or have suffered because of it. Let us consider these issues in detail.

## Level of Consumption versus Quality of Life and the Environment

An increase in monetary income in India and China does not mean that the average quality of life has necessarily improved in those countries. Life in rural areas often provided nonmonetary benefits—personal security, tranquility, better air quality, the benefits of having family close, and so on—that are not captured by economic indicators of well-being. Life in the city for new immigrants often brings increased personal insecurity with dramatic increases in crime and violence, negative health outcomes associated with polluted air and water, dangerous work environments, and deterioration in diet associated with the consumption of fast food and low-quality street foods.

The kind of unregulated development seen in India and China in recent years has also brought with it massive environmental destruction. For example, to power its expansion, China constructed the massive Three Gorges electric dam project on the Yangtze River. The lake it created has displaced more than a million people and destroyed 13 cities and 140 towns, including historical sites and valuable agricultural land. Lack of regulation means that dangerous and

Workers stretch as far as the eye can see in the Cankun Factory, Xiamen City, China.

SOURCE: © Edward Burtynsky, courtesy Nicholas Metivier, Toronto/Howard Greenberg & Bryce Wolkowitz, New York

environmentally destructive industries, such as the scavenging of waste from electronic devices and the breaking up of decommissioned ships in vulnerable marine environments, are commonplace.

Agricultural expansion has denuded vast territories and resulted in the rapid spread of deserts. China is rapidly exceeding the carrying capacity of its ecosystem. Winds carry soil from highly eroded land in the northwest as far away as South Korea and Japan, while air and water pollution affect the health of hundreds of millions of families. At the same time, industrial development has claimed tremendous water resources previously devoted to agriculture. The Yellow River no longer reaches the sea for part of the year or even the downstream agricultural province of Shandong. This situation has imperilled agriculture in an important food-producing region. As renowned environmentalist Lester Brown concludes, "China is on the verge of a massive ecological meltdown" (2003: 11, 37).

## Absolute Poverty and Global Income Inequality

Many parts of the world have not witnessed the kind of income growth that China and India have enjoyed. In fact, as Stiglitz notes, in the last decade of the twentieth century, "the number of people living in poverty has actually increased by almost 100 million. This occurred at the same time that the total world income increased by an average of 2.5 percent annually" (Stiglitz, 2003: 5).

Measuring the gap at the global level between people with high and low income is difficult. Various experts use different methods and come up with different results. Nevertheless, as a leading researcher states, "the most basic fact about world inequality is that it is monstrously large; that result is inescapable, whatever the method or definition" (Sutcliffe, 2005; see Box 9.2). Branko Milanovic, a leading economist with the World Bank, notes that the top 5 percent of individuals in the world receive about one-third of total world income, while the top 10 percent get one-half. On the other hand, the bottom 5 and 10 percent of people in the world get just 0.2 and 0.7 percent of world income, respectively. Looked at another way, the ratio of the richest 5 percent compared with the poorest 5 percent of world citizens is 165 to 1. The richest 5 percent earn in 48 hours about what the poorest 5 percent earn in an entire year (Milanovic, 2005: 15).

A recent international project to measure the direction of change in global inequalities provides us with a more accurate estimate of global inequalities than we have had up to now. The International Comparison Program includes data from 146 national statistical agencies and major financial and development organizations, including the United Nations, the World Bank, and the International Monetary Fund. A key finding of the project is that price levels in most Asian countries, notably China, India, Indonesia, and the Philippines—countries with about 38 percent of the world's population—are much higher than was formerly assumed. This means that they have many more poor people than previously thought, with new estimates bringing incomes down some 40 percent in China and India, 17 percent in Indonesia, 41 percent in the Philippines, 32 percent in South Africa, and 24 percent in Argentina. Average incomes did not

---

| BOX 9.2 | IF 100 PEOPLE LIVED ON EARTH |
| --- | --- |

If the earth's population was shrunk to exactly 100 people, and all proportions were kept the same, there would be:
58 Asians,
10 East and West Europeans,
14 North and South Americans, and
12 Africans.

About one-third would have access to clean, safe drinking water.

One-third of the population would be children, only half of which would be vaccinated against preventable infectious diseases such as measles and polio.

Of the 67 adults, one-third would be illiterate.

20 people would receive 75 percent of the entire world's available income.

Only 7 people would own an automobile.

One person would have control over nuclear weapons.

One-third of the available land would be desert, tundra, pavement, and other wasteland; about one-eighth would be suitable for crops.

SOURCE: Reprinted with permission from the Sustainability Institute.

decline in all of the poorer economies, but increases in Russia, Egypt, Nigeria, and Lebanon were more modest than declines in the Asian countries. Milanovic (2008) concludes that global inequality is much greater than even the most pessimistic analysts thought.

## Trends in Inequality within and between Countries

What is the *trend* in global income inequality? Is it decreasing or increasing, and if so, for what time period? Scholars have marshalled evidence that gives us a good idea of inequality trends since the 1930s. The data are better for the developed countries, but trends are apparent for the global south, too.

Considering inequality within developed countries, the gap between the rich and poor decreased from the 1930s to the 1960s. This was the period when the welfare state was being constructed and Keynesian economic policies were being implemented (Bornschier, 2002: 102). For the global south, the same trend is apparent for only some countries. Brazil and Mexico saw increased gaps between rich and poor between 1950 and 1970. The gap between rich and poor countries was quite stable during these decades.

After the 1970s, when neoliberal policies were implemented, the picture becomes less rosy. Inequalities within countries substantially increased. Between countries, the gap also increased, especially during the 1980s (Bornschier, 2002: 108–10; Braun, 1997). Neoliberal policies were probably not the only factor contributing to this outcome. Other causes of the growing gap between rich and poor include the increasing penetration and integration of national economies by transnational corporations and the ongoing massive technological shift away from industrial production to the digital information economy, especially in the developed countries. Nevertheless, neoliberalism helped to widen the gap between rich and poor.

## Growth Needs Strong States

Neoliberal policies have not stimulated growth in the global south. To the contrary, growth rates were higher in the decade before the introduction of SAPs (an average of 2.5 percent between 1960 and 1979) than in the era when SAPs were imposed by international lending agencies (0.0 percent between 1980 and 1998; Brym et al., 2005: 1). But what does history teach us about the policies the *rich* countries followed to encourage industrialization? Did they follow the tenets of neoliberalism? Aside from Britain, the first industrializing country, they did not. As French political economist François Chesnais (2004) notes, "the United States, France, Germany and the other industrialised countries [including Japan] benefited from selective *protection* of their home market for over a century or more" (my emphasis). This gave them time to grow until they could compete with Britain in world markets. Only the countries of the global south that fell under the sway of neoliberalism have lacked the opportunity to nurture their industrial and technological base. "Time has been denied to them," writes Chesnais.

Contrary to neoliberal theory, minimal state involvement is about the last thing industrializing countries need. In recent decades, the rapid industrialization of the "Asian tigers"—South Korea, Taiwan, Singapore, and, later, China and India—depended on strong states and considerable state involvement in the economy. For example, governments in South Korea and Taiwan after World War II were highly centralized and authoritarian. They succeeded in carrying out sweeping land reforms that eliminated the class of powerful landowners—the same class that opposed protectionist policies in Latin America. The governments of these two countries opted for a strong industrial policy that marshalled the resources of the state to develop infrastructure and use state credit to fund investment in key industrial sectors. They kept control of industrial development by preventing foreign corporations from taking over their expanding industries. They also used their power to repress labour movements, which kept wages down and made emerging industry highly competitive in the world market.

China followed suit. The all-powerful Communist Party organized a top-down transformation of the economy to encourage foreign investment—but on their terms rather than terms dictated by neoliberal institutions. The Communist Party organized massive infrastructure projects that encouraged industrial investment. It kept wages low and used violence to prevent the formation of independent labour organizations.[1]

## Women under Neoliberalism

Other signs exist that neoliberalism has failed to produce the results claimed by its advocates. The dismantling of many national banks by IMF policy prescription undermined cheap credit to small farmers and imperilled rural incomes in many poor countries (Rodriguez Gomez and Torres, 1996: 157–58). Trade liberalization encouraged the import of heavily subsidized agricultural commodities from the developed countries. They undermined rural incomes, as prices for food produced by small farmers plummeted in the face of an incoming tide of low-cost food. Because of such policies, millions of rural poor have been forced off the land and into already overcrowded towns and cities. Millions more migrated to the developed world, some illegally and at great danger to themselves. Such migrants have become the source of a huge global economy in recent years. They typically do menial work and send money back to family members in Mexico, the Philippines, and elsewhere.

In some parts of the global south, such as India and Thailand, neoliberal policies have been especially hard on women, partly because women form the bulk of the agricultural workforce (Shiva, 1993: 232). Elsewhere, in countries as diverse as Nicaragua and Nigeria, women have had to raise families on their own as their husbands are forced to migrate to the cities or to the developed world in search of cash income. Evidence suggests that these circumstances are breaking down long-standing patriarchal structures and forging new ties of solidarity among women as they strive to cope with the new realities, but the change involves much suffering.

Since 1999, the World Bank and the IMF have implemented policies that they believe promote gender equity. However, critics point out that these new policies have been weakly implemented and have done little to eliminate gender barriers for women wanting to access the paid workforce or engage in production for export markets. Nor do they tackle the substantial gender inequality that exists in the households of the global south (Brym et al., 2005).

## STATE VIOLENCE, WAR, AND THE PRODUCTION OF POVERTY

Military aggression and war have helped undermine development in much of the post–World War II era, and they therefore deserve to be discussed at some length. During the Cold War, mutually assured destruction by nuclear weapons made military confrontation between the Soviet Union and the United States out of the question. Nevertheless, both countries used their economic and military might to reshape the world during this period.

Under the guise of making the world "safe for democracy" and "fighting communism," the United States was directly or indirectly involved in a series of military *coups d'état* in Latin America and elsewhere from the 1950s to the late 1970s, beginning with the CIA-organized invasion of Guatemala in 1954. The government it had installed at that time prepared the ground for a series of pro-American regimes that have carried on continual campaigns of **state terrorism** that have killed many tens of thousands of Guatemalans, often with unspeakable brutality (Falla, 1994). More than a million citizens have been forced to flee the violence in their country. For most of the decades that followed, Washington provided military aid, training, and diplomatic support for these regimes (Gareau, 2004: 63). When it became politically impossible for Washington to provide such assistance because of the Guatemalan military's gross human rights abuses, the Israeli government stepped in to provide military aid and training (Marshall, Scott, and Hunter, 1987).

The "domino theory" held that if one country fell under communist influence, its neighbours would soon follow suit. Operating with the domino theory in mind, the United States began a decade-long military intervention in Vietnam in the 1960s. This intervention followed years of French colonial domination. America's undeclared war killed more than a million North Vietnamese military personnel, between 500 000 and two million civilians, and more than 58 000 American military personnel. The war destroyed Vietnam's economic infrastructure; the country has only recently shown signs of recovery and economic expansion.

The main American rival on the world stage at this time was the Soviet Union, which also sought to extend its influence and promote the economic model it favoured. In so doing, it used military force to block efforts to democratize and liberalize authoritarian communist regimes within its sphere of influence (Hungary in 1956, Czechoslovakia in 1968) while lending its support to pro-Soviet governments elsewhere in Eastern Europe with strong authoritarian tendencies. Throughout the Cold War, the Soviet Union provided military equipment, training, and in-country advisers to various authoritarian regimes in the Middle East, notably Syria, Algeria, and Iraq under Saddam Hussein, as it competed with the United States for influence in the region. It refrained from supplying the most advanced weaponry to these states, however, for fear that doing so would drag it into direct military confrontation with the Americans (Antonenko, 2001).

Soviet economic and military aid also assisted the struggles of different movements around the globe to remove colonial and neocolonial domination. It bolstered the Vietnamese war effort against the United States, helped the Cubans resist the American economic blockade of that country, and provided arms and materiel to Angola, Mozambique, and Nicaragua in their war against "contra" mercenary armies and the apartheid South African government. Such countries as Cuba and Nicaragua turned to the Soviet Union for military aid only after the United States had fostered economic destabilization and engaged in covert military operations with the intention of bringing down these governments.

In the 1970s the United States, with the help of allies, such as France, provided military equipment, extensive training, and expertise to help install military governments in Brazil, Uruguay, Chile, Argentina, and the Dominican Republic. When these oppressive military regimes came to power, they typically forged strong ties with multinational corporations while suppressing trade unions and popular organizations and groups that opposed them. The oppression they unleashed was brutal. In Argentina, the number of citizens killed by the pro-American dictatorships exceeded 30 000 people, with members of the younger generation the principal victims (Marchak, 1999). Increasingly, the tactics of repression developed by these dictatorships in Latin America are being used in other part of the world to stamp out dissent.

In the 1970s, popular struggles against a staunchly pro-American dictatorship in Nicaragua, and European colonial regimes in Angola and Mozambique, were successful in establishing governments that sought to redistribute land and wealth, and establish more democratic forms of popular participation. Indeed, in their first years in power, they made dramatic strides in combating illiteracy and expanding healthcare (Vilas, 1986).

In the 1980s, the U.S. government sponsored illegal arms deals to covert armies to fight the revolutionary government in Nicaragua and support the South African government in its campaign to destabilize Mozambique and Angola (Gareau, 2004; Marshall, Scott, and Hunter, 1987). In Mozambique, the South African strategy of destabilization was responsible for destroying 718 health facilities and schools accommodating 300 000 students between 1981 and 1986 (Gareau, 2004: 139–40). In Nicaragua, more than 50 000 people were killed or wounded

in what was called the "contra war." In southern Africa, a task force appointed by the secretary general of the United Nations estimated that damage to Mozambique, Angola, and Zimbabwe from South Africa's destabilization campaign amounted to $60 billion (1988 prices) between 1981 and 1988, an immense sum for such desperately poor countries. Moreover, 1.5 million people died from violence or violence-related disease and famine, and half the population of Mozambique and Angola was displaced (Gareau, 2004: 141).

In the twenty-first century, war has continued to plague parts of the global south, particularly sub-Saharan Africa and the Middle East, and has undermined the benefits that might come from development assistance. Post-communist Russia has become a major arms vendor. The Russian defence industry now depends on arms exports for its survival, and private interests in Russia increasingly act without government support to penetrate the lucrative Middle East arms market (Antonenko, 2001). New actors have also emerged to pursue self-serving policies that fuel war, economic turmoil, and social disruption and dislocation, China chief among them. For example, China's pursuit of oil in Sudan has led it to support the Sudanese regime, which is responsible for the ongoing genocide in Darfur.

# RESISTANCE TO THE NEOLIBERAL NEW WORLD ORDER

## GOVERNMENT RESISTANCE

We end our discussion by considering how governments and people in the global South, and most recently in the developed North as well, have resisted neoliberal policies.

Such resistance has been particularly acute in Latin America. Since 2000, Argentina, Brazil, Bolivia, Ecuador, and Venezuela have elected governments that oppose neoliberalism. These governments have been deeply concerned with the increasing concentration of land ownership, the concomitant spread of landlessness, and skyrocketing urban poverty in recent decades. They have sought to aid the landless and the urban poor, and in some cases to nationalize key resource industries and capture the profits that for decades went largely to transnational companies with little local benefit. The Chavez government in

Women members of the Movimento Sem Terra (MST), Brazil's Landless Workers Movement, protest against then United States president George W. Bush's visit to Brazil. The march also marked support of International Women's Day, and thousands of protesters participated. SOURCE: © Cazalis/Corbis.

Venezuela has used its oil wealth to provide substantial aid to other poor countries in Latin America. In fact, it has provided more aid than has the United States, which has an economy 90 times the size of Venezuela's ("Chavez," 2007).

## POPULAR RESISTANCE

In civil society as well, broad-based organizations have challenged the neoliberal development model. Most prominent among these is the World Social Forum, which first brought together representatives from around the world in Porto Alegre, Brazil, in 2001. Their statement of principles set out their aims as follows:

> The alternatives proposed at the World Social Forum stand in opposition to a process of globalisation commanded by the large multinational corporations and by the governments and international institutions at the service of those corporations' interests, with the complicity of national governments. They are designed to ensure that globalisation in solidarity will prevail as a new stage in world history. This will respect universal human rights, and those of all citizens—men and women—of all nations and the

environment and will rest on democratic international systems and institutions at the service of social justice, equality and the sovereignty of peoples. (World Social Forum, 2009)

Another notable example of popular resistance to neoliberalism is *Via Campesina*, an international organization of peasant farmers, rural women, and landless workers that seeks to achieve social justice and gender parity in the context of sustainable agricultural production (Borras, 2008). In 2007, hundreds of delegates from 86 countries met in the small village of Nyéléni in the African nation of Mali and set out their principles (see Box 9.3).

Popular resistance to neoliberalism worldwide often takes the form of sit-ins, demonstrations, and strikes by students, nongovernmental organizations, unions, peasant associations, and trade unions. Increasingly, however, resistance to neoliberalism has entered formal politics. For example, the 2008 American presidential race sparked debate over the damage done to people and the environment by the North American Free Trade Agreement, and the 2012 campaign raised the question of whether the level of economic inequality had grown too high. It is impossible to know where such debate will lead or what it will eventually achieve. However, the aftermath of

| BOX 9.3 | **EXCERPT FROM THE *DECLARATION OF NYÉLÉNI*, MALI, 2007** |
|---|---|

What are we fighting for?

A world where ...

... all peoples, nations and states are able to determine their own food producing systems and policies that provide every one of us with good quality, adequate, affordable, healthy, and culturally appropriate food;

... recognition and respect of women's roles and rights in food production, and representation of women in all decision-making bodies;

... all peoples in each of our countries are able to live with dignity, earn a living wage for their labour and have the opportunity to remain in their homes;

... where food sovereignty is considered a basic human right, recognised and implemented by communities, peoples, states and international bodies;

... we are able to conserve and rehabilitate rural environments, fish stocks, landscapes and food traditions based on ecologically sustainable management of land, soils, water, seas, seeds, livestock and other biodiversity;

... we value, recognize and respect our diversity of traditional knowledge, food, language and culture, and the way we organise and express ourselves;

... there is genuine and integral agrarian reform that guarantees peasants full rights to land, defends and recovers the territories of indigenous peoples, ensures fishing communities' access and control over their fishing areas and eco-systems, honours access and control over pastoral lands and migratory routes, assures decent jobs with fair remuneration and labour rights for all, and a future for young people in the countryside;

... where agrarian reform revitalises interdependence between producers and consumers, ensures community survival, social and economic justice and ecological sustainability, and respect for local autonomy and governance with equal rights for women and men ... where it guarantees the right to territory and self-determination for our peoples;

... where we share our lands and territories peacefully and fairly among our peoples, be we peasants, indigenous peoples, artisanal fishers, pastoralists, or others;

... in the case of natural and human-created disasters and conflict-recovery situations, food sovereignty acts as a kind of "insurance" that strengthens local recovery efforts and mitigates negative impacts ... where we remember that affected communities are not helpless, and where strong local organization for self-help is the key to recovery;

... where peoples' power to make decisions about their material, natural and spiritual heritage are defended;

... where all peoples have the right to defend their territories from the actions of transnational corporations;

What are we fighting against?

Imperialism, neoliberalism, neo-colonialism and patriarchy, and all systems that impoverish life, resources and eco-systems, and the agents that promote the above such as international financial institutions, the World Trade Organisation, free trade agreements, transnational corporations, and governments that are antagonistic to their peoples;

The dumping of food at prices below the cost of production in the global economy;

The domination of our food and food producing systems by corporations that place profits before people, health and the environment;

Technologies and practices that undercut our future food-producing capacities, damage the environment and put our health at risk. Those include transgenic crops and animals, terminator technology, industrial aquaculture and destructive fishing practices, the so-called white revolution of industrial dairy practices, the so-called 'old' and 'new' Green Revolutions, and the "Green Deserts" of industrial bio-fuel monocultures and other plantations;

The privatisation and commodification of food, basic and public services, knowledge, land, water, seeds, livestock and our natural heritage;

Development projects/models and extractive industry that displace people and destroy our environments and natural heritage;

Wars, conflicts, occupations, economic blockades, famines, forced displacement of people and confiscation of their land, and all forces and governments that cause and support them; post disaster and conflict reconstruction programmes that destroy our environments and capacities;

The criminalization of all those who struggle to protect and defend our rights;

Food aid that disguises dumping, introduces GMOs into local environments and food systems and creates new colonialism patterns;

The internationalisation and globalisation of paternalistic and patriarchal values that marginalise women, diverse agricultural, indigenous, pastoral and fisher communities around the world.

SOURCE: *La Via Campesina*, 2007.

the 2008–09 global financial meltdown suggests that the neoliberal model may have run its course and that new opportunities for constructing a sounder and more just global economic system are at hand.

A telling sign that people are questioning the legitimacy of the neoliberal order emerged in 2011. A blog posted by the Vancouver-based magazine *Adbusters* called for the occupation of Wall Street, the centre of American finance, demanding that "Barack Obama ordain a Presidential Commission tasked with ending the influence money has over our representatives in Washington. It's time for Democracy Not Corporatocracy; we're doomed without it" (Chappel, 2011). In just a few months, the Occupy Wall Street Movement saw protests spread from a few major North American cities to more than 750 locations around the globe ("Occupy Protests around the World," 2011).

The Occupy Wall Street movement resonated not only with the poor but also with broad sections of the middle class. Many Americans were disgusted by the failure of government to prosecute any of the wealthy people believed to be at the heart of decisions that brought on the financial crisis in 2008, while millions remained unemployed or lost their homes. Elsewhere, government austerity measures in the face of economic slowdown and skyrocketing unemployment were the most prominent motivators. Everywhere, stark economic inequalities brought on by three decades of neoliberal policies provoked anger and spurred tens of thousands to demonstrate in the streets.

The Occupy Wall Street movement, together with the democracy movement that swept much of

SOURCE: Artist rendering by Katherine Ball.

the Middle East and North Africa in 2011, suggest that, despite the seemingly overwhelming power of global elites and the economic model they have imposed, it is ultimately people who make history.

## SUMMARY

1. Global inequality is perhaps the most pressing issue of our times.

2. Stages of economic growth theory posits that societies proceed through various stages of development much as biological organisms do. Contemporary American market society is considered the ultimate stage.

3. Modernization theory argues that value orientations determine the success of development in a particular country. Countries in which people have a high need for achievement and value competitive behaviour are said to have a higher likelihood of success in the development process.

4. Dependency theory stresses the role of structural relationships of exploitation between rich and poor regions of the globe as important in blocking the development of the latter.

5. According to Jared Diamond, environmental factors, including the geographical features of different continents and the biological resources available to early peoples, were fundamentally important in determining which part of the globe came to dominate other parts of the globe.

6. Marxist development theory places particular weight on class structure and conflict between fundamental classes within each historical epoch as central to determining development outcomes.

7. A historical and holistic approach helps us understand the divergent development of different parts of the globe.

8. Significant structural barriers have blocked or retarded the economic development of many countries.

9. Not all countries in the global south are the same; different class structures and political arrangements have produced different development outcomes.

10. Policies promoted by the International Monetary Fund and the World Bank have helped to undermine rural livelihoods in some parts of the world and have not effectively addressed the severe disadvantages women face in several regions of the global south.

11. Certain factors have allowed for the rapid development of a few formerly poor countries, but the associated costs for society and the environment have often been high.

12. War and military aggression, often sponsored by developed countries, have had a major negative impact on development in the global south.

13. Today there is general agreement that global inequalities are staggering, and new evidence indicates that the gap between rich and poor countries is wider than earlier believed.

14. Resistance to the dominant development model is growing and is particularly strong in Latin America. The Occupy Wall Street movement suggests this resistance is taking on global dimensions.

## QUESTIONS TO CONSIDER

1. Do you think global inequality will change over the next 25 years? In what ways? Why do you think these changes will occur? If you think global inequality will remain the same, explain why.

2. Should Canadians do anything to help alleviate global poverty? Why or why not? If you think Canadians should help end global poverty, then what should we do?

3. What circumstances allowed some countries to escape underdevelopment in the late twentieth and early twenty-first centuries?

## GLOSSARY

**Capitalism** (p. 212) is an economic system based on profit seeking in competitive markets. It is associated with dynamic technological development, the development of class inequality, and accelerating environmental destruction.

**Deindustrialization** (p. 230) is a process, linked to neoliberal policies, that facilitates businesses moving to the lowest wage jurisdictions nationally or abroad, resulting in social dislocation and economic decline in older industrial regions.

**Dependency theory** (p. 214) is an explanation of uneven global development that stresses the exploitative relationships that have existed between Europe and the global south, to the detriment of the latter (see underdevelopment).

**Income inequality** (p. 221) is the difference in income earned by high and low income earners, whether within a country or among countries.

**Modernization theory** (p. 214) argues that economic growth and development can best be achieved if the values underlying market capitalism are aggressively fostered.

**Neoliberal theory** (p. 220) calls for the elimination of government involvement in the economy, which presumably allows free markets to achieve economic growth and development.

**Purchasing power parity** (p. 213) is the number of units of a country's currency needed to buy the same amount of goods and services in the domestic market as a U.S. dollar would buy in the United States.

**Stages of development** (p. 214) in W. W. Rostow's theory are the developmental phases through which societies supposedly pass. Rostow believed that modern American capitalism represents a final developmental stage characterized by sustained economic growth.

**State terrorism** (p. 224) is a deliberate act of physical or psychological violence perpetrated by state organizations (the army, secret police, etc.) to intimidate and coerce certain groups by causing fear, anxiety, panic, and horror.

**Structural adjustment programs (SAPs)** (p. 220) are policies imposed on debtor countries by the World Bank that entail privatization of state enterprises, opening of debtor economies to imports and capital from developed countries, eliminating social poverty reduction programs, and meeting debt obligations to the financial institutions of the rich countries.

**Terms of trade** (p. 217) refers to the ratio of the price of exports to the price of imports.

**Underdevelopment** (p. 216) is the idea that the development of Europe required the exploitation of the global south and undermined its economic development.

The **Washington consensus** (p. 220) is the shared view of the International Monetary Fund, the World Bank, and the U.S. Treasury Department that emerged in the late 1970s promoting a neoliberal approach to economic development and stabilization in the global south.

## SUGGESTED READING

Collier, Paul. (2008). *The Bottom Billion: Why the Poorest Countries Are Failing and What Can Be Done about It*. Toronto: Oxford University Press. Argues that the challenge of lifting the world's poorest billion people out of poverty is akin to rebuilding Europe after World War II, requiring not only immediate aid but also trade and security effectively promoted by multilateral institutions.

Griesgraber, Jo Marie, and Bernard Gunter, eds. (1996). *Development: New Paradigms and Principles for the Twenty-First Century (Rethinking Bretton Woods)*. London: Pluto Press.

A critique of the Washington consensus approach to development and a detailed proposal for equitable, sustainable, and participatory development.

Veltmeyer, Henry, ed. (2008). *New Perspectives on Globalization and Antiglobalization: Prospects for a New World Order*. Aldershot, UK: Ashgate. Eleven specialists in the political economy of international relations and globalization analyze the diverse dimensions of the globalization process.

## NOTE

1. As transnational manufacturing firms shifted investment to low-cost labour markets, the **deindustrialization** of many developed countries took place, devastating communities in the north of England and the north-central United States (Bluestone and Harrison, 1982, 1988). Canadian workers and communities in Ontario and Quebec have not been immune to these forces (Winson and Leach, 2002). Investment has not shifted to all low-wage countries, however, because few can offer the massive infrastructure, disciplined low-cost labour force, and political stability that China can.

# Politics

# CHAPTER 18

# POLITICS AND SOCIAL MOVEMENTS

**Robert J. Brym**
UNIVERSITY OF TORONTO

# INTRODUCTION

I almost caused a small riot once. It happened in Grade 11, shortly after I learned that water combined with sulfur dioxide produces sulfurous acid. The news shocked me. To understand why, you have to know where I lived: in Saint John, New Brunswick, about 100 metres (110 yards) downwind of one of the larger pulp and paper mills in Canada. Acrid waves of sulfur dioxide billowed day and night from the mill's imposing smokestacks. The town's pervasive rotten-egg smell was a longstanding complaint in the area. But, for me, disgust turned to upset when I realized the fumes were toxic. Suddenly it was clear why many people I knew—especially people living near the mill—woke up in the morning with a kind of "smoker's cough." By the simple act of breathing, we were causing the gas to mix with the moisture in our bodies and form an acid that our lungs tried to expunge, with only partial success.

Twenty years later, I read the results of a medical research report showing that area residents suffer from rates of lung disease, including emphysema and lung cancer, significantly above the national average. However, even in 1968 it was evident a serious problem was brewing in my hometown. I therefore hatched a plan. Our high school was about to hold its annual model parliament. The event was notoriously boring, partly because, year in, year out, virtually everyone voted for the same party, the Conservatives. But here was an issue, I thought, that could turn things around. The pulp and paper mill was owned by K.C. Irving, an industrialist so powerful that his companies were said to control 40 percent of New Brunswick's economic output. *Forbes* magazine in the United States annually ranked Irving among the wealthiest men in the world. I figured that once I told my fellow students the political implications of the fact that water combined with sulfur dioxide produces sulfurous acid, they would quickly demand the closure of the mill until Irving guaranteed a clean operation.

Was *I* naive. As head of the tiny Liberal Party, I had to address the entire student body during assembly on election day to outline the party platform and mobilize votes. When I got to the part of my speech explaining why K.C. Irving was our enemy, the murmuring in the audience, which had been growing like the sound of a hungry animal about to pounce on its prey, erupted into loud "boos." A couple of students rushed the stage. The principal suddenly appeared from the wings and commanded the student body to settle down. He then took me by the arm and informed me that, for my own safety,

The year 1968 was one of student rebellion worldwide. Here students run from police in Paris, France.
SOURCE: © Bettmann/Corbis.

my speech was finished. So, I discovered on election day, was our high school's Liberal Party. And so, it emerged, was my high school political career.

This incident troubled me for many years, less because of the embarrassment it caused me than because of the puzzles it presented. Why did I almost cause a small riot? Why didn't my fellow students rebel in the way I thought they would? Why did they continue to support an arrangement that was enriching one man at the cost of a community's health? Why weren't they enraged? Couldn't they see the injustice? Other people did. The year 1968 was not just the year of my political failure at Saint John High School. It was also the year that student riots in France nearly caused the fall of the government of Charles de Gaulle. It was the year in which the suppression of student strikes by the Mexican government left dozens of students dead. It was the year in which American students at Berkeley, Michigan, and other universities fought with unprecedented vigour for free speech on their campuses, an end to American involvement in the war in Vietnam, increased civil rights for American blacks, and an expanded role for women in public affairs.

I didn't know it at the time, but by asking why students in Paris, Mexico City, and Berkeley rebelled while my fellow students did not, I was raising the main question that animates the sociological study of politics and social movements. Why are some groups more successful than others in formulating their demands and getting them carried out? In other words, who gets what and under what social circumstances? That is the main issue addressed by this chapter.

**Power** is the ability of an individual or a group to impose its will on others, even if they resist (Weber, 1946 [1922]: 180). In the first section of this chapter, you will learn that the power of a group may be widely recognized as legitimate or valid under some circumstances. If it is, raw power becomes legitimate **authority** (see Box 18.1). The people who occupy the command posts of institutions are then generally seen as **authorities.** Under other circumstances, however, power flows to nonauthorities. This situation undermines the legitimacy of authority. In this case, nonauthorities form **social movements,** or collective attempts to change part or all of the social order. They may riot,

| BOX 18.1 | THREE BASES OF AUTHORITY |
|----------|--------------------------|

Max Weber (1947) argued that authority can have one of three bases:

1. *Traditional authority:* Particularly in tribal and feudal societies, rulers inherit authority through family or clan ties. In such circumstances, people believe the right of a family or clan to monopolize leadership derives from a god's will.

2. *Legal-rational authority:* In modern societies, authority derives from respect for the law. Laws specify how a person can achieve office. People generally believe these laws are rational. If someone achieves office by following these laws, his or her authority is respected.

3. *Charismatic authority:* Sometimes, extraordinary, charismatic individuals challenge traditional or legal-rational authority. They claim to be inspired by a god or some higher principle that transcends traditional authority, such as the principle that all people are created equal. Their claim is widely believed. Charismatic figures often emerge during a **political revolution,** a concerted attempt by many people to overthrow political institutions and establish new ones. Political revolutions take place when widespread and successful movements of opposition clash with crumbling traditional or legal-rational authority (Skocpol, 1979).

petition, strike, demonstrate, and establish pressure groups, unions, and **political parties** (organizations that seek to control state power) to achieve their aims.

The terms defined above allow us to distinguish between "normal politics" and "politics beyond the rules." Normal politics is politics as it is practised when authorities are firmly in power. Politics beyond the rules is politics as it is practised when the legitimacy of authority grows weak. Sociologists have proposed various theories to explain the two types of politics. In the second and third sections of this chapter, I evaluate these theories using mainly Canadian data.

Finally, in the chapter's concluding section, I place our discussion in historical context. How has politics developed over the past 300 years? What developments can we reasonably expect in the near future? This section will help you to better understand your political options in coming years.

## POWER FROM ABOVE: NORMAL POLITICS

In 1998, the RCMP used pepper spray to disperse Vancouver crowds demonstrating against visiting Indonesian President Suharto. The incident caused a scandal because it was widely seen as excessive use of force sanctioned by the prime minister. The solicitor general, who is responsible for the RCMP, was forced to resign over the incident.

This incident illustrates the use of **force** or coercive power by authorities. Paradoxically, the use of force by authorities is a sign of their weakness: If authorities are truly in a position of strength, their

rule will be widely recognized as legitimate. They will not need to use force to impose their will because most people agree with their policies. Here, politics will be routine, nonviolent, or "normal." To be sure, minor outbursts of violence occur even under normal politics. However, such events are unusual in Canada today. They rarely result in fatalities. For the most part, Canadian politics today is normal politics.

Power is exercised in all social settings, from the family to the classroom to the workplace. However, the ultimate seat of power in society is the state. The **state** is a set of institutions that formulate and carry out a country's laws, policies, and binding regulations. Why is the state's power "ultimate?" Because its authority stands above all others, and if the state needs to use force to maintain order or protect its borders, most people will regard its actions as legitimate.

In democratic countries, such as Canada, the government is formed by the elected members of the political party that wins the most seats in a general election (see Figure 18.1). It comprises the head of the party, who becomes prime minister, and the cabinet ministers whom the prime minister selects to advise him or her. It is the job of the government to initiate policies, propose laws, and see that they are enforced. That is why the government is also called the *executive* branch of the state. Proposed laws are turned into operating statutes by the *legislature*, which consists of all the people elected to Parliament. It is the responsibility of the *judiciary* or court system to interpret laws and regulations, that is, to figure out whether and how particular laws and regulations apply in disputed cases. The state's *administrative apparatus or bureaucracy* undertakes

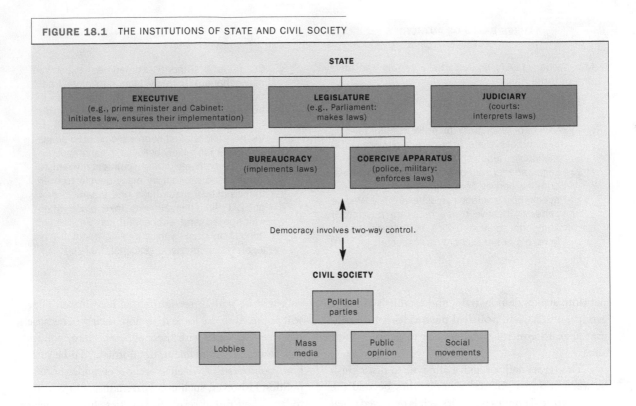

**FIGURE 18.1**    THE INSTITUTIONS OF STATE AND CIVIL SOCIETY

enforcement of laws. If laws are broken or the state's security is jeopardized, it is the role of the *coercive apparatus*—the police and military—to enforce the law and protect the state.

The state, then, is a set of institutions that exercise control over society. However, individuals in **civil society,** the private sphere of life, also exercise control over the state through a variety of organizations and institutions. We have already noted how social movements may influence the state. In addition, the mass media are supposed to keep a watchful and critical eye on the state and help to keep the public informed about the quality of government. Pressure groups or "lobbies" are formed by trade unions, manufacturers' associations, ethnic groups, and other organizations to advise politicians of their members' desires. Lobbies also remind politicians how much their members' votes and campaign contributions matter. Finally, political parties regularly seek to mobilize voters as they compete for control of government.

How democratic is the Canadian state? Does the interaction between state and civil society ensure that every citizen has a roughly equal say in the determination of laws and policies? Or, as George Orwell asked in *Animal Farm*, are some citizens more equal than others? Do we, as Abraham Lincoln claimed for the Americans, enjoy "government of the people, by the people, for the people?" Or is it more accurate to say, in the words of one wit, that we are subjected to "government of the people, by the lawyers, for the business owners"? These are among the chief questions asked by sociologists who study the state and its operations. It is now time to consider them in detail.

## PLURALIST THEORY

**Pluralist theory** is one interpretation of the relationship between state and civil society (Dahl, 1961; Polsby, 1959). According to pluralists, we live in a heterogeneous society with many competing interests and centres of power. For example, the interests of parents with school-age children may differ from the interests of pensioners. Parents may want school budgets to grow. Pensioners may want them to shrink. Because of such heterogeneity, no one group can control politics, according to the pluralists. They argue that, over time, all voters and interest groups influence the political process almost equally. Sometimes one category of voters wins a political battle, sometimes another. Most often, however, politics involves negotiation and compromise among competing groups. According to the pluralists, because no one group of people is always able to control the political agenda or the outcome of political conflict, democracy is guaranteed.

## ELITE THEORY

Elite theorists, C. Wright Mills (1956) foremost among them, sharply disagree with the pluralist account. According to **elite theory**, *elites* are small groups that occupy the command posts of a society's institutions. In the United States, the country that Mills studied, the most powerful elites are the people who run the country's several hundred biggest corporations, the executive branch of government, and the military. Mills wrote that the men who control these institutions (they are almost all men) make the important decisions that profoundly affect members of society. Moreover, they do so without much regard for elections or public opinion.

Mills showed how the corporate, state, and military elites are interconnected. People move from one elite to another over their careers. Their children intermarry. They maintain close social contact. They tend to be recruited from the upper-middle and upper classes. However, Mills denied that these similarities and interconnections turn the three elites into a **ruling class,** that is, a self-conscious and cohesive group of people, led by corporate executives and owners of big business, who act to advance their common interests. The three elites are independent of each other, Mills insisted. They may see eye-to-eye on many issues, but each has its own jealously guarded sphere of influence, and conflict between elite groups is therefore common (Mills, 1956: 277).

### The Elitist Critique of Pluralism

Most political sociologists today question the pluralist account of democratic politics because research has established the existence of large, persistent, wealth-based inequalities in political influence and political participation.

John Porter's classic, *The Vertical Mosaic* (1965), was the first in a series of Canadian studies that demonstrate the weaknesses of pluralism and corroborate some aspects of elite theory (Brym, 1989; Clement, 1975; Olsen, 1980). These studies show that a disproportionately large number of people in Canada's political and other elites come from upper- and upper-middle-class families. For example, about 40 percent of Canadian prime ministers, premiers, and Cabinet ministers were born into the richest 10 percent of families in the country (Olsen, 1980: 129). In their youth, members of Canada's elites are likely to have attended expensive private schools. As adults, they tend to marry the offspring of other elite members and belong to exclusive private clubs. In

the course of their careers, they often move from one elite to another. Arguably, people with this sort of background cannot act dispassionately on behalf of all Canadians, rich and poor.

Controversy persists over whether Canada's elites form a ruling class. Porter (1965), like Mills (1956), noted frequent conflict among elites. He argued against the view that a ruling class controls Canada. His top students disagreed. They argued that the interests of large corporations dominate Canadian political life (Clement, 1975; Olsen, 1980). However, both Porter and his students did agree on one point: contrary to pluralist claims, Canada's well-to-do consistently exercise disproportionate influence over political life in this country.

Studies of political participation in Canada add weight to the elitist view (Blais, Gidengil, Nadeau, and Nevitte, 1997; Frank, 1994; Mishler, 1979: 88–97). Many surveys show that political involvement decreases with social class. For example, the likelihood of voting falls with a person's class position. The likelihood of phoning or writing a member of Parliament, helping a candidate in an election campaign, contributing money to a political party, and running for office declines even more steeply as we move down the class hierarchy. As intensity of political participation declines, so does political influence. Consequently, although political apathy and cynicism are high among Canadians, the poorest Canadians are the most politically apathetic and cynical of any income category. They have less interest in politics than do the well-to-do, and they are more likely to think that government does not care what they think (see Figure 18.2). As a leading political sociologist wrote, "The combination of a low vote and a relative lack of organization among the lower-status groups means that they will suffer from neglect by the politicians who will be receptive to the wishes of the more privileged, participating, and organized strata" (Lipset, 1981: 226–27; see Box 18.2).

### The Marxist Critique of Elite Theory

Although compelling in some respects, elite theory has its critics, Marxists foremost among them. Some Marxists, known as "instrumentalists," deny that elites enjoy more or less equal power. Actually, they say, elites form a ruling class dominated by big business. From their point of view, the state is an arm (or "instrument") of the business elite. Big business gains control of the state in three main ways. First, members of wealthy families occupy important state positions in highly disproportionate numbers. Second,

**FIGURE 18.2**   POLITICAL CYNICISM AND DONATIONS BY ANNUAL HOUSEHOLD INCOME, CANADA

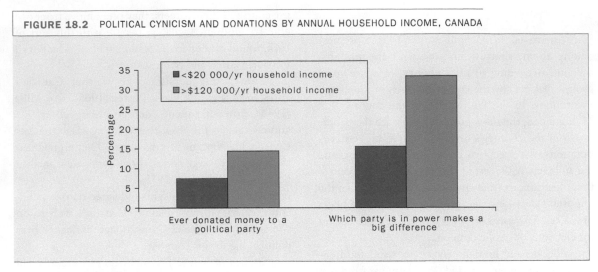

- ■ <$20 000/yr household income
- ■ >$120 000/yr household income

Percentage

Ever donated money to a political party

Which party is in power makes a big difference

SOURCE: "Canadian Election Panel Study" (2010).

government officials rely mainly on the representatives of big business for advice. Third, political parties rely mainly on big business for financial support. According to some Marxists, members of different elites may disagree about specific issues. However, as a result of the three control mechanisms listed above, they always agree about one issue: the need to maintain the health of the capitalist system (Miliband, 1973 [1969]).

A second group of Marxists, known as "stucturalists" offers a somewhat different interpretation of why the state in capitalist society is necessarily biased in favour of big business. For the structuralists, it is not so much the social origins of high government officials or the social ties linking them with big business that encourages the state to act with a pro-capitalist bias. Rather, they argue, the capitalist state acts as an arm of big business because it is constrained to do so by the nature of the capitalist system itself. For example, if the Canadian government doubled the corporate tax rate, investment would be redirected to countries with regimes that are kinder to company profits. Such a move would cost Canada jobs and prosperity. It would be highly unpopular. The government could easily fall. Fearing such outcomes, governments in capitalist societies find their field of action restricted to policies that ensure the well-being of big business. According to the structuralists, it is the very fact that the state is embedded in a capitalist system that forces it to act in this way (Poulantzas, 1975 [1968]).

It follows from both the instrumentalist and the structuralist positions that ordinary citizens,

Karl Marx predicted that capitalism would create a large mass of impoverished workers who would eventually take over the state, eliminate private property, and forge a communist society. After the revolution of 1917, the Soviet Union became the first self-proclaimed communist society. This early May Day poster reads: "Workers of all countries unite. The 1st of May work holiday. Long live the international unity of the proletariat!"
SOURCE: © Corbis.

**BOX 18.2**    **DEFEATING POLITICAL CYNICISM: TECHNOLOGY, ORGANIZATION, AND THE OBAMA EFFECT**

Turnout in the American presidential election of 1996 reached an all-time low. Just 48 percent of the voting-age population went to the polls. However, in subsequent elections, turnout increased, reaching 56 percent in 2008. Why the upturn? At 61 percent in the 2011 federal election, Canadian voter turnout remains higher than voter turnout in the United States, but for more than a decade, Canadian voter turnout dropped while American voter turnout increased (see Figure 18.3). Why the different trends in the two countries?

The competitiveness of elections in the United States and Canada may be part of the answer. Big fights tend to draw big crowds, and recent American presidential elections have been intensely competitive. Over the same period, Canadians were arguably presented with less stark party alternatives than Americans were. Canadian cynicism about politics may have remained high because less seemed to be at stake in Canadian elections. The result: persistently declining voter turnout in Canada.

Another factor that has contributed to the recent American upturn in voter turnout is that technological and organizational improvements encourage more people to vote in the United States.

Party organizers now use the Internet intensively to solicit donations, recruit volunteers, and communicate with them. They employ census and survey data to identify persuadable voters. Then, they send entire armies of the party faithful out to contact persuadable voters face-to-face and encourage them to vote (McDonald 2008a, 2008b). Canadian federal elections seem to be less technologically and organizationally advanced than American presidential elections are. Persistent declines in Canadian voter turnout may result from the technological and organizational lag.

Finally, the "Obama effect" is partly responsible for the most recent uptick in American voter turnout. President Barack Obama is, of course, a young, attractive, inspirational leader. In the 2008 presidential election, his message of hope and change appealed strongly to the most cynical age cohort: youth. Voters between the age of 18 and 29 supported Obama over McCain by a two-to-one margin, and they came out to the polls in droves ("United States," 2008). Meanwhile, voter turnout among Canadian youth is the lowest among all age cohorts (see Figure 18.3). We await our Obama.

**FIGURE 18.3**   VOTER TURNOUT, CANADIAN FEDERAL ELECTIONS

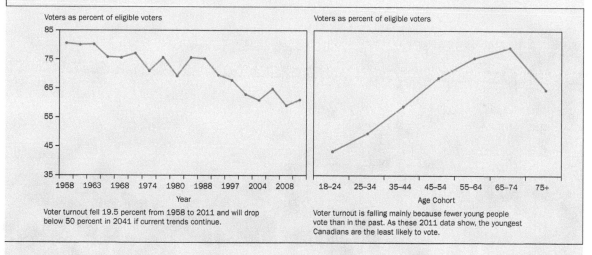

Voter turnout fell 19.5 percent from 1958 to 2011 and will drop below 50 percent in 2041 if current trends continue.

Voter turnout is falling mainly because fewer young people vote than in the past. As these 2011 data show, the youngest Canadians are the least likely to vote.

SOURCE: "Estimation of Voter Turnout by Age Group and Gender", Elections Canada, 2012. This reproduction is a copy of the version available at www.elections.ca. Reproduced with the permission of Elections Canada, but adaptation rests with the author.

and especially members of the working class, rarely have much influence over state policy. According to Marxists, true democracy can emerge only if members of the working class and their supporters overthrow capitalism and establish a socialist system in which economic differences between people are eliminated or at least substantially reduced.

## POWER-BALANCE THEORY

Pluralists assume that all major groups in society enjoy approximately equal power. Elitists assume that members of the upper class enjoy the most power. Both approaches, however, assume that the distribution of power in society does not change much over time, except in those rare instances when revolutions take place.

In contrast, power-balance theorists argue that the distribution of power in society changes significantly more frequently. **Power-balance theory** allows that power is usually concentrated in the hands of the wealthy. However, adherents of this approach also note that other classes sometimes gain power. This has big implications for political life. Among other things, the distribution of power determines how democratic a society is.

To make their case, power-balance theorists first measure variations in the social distribution of power. They then show how those variations are reflected in the successes and failures of different political parties and the rejection and adoption of different state policies. Along with the pluralists, they recognize that society is truly democratic only when power is widely distributed. Along with the elitists, they recognize that society is not very democratic when power is highly concentrated in the hands of a few wealthy citizens. However, by treating the distribution of power as a variable,

they improve our understanding of the relationship between power and democracy.

We can better understand power-balance theory by examining Canadian politics in comparative perspective. We first note that a group's power is partly determined by the degree to which it forms organizations to further its interests. For example, unionized blue-collar and white-collar workers are more powerful than their nonunionized counterparts are. That is because unions allow workers to speak with one voice. Unions enable workers to effectively bargain with employers and governments for improved wages, working conditions, and social policies. Moreover, if bargaining fails, they can go out on strike to try to force the issue.

If level of unionization increases working-class power, that should be reflected in the political behaviour of citizens and the policies adopted by governments. And, in fact, it is. Compare Sweden and Canada (Casper, McLanahan, and Garfinkle, 1994; Korpi, 1983; Myles, 1989; O'Connor, 1996; O'Connor and Brym, 1988; O'Connor and Olsen, 1998; Olsen, 2002; Olsen and Brym, 1996). In Sweden, more than three-quarters of blue- and white-collar workers are

The peak year of strike activity in Canada was 1919. In that year, 17.3 strikes took place for every 100 000 nonagricultural workers in the country. This photo was taken on "Bloody Saturday," June 21, 1919, during the Winnipeg General Strike. It shows a violent confrontation between rioters and Mounties and special police.
SOURCE: LAC C-33392.

union members. In Canada, about three in ten non-agricultural workers are members of unions. Several consequences follow:

- 61.4 percent of Canadians voted in the 2011 federal election, compared with 84.6 percent of Swedes in the 2010 Swedish federal election ("Voter Turnout," 2011; Statistics Sweden, 2011). The difference is largely due to the fact that working-class Swedes are more likely to vote than working-class Canadians are.

- The Swedish socialist party has formed the government almost continuously since World War II. In contrast, Canada's socialist party, the NDP, has never formed the federal government or even had a representative in the federal cabinet. The parties that have formed Canada's federal governments (Liberals, Progressive Conservatives, and Conservatives) are those that are most strongly supported by business (see Figure 18.4).

- Swedish governments have acted more vigorously than Canadian governments have to eradicate poverty and equalize incomes. Thus, fewer than 4 percent of Swedes are classified as living below the poverty line (as defined by the low income cutoff; see Chapter 6, Social Stratification). The comparable figure for Canadians is about 15 percent. In Sweden, about 20 percent of all income goes to the top 10 percent of income earners. The comparable figure for Canada is

about 30 percent of all income. And in Sweden, a broader range of retired people receive more generous pensions and more frequent cost-of-living adjustments than do pensioners in Canada.

- Since women are disproportionately concentrated in low-income, low-status jobs (see Chapter 7, Gender Inequality), they benefit more than men do when the working class is more powerful. As a result, the ratio of women's to men's earnings is about 80 percent in Sweden and 67 percent in Canada. Moreover, in Sweden, the ratio of women to men who live below the poverty line is just above 90 percent, while in Canada the comparable figure is nearly 130 percent. Finally, parental benefits are superior in Sweden and child-care facilities are more widely available and affordable.

We thus see that elections matter a great deal in the lives of ordinary people. Elections determine the types of parties that get elected. Elected parties, in turn, shape government policies. The outcome of any particular election depends on the appeal of party leaders, their effectiveness in presenting issues to the public, and myriad other short-term factors (Clarke, Jenson, Le Duc, and Pammett, 1996; see Figure 18.5). However, when considering the types of parties that get elected over several decades, as we did previously, we see that the distribution of power between classes and other groups shapes the character of politics in a country.

The preceding analysis also implies that Sweden is more democratic than Canada is. True, citizens of both countries are legally free to vote and influence their governments. But because the working class is more powerful in Sweden, Swedes' legal right to vote and influence governments has been turned into real political influence on a wider scale. In general, only if more citizens wield more clout can society become more democratic.

## STATE-CENTRED THEORY

Power-balance theory suggests that democratic politics is a contest among various classes and other groups to control the state for their own advantage. When power is substantially redistributed—when, for example, a major class gets better organized while another major class becomes less socially organized—old ruling parties usually fall and new ones take office.

Note, however, that a winner-take-all strategy would be nothing short of foolish. If winning parties monopolized the spoils of office, passing laws

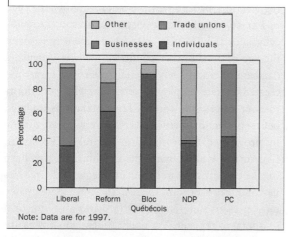

**FIGURE 18.4** CONTRIBUTIONS TO FEDERAL POLITICAL PARTIES BY SOURCE

Note: Data are for 1997.

SOURCE: Elections Canada, "Contributions to Registered Political Parties, By Donor Category (Dollars)," from http://www.elections.ca /ecFiscals/1997/table03_e.html, 1997. Reproduced with the permission of the Minister of Public Works and Government Services Canada, 2011.

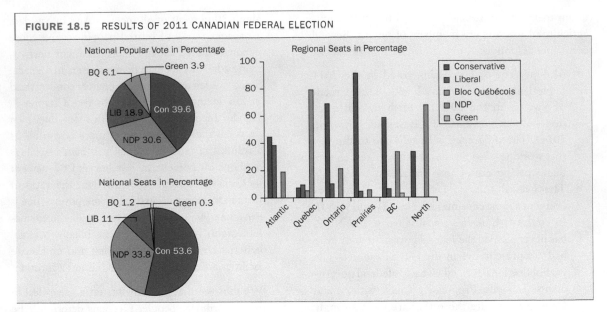

FIGURE 18.5    RESULTS OF 2011 CANADIAN FEDERAL ELECTION

SOURCE: Data used to create the above chart was taken from the website of Elections Canada, www.elections.ca, 2011. It is used with the permission of the Chief Electoral Officer. Adaptation and analysis are the responsibility of the author.

that benefit only their supporters, they might cause massive outrage and even violent opposition. Yet allowing opponents to become angry, organized, and resolute would be counterproductive. After all, winners want more than just a moment of glory. They want to be able to enjoy the spoils of office in a stable political environment over the long haul. To achieve such stability, it is crucial that people who *lose* elections are given a say in government. To a degree, the party in power must attend to the wants of losing minorities. That way, even determined opponents are likely to recognize the legitimacy of the government and its right to rule. Pluralists thus make a good point when they say that democratic politics is about accommodation and compromise; they only lose sight of the fact that accommodation and compromise typically give more advantages to some than to others, as both elite theorists and power-balance theorists stress.

There is, however, more to the story of politics than conflict between classes and between other groups. Theda Skocpol and other **state-centred theorists** have shown how the state itself can structure political life independently of the way power is distributed among classes and other groups at a given time (Block, 1979; Evans, Rueschemeyer, and Skocpol, 1985; Skocpol, 1979). Their argument is a valuable supplement to power-balance theory.

To illustrate how state structures shape politics, consider the problem of nonvoting in the United States. In presidential elections, voter turnout fell more or less steadily between the end of World War II and 1996, when it stood at just 48 percent of the voting age population. Turnout increased in 2000 (50 percent), 2004 (55 percent), and 2008 (56 percent), but the United States still has one of the lowest voter turnouts of any rich democracy in the world (Piven and Cloward, 1989: 5). How can we explain this?

The high rate of nonvoting is largely a product of voter registration law—a feature of the American political structure, not of the current distribution of power. In every democracy, laws specify voter registration procedures. In some countries, such as France, citizens are registered to vote automatically once they receive state-issued identity cards at the age of 18. In other countries, such as Canada, a database of citizens who are eligible to vote was first created by state-employed canvassers who went door-to-door to register voters. The database is updated between elections with information supplied mainly by provincial, territorial, and federal data sources. Only in the United States do individual citizens have to take the initiative to go out and register themselves in voter registration centres. In some states, they must present state-issued ID (a driver's license or a passport) to register. Yet many American citizens are unable or unwilling to register. As a result, the United States has a proportionately smaller pool of eligible voters than the other democracies do. Only about 65 percent of American citizens are registered to vote (Piven and Cloward, 1989: 256–59).

Apart from shrinking the pool of eligible voters, American voter registration law has a second important consequence. Because some *types* of people are less able and inclined than others to register, a strong bias is introduced into the political system. Specifically, the poor are less likely to register than the better-off are. People without much formal education are less likely to register than the better educated are. Members of disadvantaged racial minority groups, especially African Americans, are less likely to register than whites are. Such people are less likely than others are to have the knowledge, time, and money needed to register, let alone a driver's license or a passport. Thus, American voter registration law is a pathway to democracy for some but a barrier to democracy for others. The American political system is less responsive than other rich democracies are to the needs of the disadvantaged. That is partly because, as state-centred theory suggests, the law requires citizen-initiated voter registration. As a result, many disadvantaged people are effectively disenfranchised.[1]

Big shocks sometimes rock state structures. In general, however, they are resistant to change. The foundations of state structures are anchored by constitutions, which can be altered only by large majorities of federally elected representatives and state- or provincial-level legislatures. Their upper stories are girded by laws, regulations, and policies, some of which help to keep potentially disruptive social forces at bay. American voter registration law is a case in point.[2] And then there are the many

ideological reinforcements. All states create anthems, flags, ceremonies, celebrations, sporting events, and school curricula that stimulate patriotism and serve in part to justify existing political arrangements.

In sum, each school of thought reviewed above makes a useful contribution to our appreciation of normal democratic politics (see Table 18.1). Pluralists teach us that normal democratic politics is about compromise and the accommodation of all group interests. Elite theorists teach us that, despite compromise and accommodation, power is concentrated in the hands of higher-status groups, whose interests the political system therefore serves best. Power-balance theorists teach us that, despite the concentration of power in society, substantial shifts in the distribution of power often occur, and they have discernible effects on voting patterns and public policies. Marxists highlight the rare occasions when political power is rapidly redistributed by revolutionary upheavals. And state-centred theorists teach us that, despite the influence of the distribution of power on political life, state structures exert an important independent effect on politics, too.

## POWER FROM BELOW: POLITICS BEYOND THE RULES

### RELATIVE-DEPRIVATION THEORY

All five theories of democracy reviewed above focus on normal politics. We know, however, that politics is sometimes anything but normal. Routine political

**TABLE 18.1**  FIVE SOCIOLOGICAL THEORIES OF DEMOCRACY COMPARED

|  | PLURALIST | ELITE | MARXIST | POWER BALANCE | STATE-CENTRED |
|---|---|---|---|---|---|
| How is power distributed? | dispersed | concentrated | concentrated | concentrated | concentrated |
| Who are the main power holders? | various groups | elites | ruling class | upper class | state officials |
| On what is their power based? | holding political office | controlling major institutions | owning substantial capital | owning substantial capital | holding political office |
| What is the main basis of public policy? | the will of all citizens | the interests of major elites | capitalist interests | the balance of power between classes, etc. | the influence of state structures |
| Do lower classes have much influence on politics? | yes | no | rarely | sometimes | sometimes |

processes can break down. Social movements can form. Large-scale political violence can erupt. As Vladimir Lenin, the leader of the Russian revolution of 1917, said, people sometimes "vote with their feet."

Until about 1970, many sociologists argued that social movements tend to emerge when people experience **relative deprivation.** People feel relatively deprived when they experience an intolerable gap between the social rewards they think they deserve and the social rewards they expect to receive. (Social rewards are widely valued goods, including money, education, security, prestige, and so on.) Accordingly, people are most likely to rebel against authority when rising expectations (brought on by, say, rapid economic growth and migration) are met by a sudden decline in social rewards (because of, say, economic recession or war; Davies, 1969). In addition, until about 1970, many sociologists held that the people who lead and first join social movements are likely to be outsiders who lack strong social ties to their communities.

A large body of research has now discredited these ideas. For example, we now know that the leaders and early joiners of social movements are usually well-integrated members of their communities, not socially marginal newcomers. In the 1930s, for example, Saskatchewan farmers and workers formed the Cooperative Commonwealth Federation (CCF) to protest federal government policy toward the West in general and Western agriculture in particular. The movement's leaders and early recruits were not outsiders. The workers were mainly local trade union activists. The farmers had been involved in the establishment of community-owned retail stores, credit unions, and marketing cooperatives (Lipset, 1971).

Much research also calls into question the idea that relative deprivation leads to the formation of social movements. For example, sociologists have compared measures of relative deprivation with the frequency of demonstrations, strikes, and acts of collective violence in France, Italy, Germany, and England. They have found that, in general, outbreaks of collective unrest do not increase with mounting relative deprivation (Lodhi and Tilly, 1973; Snyder and Tilly, 1972; Tilly, 1979a; Tilly, Tilly, and Tilly, 1975).

## RESOURCE MOBILIZATION THEORY

Because of the inadequacies of relative deprivation theory noted above, an alternative approach to the study of social movements gained popularity. **Resource mobilization theory** is based on the idea

that social movements emerge only when disadvantaged people can marshal the means necessary to challenge authority (Jenkins, 1983; McCarthy and Zald, 1977; Oberschall, 1973; Tilly, 1978). Foremost among the resources they need to challenge authority is the capacity to forge strong social ties among themselves. Other important resources that allow disadvantaged people to challenge authority include jobs, money, arms, and access to means of spreading their ideas.

You can appreciate the significance of resource mobilization theory by considering patterns of strike activity in Canada. When blue-collar and white-collar workers go out on strike, they are withholding their labour to extract concessions from employers or governments in the form of higher wages and improved social welfare benefits. When are workers most inclined to challenge the authority of employers and governments in this way? Research shows that in Canada since World War II, strike activity has been high when (1) unemployment is low, (2) union membership is high, and (3) governments have been relatively generous in their provision of social welfare benefits. Low unemployment indicates a strong economy. Workers are inclined to strike when business activity is robust because they know employers and governments can afford to make concessions. (Employers make bigger profits and governments collect more taxes during economic booms.) A high level of unionization is also conducive to more strike activity because unions provide workers with leadership, strike funds, and coordination. Thus, as resource mobilization theory predicts, strong social ties among workers (as indicated by a high level of unionization) and access to jobs and money (as indicated by a booming economy) increase challenges to authority (as indicated by strikes).[3]

Figure 18.6 shows the pattern of strike activity in post-World War II Canada. It supports the arguments of resource mobilization theory. Until 1974, the trend in strike activity was upward. (In the 1970s, Canada was, in fact, one of the most strike-prone countries in the world.) This was a period of growing prosperity, low unemployment, expanding state benefits, and increasing unionization. With increasing access to organizational and material resources, workers often challenged authority in the three decades after World War II. In 1973, however, economic crisis struck. Oil prices tripled, and then tripled again at the end of the decade. Inflation increased and unemployment rose. Soon, the government was strapped for funds and

**FIGURE 18.6** WEIGHTED FREQUENCY OF STRIKES, CANADA, 1946–2008

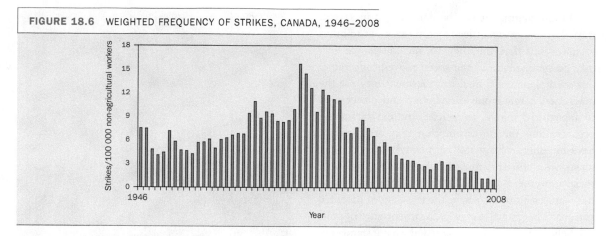

SOURCES: Canada Department of Labour (1970, 1973, 1985); Human Resources Development Canada (1995, 1998, 2006); International Labour Organization (2012).

had to borrow heavily to maintain social welfare programs. Eventually, the debt burden was so heavy that the government felt obliged to cut various social welfare programs. Unionization reached a peak in 1978, stabilized, and then began to fall (see Figure 18.7). Thus, in the post-1973 climate, the organizational and material resources of workers fell. As a result, strike activity plummeted. In 1974, nearly 16 strikes took place for every 100 000 Canadian workers. By 2006, that figure had fallen to just over 1 (Brym, 2008).

## FRAMING DISCONTENT

As you have seen, resource mobilization theory is a useful approach to the study of social movements, such as the strike movement in Canada. Even so, the emergence of a social movement sometimes takes sociologists by surprise. In addition, the failure of an aggrieved group to press its claim is sometimes equally unexpected. And movements that do emerge are successful to varying degrees. It seems, therefore, that something lies between (1) the capacity of disadvantaged people to mobilize resources for collective action and (2) the recruitment of a substantial number of movement members. Sociologists call that "something" **frame alignment** (Goffman, 1974; Snow, Rochford, Worden, and Benford, 1986). Frame alignment is the process by which individual interests, beliefs, and values either become congruent and complementary with the activities, ideas, and goals of the movement or fail to do so. Thanks to the efforts of scholars operating mainly in the symbolic interactionist tradition (see Chapter 1, Introducing Sociology, and Chapter 3, Socialization), frame alignment has recently become the subject of sustained sociological investigation.

**FIGURE 18.7** PERCENTAGE OF NONAGRICULTURAL WORKERS UNIONIZED, CANADA AND THE UNITED STATES, 1925–2010

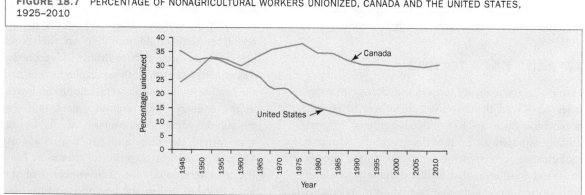

SOURCES: Bureau of Labor Statistics (2012); Canada Department of Labour (1973); Human Resources Development Canada (1995, 1998); Human Resources and Skills Development Canada (2011); Mayer (2004); Statistics Canada (2008).

Frame alignment can be encouraged in several ways. Social movement leaders can reach out to other organizations that, they believe, include people who may be sympathetic to the social movement's cause. For example, an anti-nuclear movement may use the mass media, telephone campaigns, and direct mail to appeal to feminist, anti-racist, and environmental organizations on the assumption they are likely to have members who would agree at least in general terms with the anti-nuclear platform. In addition, social movements can idealize values that have so far not featured prominently in the thinking of potential recruits. They can also elevate the importance of positive beliefs about the movement and what it stands for. For example, in trying to win new recruits, movement members might emphasize the seriousness of the social movement's purpose. They might analyze in a clear and compelling manner the causes of the problem the movement is trying to solve. Or they might stress the likelihood of the movement's success. By doing so they might increase the movement's appeal to potential recruits and win them over to the cause. Social movements can also stretch their objectives and activities to win recruits who are not initially sympathetic to the movement's original aims. This may involve watering down the movement's ideals. Alternatively, movement leaders may decide to take action calculated to appeal to nonsympathizers on grounds that have little or nothing to do with the movement's purpose. When rock, punk, or reggae bands play at nuclear disarmament rallies or gay liberation festivals, it is not necessarily because the music is relevant to the movement's goals. Nor do bands play just because movement members want to be entertained. The purpose is also to attract nonmembers. Once attracted by the music, nonmembers may make friends and acquaintances in the movement and then be encouraged to attend a more serious-minded meeting.

## REFRAIN: BACK TO 1968

Frame alignment theory stresses the interaction strategies employed by movement members to recruit nonmembers who are like-minded, apathetic, or even initially opposed to the movement's goals. Resource mobilization theory focuses on the broad social-structural conditions that facilitate the emergence of social movements. One theory usefully supplements the other.

The two theories certainly help clarify the 1968 high school incident I described at the beginning of

The Assembly of First Nations, which represents 633 Aboriginal groups, demands that Aboriginal Canadians have the right to formulate their own laws and reject some Canadian laws. Here, Aboriginal peoples protest certain taxes outside a government office.
SOURCE: © Dick Hemingway.

this chapter. It now seems clear that two main factors prevented me from influencing my classmates in New Brunswick when I spoke to them about the dangers of industrial pollution:

1. Disadvantaged people in New Brunswick were relatively powerless. They had access to few resources they could mobilize on their own behalf. That is because New Brunswick's economy was underdeveloped. Both per capita income and the level of unionization were among the lowest in the country. The unemployment rate was among the highest. In contrast, K. C. Irving, who owned the pulp and paper mill against which I railed, was so powerful that most New Brunswickers could not even conceive of the need to rebel against the conditions of life that he helped to create for them. He owned most of the industrial establishments in the province—the oil refinery and a network of gas stations, the dry

docks, the pulp mills, the mines, and the logging operations. Every daily newspaper, most of the weeklies, all of the TV stations, and most of the radio stations were his, too. Little wonder we rarely heard a critical word about his operations. Many people also believed that Irving could make or break provincial governments single-handedly. Should I therefore have been surprised that mere high school students refused to take him on? In their conservatism, my fellow students were only mimicking their parents, who, on the whole, were as powerless as Irving was mighty (Brym, 1979).

2. Many of my classmates did not share my sense of injustice. Most of them regarded K. C. Irving as the great provider. They thought his pulp and paper mill, as well as his myriad other industrial establishments, gave many New Brunswickers jobs. They regarded that fact as more important for their lives and the lives of their families than the pollution problem I raised. Frame-alignment theory suggests I needed to figure out ways of building bridges between their understanding and mine. I did not. I therefore received an unsympathetic hearing.

## THE HISTORY AND FUTURE OF SOCIAL MOVEMENTS

### I. THE RICH COUNTRIES

Three hundred years ago, social movements were typically small, localized, and violent. In Europe, poor residents of a particular city might riot against public officials in reaction to a rise in bread prices or taxes. Peasants on a particular estate might burn their landowner's barns (or their landowner) in response to his demand for a larger share of the crop. Then the reach of the state grew, soon encompassing most aspects of life. The state taxed nearly all its citizens at higher and higher rates as government services expanded. It imposed a uniform language and a common curriculum in a compulsory education system. It drafted most young men for army service. It instilled in its citizens all the ideological trappings of modern nationalism, from anthems to flags to historical myths. And in the process, social movements changed. They became national in scope, typically directing themselves against central governments rather than local targets. They grew in size, partly because potential recruits were now literate and could communicate using the printed word, partly

because big new social settings—factories, offices, densely populated urban neighbourhoods—could serve as recruitment bases. And, in most cases, social movements became less violent. Their size and organization often allowed them to stabilize, bureaucratize, and become sufficiently powerful to get their way without frequent resort to extreme measures (Tilly, 1978, 1979a, 1979b; Tilly, Tilly, and Tilly, 1975).

Social movements often used their power to expand the rights of citizens. We can identify four stages in this process. In Britain, for example, rich property owners struggled against the king in the eighteenth century for **civil citizenship:** the right to free speech, freedom of religion, and justice before the law. The male middle class and the more prosperous strata of the working class struggled against rich property owners in the nineteenth century for **political citizenship:** the right to vote and run for office. In early-twentieth-century Britain, women and poorer workers succeeded in achieving these same rights despite the opposition of well-to-do men in particular. During the remainder of the century, blue- and white-collar workers struggled against the well-to-do for **social citizenship:** the right to a certain level of economic security and full participation in the social life of the country by means of the creation of the modern welfare state (Marshall, 1965).

In the last third of the twentieth century, the struggle to broaden citizenship rights entered a new phase, which we now examine in greater detail. The broadening of the struggle for citizenship rights was signalled by the emergence of so-called **new social movements** in the 1960s and 1970s (Melucci, 1980, 1995). What is new about new social movements is the breadth of their goals, the kinds of people they attract, and their potential for going global. I will consider each of these issues in turn.

### Goals

Some new social movements, such as the peace movement, the environmental movement, and the human rights movement, promote the rights not of specific groups but of humanity as a whole to peace, security, and a clean environment. Other new social movements, such as the women's movement and the gay rights movement, promote the rights of particular groups that have been excluded from full social participation. Accordingly, gay rights groups have fought for laws that eliminate all forms of discrimination based on sexual orientation. They have also fought for the repeal of laws that discriminate on the basis of sexual orientation, such as anti-sodomy laws and laws that negatively affect parental custody of children (Adam, Duyvendak, and Krouwel, 1999).

Since the 1960s, the women's movement has succeeded in getting admission practices altered in professional schools, winning more freedom of reproductive choice for women, and opening up opportunities for women in the political, religious, military, educational, medical, and business systems (Adamson, Briskin, and McPhail, 1988; see Box 18.3).

The emergence of the peace, environmental, human rights, gay rights, and women's movements marked the beginning of a fourth stage in the history of social movements. This fourth stage involves the promotion of **universal citizenship**, or the extension of citizenship rights to all adult members of society and to society as a whole (Roche, 1995; Turner, 1986: 85–105).

## Membership

New social movements are also novel in that they attract a disproportionately large number of highly educated, well-to-do people from the social, educational, and cultural fields—teachers, professors, journalists, social workers, artists, actors, writers—and student apprentices to these occupations. Such people are predisposed to participate in new social movements for several reasons. Their higher education exposes them to radical ideas and makes those ideas appealing. They tend to hold jobs outside the business community, which often opposes their values. And they often get personally involved in the problems of

---

### BOX 18.3    THE WOMEN'S MOVEMENT AND ELECTORAL POLITICS

The women's movement was the first new social movement.

At the beginning of the twentieth century, women began to play a smaller role in domestic and farm work and started to enter the paid labour force in significant numbers. Owning more of their own economic resources, they became more independent-minded. They began to realize they might free themselves of oppressive authority in the home. They also started to understand there was nothing inevitable about their receiving less pay and working in worse conditions than men with comparable jobs did (Strong-Boag, 1986: 179).

Formulating a program for social change requires such resources as time, money, and education. Not surprisingly, therefore, the "first wave" of the women's movement comprised highly educated professionals. A group of women with just that social profile established the Canadian Woman Suffrage Association in Toronto in 1883. By demonstrating, petitioning, and gaining the support of influential liberal-minded men, women won the right to vote federally in 1918, in all provinces and territories but Quebec and Northwest Territories by 1925, in Quebec in 1940, and in the Northwest Territories by 1951.

Along with the right to vote, women won the right to run for public office. They immediately exercised that right, running mainly on the CCF and Liberal tickets. A woman was first elected to provincial office in Alberta in 1917 and to the federal Parliament in 1921.

In provincial and territorial legislatures and the federal Parliament, women sought institutional reform through government action. Specifically, they pursued equitable pay for women, easier access to higher education, protection from domestic violence, and a fair share of family assets and child support in case of divorce or desertion. However, progress was slow on all these fronts. That was partly because women's representation in the country's legislatures remained meagre. In 2012, women composed just 25 percent of federal MPs (Bashevkin, 1986; "Women in National Parliaments," 2012). Moreover, some female MPs were hardly advocates of women's rights.

Involvement in electoral politics requires time and money. Women are disadvantaged in this regard. On average, they have lower socioeconomic status than men do, and they are saddled with more domestic responsibilities. These factors prevent many women from running for office.

Public policy analysts note that female political participation can increase if such barriers are removed (Boyd, 2011: 175–76; Brodie, 1991). For example, laws could be passed that would allow candidates to take unpaid leave from their jobs to contest nominations and elections, set spending limits for nomination and election campaigns, make contributions for nomination campaigns tax deductible, treat child-care and housekeeping costs as reimbursable campaign expenses, and so on. Additionally, laws could be enacted that make government subsidies to political party campaigns dependent on

*(continued)*

BOX 18.3    *(continued)*

the proportion of their elected candidates that are women. In such a system, party subsidies would increase with the proportion of women elected.

Despite the existence of viable ideas for increasing women's participation in electoral politics, progress has been slow. Therefore, many feminists have developed a strategy that is oriented less toward established political institutions and more toward grassroots action. The new strategy sought to achieve change not just "from above," by means of party politics but also "from below," by creating a whole network of new organizations, such as study groups, consciousness-raising circles, women's bookstores, rape crisis centres, abortion clinics, shelters for battered women, and opportunities to publicize the importance of feminist aims, such as International Women's Day marches.

It was not only slow progress on the established political front that led women to create this network of new organizations. Many "second-wave" feminists were deeply involved in the student movement of the 1960s and 1970s. They were appalled to discover that, despite much rhetoric about liberation and equality, men controlled the student movement and often refused to allow feminist issues to become part of their agenda. To pursue their aims, they felt it was necessary to create new organizations run by women.

Today, the women's movement operates both at the grassroots level and within established political organizations to achieve its aims. It is internally differentiated. *Liberal feminists* believe that women can participate fully in society if they achieve equality of opportunity with men. They therefore advocate policies aimed at pay equity and the elimination of gender discrimination in the workplace. *Radical feminists* hold that male domination is rooted in the family. They champion free and safe contraception and abortion, an equitable division of domestic labour, and the like. *Socialist feminists* maintain that legal equality is not enough to ensure that women can participate fully in society. In addition, they argue, the state should provide affordable and accessible daycare facilities and other services. These services, they say, could alleviate the economic burdens that prevent most women, especially those from the working class, from taking full advantage of available opportunities for education and employment. *Anti-racist and postmodernist feminists* have criticized liberal, socialist, and radical feminists for generalizing from the experience of white women and failing to see how women's lives are rooted in particular historical and racial experiences. These new currents have done much to extend the relevance of feminism to previously marginalized groups. Thus, despite their different emphases, the various types of feminism share a strong desire to see members of a previously marginal group expand their citizenship rights and become full participants in society.

their clients and audiences, sometimes even becoming their advocates (Brint, 1984; Rootes, 1995).

## Globalization Potential

Finally, new social movements possess more potential for globalization than old social movements did. In the 1960s, social movements were typically *national* in scope. That is why, for example, the intensity and frequency of urban race riots in the United States in the 1960s did not depend on such local conditions as the degree of black–white inequality in a given city (Spilerman, 1970, 1976). Instead, congressional and presidential action (and lack of action) on civil rights issues, national TV coverage of race issues, and growing black consciousness and solidarity helped to create the view among African Americans that racial problems are nationwide and can be solved only by the federal government.

Many new social movements that gained force in the 1970s increased the scope of protest still further. For example, members of the nuclear disarmament and environmental movements viewed federal legislation as a necessary but insufficient solution to the issues that troubled them. Once they recognized that, say, the condition of the Brazilian rain forest affects climatic conditions worldwide and that the spread of weapons of mass destruction can easily destroy all of humanity, movement activists pressed for international agreements binding all countries to stop environmental destruction and nuclear proliferation. Social movements went global.

The globalization of social movements was facilitated by the ease with which people in various national movements could travel and communicate with like-minded activists from other countries. In the age of CNN, inexpensive jet transportation, fax machines, and email, it is possible not only to see the connection between apparently local problems and their global sources but also to act locally and globally. Greenpeace, for instance, is a highly successful environmental movement that originated in Vancouver in the mid-1970s and now has offices in 41 countries, with its international office in Amsterdam ("Greenpeace," 1999). A more recent global initiative with roots in Vancouver is the Occupy Movement.

On July 13, 2011, Kalle Lasn, editor of the Vancouver-based anti-consumerist magazine *Adbusters*, created a hashtag on Twitter, #OCCUPYWALLSTREET, and designed a poster of a ballerina dancing on the back of the bronze sculpture of a bull (symbolic of a profitable market) racing up Wall Street in Manhattan (Yardley, 2011). The poster called for people to go to the centre of the financial universe and protest the growing wealth and greed of the richest 1 percent of society and their role in causing the world financial crisis of 2008–09. Thousands did, and within days, demonstrations and encampments were sprouting in cities around the world. It was the most remarkable evidence of the globalization of social movements ever observed. Although nearly all of the protests had died down by the end of 2011 (St. John's, Newfoundland and Labrador, was the last Canadian holdout), the movement succeeded in

influencing global political discourse. One poll found that two-thirds of Americans surveyed in December 2011 believed that conflict between the rich and the poor was the main conflict in society—an increase of 19 percent since 2009 (Pew Research Center, 2012). The Occupy Movement helped to put class conflict back on the political agenda of the United States and other countries.

The globalization of social movements can be further illustrated by coming full circle and returning to the anecdote with which I began this chapter. In 1991, I visited my hometown. I had not been back in years. As I entered the city, I vaguely sensed that something was different. I could not define the change precisely until I reached the Irving pulp and paper mill. Suddenly, it became obvious: the rotten-egg smell was virtually gone. I subsequently discovered that in the 1970s a local woman whose son developed a serious case of asthma took legal action against the mill and eventually won. The mill owner was required by law to install a "scrubber" in the main smokestack to remove most of the sulfur dioxide emissions. Soon, the federal government was putting pressure on the mill owner to purify the polluted water that poured out of the plant and into the St. John River and the Bay of Fundy. Apparently, local citizens and the environmental movement had caused a change in the climate of opinion, influencing the government to force the mill owner to spend millions of dollars on a cleanup. It took decades, but what was political heresy in 1968 eventually became established practice because environmental concerns had been amplified by the voice of a movement that had grown to global proportions. In general, as this case illustrates, globalization helps to ensure that many new social movements transcend local and national boundaries and that many of them—but, as you will now learn, not all—promote universalistic goals.

## II. THE OTHER 85 PERCENT

With variations, the pattern of social movement evolution sketched previously applies to the 20 or so rich countries of North America, Western Europe, Oceania, and Japan. As we have seen, social movements in these rich countries typically sought to broaden democracy through the expansion of citizenship rights. In contrast, social movements in the other 85 percent of the world (by population) developed differently. They focused less on broadening the bases of democracy than on ensuring more elemental human rights, notably freedom from colonial rule and freedom to create the conditions for independent economic growth.

SOURCE: © Monica E/Occupy Together/www.occupytogether.org.

NEL

The "other 85 percent" of the world is relatively weak economically, politically, and militarily because it began substantial industrialization only after World War I and in some cases after World War II. This circumstance allowed the early industrializers (Britain, France, Japan, Russia, the United States, and so on) to carve up most of Asia, Africa, and South America into colonies, protectorates, mandates, spheres of influence, and other administrative forms of subjugation. The nineteenth century was the age of imperialism. The early industrializers used the rest of the world as a captive market for their manufactured goods and a source of inexpensive raw materials and labour. They enriched themselves even as they limited economic growth and well-being in the less-developed countries.

Events in the Muslim world were, in many respects, typical and thus illustrate the problem (Hourani, 1991: 265–349). Already by the 1830s the armed forces of France had taken control of part of Algeria, those of Britain had taken control of part of the Arabian peninsula, and those of Russia had taken over the Muslim lands of the Caucasus. A century later, almost the entire Middle East and North Africa were under British and French control. Egyptian cotton fed the looms of Lancashire. Iraqi oil supplied half of France's needs. British and French ships brought European machinery and textiles to the region. British and French financiers profited handsomely from their control of local banking. Some indigenous merchants and landowners benefited from the new economic relations too. However, the growing number of peasants and urban workers remained poor and powerless.

In the world's rich countries, a strong bourgeoisie—an affluent and politically powerful class of merchants, industrialists, and financiers—did much to promote the growth of democracy in its early stages (Moore, 1967). In contrast, in the Muslim countries and the rest of the less economically developed world, the bourgeoisie was small, weak, and dependent on imperial interests. Consequently, democratic ideals had little chance to sink deep roots. Instead, European and (especially after World War II) American domination of less-developed countries bred resentment, resistance, and revolt. Peasants, urban workers, intellectuals, and military officers were increasingly attracted to anti-imperialist independence movements based on various forms and mixes of socialism and nationalism (Brym, 1980: 50–53; Wolf, 1999 [1969]).

In the Muslim world, Islam was an additional source of anti-imperialist sentiment. In 1928, the Society of the Muslim Brothers was formed in Egypt ("Muslim Brotherhood Movement," 2002). It served as a prototype for other, similar groups. The Muslim Brotherhood argued against Western values and imperialist domination. It called for a return to the teaching of the Qur'an, strictly interpreted, and demanded that Egypt become an Islamic state based on religious law (shari'a). This type of thinking became popular in Egypt and throughout the Muslim world in the twentieth century, gaining impetus especially in Iran from the 1960s on and then spreading to Algeria and as far afield as Afghanistan and Sudan by the end of the century.

Growing popularity did not translate into widespread political ascendance until recent times. After World War II, almost all Middle Eastern and North African countries were authoritarian regimes that suppressed the Muslim Brotherhood and forced its popularity to flow underground. There, it branched into several streams, two of the most notable of which were an extremist current exemplified by al Qaeda and a more liberal current exemplified by political parties that a plurality of Moroccans, Tunisians, and Egyptians favoured in national elections held in 2011 and 2012.

## Extremist Political Islam: al Qaeda

A clear line of intellectual influence leads from the early Muslim Brothers to the assassins of Egypt's President Anwar Sadat in 1981 after he made peace with Israel to Osama bin Laden and al Qaeda (Worth, 2001). Al Qaeda's chief aims are to remove all Western (especially American) influence from areas with Muslim majorities, create in their place societies based on a fundamentalist interpretation of Islamic law, and destroy Israel as a Jewish state.

It is noteworthy that, however much al Qaeda is influenced by ideas dating back nine decades, it is every inch a global movement that relies on modern technology for its successes. Al Qaeda has placed operatives in as many as 60 countries. It finances itself through a complex international network of legitimate businesses, charitable and relief organizations, private donors, and opium trafficking operations (Shahar, 2001). Bin Laden communicated with his operatives via satellite telephone until U.S. law enforcement authorities inexplicably revealed they were tapping calls from his base in Afghanistan. Once he learned of these taps, he increased his use of another, more effective means of global communication—sending messages that are easily encrypted but difficult to decode via the Internet (Kelley, 2001; McCullogh, 2000).

Some analysts think such messages were used to help plan and coordinate the complex, virtually simultaneous jet hijackings that resulted in the crash of an airliner in Pennsylvania and the destruction of the World Trade Center and part of the Pentagon on September 11, 2001, killing some 3000 people.

## Liberal Political Islam: Morocco, Tunisia, and Egypt

In late 2010, Mohamed Bouazizi, a 27-year-old Tunisian street vendor, set himself on fire to protest harassment and humiliation by local officials. His action catalyzed widespread and often violent anti-regime demonstrations that first overthrew the Tunisian government and then spread with similar effect to Egypt and Libya, while also rocking other governments throughout the region. Bouazizi and those inspired by him objected to the authoritarianism, corruption, economic stagnation, unemployment, and poverty that characterizes most of the Middle East and North Africa. They initiated what came to be called the "Arab Spring" (see Box 18.4).

The most popular political parties that emerged from national elections held in Morocco, Tunisia, and Egypt in 2011 and 2012 were those organized by the Muslim Brotherhood, now free to run for office. These parties are unlike anything most Westerners had expected, let alone seen. On the one hand, the parties now in the ascendant in the region insist that Islam should form the basis of politics and law. They are suspicious of Western intentions. On the other hand, they have repeatedly and publicly stated their support for democratic elections and their tolerance of religious and ethnic minorities. Exactly how such apparently liberal Islamic parties will act once in office is unclear as of this writing. However, they have given hope to many people in the region and beyond that the dark era of authoritarianism that characterized the Middle East and North Africa for so long is at last beginning to lift (Andersen, Brym, and Araj, 2012).

As recent events in the Middle East and North Africa illustrate, a wide range of reactions against Western power and influence now grips much of the developing world. In its extreme forms, the

---

**BOX 18.4    WILL THE REVOLUTION BE TWITTERED?**

Some observers claim that Facebook and Twitter made the Arab Spring possible because they allowed the powerless to express their grievances and coordinate their actions with ease. However, such claims probably overstate the beneficial effects of new communications technology on global social movements. Most Facebook friends are really acquaintances, and most Twitter followers don't know the people they are following personally. It is relatively easy to get such socially distant people on networking sites to participate in certain actions—but only if participation requires little sacrifice. Thus, the Facebook page of the Save Darfur Coalition has nearly 1.3 million members, but they have donated an average of just nine cents each to the organization (Gladwell, 2010). Big sacrifices in the name of political principles require strong social ties, not the weak ties offered by Twitter accounts and Facebook pages. Typically, when individuals join a movement, they attract clusters of friends, relatives, and members of the same unions, cooperatives, fraternities, college dorms, churches, mosques, and neighbourhoods. This pattern occurs because involvement in a social movement is likely to require big sacrifices, and you need to be close to others before you can reasonably expect them to share your ideas and willingness to sacrifice for a cause (McAdam, 1982).

A protester in Tahrir Square, Cairo, Egypt, in 2011, helping to overthrow the authoritarian regime of President Hosni Mubarak.
SOURCE: © Patrick Baz/Getty Images.

anti-Western reaction has no respect for minority rights, multiculturalism, elections, relatively open markets, and many of the other freedoms we enjoy and often take for granted in the West. In its more moderate forms, it shares many of the West's fundamental values. Yet regardless of its orientation, the anti-Western reaction is everywhere based on the desire of people to restore the independence and dignity they lost when the industrialized world showed up on their doorstep uninvited. One of the great tasks the West faces in the twenty-first century is to defend itself against violence while doing its utmost to remove the ultimate source of that violence: the gap between rich and poor countries that opened up at the time of the Industrial Revolution and that has widened ever since. Whether we are up to the task is anyone's guess.

## SUMMARY

1. Democracy involves a two-way process of control between the state (the set of institutions that formulate and carry out a country's law, policies, and binding regulations) and civil society (the private sphere, consisting of social movements, political parties, and so on).

2. The level of democracy in a society depends on the capacity of civil society to influence the state through citizen support of social movements, political parties, and other groups. That capacity increases as power becomes more widely distributed in society.

3. Although pluralists correctly note that democratic politics is about negotiation and compromise, they fail to appreciate how advantaged groups tend to have more political influence than others do.

4. Although elite theorists are right to note that power is concentrated in the hands of advantaged groups, they fail to appreciate how variations in the distribution of power influence political behaviour and public policy.

5. While power-balance theorists focus on the effect of changes in the distribution of power in society, they fail to appreciate what state-centred theorists emphasize—that state institutions and laws also affect political behaviour and public policy.

6. The degree to which power is widely distributed influences the success of particular kinds of parties and policies. Widely distributed power is associated with the success of labour parties and policies that redistribute wealth.

7. Research does not support the view that social movements emerge when relative deprivation spreads.

8. Research suggests that people are more inclined to rebel against the status quo when they are bound by close social ties to many other people who feel similarly wronged and when they have the money and other resources needed to protest.

9. For social movements to grow, members must engage in frame alignment, making the activities, goals, and ideology of the movement congruent with the interests, beliefs, and values of potential new recruits.

10. The history of democracy is a struggle for the acquisition of constantly broadening citizenship rights—first the right to free speech, freedom of religion, and justice before the law, then the right to vote and run for office, then the right to a certain level of economic security and full participation in the life of society, and finally the right of marginal groups to full citizenship and the right of humanity as a whole to peace and security.

11. In the developing world, social movements have focused less on broadening the bases of democracy than on ensuring more elemental human rights, notably freedom from colonial rule and freedom to create the conditions for independent economic growth. In some cases these movements have taken extreme, anti-democratic forms.

## QUESTIONS TO CONSIDER

1. Have you ever participated in a social movement or been actively involved in a political party? If so, explain how your political choices (which party you joined, your level of participation, the timing of your recruitment) were influenced by the sociological factors discussed in this chapter. If you have never participated in a social movement or been actively involved in a political party, explain how the sociological factors discussed in this chapter influence you to remain politically inactive.

2. How would you achieve a political goal? Map out a detailed strategy for reaching a clearly defined aim, such as a reduction in income tax

or an increase in university funding. Who would you try to recruit to help you achieve your goal? Why? What collective actions do you think would be most successful? Why? To whose attention would these actions be directed? Why? Write a manifesto that frames your argument in a way that is culturally appealing to potential recruits.

3. Do you think that social movements will be more or less widespread in the twenty-first century than they were in the twentieth? Why or why not? What kinds of social movements are likely to predominate?

4. Do you think that the twenty-first century will be more or less democratic than the twentieth? Why or why not?

## GLOSSARY

**Authorities** (p. 440) are people who occupy the command posts of legitimized power structures.

**Authority** (p. 440) is power that is widely viewed as legitimate.

**Civil citizenship** (p. 453) recognizes the right to free speech, freedom of religion, and justice before the law.

**Civil society** (p. 442) is the private (nonstate) sphere of social life.

**Elite theory** (p. 443) maintains that well-to-do people consistently have more political influence than people who are less well-to-do have and that society is therefore not as democratic as it is often portrayed.

**Force** (p. 441) is coercive power.

**Frame alignment** (p. 451) is the process by which individual interests, beliefs, and values either become congruent and complementary with the activities, goals, and ideology of a social movement.

**New social movements** (p. 453) are post-1950s movements that attract a disproportionately large number of highly educated people in the social, educational, and cultural fields and universalize the struggle for citizenship.

**Pluralist theory** (p. 442) holds that society has many competing interests and centres of power and that no one interest or power centre predominates in the long run.

**Political citizenship** (p. 453) recognizes the right to run for office and vote.

**Political parties** (p. 441) are organizations that seek to control state power.

A **political revolution** (p. 441) is a concerted attempt on the part of many people to overthrow existing political institutions and establish new ones. Political revolutions take place when widespread and successful movements of opposition clash with crumbling traditional or legal-rational authority.

**Power** (p. 440) is the ability of an individual or a group to impose its will on others, even if they resist.

**Power-balance theory** (p. 446) suggests that social movement formation and success depend on how powerful authorities are, compared with partisans of change. It also holds that societies with widely distributed power are more democratic and more egalitarian than are societies with narrowly held power.

**Relative deprivation** (p. 450) is an intolerable gap between the social rewards people feel they deserve and the social rewards they expect to receive.

**Resource mobilization theory** (p. 450) holds that social movements crystallize and succeed in achieving their goals to the degree that they have access to scarce resources, such as money and effective communication facilities.

A **ruling class** (p. 443) is a self-conscious and cohesive group of people, led by corporate executives and owners of big business, who act to advance their common interests.

**Social citizenship** (p. 453) recognizes the right to a certain level of economic security and full participation in social life.

**Social movements** (p. 440) are enduring collective attempts to change part or all of the social order by means of rioting, petitioning, striking, demonstrating, and establishing pressure groups, unions, and political parties.

The **state** (p. 441) is a set of institutions that formulate and implement a country's laws, policies, and binding regulations. It consists of an executive branch (which initiates laws), a legislative branch (which makes laws), a judicial branch (which interprets laws), and an administrative and coercive apparatus (which enforces laws and protects state security).

**State-centred theory** (p. 448) shows how the state structures political life independently of the way power is distributed among classes and other groups at a given time.

**Universal citizenship** (p. 454) recognizes the right of marginal groups and the rights of humanity as a whole to full citizenship.

## SUGGESTED READING

Baer, Doug, ed. (2002). *Political Sociology: Canadian Perspectives.* Toronto: Oxford University Press. This useful compendium of Canadian materials covers major issues and debates.

Tilly, Charles and Sidney Tarrow. (2007). *Contentious Politics.* Boulder CO: Paradigm Publishers. An accessible and innovative introduction to political sociology by two grand masters.

Wolf, Eric. (1999 [1969]). *Peasant Wars of the 20th Century.* Norman, OK: Oklahoma University Press. The best introduction to social movements in the developing world.

## NOTES

1. In addition, fewer than 13 percent of the American working class are unionized, making it the least organized working class in any of the world's rich countries.

2. For example, in the 1890s, a coalition of white and black southern farmers threatened the established American political parties. It was precisely for this reason that American electoral laws were made more restrictive.

3. Some of these generalizations do not apply to countries with a long tradition of labour government. For example, since World War II, Sweden has experienced high levels of unionization and low strike rates. That is because Swedish workers and their representatives are involved in government policymaking. Decisions about wages and benefits tend to be made in negotiations among unions, employer associations, and governments rather than on the picket line.

# Mass Media

# Mass Media

## SOCIAL MEDIA AND REVOLUTION

In 2011, people living in Tunisia, Egypt, and Libya overthrew their despotic and corrupt governments. These revolutions were unique in their use of social media as an organizing tool. Ayat Mneina, a Libyan-born University of Manitoba student, describes how she helped in the fight for political freedom in her home country:

**Ayat Mneina**

*Used with permission of Ayat Mneina*

*The resentment toward the regime and the desire for change are sentiments I share with the youth in Libya. Upon seeing the uprisings take place in neighbouring Tunisia and Egypt in January, a friend (Omar Amer) and I made a conscious decision to get involved if the youth of Libya were ever to take action.*

*We decided to observe social media outlets used by Libyan youth, predominantly Facebook, to gauge the potential for action. We simultaneously monitored the use of social media, including Twitter, by Tunisian and Egyptian youth in case we had to mobilize.*

*Within weeks of the Jasmine Revolution in Tunisia, Facebook groups emerged calling for a Day of Rage in Libya, setting the date for February 17, 2011. Although we could not predict whether or not the youth would in fact take to the streets, as the day grew near we equipped ourselves with a Twitter account (called @ShababLibya), a small network of friends and relatives on the ground who we could contact for updates, a Skype account, a YouTube account, a Gmail account, and a Facebook account and page all complementing our effort—which we chose to call the Libyan Youth Movement (ShababLibya).*

*Because of premature protests occurring on February 15–due to the arrest of a young human rights lawyer named Fathi Terbil and reports of increased security in the resistance stronghold of Benghazi–we grew skeptical about the upcoming Day of Rage. On the evening of the 16th, we received confirmation from several sources that youth were in fact planning to take to the streets the next morning. Fully equipped with caffeine, laptops, and our complete toolbox of social media, we began the task of filling the void that existed because independent and international media were not allowed to operate in Libya.*

*Overnight, we found ourselves tweeting urgent messages to the world and international media calling for the coverage of what we soon understood was the brutal and indiscriminate murder of innocent, unarmed protesters across the country. The images, reports, and accounts we received were unlike anything we could have prepared for, and in the next week we became the number one source of information on the Libyan uprising. We tweeted and posted reports as we received them, confirmed from the ground based on accounts from at least three people. We also provided media outlets with interviews and contacts with protesters on the ground, and we were even able to deliver coordinates of Gaddafi forces to NATO. We rallied for international support, and effectively became the voice of the Libyan youth during the revolution. I have seen our humble efforts thrive and grow to include more than 49,000 followers on Twitter, nearly 23,000 subscribers to our Facebook page, a website that sees thousands of visitors every week (www.shabablibya.org), and a handful of dedicated volunteers located around the globe who have tirelessly given their time and effort to this cause.*

At the same time, people in Libya were using their mobile phones to record the fighting and to post their videos on YouTube. Outside reporters were not allowed to work freely in the parts of Libya controlled by Gaddafi, so these videos were important in helping to convince other countries to provide support to the revolution.

Social media have played a prominent role in other political events. Repressive governments control their local media and constantly transmit government propaganda. Satellite TV helped to break this control—the Al Jazeera network gave many people in the Middle East their first real look at the outside world and showed the harm being done by their own repressive regimes. The Internet and the World Wide Web further opened up the world and for the first time enabled two-way communication inside and outside these countries. Cellphones enabled people who could not afford computers to access the Internet and to share information through social media. Revolutionaries no longer needed to seize state radio and television stations to get their message out. The transformation of media communication from "one-to-many" to "many-to-many" (Zakaria, 2011) made it possible for citizens to use the media to organize against the state.

People do not need social media to overturn oppressive governments—revolutions occurred long before the Internet. However, social media help people to get their message out and to mobilize others. Social media allow opponents to share information without

the knowledge of the government and also to send news about their situation to the rest of the world.

Repressive governments do not just passively allow their opponents to use social media. More than 40 countries, including China, Iran, and Cuba, restrict Internet access (Canada Centre for Global Security Studies, 2011), and during times of crisis, governments may try to shut down the Internet and other social media entirely. During protests in 2009, the Iranian government shut down Tehran's cellphone network on days when demonstrations were planned and severely restricted Internet use. In 2011, the Egyptian government also tried shutting down social media in an unsuccessful attempt to save the regime of Hosni Mubarak.

While the Internet is a valuable tool, people cannot just dial up a revolution. The efforts in Egypt, Tunisia, and Libya would not have been successful without the courage of thousands of local residents who were willing to give their lives to change their government. Gaddafi would likely still be in power in Libya if the rebels had not also received military assistance from NATO. However, this support would probably not have happened without the work of people like Ayat Mneina, who collected information and put together a story that attracted the attention of individuals and governments around the world. The social media message is part of a media ecosystem that can help to amplify a message to enough audiences that a huge undertaking like a revolution becomes possible (Zuckerman, 2011).

Before reading on, test your knowledge of the media by taking the quiz in Box 17.1. on page 478.

(*Source:* Used with permission of Ayat Mneina)

## Critical Thinking Questions

1. Think of a political issue that you and your friends are interested in (tuition fees, student loan policies, environmental issues,). How could you use social media to help promote your views on this issue?

2. In the 2008 U.S. presidential election, Barack Obama based much of his campaign strategy on organizing support through social media. Do you think young voters would be more receptive to political participation if more politicians follow President Obama's example?

3. Do any of your friends or classmates come from countries with repressive governments? If so, are any of them involved in using social media to help people who oppose these governments?

93

What impact are the media having on our culture, our social institutions, and our communities?

## LEARNING OBJECTIVES

### AFTER READING THIS CHAPTER, YOU SHOULD BE ABLE TO

**LO-1** Understand what is meant by the term *mass media*.

**LO-2** Consider how the impact of the media is explained by functionalist, conflict, feminist, interactionist, and postmodern theories.

**LO-3** Understand how new media both bring people together and keep them apart.

**LO-4** Understand how social media sites profit from the information you provide them.

**LO-5** Think about the role played by the media in globalization.

## LO-1 WHAT ARE THE MASS MEDIA?

**mass media** Any technologically based means of communicating between large numbers of people distributed widely over space or time.

The media connect those who produce messages with those who receive them. The **mass media** can be defined as any technologically based means of communicating between large numbers of people distributed widely over space or time (Pavlik and McIntosh 2011:18).

Traditionally, the mass media have involved one-way communication in which a single source sent out a message to a large number of people who passively received that message. Think of the early days of television when there were only one or two channels and families gathered in their living rooms to watch their favourite programs. There was no opportunity for direct interaction between the media and members of the audience and little choice of programs.

## BOX 17.1 SOCIOLOGY AND EVERYDAY LIFE

### How Much Do You Know About the Media?

| True | False | |
|------|-------|---|
| T | F | 1. You do not need to be concerned about your privacy when using social media sites such as Facebook. |
| T | F | 2. Canadians spend more time watching television than using the Internet. |
| T | F | 3. Canadian radio stations can broadcast any songs they wish. |
| T | F | 4. When people design their online avatars in virtual worlds such as Second Life, they are not bound by our real-life cultural preferences about body size, hairstyles, and dress. |
| T | F | 5. While Internet dating sites are becoming more common, most people still meet their partners through traditional means such as family, school, and church. |

For answers to the quiz about the media, go to **www.nelson.com/sociologyinourtimes6e.**

The nature of the media has changed dramatically. Social media such as blogs, Facebook, and Twitter allow many individuals or groups to send out messages to many others, and the monopoly of those who control transmission has been broken. We have access to hundreds of television channels and millions of websites, there are countless YouTube videos to watch, and we can communicate directly with people anywhere in the world, thanks to the **Internet**—the network infrastructure that links together the world's millions of computers.

Over the past decade, the development of smartphones, tablets, and other portable devices has meant that we can stay constantly connected with family and friends and with the vast range of information available on the **World Wide Web**—the computer language that allows us to access information on the Internet. There used to be a clear separation of the different media, but media convergence has blended them together. Now we can watch movies and television programs, read novels and online newspapers, listen to music, and send text and voice messages on the same digital media device. We now live in a world where anyone can become a publisher or broadcaster through blogs, YouTube videos, or publishing services such as Amazon's CreateSpace—and the traditional media will have to adapt to this new reality.

In this chapter, we will discuss some of the ways in which we are affected by the media and how new media technology is changing many aspects of our lives.

> **Internet** The network infrastructure that links together the world's millions of computers.

> **World Wide Web** The computer language that allows us to access information on the Internet.

## SOCIOLOGICAL PERSPECTIVES ON THE MASS MEDIA  `LO-2`

The media play an important role in our lives. Media theorist Douglas Kellner has set out some of the ways the media affect us:

> Radio, television, film, and the other products of media culture provide materials out of which we forge our very identities; our sense of selfhood; our notion of what it means to be male or female; our sense of class, of ethnicity and race, of nationality, of sexuality; and of "us" and "them." Media images help shape our view of the world and our deepest values: what we consider good or bad, positive or negative, moral or evil. Media stories provide the symbols, myths, and resources through which we constitute a common culture and through the appropriation of which we insert ourselves into this culture. Media spectacles demonstrate who has power and who is powerless, who is allowed to exercise force and violence, and who is not. They dramatize and legitimate the power of the forces that be and show the powerless that they must stay in their places or be oppressed . . .
>
> The media . . . contribute to educating us how to behave and what to think, feel, believe, fear, and desire—and what not to do. The media . . . show us how to dress, look, and consume: how to react to members of different social groups; how to be popular and successful and how to avoid failure; and how to conform to the dominant system of norms, values, practices, and institutions. Consequently, the gaining of critical media literacy is an important resource for individuals and citizens in learning how to cope with a seductive cultural environment. (2011:7)

The Center for Media Literacy defines **media literacy** as the ability to access, analyze, evaluate, and create media in a variety of forms (2011). Sociology provides many of the tools we need to become media literate and to understand the role of the media in our society. Different sociological theories provide us with a variety of perspectives that help us to explain how the media operate in our society and to understand the impact the media have on our attitudes and behaviour.

> **media literacy** The ability to access, analyze, evaluate, and create media in a variety of forms.

## Functionalist Perspectives on the Media

**FUNCTIONS OF THE MEDIA** Charles Wright was one of the earliest sociologists to analyze the media from a functionalist perspective. Wright (1959) described four functions of the mass media:

- *Surveillance.* The media tell us what is happening in the world. By warning us about imminent storms, reporting the latest economic news, or telling us about the newest Hollywood movies, the media play an important role in informing the public.
- *Interpretation.* The media also interpret what is going on and tell us how we should respond to events. In editorials and in the selection of news stories, the media advance a particular agenda. Many parts of the mass media advocate particular political perspectives and try to influence how citizens vote.
- *Socialization.* The media transmit information, values, and norms from one generation to another and to newcomers. We can learn about society's rules, customs, and ways of behaving from the media.
- *Entertainment.* The media provide us with content that we find interesting and enjoyable. Many of us spend a significant part of our day being entertained by television, video games, radio programs, and recorded music.

Most would agree that the media do indeed fill these functions. The media sometimes do an excellent job of telling us what is going on—people around the world instantly learned of disasters like the 2011 earthquake and tsunami in Japan and the 2008 economic collapse. However, media coverage can be selective, so we learn more about some events than others. For example, while a terrorist bombing in a Western industrialized country will receive massive coverage in the media, atrocities elsewhere in the world may remain virtually uncovered—most Canadians are unaware of mass atrocities going on in countries such as the Democratic Republic of the Congo because the media do not want to spend money covering conflicts in little-known countries. Coverage of the Rwandan genocide took a back seat to the massive coverage of the O.J. Simpson murder trial in California and other events such as the war in the former Yugoslavia (Jackson, Nielsen, and Hsu, 2011).

One important form of socialization is that the media share images and experiences that allow us to imagine ourselves as part of a nation state. The invention of the printing press played an important role in developing a unified culture in France and other European countries (Straw, 2011). For centuries, France consisted of decentralized regional cultures with little sense of a national identity. Print media helped to standardize the French language, and the news and entertainment media contributed to a shared identity throughout the country. Straw also reports that the media, particularly television, drew the regions of Quebec together following

These early CBC logos highlight the organization's mandate of reflecting Canada and its regions.

the Quiet Revolution of the 1960s. The media play the same role everywhere in the world through broadcasting events such as the Olympics, legislative sessions, and national elections.

In many countries, the media have a legislated nation-building mandate. Canada's *Broadcasting Act* specifically gives the Canadian Broadcasting Corporation (CBC) the mandate to be "predominantly and distinctively Canadian, reflect Canada and its regions to national and regional audiences, while serving the special needs of those regions," to "actively contribute to the flow and exchange of cultural expression," to "contribute to shared national consciousness and identity," and to "reflect the multicultural and multiracial nature of Canada." (See Box 17.2.)

## BOX 17.2    POINT/COUNTERPOINT

### Should We Regulate the Media?

Many countries strictly regulate their media. China has imprisoned hundreds of journalists over the past decade, and "The Great Firewall of China" (formally named the Golden Shield Project) is one of many ways the Chinese government restricts free access to the Internet. Iran, Cuba, and several other countries are also known for their harsh treatment of journalists who are critical of the government.

Many other governments have also passed laws regulating the media. While Canadian media regulations may not censor free political expression, they do restrict who can own media companies, they regulate the use of the airwaves, and they put restrictions on media content. Children cannot view certain types of movies, and tobacco advertising is prohibited. One of the most interesting laws regulates the music played by Canadian radio stations.

In 1971, the Canadian government passed legislation specifying the amount of Canadian music that must be played on Canadian radio. York has explained why this legislation was passed:

The average Top Forty station was programmed by an American broadcasting consultant, who told the station what to play, how to play it, and who to hire and fire. The station played either English or American records or both; it employed primarily American deejays; and it modeled itself after the best (or worst, whichever way you personally hear it) U.S. stations in Boston, Chicago and New York. The yardstick of success was just how close you could come to sounding exactly like these American stations. (Ranson, 2008)

In the 1950s and 1960s, few Canadian musicians were as popular as those from the United States and England. This situation changed when the Canadian Radio-television and Telecommunications Commission (CRTC) required radio and television stations to promote Canadian culture by broadcasting a regulated amount of content written and performed by Canadians. Television stations must broadcast material with 60 percent Canadian content (50 percent during evening hours), and radio stations must play music with 35 percent Canadian content. These regulations have had a positive impact. Canadian popular musicians flourished, and many have become international stars (Ranson, 2008). For example, Arcade Fire won the Grammy Award for best album of 2010, and in December 2011, four of the seven best-selling albums in North America were recorded by Canadian artists—Michael Bublé (#1), Justin Bieber (#3), Nickelback (#6), and Drake (#7).

While this effort to promote Canadian artists was successful, in 1999 the CRTC decided not to regulate the Internet. The CRTC felt that regulation would stifle creativity and innovation and that most of the content of the Internet at that time was mainly text-based and did not involve broadcasting content (CRTC, 2011). The CRTC also felt that enough Internet content was being produced in Canada, so no regulation was necessary at that time.

The CRTC revisited this issue in 2009, and several groups, including those representing actors, urged the CRTC to regulate online content in the same way as it regulates television and radio because they felt the new media are just providing alternate platforms for viewing and listening to cultural products. While it is easy to control the content produced by radio and television stations operating in Canada, however, Internet content can be transmitted from anywhere in the world. Transmitting radio over the Internet requires few resources other than a computer, a microphone, and some MP3 files—all of which are very portable, so regulation would likely be futile (Ranson, 2008). Thus, Internet content is still not regulated.

What are your views on this issue? Now that we are able to access radio and video broadcasts from anywhere in the world, should the federal government try to regulate content on the Internet to protect Canadian artists?

Building a national consciousness is not always positive. The 1994 genocide in Rwanda was spread by radio stations and newspapers that promoted hatred against the Tutsi minority, and the media were heavily used by the Nazis to promote their vision of German racial superiority prior to World War II (Jackson, Nielsen, and Hsu, 2011).

Bookman (2011) has pointed out that today's interactive media also allow us to become members of very different types of imagined communities. These include online communities such as Second Life and FarmVille, as well as communities organized around interests such as cooking, sports, and environmental issues that can include members from around the globe.

**OTHER FUNCTIONS OF THE MEDIA**  Wright's four categories do not exhaust the functions of the media. For example, new forms of social media give the public a forum to express their views and perspectives. Traditional mass media tightly control what is transmitted, but we are now living in an era when anyone can set up a website, write a blog, or comment on a news story. As you read in Ayat Mneina's story in the chapter introduction, people can be mobilized through these sites. The July 2011 edition of the Vancouver-based anti-consumer magazine *Adbusters* included the message "What is our one demand? . . . #OCCUPYWALLSTREET, September 17" (Mickleburgh, 2011), which precipitated the Occupy movement in 2011. This movement spread quickly to many other cities throughout North America and Europe and at least temporarily drew attention to the increasing degree of inequality in Western countries. And some politicians follow public sites and even analyze Twitter feeds to help them develop policies that might appeal to voters.

The media can also link people through means such as Facebook, dating sites, and sales sites such as eBay. The importance of being able to stay close to people who are important to us is shown by the fact that in 2011, Skype reported 300 million minutes of video calls each day, an increase of 900 percent since 2007 (Caukin, 2011).

The media also have a **status conferral** function—attention by the media can give people high status. This status can apply to people who have made real contributions to society and deserve recognition, but today's mass media also confer "star" status on people who have no particular talent but are simply "famous for being famous."

> **status conferral** The process of giving prominence to particular individuals by focusing media attention on them.

The Occupy movement spread to many Canadian cities, including to this site in Toronto. Did this movement make you more aware of income inequality in Canada?

NEL

The celebrity socialite is not a new phenomenon, but reality television and the new social media have magnified the popularity of people such as the Kardashians (Gerds, 2011). Reality television shows enhance celebrity by showing us the details of their homes, cars, parties, holidays, and other personal details that make fans feel they have a close relationship with the celebrity, many of whom have blogs they use to reinforce these intimate ties with fans. Fans can respond to the blog postings, which helps them believe that they have a mutual relationship with the celebrity. Frequent tweets by the stars also give fans the sense that they are part of the celebrity's life. People grieved the deaths of celebrities such as Princess Diana and Michael Jackson as if they were close friends rather than people who were known only through media images (Hodkinson, 2011). The fact that people feel they are friends with people they will never meet blurs the distinction between reality and fiction—an issue that will be discussed later in this chapter when we discuss postmodern theories of media.

**DYSFUNCTIONS OF THE MEDIA** The media can also be *dysfunctional*. More than 60 years ago, long before the development of the Internet and the 24-hour global news cycle, Paul Lazarsfeld and Robert Merton (1948) coined the term *narcotization* to describe a situation in which people become so overwhelmed by the amount of information they receive that they become numb and do not act on the information. Nonstop broadcasts of scenes from a natural disaster such as the earthquake in Japan in 2011 can mobilize people to contribute to relief efforts, but as the bad news continues, people become desensitized and their attention moves on to other things.

Another dysfunction is that the free flow of news can threaten the status quo. News of what is happening elsewhere can be contagious. For example, the overthrow of the Tunisian government in 2011 quickly led to the successful revolutions in Egypt and Libya and to unsuccessful movements in several other countries, including Bahrain and Syria.

The media can also deliberately distort the news to sway public opinion. For example, Anderson and Robertson have documented the way in which the media have perpetuated stereotypes that have reinforced notions that "degrade, denigrate, and marginalize" Aboriginal people (2011:6). For nearly 150 years, the media have contributed to the marginalization of Aboriginal people by portraying them as inferior and by failing to present the Aboriginal case in discussions of issues such as land claims. Thus Aboriginal people have been largely excluded from the nation-building narrative presented by mainstream newspapers.

Other distortions, which are mainly being spread through the Web rather than through traditional media, include claims that the U.S. government was behind the 9/11 attacks on the World Trade Center and that President Obama is not legally the president because he was born outside the United States. These stories survive because the new media provide so many possible sources of information that almost every bias and interest can find support online.

The impact of these false stories may also be greater because of the new media. A person who watches network news or reads a mainstream newsmagazine will be exposed to a variety of issues and perspectives. However, if news comes through a customized daily news feed—what MIT Media Lab founder Nicholas Negroponte (1995) has called "The Daily Me"—the recipient may be exposed only to points of view he or she already supports. This new information will reinforce these beliefs rather than encouraging the recipient to consider alternative views. However, there has not yet been sufficient research to know whether the Internet will lead to selective exposure to a narrow range of opinions or whether people will use its power to find sources that challenge their views.

## Conflict Perspectives on the Media

Conflict theorists argue that the media help the dominant class control society by reinforcing its capitalist ideology and by encouraging a mass consumer culture that allows those who own the means of production to sell us unnecessary products and services.

**MASS MEDIA AND MASS DECEPTION** Max Horkheimer and Theodor Adorno (1972) were two of the earliest critics of the mass media. During the 1940s, they asserted that the *culture*

Image courtesy of The Advertising Archives

Conflict theorists believe that capitalism uses the media to create false needs for consumer products. One example of this is advertising for makeup products that try to sell people on the ideal of everlasting youth and beauty.

*industry* has turned artistic expression into just another marketable commodity—a commodity that keeps people passively entertained and politically apathetic. Consumption of this mass media culture destroys individual creativity and prevents consumers from taking a critical approach to their life situation. While "true" artistic activities may lead to independent thought and criticism of existing social arrangements, monopoly capitalism has used popular culture to promote its own values and to help preserve the status quo. According to these critics, the culture industry has been responsible for the mass deception and control of the public.

Through advertising and the images created by the popular media, capitalism also creates false needs for consumer products while people's true needs—including freedom and creativity—are ignored. And of course these products are manufactured and sold by the capitalist system that created the need for them. These false needs keep workers motivated to work even harder for their capitalist employers.

The mass culture industry also provides workers with a way of escaping the boredom and routine that define their lives. The cultural products the workers consume are standardized and follow a consistent formula so that the consumer does not have to think much about them or engage with them intellectually. People can just come home after work and absorb media products such as television programs without engaging with others, without thinking about their problems, and without thinking critically about their lives under capitalism.

**MEDIA CONCENTRATION** Conflict theorists are critical of the fact that members of the dominant class control the media. They feel the media exploit the working class by promoting the cultural values and beliefs of the rich and powerful and by creating a false consciousness among workers. The media in most democratic countries claim to be objective, but conflict theorists reject this claim. For example, Herman and Chomsky (1998) describe the reasons why concentrated capitalist control means that stories critical of capitalism will not appear in the popular media. These include the following: Massive media companies profit from capitalism; their advertisers would not allow them to be critical of corporations; and governments and other organizations, such as pressure groups and corporations, influence media organizations. These factors mean that the public does not receive any information that would seriously threaten the interests of the dominant class.

The Senate has concluded that the ownership of media is more highly concentrated in Canada than in most other countries and has recommended that the government take steps to ensure that media concentration is limited (Parliament of Canada, 2006). However, since the Senate report, there has been even more concentration: Shaw recently purchased the broadcasting assets of Canwest, and Bell bought the portion of CTV network it did not already control. Both of these transactions are examples of media convergence as telecommunications companies (Shaw and Bell) have merged with media companies (Canwest and CTV). All the largest media companies show this convergence. For example, Rogers Communications provides cellular and home phone service, Internet, and cable television. Along with these telecommunications services, Rogers owns 54 radio stations and two television networks; 70 magazines, including *Maclean's* and *Chatelaine*; and several television channels, including The Shopping Channel and Rogers Sportsnet. Rogers also owns the Toronto Blue Jays baseball team. In 2011, Rogers and Bell each purchased 37.5 percent of the Toronto Maple Leafs, the Toronto Raptors, and the Toronto FC soccer club.

Thus, Rogers (and its major competitors Bell, Telus, and Shaw) owns some of the content as well as the means of distributing that content. Content can easily be shifted from one platform to another, and advertising can be targeted to very specific audiences. This gives these corporations a very powerful place in the digital world. They have always been hugely profitable, as they spent many years as monopolies—for decades, in many areas, people had only one choice of a cable television provider, so the companies that received these licences were guaranteed large profits. While some of their business has now been deregulated, the massive cost of entering the market helps to limit competition.

Why is media concentration an issue? Those who control the media control the message, and if ownership is concentrated, there will be less likelihood of diverse messages. Conflict theorists such as Hall (1982) believe that the media support the values and interests of the dominant class. For example, while the Fox News Network describes itself as "fair and balanced," it actually has a very deliberate right-wing bias (Martin, 2008) and vigorously supports America's economic elites. While television networks such as Fox (and Sun News, its Canadian counterpart) do not hide their ideological bias, conflict theorists believe that other media that claim to be objective are also biased. For example, Parenti argues that

> [Media bias] moves in more or less consistent directions, favoring management over labor, corporations over corporate critics, affluent whites over low income minorities, officialdom over protestors . . . privatization and free market 'reforms' over public sector development, U.S. dominance of the Third World over revolutionary or populist social change, and conservative commentators and columnists over progressive or radical ones. (2001)

How is media reporting biased? The media report some stories, ignore others that might challenge the dominant view of the world, and discredit stories that do not support the message of the established elites. They may also use loaded words: "freedom fighter" is a positive label, while "terrorist" is a negative label used to describe the same behaviour. Referring to "Third World" countries implicitly adopts the perspective that these countries are inferior to industrialized Western countries. The media also often deal with issues and events at a superficial level, which has the effect of supporting the status quo. Election campaigns focus on things like the latest poll results or a candidate's bus breaking down rather than on fundamental issues like inequality or the environment. Crime stories provide us with all the gruesome details, and the discussion is often racialized so that particular racial groups are blamed, deflecting attention from the social causes of crime.

While media concentration has been an important concern, the new social media have begun to change the situation. The chapter introduction showed how social media were able to break the media monopoly of repressive governments, and anyone can set up a blog to get out information that might not be published or broadcast by media conglomerates. The music industry has much less control over its products since downloading became possible, and individual artists are now able to sell their work online without going through a record company.

## Interactionist Perspectives on the Media

Symbolic interactionists tell us that individuals continually negotiate their social realities. In his looking-glass-self theory, Charles Horton Cooley (1922/1902) proposed that a person's sense of self is derived from the perceptions of others. According to Cooley, we use our interactions with others as a mirror for our own thoughts and actions; our sense of self depends on how we interpret what they do and say. Consequently, our sense of self is always developing as we interact with others.

Cooley developed his theory more than a century ago, so it is interesting to see how it applies to our new social media. Do these social media affect our sense of self? Does interacting with others online have positive or negative effects on our self-concepts? Do our online representations affect our sense of self and our behaviour?

**SOCIAL MEDIA AND GENDER IDENTITY** Shapiro has studied the impact of the Internet on transgendered people. The Internet has made it easier for everyone to learn more about transgenderism, which makes it easier for the transgendered to work out new identities. It has also helped them to "shape their own gender identity and self-esteem and manage feelings of fear, isolation, and anger" (Shapiro, 2010:107).

Differently gendered people can feel isolated because they are afraid of public stigmatization (Schrock et al., 2004). However, the Internet can help them construct their identities by providing them with information through blogs and information sites. Perhaps more importantly, online discussion forums provide a way of discussing their lives with others who share the same experience. The importance of this contact is apparent in the expression of joy posted by a cross-dresser who had just discovered an online news group:

> just couldn't resist sharing my *elation* at having found you! I stumbled across the group by accident during lunch today and my heart skipped, then skipped again, and again. i've been a t-something as long as i can recall, but never had much hope of meeting anyone else. it's so *good* to see you all out there. (Schrock et al., 2004:66)

This contact can help people construct their gender identities. Hill asked members of Toronto's trans community (including cross-dressers, transsexuals, and transgendered persons) how they came to their sense of identity as trans persons. Many of his respondents reported that communications technologies had played an important role in this process. For example, Miqqi said:

> The biggest impact on the transgender world has been the Internet . . . I cannot overestimate its importance. It is . . . more than anything else how contact has been made for hundreds and hundreds of people who are isolated and otherwise out of contact. (Hill, 2005:39)

Another respondent, Melisa, who had been very isolated in a small northern community, described how she began to develop her trans identity based on her online contacts:

> I got on the Internet and the first thing I did, you know, was talk to anybody I could talk to about it . . . I wanted to talk to anybody or anything I could just to get some kind of rationale behind it, the vocabulary, do something with it . . . To build a story, to build a way to talk about it . . . It was something I could never do before. (Hill, 2005:41)

This research suggests that new social media can affect how people develop their identity, particularly for people who are isolated from other role models.

**VIRTUAL IDENTITIES AND REALITY** Many people blur the difference between reality and simulation by using the virtual world to experiment with their identity. Audrey, a subject interviewed by Sherry Turkle, told her that creating avatars and Facebook profiles is a "performance of you":

> Making an avatar and texting. Pretty much the same. You're creating your own person; you don't have to think of things on the spot really, which a lot of people can't really do. You're creating your own little ideal person and sending it out. Also on the Internet, with sites like MySpace and Facebook, you put up the things you like about yourself, and you're not going to advertise the bad aspects of you . . . You can write anything about yourself; these people don't know. You can create who you want to be . . . maybe in real life it won't work for you, you can't pull it off. But you can pull it off on the Internet. (2011:191)

Audrey uses her online virtual life to help construct her real identity. She uses Facebook and Second Life to try different styles—flirting one day and being witty on another—and notes how others respond. If the new style gets a poor response, she changes it, and if her online friends respond positively, she incorporates that into her real-life identity. One of Turkle's respondents came out as gay online to help him deal with this process in real life. Another, who needed a prosthetic leg following a car accident, practised sexual intimacy through her online avatar (which also had a prosthetic leg) before considering a sexual relationship in real life. The Internet's anonymity means that these identity experiments are much less risky than if they were done in real life. Just as a pilot can safely learn to fly and to handle aircraft emergencies in a flight simulator, some people can learn to handle real-life problems by practising online.

We know that people create idealized images of themselves when they create avatars on sites such as Second Life (LeBlanc, 2011). Yee and Bailenson (2007) have addressed the interesting question of whether the process works the other way as well—do our avatars also affect our real-life behaviour?

Yee and Bailenson assigned volunteers to either attractive or unattractive avatars and asked the volunteers to interact online with other avatars. They wanted to see whether their subjects conformed to the stereotypes of their avatars. They found that those with attractive avatars were more confident and friendlier toward others than were subjects with unattractive avatars. They chatted more often with the other avatars and positioned themselves much more closely to their companions than did the unattractive avatars. In a second experiment, taller avatars did better in a negotiation than shorter avatars. The finding that the nature of our avatars affects the way we behave may help to explain why virtual communities are friendlier and more intimate than real life because people tend to create attractive avatars.

This effect also spills over into our real lives. Yee, Bailenson, and Duchenault (2009) found that the effects of the height of avatars continued when the volunteers later engaged in face-to-face real-life negotiations. Yee and his colleagues conclude that, "Together these studies suggest that neither the virtual nor the physical self can ever be truly liberated from the other. What we learn in one body is shared with other bodies we inhabit, whether virtual or physical" (2009:309). As more people spend more time online with their digital avatars, it will be interesting to see what impact this will have on behaviour and on our interactions with others.

The new media raise some interesting questions concerning the meaning of the "self" in a digital world. Nancy Baym asks where our true selves reside: "[W]hat if the selves enacted through digital media don't line up with those we present face to face, or if they contradict one another? If someone is nurturing face to face, aggressive in one online forum, and needy in another online forum, which is real? Is there such a thing as a true self anymore? Was there ever?" (2010:3). Of course, sociologists such as Goffman (1959) long ago showed us that all of us present ourselves in different ways depending on the circumstances, so perhaps this is not just limited to our digital worlds.

## Feminist Perspectives on the Media

Gender scripts are our "blueprints for behavior, belief, and identity" (Shapiro, 2010:9). These scripts guide how we perform gender roles, and one of the ways we learn about these scripts is through the media. Many feminists are critical of the media's stereotyping of women, and research supports their view that television shows, newspaper stories, advertisements, movies, songs, and video games use sexist imagery to define women. If the media help us define our gender identities, the distorted mirror they hold up to women will have a negative impact.

Some of this bias can be attributed to the fact that the majority of people working in the media are male, and this male overrepresentation is particularly great at the senior management level (Straw, 2011). Advertising has been particularly criticized for being sexist, and most of the people employed in advertising agencies, particularly those who create the ads, are white males (Leiss et al., 2006).

**WOMEN IN THE NEWS** Since 1995, the Global Media Monitoring Project (2010) has reported on the representation of women in the media. Its first study, which looked at 71 countries (now expanded to 108 countries), found that women were greatly underrepresented in newspaper, television, and radio stories in every country. Between 1995 and 2010, the percentage of stories that mentioned women increased from 17 percent to 24 percent. However, this meant that women were still neglected in media reports. The study also found that media reports stereotyped women's social roles. Women were more likely to appear in stories dealing with science and health than in stories dealing with politics or the economy. Women were underrepresented in all occupational categories except homemakers and students, so their role in other occupations and professions was minimized. Stories about women were more likely to mention their age and their family status than were stories about men. Thus, the media play an important role in reinforcing unequal gender stereotypes around the globe (Global Media Monitoring Project, 2010).

**WOMEN IN ADVERTISING** Gender roles are an important part of media advertising. While most products are designed to have some practical use, marketers also try to give their products a symbolic value that will encourage consumers to buy (Hodkinson, 2011). Consumers are invited to associate themselves with the image presented in advertising.

The image that many advertisers wish to hold up to women was illustrated by American feminist leader Gloria Steinem. Steinem, the founding editor of *Ms.* magazine, described a conversation she had with Leonard Lauder, president of the Estée Lauder cosmetics company:

> *Ms.* isn't appropriate for his ads anyway, he explains. Why? Because Estée Lauder is selling a "kept-woman mentality."
>
> I can't quite believe this. Sixty percent of the users of his products are salaried, and generally resemble *Ms.* readers. Besides, his company has the appeal of having been started by a creative and hardworking woman, his mother, Estée Lauder.
>
> That doesn't matter, he says. He knows his customers, and they would *like* to be kept women. That's why he will never advertise in *Ms.* (2011:241)

The lack of advertising from Estée Lauder and other companies led to the eventual sale of the magazine.

One of the few companies that did use a feminist message was a tobacco company. During the 1960s and 1970s, advertising for Virginia Slims cigarettes used the slogan "You've Come a Long Way, Baby" to co-opt the progressive image of the feminist movement as a way of attracting women to their product.

Despite decades of criticism, advertisers continue to show women in the role of caregivers or sex objects (Leiss et al., 2006). Current ads for GoDaddy.com—a company that registers Internet domain names—portray several female athletes, including Danica Patrick, in a sexualized manner. When not doing these commercials, Patrick has been breaking down stereotypes in the very dangerous, male-dominated sport of high-performance auto racing, but in the ads she is depicted only as an attractive, scantily clad woman. Other advertisements have depicted women as needing a man's help—sink stains required the help of the Ajax White Knight, and dirty floors and doors led to a call for Mr. Clean to rescue the woman of the house (O'Reilly, 2011). While women prefer advertising that shows them in more egalitarian roles (Leiss et al., 2006), advertisers still persist in showing women in these traditional ways.

Erving Goffman (1979) went beyond the content of the ads to look at other ways in which advertisers engage in gender stereotyping. He looked at the details of print advertisements and found several ways in which women and men were portrayed differently. Women were more often sitting down or even lying on the floor or a bed, while men were more often standing. Men were authorities, while women were more often in subordinate positions—men were shown instructing women or as doctors who had authority over female nurses. The exception to this was ads showing a kitchen, where women were in charge and were typically shown cooking for or serving men. If men were shown doing household chores, they were typically doing an incompetent job, often under the scrutiny of a woman.

The media perpetuate traditional gender roles, despite the dramatic changes in the role of women over the past 40 years. Why should we be concerned about this depiction of women? Media stereotypes may make it harder for women to move into nontraditional roles and to break through the glass ceiling that still exists in many occupations. The way the media portray ideals of personal appearance also influences how people think about themselves and the improvements that they believe their bodies require. Researchers have found, for example, that the media ideal of thin female bodies can lead to body dissatisfaction and depression among those who are most exposed to these idealized images (Mastro and Stern, 2006). If this view is correct, media framing plays an important role in the growing phenomenon of young women opting for cosmetic surgery.

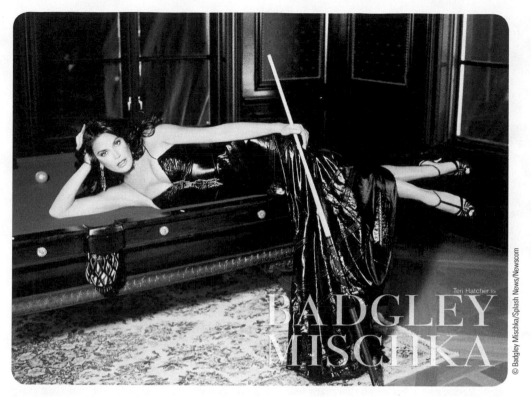

This shoe advertisement, featuring actor Teri Hatcher, shows how advertisers use gender stereotypes to market their products.

## Postmodern Perspectives on the Media

The new social media are postmodern developments, so it should not be surprising that we can use the tools of postmodern theory to analyze some of the latest media trends. We can consider several examples of the way postmodern scholars have analyzed new media.

**CREATING AVATARS IN SECOND LIFE** Cathie LeBlanc (2011) used a postmodern framework to help us understand how participants design their avatars in Second Life. Postmodern theorist Michel Foucault showed that we live in a society where technologies make widespread surveillance possible in many different social settings. Because people feel they are always being watched, they govern their own behaviour through self-surveillance. While some have predicted that virtual environments such as Second Life will enable people to freely choose the bodies of their avatars without concern for physical limitations or cultural constraints, LeBlanc believes that self-surveillance will enforce social constraints on the appearance of avatars.

When people first move into the Second Life environment, they can select a default body, but the default body of a newcomer reduces their status in the virtual world, so most quickly customize their avatar as it becomes clear that the avatar's external appearance matters. The expectation is that Second Life residents will design an avatar to match their idealized view of who they really are and that this avatar will also meet conventional standards of attractiveness.

Avatars are designed by Second Life residents who are sitting outside the online environment looking at their on-screen representations. Like a cosmetic surgeon, residents can change those aspects of their avatar that do not match their view of who they are or would like to be. As residents of Second Life move through their online world, they see both the landscape and the back of their avatar. This creates a feeling that the body is "both a subject and an object" (LeBlanc, 2011:116). This sense of detachment reinforces a self-surveillance that enforces the norms of the virtual community.

*second life fat squad        second life, march '08*

Used with permission of Marissa Ashkenaz

These rather normal-looking avatars are the "plus-sized" bodies that generated hostile comments on Second Life. Why do you think people responded so negatively to the appearance of these avatars?

What are these norms? Despite the hope that virtual space would enable people to free themselves from real-life bodily constraints, what actually happens is that external appearance becomes as important online as it is in the real world. Just as people use cosmetic surgery, makeup, tattoos, piercings, and clothing to try to communicate who they are in real life, online residents are bound by cultural constraints. In effect, self-surveillance is even more explicit online than it is in the real world. This explains one researcher's finding that in Second Life, "Almost everyone was thin, beautiful, well dressed, and had chosen features typical of North American societies' Anglo-European ideals including skin tone, facial and body structure" (Shapiro, 2010:89).

Thus, people who could be whatever they wanted chose to follow the familiar cultural norms they had learned in the real-life world. It seems likely that this was largely the result of self-surveillance, but there was also pressure from others online to use attractive avatars. For example, one researcher found that many fellow Second Lifers were hostile toward the plus-sized avatars that she and several friends used (Ashkenaz, 2008). Typical of the comments were the following:

Kess also experienced some biting comments from her friends about her new weight gain:

Grow: Hi fatass :P

*Then later on:*

Grow: Kess you put on weight over xmas, hun.

Jad: Eat too much for xmas, kess?

### FANTASY FOOTBALL

For the fantasy football fanatic, the seventh day is hardly an occasion for rest. From the moment he wakes, the clock begins ticking toward kickoff. There are statistical match-ups to analyze; weather and injury reports to consult; imaginary rosters to juggle. He is still a fan, but a very different kind of fan, and while he may not be alone in managing and cheering on his particular fantasy squad, he is not at all alone in his quest for fantasy success. (Serazio, 2008:229)

Fantasy sports have become a significant part of North American culture. Fantasy sports leagues enable people to draft real players onto their fantasy teams. The fantasy "owners" decide who is going to play and can trade players to other teams. The results are based on the performance of each of their chosen players in actual games.

Websites, magazines, talk shows, apps, and statistical services are dedicated to fantasy sports (Harper and Ploeg, 2011). The Internet has had a huge impact on fantasy sports because it enables the real-time tracking of statistics so that participants do not have to spend time making these calculations.

The blending of real performance with the fantasy ownership of a team has changed the way people watch and relate to the game (Serazio, 2008). While sports fans normally cheer for a favourite team and often identify strongly with that team, fantasy team owners are concerned

NEL

about the performance of the individual players who make up their virtual teams. And of course these teams are not really "teams" in the sense of being a group of people who work together to attain the common goal of winning but exist only in the simulated realm of fantasy. To the participants, however, the results of their fantasy teams do feel very real and can have real consequences if there are financial prizes for the best teams.

Jean Baudrillard (1995) developed the notion of **hyperreality**—a situation in which the distinction between reality and simulation has become blurred. We are saturated in media that have become a central part of our lives and that help to define our experiences and our understanding of the world. Manufactured images and representations are part of our reality and in turn affect the way we interpret subsequent images.

Harper and Ploeg argue that fantasy sports illustrate the world of hyperreality: "Reality is no longer diametrically opposed to fantasy; it is indistinguishable from it. Ironically, in *fantasy sports*, fans abandon the dichotomized framework of fantasy/reality and, instead, embrace the paradigm of the hyperreal" (2011:156).

> **hyperreality** A situation in which the distinction between reality and simulation has become blurred.

**FARMVILLE** The Internet game FarmVille provides another example of hyperreality in which players can sometimes lose track of the difference between their real and virtual lives. Emily Hall (2011) describes how the designers have built into the game many ways of rewarding players through awards and prizes. This recognition can lead some players to feel that they get more appreciation from their simulated work in FarmVille than from their real jobs. Life online can be simpler than real life, and players can become very absorbed in the game as they build up their farms, add decorations that show their prosperity, and receive gifts from their online neighbours.

The creators of FarmVille have developed ways of keeping players involved and expanding the numbers playing the game. Crops grow in real time, so individual participants must keep checking online in order to harvest them at the proper time. Players have incentives for bringing new people into the game, and players are encouraged to create communities where people are farming with their real-life friends as their online neighbours. Players can also join co-ops whose members are rewarded for accomplishing collective goals. This places pressure on each member to stay involved with the game because all co-op members will suffer if one fails to do his or her part.

These techniques have helped FarmVille become the most popular online game. According to Patrick Liskiewicz, a game that he feels is actually boring and difficult to play has become a huge success because game developers have built in social pressures to play:

> My mother began playing *Farmville* last fall, because her friend asked her to join and become her in-game neighbor. In *Farmville*, neighbors send you gifts, help you tend your farm, post bonuses to their Facebook pages, and allow you to earn larger plots of land. Without at least eight in-game neighbors, in fact, it is almost impossible to advance in *Farmville* without spending real money. This frustrating reality led my mother—who was now obligated to play because of her friend—to convince my father, two of her sisters, my fiancée and (much to my dismay) myself to join *Farmville*. Soon, we were all scheduling our days around harvesting, sending each other gifts of trees and elephants, and posting ribbons on our Facebook walls. And we were convincing our own friends to join *Farmville*, too. Good times.
>
> The secret to *Farmville*'s popularity is neither gameplay nor aesthetics. *Farmville* is popular because it entangles users in a web of social obligations. When users log into Facebook, they are reminded that their neighbors have sent them gifts, posted bonuses on their walls, and helped with each others' farms. In turn, they are obligated to return the courtesies . . . We play *Farmville*, then, because we are trying to be good to one another. We play *Farmville* because we are polite, cultivated people. (2010)

Zynga, the corporation that owns FarmVille, makes hundreds of millions of dollars each year, most of which comes from participants who use real money to buy land, animals, and other in-game products, so these strategies are used to increase their profits. Here again, the difference between the real and the simulated is blurred as real-life social relations are manipulated by the creators of a simulated world in order to make real-life profits (Hall, 2011).

Finally, consider a recent tragic consequence of the hyperreality created by FarmVille. A man in England robbed a blind man to obtain money so he could buy animals for his virtual farm and then killed a family friend so he could pay back the money before his victim reported him to the police (Osuh, 2011).

## TIME TO REVIEW

- Describe the role played by social media in the 2011/12 revolutions in the Middle East and North Africa.
- What are the functions and dysfunctions of the media?
- Discuss how conflict theorists feel the media support capitalist societies. What role does media concentration play in this support?
- How do interactionists help us to understand the way the new media helps people develop their identities?
- Discuss how stereotyped gender roles are used in advertising to promote products.
- How do online games fit Baudrillard's notion of hyperreality?

## CONCEPT SNAPSHOT

| | |
|---|---|
| **FUNCTIONALIST PERSPECTIVES**<br>**Key thinker:** Charles Wright | Functionalists have shown that the media help us to learn what is happening in the world; suggest how we should interpret and respond to these events; teach us about our society's rules, customs, and ways of behaving; and keep us entertained. The media also provide us with community forums, link people together, and confer status on certain individuals. The media also have dysfunctions, including misinforming us and "narcotizing" us to the extent that we do not respond to social issues. |
| **CONFLICT PERSPECTIVES**<br>**Key thinkers:** Max Horkheimer, Theodor Adorno | Conflict theorists argue that the media help the dominant class control society by reinforcing capitalist ideology and by encouraging a mass consumer culture that allows those who own the means of production to sell us unnecessary products and services. Conflict theorists are highly critical of the fact that the conventional media are dominated by a few very large corporations that control the message that goes out to media consumers. |
| **INTERACTIONIST PERSPECTIVES**<br>**Key thinkers:** Sherry Turkle, Jeremy Bailenson | Interactionists tell us that individuals continually negotiate their social realities. The media, particularly the new social media, play an important role in creating our sense of self. Many people are now experimenting with identities online through the persona they put on their Facebook pages and through avatars in online games and virtual reality communities. |
| **FEMINIST PERSPECTIVES**<br>**Key thinkers:** Gloria Steinem, Erving Goffman | Feminist sociologists have been critical of the stereotyped manner in which women are portrayed in the media. Most stories in the media focus on males and women are depicted in typical gender-linked roles. This is especially true in advertisements, where women tend to be depicted as traditional homemakers and caregivers or as sex objects. These media stereotypes may make it more difficult for women to move into non-traditional social roles. |
| **POSTMODERN PERSPECTIVES**<br>**Key thinkers:** Michel Foucault, Cathie LeBlanc, Jean Baudrillard | Postmodern theorists have approached the media in several different ways. One of the most interesting of these is Baudrillard, whose theory of hyperreality points out how the distinction between reality and simulation has become blurred. Manufactured images and representations are part of our reality and in turn affect the way we interpret subsequent images. |

## THE IMPACT OF SOCIAL MEDIA    LO-3

In this section, we will look at some of the ways in which new media technologies are reshaping the ways we interact with each other. Texting is replacing face-to-face contact, and we are increasingly likely to meet our romantic partners online rather than through family or school. It is important to think about the impact of these changes on our culture and our social relationships.

### Alone Together: Do Social Media Bring Us Together or Keep Us Apart?

Sherry Turkle was one of the first to study computer culture. When she began her work in the 1980s, phones were mounted on kitchen walls, people were playing simple video games that plugged into their television sets, and a few hobbyists were building and programming their own home computers. Turkle was interested in learning how these tools were shaping individuals and their cultures.

The relationship between people and their communication devices changed dramatically in the 1990s and continues to rapidly evolve. Many of us are connected all the time and communicating electronically is becoming the way we live rather than just something we do. The Internet has dramatically increased the scope of possible relationships, as it is now just as easy to communicate with people halfway around the world as with the people next door. Your parents' old wall-mounted telephones were just a means of communication, but our portable devices have become a "portal that enable[s] people to live parallel lives in online worlds" (Turkle, 2011:xi).

What impact has this had on our lives? Do social media hold us together or keep us apart? Two facets of social media are having a dramatic impact on our social relationships: Mobile devices mean that we can always be contacted, and we can develop online identities in addition to living our "real" lives.

**WE ARE ALWAYS AVAILABLE** Mobile connections such as smartphones mean that people are no longer tethered to their computers but can carry their online lives with them everywhere. This means that we can always be available to others and have difficulty escaping this contact even if we wish to do so.

Some people have become dependent on this constant connection. In 2011, when a problem affected many subscribers' use of their BlackBerry smartphones for several days, many called it a "disaster" and filed lawsuits against the manufacturer. Some of Turkle's respondents describe the loss of a cellphone as feeling "like a death" (2011:16).

Communications professor Danna Walker required her students to avoid all electronic media for 24 hours. Many of the students found this painful. One wrote, "I was in shock . . . I honestly did not think I could accomplish this task. The 24 hours I spent in what seemed like complete isolation became known as one of the toughest days I have had to endure" (2007). Walker commented that another "apparently did not see the irony in this statement: 'I felt like I would be wasting my time doing the project. I did not want to give up my daily schedule, which mainly includes lying on my couch, watching television and playing The Sims 2 . . . computer game" (2007). Another said, "There was a moment in my day when I felt homeless . . . I couldn't go home because I knew that would be too tempting . . . I was walking down the street literally with nowhere to go, and I just didn't know what I was going to do" (2007).

The fact that we can be constantly available to friends and family might help us to strengthen our relationships with these significant others. However, Turkle concluded that the new media may actually be keeping us apart: "We are increasingly connected to each other but oddly more alone: in intimacy, new solitudes" (2011:19).

Think of how some people pay more attention to their mobile phones than to the people they are with. Face-to-face conversations are routinely interrupted by the beep or buzz of the mobile device

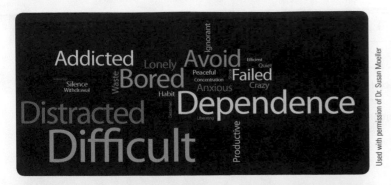

The first of these word clouds shows the feelings of students who had spent 24 hours without media. The second shows their responses to a question about the advantages of unplugging. What lesson can you draw from these two word clouds?

as a text message is given priority over face-to-face communication because our new cultural norms demand an instant response. The average teenager sends more than 3300 text messages each month, and teenage girls send an average of 4050 (Nielsen, 2010). While each text message may not take long, sending more than a hundred texts a day takes an enormous amount of time. The time spent using social media—whether responding to hundreds of texts each day, spending hours in virtual reality, or playing an online game—is time that is not spent interacting with other people. Face-to-face relationships are being replaced by networked relationships. This point was highlighted by another of Danna Walker's students who had to give up electronic media for a day: "My mother is thrilled that I'm doing this . . . to her it means I get to spend the day with her. I bite, and we walk into town for some brunch. I draw out the brunch as long as possible" (2007).

The ability to chat online certainly broadens our range of contacts. People can keep in touch with hundreds of Facebook friends. However, we can ask whether having many brief contacts with a broad range of "friends" is as meaningful as more intimate personal relationships with fewer people.

Technology can be used to keep people at a distance: "Texting puts people not too close, not too far, but at just the right distance" (Turkle, 2011:15).

Turkle also discusses an extreme form of distancing one's self from others when she describes an interview with a reporter from *Scientific American* who accused her of intolerance because she did not think it was appropriate that people might someday have sexual relationships with robots and even marry them. Turkle subsequently interviewed several people who would have welcomed such relationships because they came without the risks inherent in relationships with other humans. Real-life marital partners can cheat, become alcoholics, and be judgmental about their partner's behaviour. Robotic spouses would be completely predictable and could be programmed to do whatever their partners/owners wished. Many young people have been raised with robotic pets, and some seniors now have robot companions to keep them from getting lonely.

**WE CAN LIVE ALTERNATIVE LIVES** Social media can provide us with online lives that may be more satisfying to some people than their real lives. Consider the promises made by Second Life (secondlife.com): "Who will you meet in Second Life? Where will you explore? What will you discover? Who will you be? Anything is possible in Second Life. A whole new world is waiting."

To someone who is lonely and unhappy, the promise of virtual reality can be compelling. A new identity, a glamorous appearance, and the chance to live an adventurous lifestyle lie ahead.

Your Second Life avatar can help you live your dreams, and you are in control in a way that would never be possible in the real world.

Consider Pete, one of Turkle's interview subjects. Pete was a 46-year-old man who was devoted to Second Life. His online avatar is a handsome young man who had married a young and beautiful avatar, Jade, at a wedding attended by their virtual best friends. While Pete has never met the anonymous woman (or man) who is behind Jade, he shares with Jade a relationship that is both socially and physically intimate. Pete prefers his Second Life to his "real life": "Second Life gives me a better relationship than I have in real life. This is where I feel most myself. Jade accepts who I am. My relationship with Jade makes it possible for me to stay in my marriage, with my family" (2011:159). To Turkle, "The ironies are apparent: an avatar who has never seen or spoken to him in person and to whom he appears in a body nothing like his own seems, to him, most accepting of his truest self" (2011:159).

While Pete used his online life to help cope with an unhappy family situation, others who are dissatisfied with their real lives may completely withdraw into their online worlds. Adam was another of Turkle's respondents. He got little satisfaction from his life and turned to online games such as Quake and Civilization:

> These games take so long, you can literally play it for days. One time when I played it, I had just got the game and I got so addicted, I stayed home the next day and I played . . . I think it was like noon the next day, or like nine o'clock the next day, I played all night long. And I ended up winning. You get so advanced. You get super-advanced technology. (2011:222)

Adam felt good only when he was playing games, and he was emotionally attached to the bots he played with. He was letting the rest of his life slip away, and his difficulties dealing with reality turned him even more toward the virtual world.

## How Social Media Affect Our Lives

Even those who are not hooked on virtual worlds or online games can be affected by the demands and distractions of the new media. Many of our activities require concentration, but it can be difficult to focus on a task when texts and emails keep arriving and any fleeting thought can lead us to waste minutes or hours tracking something down on the Internet. Many of our students have told us how difficult it can be to study when their friends expect an immediate response to text messages. The Internet has been an invaluable resource that has helped us write this text—we no longer need to walk to the library to find the most recent crime rates or to read an article in an academic journal—but it is also a source of distraction that makes it more difficult to meet deadlines. Sometimes watching cat videos or checking the latest hockey scores is more interesting than writing about how to conduct survey research or why social class affects educational success.

There are other, more serious consequences of distractions. An iPhone app named Type n Walk uses the iPhone camera to show the ground ahead of you so you do not walk into a tree or a lamppost while you are texting on your phone. Hundreds of people are killed each year in North America because drivers continue to text and talk on cellphones while they are driving despite a vast amount of evidence showing that this practice is at least as dangerous as drunk driving. For some people, the need to be in constant contact with others outweighs the need to walk or drive safely.

Some researchers have studied problematic Internet use (Tokunaga and Rains, 2010), which consists of behaviours such as not being able to control the amount of time spent using the Internet, a preference for online interaction over in-person interaction, and withdrawal when the Internet is not available. Some consider the Internet addictive—South Korea has set up Internet addiction recovery programs for young people, and 12-step recovery programs for Internet addiction are even available online (Blascovich and Bailenson, 2011).

Elias Aboujaoude (2010) suggests that virtual technology may have a much more profound impact than earlier forms of mass media—in the 18th century, the new popularity of novels led to fears of "reading mania" (Korkeila, 2010)—because the new media have immersive and interactive qualities that the earlier media did not have. Blascovich and Bailenson (2011) speculate that 3-D immersive virtual reality experiences are potentially much more addictive than current online games and activities because the experiences are closer to those of real life. Online avatars will look like humans and will be controlled as easily as we control our own bodies, so the line between real and simulation will continue to fade.

While there may be negative effects, the popularity of social media show that most people who use it consider it a valuable part of their lives. Families share news and photos on social media, and friends can stay in touch with each other, even if they live in different cities. The earlier discussion of the impact of the Internet on the transgendered and transsexual community shows how important it can be for people to be able to meet like-minded others online. The ability to have friends and role models from anywhere in the world can be liberating to people whose physical condition, sexual preferences, or other characteristics make them different. The GimpGirl Community, established online by women with disabilities, is another example of how the Internet enables people to set up networks of friendship and support from hundreds of communities to interact with one another.

**WILL YOU MEET YOUR PARTNER ON THE INTERNET? THE RISE OF ONLINE DATING** The Internet has dramatically changed the way many people meet their partners. In the 1940s and 1950s, most heterosexual couples met through family, friends, and school (Rosenfeld and Thomas, 2012). The family and school have steadily declined as sources of connection since then, but friends are still very important in making introductions, and the proportion of people who meet their future partners in bars and restaurants has doubled since the 1940s. The most significant change has been that in just over a decade, the percentage of people who met their partners on the Internet jumped from zero to 22 percent and it is now the third most common way of meeting (see Figure 17.1). These people meet through dating sites, online personal ads, online gaming sites, and sites focused on interests such as religion or hobbies.

Same-sex couples were much more likely to meet over the Internet: 61 percent of same-sex couples met online (see Figure 17.2 on page 498). Rosenfeld and Thomas believe this is because the Internet may be particularly useful to people facing thin dating markets—those who are seeking partners who are harder to find and where relationships may meet with social disapproval from some people. Parents will not be helpful in introducing a gay or lesbian child to a future partner if they disapprove of same-sex marriage or if their child has not come out to them. However, the Internet allows for a very efficient search process far beyond local neighbourhoods and friendship groups. Older heterosexuals also have a limited range of potential partners because most people in their age group already have partners and also have much higher than average rates of finding partners online. Rosenfeld and Thomas found that couples who met online were just as satisfied with their relationships as people who met in other ways and were no more likely to break up their relationships.

**WILL ONLINE DATING BROADEN OUR SOCIAL TIES?** How will digital media transform our social relationships? A Super Bowl ad for telecommunications company MCI told us, "There is no race, there are no genders, there is no age, there are no infirmities, there are only minds. Utopia? No, the Internet" (Baym, 2010:34). However, others feel social media will just reinforce our existing social networks. Those who favour this view cite research on the impact of the telephone, which increased people's ability to communicate but did not change people's social networks because they used the phone to communicate with their existing network of friends and relatives. Rosenfeld and Thomas examined the impact of the Internet on dating and marriage.

| FIGURE 17.1 | THE CHANGING WAYS AMERICANS MEET THEIR PARTNERS: HETEROSEXUAL COUPLES |

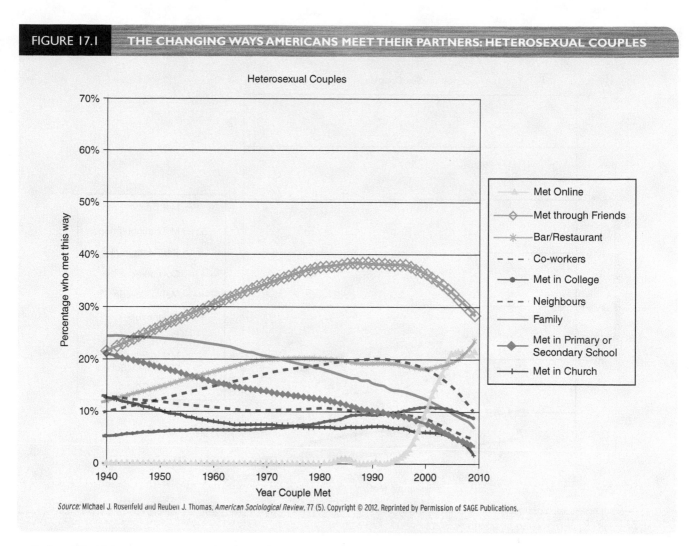

Source: Michael J. Rosenfeld and Reuben J. Thomas, *American Sociological Review*, 77 (5). Copyright © 2012. Reprinted by Permission of SAGE Publications.

Before World War II, most people chose their mates from their local neighbourhoods, schools, and churches. Because these institutions were homogeneous, people married partners with very similar class and race backgrounds. Does the broader reach of the Internet mean that people will meet potential partners who come from more diverse economic, racial, and religious backgrounds?

The Internet has had a limited effect on broadening social contacts. While couples from different religions were more likely than those from the same religion to have met online, the opposite was true for couples from different racial backgrounds, although the latter difference was not strong. There were only very small class differences between those who met online and those who met in other ways (Rosenfeld and Thomas, 2012).

**DO PEOPLE TELL THE TRUTH ABOUT THEMSELVES ONLINE?** While people are able to hide their identities in much of the online universe, this does not work in online dating, where the ultimate goal is a real-life romantic relationship. Those seeking a romantic attachment online face a dilemma. To attract potential partners, a person wants to create a positive impression. For online dating, physical attractiveness is particularly important in self-presentation, so people may use their most flattering photographs, photographs taken several years ago, or photographs that have been digitally altered (Toma and Hancock, 2010). However, the person must take care in constructing an online image. If reality is distorted too much, the potential partner may be very disappointed at the first face-to-face meeting—it is immediately obvious if

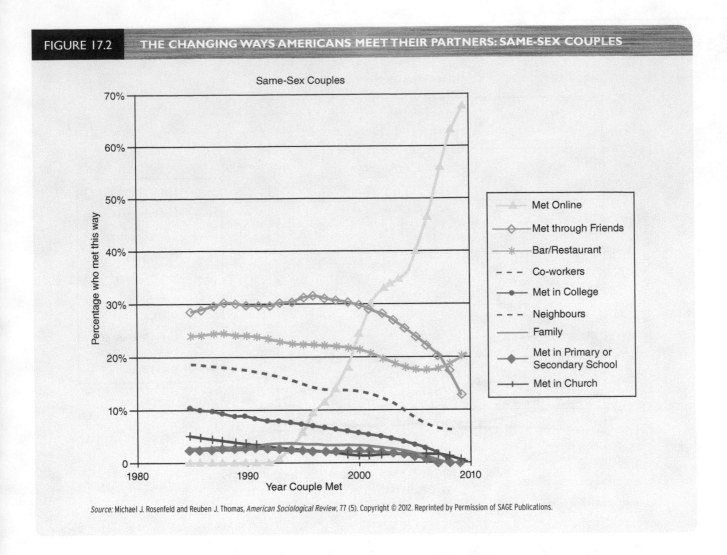

**FIGURE 17.2**     **THE CHANGING WAYS AMERICANS MEET THEIR PARTNERS: SAME-SEX COUPLES**

Same-Sex Couples

Legend:
- Met Online
- Met through Friends
- Bar/Restaurant
- Co-workers
- Met in College
- Neighbours
- Family
- Met in Primary or Secondary School
- Met in Church

*Source:* Michael J. Rosenfeld and Reuben J. Thomas, *American Sociological Review*, 77 (5). Copyright © 2012. Reprinted by Permission of SAGE Publications.

a man is 20 cm shorter or 40 kg heavier than his dating profile had claimed, or if he really does not own a Ferrari and live in a mansion.

Toma and Hancock (2010) assessed the accuracy of daters' online reports of physical attractiveness. Those who were the least attractive were the most likely to enhance their online photographs and to lie about height, weight, and age. They were slightly more likely than more attractive online daters to lie about factors such as income and occupation. On the other hand, attractive daters posted more photographs of themselves, presumably to showcase their desirability.

Given the possibility of distortion, how do those seeking a partner reduce the chance of being disappointed when they actually meet their online contact? In relationships that begin through social contacts, some information about a potential partner can often be obtained from family, friends, and co-workers. Also, when we meet people in person, we know how they look, and we can use nonverbal cues to give us some clues about their personality.

These information sources are not available in online dating, but there are other ways of checking out another person (Gibbs, Ellison, and Lai, 2011). Networking sites such as Facebook and LinkedIn, public records (such as property tax assessments), and Google searches provide information about potential partners. Some online daters also ask direct questions and disclose more of their own personal information in online conversations in the hope of getting their potential partner to disclose more of their information.

Toma and Hancock used computerized linguistic analysis to find clues to the truthfulness of potential partners. These clues can be found in the language people used to describe themselves. The less truthful used fewer first-person pronouns (words such as *I*), used more negatives, and had shorter self-descriptions than those who were being honest (Rosenbloom, 2011).

## PROFITING FROM SOCIAL MEDIA    LO-4

The early Internet was not about money because it was originally designed to allow scientists to communicate with one another. Businesses soon began to seek ways of profiting from Web activities, however, and the ideologies of "free" versus "profit" have battled throughout the history of the Internet. For example, early in the development of the Web, Microsoft forced computer manufacturers to include Internet Explorer in their computers. Eventually, Explorer captured 97 percent of the browser market and put most of its competitors out of business. This monopoly was broken by the courts, and other browsers, such as Firefox and Chrome, have become popular.

Another economic battle was fought after the invention of Napster, which was the first widely available means of downloading music. This had a huge impact on the music industry as millions of people began to share music online rather than purchasing it from music stores. This permanently changed the music business, although legal music sources such as iTunes have helped the music companies and the artists regain some of their profits.

The new social media are also trying to become profitable. Most users do not understand the role of Facebook (Rushkoff, 2010). They think they are *clients* of Facebook, but they are actually its *products*—because Facebook makes money by selling access to personal information. Because of the information people provide to the site, Facebook can charge a premium for ads that are tailored to the interests of a particular audience. At the end of 2011, the estimated value of Facebook was $100 billion; Zynga, the producer of FarmVille, was valued at almost $10 billion. However, both declined in value in 2012 as questions arose about their ability to make profits (see Box 17.3).

There are many ways of profiting from the new media . Many corporations, including Nike, Nissan, and Sears, have become part of Second Life with stores, showrooms, and virtual products. They hope to use the site to get potential customers interested in their real-life products. Movies have had virtual premieres complete with red carpets and glamorous virtual stars. Religious institutions are also becoming part of Second Life, so we now see virtual missionaries who try to spread the faith online. According to one religious spokesperson, "This virtual Second Life is becoming populated with churches, mosques, temples, cathedrals, synagogues, places of prayer of all kinds. And behind an avatar, there is a man or woman, perhaps searching for God and faith, perhaps with very strong spiritual needs" (quoted in Rhoten and Lutters, 2009).

IBM has more than 50 "islands" in Second Life where it conducts meetings and other events (Rhoten and Lutters, 2009). This saves the company travel costs and is considered more personal than conference calls or video conferencing. The boundaries between real and virtual worlds were narrowed in 2007 when nearly 2000 avatars invaded one of IBM's islands to protest against the company's threats to cut employees' pay in Italy. The protest was successful in the real world, and is now commemorated in a museum on Union Island in Second Life (Rhoten and Lutters, 2009). Many other political and social issues have also been addressed in Second Life, including Palestinian statehood and the animal rights movement.

We are barely touching the surface of the commercial exploitation of the new media. Advertisers have developed a strategy of *self-endorsing*, which means that an avatar or other representation of the consumer is used in an advertisement. Ahn and Bailenson (2011) found that this was a highly effective technique. If the avatar is shown using the product, favourable brand attitude and purchase intentions increased. For example, if the avatar was shown wearing a particular brand of clothing, the research subjects were more likely to prefer that brand to others representing similar products. The closer avatars were in appearance to the consumer, the more positive the brand attitude.

## BOX 17.3    POINT/COUNTERPOINT

### New Media and Privacy

You have just tweeted a friend that you're going for coffee. As you pass a coffee shop, a coupon arrives on your phone offering 50 cents off a large cup of coffee. A friend who is travelling to Paris uses an online site to book a hotel room. Because she is using a Mac computer, the hotels that come up on the booking list are more expensive than if she had used a PC. A new college graduate has submitted a resumé for a job. The potential employer looks at the applicant's Facebook site, finds photos of the applicant using soft drugs at parties, and decides not to hire the person. In each of these cases, information that a person might expect to be private has been used by a third party. In the first two cases, the information was sold to an advertiser.

Online sites such as Facebook, Google, and Twitter provide a useful service for hundreds of millions of users. However, from the perspective of those who own these sites, the service is actually provided to advertisers rather than to users. The commodity they provide to these advertisers is personal information about users that allows advertisers to carefully target their ad campaigns. Advertisers are interested in knowing your location, relationship status, travel plans, musical tastes, occupation, and other interests.

Search engines such as Google make billions of dollars from tracking the key words you use. If you search for terms such as *headache* or *upset stomach*, you may receive ads or coupons for remedies for these maladies. Google also tracks your information across its different products, such as Gmail and YouTube, to develop more complete profiles of users in order to personalize the service.

Facebook and other networking sites frequently change their privacy policies with little notice. In 2009, Facebook suddenly made lists of friends publicly available. This change had serious consequences for many people. For example, the Iranian government detained people who were Facebook friends with people who were critics of the government (Andrews, 2012). The people who bought shares of Facebook when they were first offered to the public in 2012 valued each of its one billion users at $100. At that time, the company was earning only an average of $1 per user, so its shareholders will be putting pressure on Facebook executives to find new ways of selling people's information that will put increasing pressure on privacy. Meanwhile, Google has

paid large fines after admitting to using its Street View camera cars to collect people's wireless data and to violating rules by bypassing privacy settings on the Safari browsers used on iPhones and computers.

While people may feel that receiving targeted advertising is an acceptable price to pay for using the services of a search engine or networking site, many of us are not aware of the other organizations that use these data. Insurance companies may search for evidence of risky activities or chronic illnesses that individuals may not report on their application forms. Law enforcement agencies and tax officials use social media sites to find information about potential wrongdoing and do not need search warrants that would be required if they were accessing the information in another fashion. Law enforcement agencies can also track people by using their cellphone records and obtain a great deal of personal information through this tracking:

> The United States Court of Appeals for the District of Columbia Circuit, ruling about the use of tracking devices by the police, noted that GPS data can reveal whether a person "is a weekly church goer, a heavy drinker, a regular at the gym, an unfaithful husband, an outpatient receiving medical treatment, an associate of particular individuals or political groups—and not just one such fact about a person, but all such facts." (Maass and Rajagopalan, 2012)

Information may last forever on the Internet. Do most people know that personal information they and their friends post online can come back to haunt them in the future when they apply for a job, run for political office, or try to convince their teenage children that they behaved perfectly when they were attending university or college? What about sites such as Banjo that allow people to track you and receive a message if you are near their location? Does it concern you that if you search for information on HIV/AIDS for a term paper, a data aggregator may infer that you have AIDS? Should people have the right to know what data are being collected about them and to prohibit companies from tracking their information without their consent? Would you prefer to pay a fee for Facebook rather than letting them sell your personal information to advertisers? These and other issues need to be worked out as new media technologies become more pervasive in our lives.

*Sources:* Andrews, 2012; Maass and Rajagopalan, 2012.

## GLOBALIZATION AND THE MEDIA  LO-5

## Media Technology and Globalization

With its dots and dashes transmitted through a wire, the telegraph seems a very primitive means of communication compared with today's media technologies. After its introduction in the 1840s, however, people predicted it would have a revolutionary impact because, for the first time, people could instantly communicate over a distance:

> Universal peace and harmony seem at this time more possible than ever before, as the telegraph binds together by a vital cord all the nations of the earth. It is impossible that old prejudices and hostilities should any longer exist, while such an instrument has been created for an exchange of thought between all nations of the earth. (Czitrom, 1982:10)

Canadian media scholar Marshall McLuhan was one of the first to recognize the potential impact of modern media technologies. McLuhan believed these technologies would create a **global village** in which people around the world share information through interactive media: "'Time' has ceased, 'space' has vanished. We now live in a global village . . . a simultaneous happening" (McLuhan, Fiore, and Fairey, 1967:63). McLuhan optimistically believed that the global village would empower people and foster the growth of democracy and equality.

Today's media make it possible to form communities of shared interest even though people have no direct contact with each other. For McLuhan, it was important that this communication was not one way and linear but decentralized and multidirectional:

> In the electric age, when our central nervous system is technologically extended to involve us in the whole of mankind and to incorporate the whole of mankind in us, we necessarily participate, in depth, in the consequences of our every action. It is no longer possible to adopt the aloof and disassociated role of the literate Westerner . . . As electronically contracted, the globe is no more than a village. (McLuhan, 1964:4–5)

McLuhan believed that media technology would change society and shape our social lives. While McLuhan's work predated the Internet by three decades, the impact of today's media has at least partly supported his views. Examples such as the global response to natural disasters such as the 2010 Haitian earthquake and the 2011 Japanese earthquake and tsunami are fostered by the fact that people around the globe could follow the disaster in real time through the mass media. Other examples of positive change are technologies that enable people in isolated rural areas anywhere on the globe to educate themselves, care for their health, and conduct business—a farmer with an Internet connection can easily find the most lucrative place to market her products rather than accepting the price offered by local buyers.

Not everyone is as positive about the impact of the media on globalization as McLuhan. Schiller (1992) argued that media technologies would lead to **cultural imperialism**—a process whereby powerful countries use the media to spread values and ideas that dominate and even destroy other cultures, and local cultural values are replaced by the cultural values of the dominant country. The dominant media culture is that of the United States, and the media enable large transnational corporations to profit from their global domination at the expense of cultural diversity. The globalization of culture means that local cultural values are replaced by Western values such as consumerism.

Cultural imperialism has occurred—many people around the world are familiar with Lady Gaga, the Disney characters, and many other products of American culture. However, the flows are becoming multidirectional as there is now a reverse flow of cultural products, such as India's Bollywood movies, which have become popular in many parts of the world, including North America. Countries including China and Brazil have very significant cultural industries that dominate their own local media and are now being exported.

The Qatar-based television news network Al Jazeera has become a significant cultural force since its establishment in 1996. Al Jazeera has transformed news reporting in many Middle

**global village**
A world in which distances have been shrunk by modern communications technology so that everyone is socially and economically interdependent.

**cultural imperialism**
A process whereby powerful countries use the media to spread values and ideas that dominate and even destroy other cultures, and local cultural values are replaced by the cultural values of the dominant country.

Indian actor Anil Kapoor is shown in Toronto at the opening ceremonies of the 2011 "Bollywood Oscars." This was the first time the event had been held in North America.

THE CANADIAN PRESS IMAGES/Dominic Chan

Eastern countries, where coverage was often limited because of restrictions imposed by dictatorial governments. It has provided a global alternative to Western media, and its English language services have provided people in Europe and North America with a very different perspective on Middle Eastern issues than they have been given by traditional news sources.

## The Digital Third World

Information and communications technologies are changing the world, but are these technologies helping people who are poor or just increasing the gap between rich and poor?

Some feel that the ability to share information from around the globe will help low-income countries develop by providing them with the opportunity to become knowledge societies that can compete with industrialized nations. New technologies will help them streamline industry and government, and their competitive advantage in wages will allow them to attract business. Technology can speed up educational reform and help build a more participatory civil society through the sharing of information and ideas. India has generated hundreds of thousands of jobs based on new information and communication technologies (Friedman, 2005). See Figure 17.3.

However, there is a danger that the move to a world linked by new information and communications technology will lead to a greater polarization between the rich, who can exploit the new technologies, and the poor, who do not have access to them. The poor may be excluded from the global information society—and this includes the poor in industrialized countries, as the "digital Third World" does not follow international borders. See Figure 17.4.

The major barrier to the spread of information and communications technology is cost. To become part of the "digital world," low-income countries must build expensive communications infrastructures. Because of these costs, high-income residents of high-income countries are most likely to have access to the Internet. In 2011, 78 percent of North Americans and 58 percent of Europeans had access to the Internet compared with 24 percent of Asians and only 11 percent of residents of Africa. However, there has been significant growth in Internet use in low-income countries. For example, even though it is still low, Internet use in Africa increased by 2500 percent between 2000 and 2011 (Internet World Stats, 2012). Similarly, mobile phone use is much lower in low-income countries but is also growing very rapidly. Between 2000 and 2008, mobile phone ownership in Africa increased from 2 percent to 28 percent of the population (Tryhorn, 2009). Despite this growth, it will take many years before access to modern communications approaches that of people in wealthier parts of the world.

Language issues also act as a barrier to Internet access in many parts of the world. Most of the content on the Internet is in English. Without multilingual sites, the name "World Wide Web" will never be accurate. A Web that is dominated linguistically by English and technologically and culturally by the United States will never reflect the point of view of people in low-income countries. The magnitude of this problem was demonstrated by Charles Kenny (2003), who searched for Web pages in Igbo, a language spoken by 17 million Nigerians. Kenny found only five sites that used the Igbo language.

Much remains to be done if low-income countries are to build on-ramps to the information superhighway. Rather than following the North American model, involving individual access to communications technology, it is likely that solutions in low-income countries will involve shared infrastructure and public access facilities, such as Internet phones accessed through individuals who make their living by sharing their phones with neighbours for a small fee. These intermediaries help to share the financial burden and are also important in helping teach unskilled people to utilize complex technology (Jensen, 2002).

| FIGURE 17.3 | WORLD CONNECTIONS |
| --- | --- |

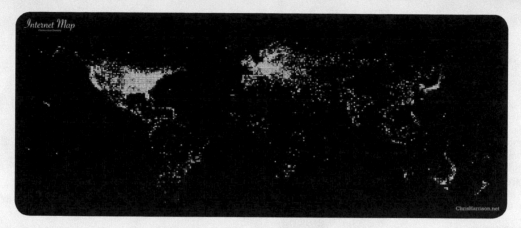

This graphic shows the relative density of Internet connectivity across the globe. You can see how North America, Europe, and Japan are far more connected than other parts of the world.

*Source:* http://www.chrisharrison.net/index.php/Visualizations/InternetMap. Used with permission of Chris Harrison.

| FIGURE 17.4 | CITY-TO-CITY CONNECTIONS |
| --- | --- |

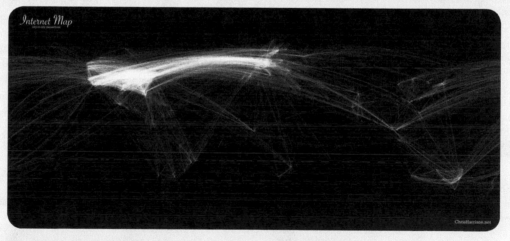

This graphic shows the network ties around the globe. North America and Europe are clearly at the core of the digital world, while other countries are on its periphery.

*Source:* http://www.chrisharrison.net/index.php/Visualizations/InternetMap. Used with permission of Chris Harrison.

## TIME TO REVIEW

- What impact does the constant connectivity of smartphones have on our lives?
- Discuss the implications of living a life online through networks such as Second Life along with your life in the 'real' world.
- What are some of the positive and negative consequences of the way people use new social media.
- How has the Internet changed the process of selecting a potential spouse?
- Describe how the pressure to make a profit can affect people's privacy rights.
- Do you think that new media will help or harm the world's poor?

## KEY TERMS

**cultural imperialism** A process whereby powerful countries use the media to spread values and ideas that dominate and even destroy other cultures, and local cultural values are replaced by the cultural values of the dominant country (p. 501).

**global village** A world in which distances have been shrunk by modern communications technology so that everyone is socially and economically interdependent (p. 501).

**hyperreality** A situation in which the distinction between reality and simulation has become blurred (p. 491).

**Internet** The network infrastructure that links together the world's millions of computers (p. 479).

**mass media** Any technologically based means of communicating between large numbers of people distributed widely over space or time (p. 478).

**media literacy** The ability to access, analyze, evaluate, and create media in a variety of forms (p. 479).

**status conferral** The process of giving prominence to particular individuals by focusing media attention on them (p. 482).

**World Wide Web** The computer language that allows us to access information on the Internet (p. 479).

**LO-1** Understand what is meant by the term *mass media*.

The media connect those who produce messages with those who receive them. The mass media are "any technologically based means of communicating between large numbers of people distributed widely over space or time" (Pavlik and McIntosh 2011:18).

© CBC

**LO-2** Consider how the impact of the media is explained by functionalist, conflict, feminist, interactionist, and postmodern theories.

Functionalist theorists believe the media exist because of the functions they play for society. For example, the media keep us informed, help societies socialize their members, and entertain us. Conflict theorists argue that the media help the dominant class control society by reinforcing capitalist ideology. Interactionist theorists show us how people use the media to help develop their individual identities. Feminist theorists have been critical of the way the media perpetuate gender stereotyping. Postmodern theorists have showed us how the media blur the distinction between reality and simulation, creating a new condition that Baudrillard called "hyperreality."

© Jen Grantham/iStockphoto

**LO-3** Understand how new media both bring people together and keep them apart.

Social media can enable us to stay connected with friends and family even though we may be living in different parts of the world. However, many people spend so much time interacting with media that they may neglect their personal relationships.

© Philip Street. Used with permission

**LO-4** Understand how social media sites profit from the information you provide them.

Companies like Facebook and Zynga (the makers of FarmVille) are worth many billions of dollars. They make money by selling information about their subscribers to advertisers or by selling things that people use in their online lives. We need to be aware of how these organizations make their money in order to ensure that we are not exploited through such factors as violations of our privacy.

**LO-5** Think about the role played by the media in globalization.

McLuhan believed that media technologies would create a global village in which people around the world shared information through interactive media. This would empower people and foster the growth of democracy and equality. Not everyone agrees with this view. There is a huge digital divide between people living in rich countries and those living in poor countries. Without action to reduce this technological gap, the disparity between rich and poor will get worse, not better.

## APPLICATION QUESTIONS

1. The chapter opener described how social media helped to overthrow Libya's repressive government. Progressive movements are not the only ones to use social media, however, as groups such as al-Qaeda and the Taliban also have a strong online presence. Using information you find on the Internet, examine how these groups make use of social media and consider how successful they have been.

2. In what ways do the media make you feel more Canadian? In what ways do the media make you feel like a citizen of the world (part of the global village) rather than like a Canadian?

3. Some people use virtual reality scenarios, such as those in Second Life, to try out new identities. Which personality trait(s) would you like to "test drive" in virtual reality?

4. People can have strong emotional attachments through their avatars in Second Life and other online worlds. If a married person's avatar has an intimate relationship with another avatar, should that be grounds for divorce in that person's real-life marriage? Why or why not?

5. Why do you think so many people are meeting their partners online? Do you think that this way of meeting is better than relying on traditional ways, such as meeting people through your family, at church, or in school? Why or why not?

# KEY FIGURES

**Theodor Adorno (1903-1969)** Philosopher Theodor Adorno was one of the earliest critics of the media. He was a member of the Frankfurt School of critical theory, which looked at the role of social factors in the oppression of the lower classes. His work with Max Horkheimer focused on the way in which the culture industry had turned into just another marketable commodity.

© INTERFOTO/Alamy

**Jean Baudrillard (1929-2007)** Postmodern scholar Jean Baudrillard is best known for his work on the way in which postmodern societies are organized around simulation, which can be more involving than reality. He developed the notion of hyperreality, which refers to a situation in which the distinction between reality and simulation has been blurred.

© INTERFOTO/Alamy

**Marshall McLuhan (1911-1980)** McLuhan was Canada's foremost media theorist. One of his best-known assertions was that because of the power of the media, we live in a global village in which people around the world share information through interactive media.

© Bettmann/Corbis

**Sherry Turkle (b. 1948)** Psychologist Sherry Turkle was one of the first scholars to study how our lives are affected by the new technology of computers and social media. Her most recent work looks at how social media may cause a flight from conversation to mere connection, thereby reducing the richness of human communication.

Peter Urban

CourseMate

? Test your comprehension and assess what you've learned with **CourseMate's** online quizzes.

For other interesting Lived Experiences, watch the video clips on **CourseMate.**

Practise what you've learned with flashcards containing key terms and definitions on **CourseMate.**

NEL

# Chapter 7

# Social Media: Implications for Social Life

SONIA BOOKMAN, University of Manitoba

## INTRODUCTION

Launched in 2004, Facebook has become an important feature of contemporary social life. With more than 800 million active users, it is the leading social networking site globally (Facebook, 2011; Levinson, 2009). Reflecting its growing popularity, a 2010 hit film told the story of how Facebook was founded. Its founder, Mark Zuckerberg, was named "Person of the Year" by *Time* magazine.

For many of us, Facebook is part of our everyday lives. We use it to create and craft profiles, add friends, post photos, and invite people to social events. On our birthdays, we eagerly anticipate the hundreds of birthday greetings that will be displayed on our Facebook wall (Eckler, 2011). We join Facebook pages and groups to meet others with similar interests and support social causes.

Facebook is a form of social media. Social media are playing an increasingly significant role in shaping the way we communicate, collaborate, and connect. This chapter explores some of the social implications of social media, bearing in mind that their influence is not yet fully understood since social media and their widespread adoption are relatively recent developments. The chapter begins with a definition and brief overview of social media. It then considers some of the key social consequences of social media for social life, focusing on how they are implicated in social relations, social activism, and surveillance.

## SOCIAL MEDIA

Social media are a category of new media that facilitate online exchanges and interaction. They encompass a diverse range of web-based and mobile services that allow people to exchange text messages, music, photos, and videos, and participate in online communities (Dewing, 2010a).

There are five main types of social media (Dewing, 2010a; Kaplan and Haenlein, 2010). *Social networking sites* are services that people use to create personal profiles, establish a list of people they are connected to, and share information. Facebook is the most prominent of these (Dewing, 2010b). *Virtual worlds* include virtual game environments, such as World of Warcraft and Second Life. Users create three-dimensional avatars (personalized graphical representations) that interact in various settings. Second Life simulates real life. Avatars own and furnish apartments, shop in malls with "Linden Dollars," and go clubbing in virtual bars. Nearly 800 000 people log on to Second Life at least once a month (Cremore, 2011), and it is growing in popularity. *Blogs* (short for "web log") and *microblogs* consist of online journals or short status updates that allow people to communicate and comment. These include the fast-growing Twitter service, which is used to send out 140-character tweets to a network of "followers." *Collective projects* include websites where people participate in the joint creation and ongoing modification of content. A well-known example is the online encyclopedia Wikipedia. Finally, *online content communities* consist of services that allow people to share media, such as photos or videos. They include YouTube and Flickr.

Social media are distinguished from traditional mass media by four key traits (Lievrouw, 2011). First, they are characterized by *hybridity* since they enable the integration and recombination of various new and old technologies. For example, Facebook is primarily a networking site, but it combines with other media technologies such as videos, as users post links to YouTube. Second, social media are *networked* and *nonlinear*. Instead of broadcasting a message from a central producer to a mass audience, as in film or broadcast television, social media are many-to-many in their connectivity. For example, Twitter allows tweets to be sent by "Tweetheart" celebrities, such as Ashton Kutcher, to millions of "followers" at once. Individuals and groups (such as TwitterMoms) in a network can also respond, comment, or view the whole conversation online (Levinson, 2009). Third, social media are *interactive*. Instead of providing people with a finished product, the content of social media is user generated and continually modified in collaborative fashion. Think of how much content on Facebook is actually contributed by users, who upload upward of 250 million photos a day (Facebook, 2011). Finally, social media are *almost everywhere all the time*, wherever an Internet or a mobile phone connection is available.

With a growing number of mobile devices, from the BlackBerry and the iPhone to wireless tablets, we can be "always on" and linked in to various networks.

Some 83 percent of Canadians enjoy Internet access and we have adopted social media quickly and widely (Ipsos Reid, 2011). According to a 2009 survey, 80 percent of Canadian Internet users engage in social media, making Canadians the top social media users in the world (Dewing, 2010b). A 2011 survey found that over half of Canadian Internet users access social networking sites, and of those, 90 percent had a Facebook account (Ipsos Reid, 2011).

While more and more Canadians are using social media, rates of use vary among different groups. For example, only 65 percent of rural dwellers are likely to be online, and they engage in fewer web-based activities than city residents do, partly owing to a lack of high-speed service (Dewing, 2010b). In addition, social media are used more extensively by young people. According to 2009 figures, of people under 35 who were online, 86 percent had a social network profile, compared with 44 percent of those over 55 (Dewing, 2010b). However, this gap is shrinking. As a 2011 survey showed, 94 percent of new social networking profiles were opened by Canadians over 35 (Ipsos Reid, 2011).

# MEDIATING SOCIAL RELATIONS

What are the implications of social media for our identities, the way we think about who we are? How do they shape the way we socialize and connect with others? Much of the initial research on the social impact of social media was contradictory. It trumpeted either social media's ability to help create liberating new identities and communities or its capacity to isolate people from one another by reducing face-to-face interaction (Woolgar, 2002: 9). Since then, however, research has produced more nuanced accounts of the way we express identities and socialize through social media (Flew and Smith, 2011).

## IDENTITY

Let's first consider the question of identity. Writing in the mid-1990s, Sherry Turkle (1995) argued that virtual worlds would enable people to construct and express their identities in new and potentially liberating ways. Examining how people engaged with virtual worlds, such as MUDs (multi-user dungeons) and MOOs (multi-user object-oriented domains), she proposed that these text-based precursors to Second Life operated as "identity workshops." Unlimited by an embodied presence, people could experiment with their identities in these spaces: "the obese can become slender, the beautiful plain, the 'nerdy' sophisticated" (Turkle, 1995: 12). In Second Life, participants design a customized avatar by selecting body type, hair colour, clothing, tattoos, and more, shaping the way they will look to others. This allows people to play with their self-presentation. For Turkle, online identity play suggests a fluidity of identity, consistent with postmodern arguments that identity is not singular and constant but variable and multiplex—an ongoing construction project, as it were (Bell, 2001: 115). Social media of all types afford ample opportunity to construct our selves as we shape and adjust our personal profiles, modify the look of our avatars, and manage our presentation of self.

However, many writers have noted the limits to online identity play. Virtual worlds are not separate from real life; we bring our embodied selves and "baggage" to the way we present our selves in online worlds. Although it is possible in principle to swap genders in virtual worlds, such as Second Life, various accounts suggest that this is not common practice (Bell, 2001). Furthermore, possibilities for identity play vary, depending on the type of social media we are using to express our selves (Baym, 2006). Facebook profiles usually correspond fairly closely with our real life identities and are contextualized in offline social contexts by displaying photos or links to local events. That is because the people we interact with on Facebook include online and many offline friends. Still, our profiles on social networking sites are carefully crafted as we construct, edit, and perform idealized versions of our selves, selecting images, "likes," and activities to shape impressions about who we are (Utz, 2010).

Recently, Turkle (2011) has reconsidered her earlier enthusiasm about online identities and possibilities for self-expression. With the growth in mobile social media technologies, she argues that we are now expected to be available at all times—to respond to Facebook messages and tweets even when on holiday or having dinner with friends. Significant amounts of time and anxiety-ridden energy go into maintaining and managing our online profiles and relationships. It is increasingly difficult to just turn off and relax. What kind of interests and life should I say I have on Facebook? Who should I be friends with online? Constant online performances not only represent but also reshape us: "Over time, such performances of identity may feel like identity itself" (Turkle, 2011: 12). Social media technologies are so much a part of us, we don't feel like ourselves without them; we are tethered. The question that continues to concern Turkle is how our identities are being reshaped by the new realities of life online.

## SOCIABILITY

Let's now consider how social media are implicated in the formation of online groups and virtual communities. In one of the most influential early accounts of online communities, Rheingold (1993) argued that the Internet was a new frontier for forging social connections, unbound by local time or location. He was enthusiastic about the potential for virtual communities to reinvigorate community building and social engagement. Based on shared interests, such virtual communities are nurtured over time, through participation in discussion and information sharing. Rheingold's version of community evokes the nostalgic image of a traditional, tight-knit circle of friends that we might find in a neighbourhood pub (Bell, 2001).

Established in 1998, the GimpGirl Community illustrates this potential. It is an online group whose members and organizers are women living with disabilities. Using a range of social media from list-servs and MOOs to Second Life, Facebook, and Twitter, the group was initiated to create a "safe, open space" where like-minded individuals could discuss issues of common concern, share information, and participate in community building (Cole et al., 2011: 1161). Members socialize and share personal writings and art. They provide emotional support and offer links to resources for women with disabilities. While disagreements occur and debates arise over group definition, these are moderated by staff members who endeavour to ensure a welcoming environment. Persisting over many years, this group forms an important part of many members' social lives and plays a significant role in the articulation of identity—what it means to be a woman with disabilities.

Not all online groups conform to this ideal of virtual community. There is a great deal of variation among online groups, just as there is offline (Baym, 2006). Some online groupings are less robust or intimately connected. For example, Twitter feeds are networks of loosely associated individuals who share an interest in a particular topic or celebrity. These groups are more temporary than Rheingold's virtual communities. People can opt out as easily as they join in, and they flit between Twitter feeds. Other groups, such as those that emerge in online gaming worlds, are more enduring and involve more intense interaction. For example, World of Warcraft encourages the development of teams in the form of clans or guilds. Members take on specific roles via their avatars and coordinate actions with others to pursue a common goal. While playing in character, members socialize online in groups that last from hours to years (Schroeder, 2011).

David Bell prefers to use the German word *bund* (covenant) to think about these kinds of online social groupings. A bund is "an elective grouping, bonded by affective and emotional solidarity, sharing a strong sense of belonging" (Bell, 2001: 107). For Bell, this concept is somewhat more open than Rheingold's version of "virtual community." It better reflects the interest-based, elective, and diverse kinds of online sociability facilitated by Facebook groups, blogging communities, and virtual gaming worlds.

While social media provide new possibilities for socializing online, it is important to remember that virtual communities do not exist in a vacuum. They are embedded in our everyday real worlds and offline social lives (see Wellman, Chapter 6). The groups that we establish online are often extensions of offline sociability and they enhance it. With social media, many of us now enjoy a mash-up of online and offline social lives that we move between with ease (Turkle, 2011).

## SOCIAL ACTIVISM

Increasingly, we use social media to debate social issues, engage in social activism, and mobilize social movements. Social media have become a means of facilitating social change. Many books are dedicated to this aspect of social media, with such titles as *Cyberactivism* (McCaughey and Ayers, 2003) and *@ Is for Activism* (Hands, 2011).

Scholars have identified two main ways in which social media facilitate social activism. First, people use social media for awareness or advocacy purposes. Second, they use social media to organize and mobilize others for political action (Harlow, 2011; Vegh, 2003). Of course, the potential of social media to enhance the effectiveness of activism depends on access to technology and know-how; it is limited by the "digital divide," which separates urban, better-educated, and higher-income people from others (Brodock, 2010).

With regard to awareness and advocacy, social media allow people to share information and draw attention to causes and issues of concern in a way that bypasses conventional media gatekeepers. Using blogs, Twitter, and independent news sites, activists create content and disseminate their own news stories. By posting reports, videos, and local news, people engage in participatory journalism (Lievrouw, 2011: 120). The creation of such independent, alternative media has played a central role in the widely studied global justice movement. In 1999, the movement held demonstrations in Seattle to coincide with the meeting of the World Trade Organization. It was here that activists set up the first Independent Media Centre (IMC). The IMC site offered streaming video and audio reports, providing in-depth coverage of the event as a counterpoint to accounts in the mainstream media (Lievrouw, 2011). Since then, a network of 175 IMCs has been established to follow movement activity and circulate news content submitted by users. Along the same lines, activists involved with the Occupy Wall Street movement developed an online *Occupied Wall Street Journal* to disseminate information. They used YouTube videos to expose incidents of violence against participants. In addition, members of the movement are establishing a social network that allows them to convene, share information, and build solidarity (Community Team, 2011).

The networked dimension of social media facilitates the organization and mobilization of social activists. Social networking sites enable people to cultivate large networks of online and offline "friends." Facebook messages travel rapidly and from many to many, unrestricted by time and space. Each Facebook user has approximately 130 "friends," so if one user posts a message requesting support for a cause, it can travel to many people quickly. This feature of social networking sites allows social movements to enlist the support and participation of interested individuals at the click of a mouse.

Such networks can be mobilized to engage in at least two kinds of collective action (Harlow, 2011). The first includes mediated online action, such as signing online petitions or conducting email campaigns. Some writers suggest that the simplicity of such online activism leads to "slacktivism," giving people the false impression that they are socially engaged by clicking "like" on a Facebook page established for a cause (Scholz, 2010). Instead of relying solely on online involvement, analysts of digital activism suggest that combining online and offline activity is important to sustaining social movements (Kavada, 2010). Indeed, many social activists use social media networks to coordinate offline protests, demonstrations, and other events. This has certainly been the case for the global justice movement, which has enlisted an array of social media to organize street protests and demonstrations around the world in a short time (Lievrouw, 2011). Social media such as Twitter also played a significant role in recent civil uprisings in Egypt and elsewhere in the Middle East and North Africa. Because of their ubiquity and mobility, technologies like Twitter quickly facilitate the mobilization of a critical mass. Much hype was generated in the mainstream media about the so-called "Twitter revolutions" based on the notion that these were new kinds of uprisings "coordinated online in real time" with social media technologies (Hands, 2011: 1). However, others caution against claims that Twitter was at the root of social activism and change (Hands, 2011).

Recent studies highlight how people use social media to initiate online activism that subsequently moves offline. For example, Harlow (2011) documents how social media, such as Facebook and Twitter, were used to generate a pro-justice and anti-violence movement in Guatemala. Following the shooting of a prominent lawyer, young Guatemalans, frustrated with high levels of violence in the country, started Facebook fan pages and groups to inform the public and call for justice. The pages brought together thousands of like-minded Facebook users, who made comments, followed threads, and built solidarity. This online "virtual" movement prompted offline "real" world action, spilling over to the streets in the form of mass demonstrations and public protests (Harlow, 2011).

## SURVEILLANCE

The same social media technologies that enable social activism are used as a means of surveillance and social control by authorities. Surveillance involves "focused systematic and routine attention to personal details for the purposes of influence, management, protection, or direction" (David Lyon, quoted in Flew and Smith, 2011: 231). Some surveillance is planned, some unintended. Targeted surveillance is facilitated by sophisticated monitoring systems that intercept communications, including text messages and tweets. These systems can also track location with mobile phone positioning technologies, scan messages for certain words, and recognize voices. Companies sell surveillance technology to law enforcement agencies around the world. Although usually employed with strict privacy protections, the authors of a recent article show how surveillance technologies have also been used to repress civil uprisings (Silver and Elgin, 2011). They give the example of Bahrain, where authorities gathered information about rights activists by monitoring their text messages and other online communications, resulting in their persecution and imprisonment.

More broadly, social media allow people, companies, and organizations to watch, profile, and monitor us. We produce a mountain of data about ourselves through social media. We take photos on our mobile phones and post them on Facebook. These photos are tagged with detailed information, such as the date, location, and names of those pictured. We share ideas in blogs and update our whereabouts on Twitter. On Facebook alone, users shared more than six billion photos, wall messages, and status updates every *week* during 2010 (Flew and Smith, 2011). This digital content is not easily deleted, and employers use it to screen candidates for jobs and monitor employee behaviour. Police use information posted by the public on sites like YouTube as evidence in crime investigations. For example, after the 2011 Stanley Cup riots in Vancouver, police gathered evidence from social media sites and set up a 2011 Riot website to track down people responsible for looting and property damage. The website asked the public to submit photos or video footage taken at the scene and identify individuals from the thousands of photos the public had already provided (Vancouver Police Department, 2011). In addition, corporations keep track of our online consumption choices and use the data we create using social media to tailor marketing strategies to particular demographic niches. For instance, PlanetOut. com is a popular online portal serving the lesbian, gay, bisexual, and transgendered communities. It functions as a meeting place, shopping mall, and newsroom for millions of members. It is presented to members as a virtual community, but it is also used by corporate marketers to solicit data used in targeted marketing (Campbell, 2005).

Sensing that we are constantly watched, we watch ourselves; we monitor our online behaviour, conforming to certain norms and the expectations of those who might see us (Turkle, 2011). Resigned to a lack of privacy, some teens remind each other not to post certain pictures and to be careful about the information they post, concerned that school officials or the police might look up their profiles. Furthermore, they realize that in a world of cut, edit, and paste, the information they generate is public and permanent. Nonetheless, it seems that most young people ignore the dangers of surveillance as they enjoy engaging in social media.

## REFERENCES

Baym, Nancy. (2006). "Interpersonal Life Online." In Leah Lievrouw and Sonia Livingstone, eds., *The Handbook of New Media: Social Shaping and Social Consequences of ICTs,* updated student ed. (pp. 35–54). London: Sage.

Bell, David. (2001). *An Introduction to Cybercultures.* London: Routledge.

Brodock, Katharine. (2010). "Economic and Social Factors: The Digital (Activism) Divide." In Mary Joyce, ed., *Digital Activism Decoded: The New Mechanics of Change* (pp. 71–84). New York: International Debate Education Association.

Campbell, John. (2005). "Outing PlanetOut: Surveillance, Gay Marketing and Internet Affinity Portals." *New Media Society,* 7 (5), 663–83.

Cole, Jennifer, Jason Nolan, Yukari Seko, Katherine Mancuso, and Alejandra Ospina. (2011). "GimpGirl Grows Up: Women with Disabilities Rethinking, Redefining, and Reclaiming Community." *New Media Society, 13* (7), 1161–79.

Community Team. (2011). "Would You Join a Facebook-Style Occupy Social network?" *CBC News,* 28 December. On the World Wide Web at http://www.cbc.ca/news/yourcommunity/2011/12/would-you-join-a-facebook-style-occupy-social-network.html (retrieved 1 August 2012).

Cremore, Lowell. (2011). "First Quarter 2011 Results for Second Life: Steady Sailing." *The Metaverse Journal* 12 May. On the World Wide Web at http://www.metaversejournal.com/2011/05/12/first-quarter-2011-results-for-second-life-steady-sailing/ (retrieved 1 August 2012).

Dewing, Michael. (2010a). *Social Media: 1. An Introduction.* Background Paper No. 2010-03-E. Ottawa: Library of Parliament.

Dewing, Michael. (2010b). *Social Media: 2. Who Uses Them?* Background Paper No. 2010-05-E. Ottawa: Library of Parliament.

Eckler, Rebecca. (2011). "This Is My Best Birthday Ever." *Maclean's Magazine* 26 September, 75.

Facebook. (2011). "Statistics." On the World Wide Web at http://www.facebook.com/press/info.php?statistics (retrieved 1 August 2012).

Flew, Terry and Smith, Richard. (2011). *New Media: An Introduction,* Cdn ed. Toronto: Oxford University Press.

Hands, Joss. (2011). *@ Is for Activism: Dissent, Resistance and Rebellion in a Digital Culture.* London: Pluto Press.

Harlow, Summer. (2011). "Social Media and Social Movements: Facebook and an Online Guatemalan Justice Movement that Moved Offline." *New Media & Society* (August 5, online), 1–19.

Ipsos Reid. (2011). *The Ipsos Canadian Inter@ctive Reid Report 2011 Fact Guide.* On the World Wide Web at http://www.ipsos-na.com/knowledge-ideas/media-content-technology/research-briefings/Default.aspx?q=the-canadian-internet-fact-guide (retrieved 1 August 2012).

Kaplan, Andreas and Michael Haenlein. (2010). "Users of the World, Unite! The Challenges and Opportunities of Social Media." *Business Horizons, 53,* 59–68.

Kavada, Anastasia. (2010). "Activism Transforms Digital: The Social Movement Perspective." In Mary Joyce, ed., *Digital Activism Decoded: The New Mechanics of Change* (pp. 101–18). New York: International Debate Education Association.

Levinson, Paul. (2009). *New New Media.* Boston: Allyn & Bacon.

Lievrouw, Leah. (2011). *Alternative and Activist New Media.* Cambridge, UK: Polity Press.

McCaughey, Martha and Michael Ayers. (2003). *Cyberactivism: Online Activism in Theory and Practice.* London: Routledge.

Rheingold, Howard. (1993). *The Virtual Community: Finding Connection in a Computerized World.* London: Secker & Warburg.

Scholz, Trebor. (2010). "Infrastructure: Its Transformations and Effect on Digital Activism." In Mary Joyce, ed., *Digital Activism Decoded: The New Mechanics of Change* (pp. 17–32). New York: International Debate Education Association.

Schroeder, Ralph. (2011). *Being There Together: Social Interaction in Virtual Environments.* Oxford, UK: Oxford University Press.

Silver, Vernon and Ben Elgin. (2011). "Torture in Bahrain Becomes Routine With Help From Nokia Siemens." *Bloomberg* 23 August. On the World Wide Web at http://www.bloomberg.com/news/2011-08-22/torture-in-bahrain-becomes-routine-with-help-from-nokia-siemens-networking.html (26 December 2011).

Turkle, Sherry. (1995). *Life on the Screen: Identity in the Age of the Internet.* New York: Simon & Schuster.

Turkle, Sherry. (2011). *Alone Together: Why We Expect More from Technology and Less from Each Other.* New York: Basic Books.

Utz, Sonja. (2010). "Show Me Your Friends and I Will Tell You What Type of Person You Are: How One's Profile, Number of Friends, and Type of Friends Influence Impression Formation on Social Network Sites." *Journal of Computer-Mediated Communication, 15,* 314–35.

Vancouver Police Department. (2011). "Riot 2011." On the World Wide Web at https://vancouver.ca/police/riot2011/index.html (retrieved 1 August 2012).

Vegh, Sandor. (2003). "Classifying Forms of Online Activism: The Case of Cyberprotests Against the World Bank." In Martha McCaughey and Michael Ayers, eds., *Cyberactivism: Online Activism in Theory and Practice* (pp. 71–96). London: Routledge.

Woolgar, Steve. (2002). "Five Rules of Virtuality." In Steve Woolgar, ed., *Virtual Society? Technology, Cyberbole, Reality* (pp. 1–22). Oxford, UK: Oxford University Press.

# The Body

# 12

# Sociology of the Body: Disability, Aging, and Death

## IN THIS CHAPTER, YOU WILL LEARN THAT

- Seemingly natural features of the human body, such as height and weight, have social causes and consequences of far-reaching importance.

- Enhancing body image to conform to prevailing norms became especially important in urban, industrial societies.

- In different times and places, people have defined and dealt with disability in different ways.

- Age is an important basis of social stratification. However, the correlation between age and the command of resources is far from perfect, and political conflicts shape the degree to which any given age cohort exercises resource control.

- Although prejudice and discrimination against older people are common in Canada, older people have wielded increasing political power in recent decades.

# NIP/TUCK

"Tell me what you don't like about yourself." With these simple words, plastic surgeons Christian Troy and Sean McNamara begin each consultation in the TV series *Nip/ Tuck*. At first, the words seem unremarkable. Why *wouldn't* we assume that prospective cosmetic surgery patients are dissatisfied with their appearance? Yet once the words sink in, they shock us. They shock us, first, when we remember how widespread the incidence of body dissatisfaction is. About four million North Americans underwent cosmetic surgery, including minimally invasive cosmetic procedures such as Botox injections, in 2008, up nearly tenfold since 1992 (American Society of Plastic Surgeons, 2009). Add to this number the many people who want cosmetic surgery but cannot afford it, and we can reasonably conclude that body dissatisfaction is not an individual idiosyncrasy but a mass social phenomenon. The plastic surgeons' words are shocking, too, because they point to dissatisfaction that is more than skin deep. Troy and McNamara don't ask prospective patients what they dislike about their bodies. They ask them what they dislike about their *selves*. Implicit in their question is the assumption that our bodies faithfully represent our selves—that weight, proportions, hairiness, and so forth, say something fundamentally important about a person's character. It is an assumption that most people share.

© FXNetworks/Courtesy Everett Collection/CP Picture Archive

Embedded in the idea that our bodies reflect our selves is a sociological principle that is the main lesson of this chapter. The human body is not just a wonder of biology; it is also a sociological wonder (Turner, 1996). Its parts, its disabilities, its aging, and its death mean different things and have different consequences for different cultures, historical periods, and categories of people. For example, a person's height, weight, and attractiveness may seem to be facts of nature. Closer inspection reveals, however, that the standards by which we define a "normal" or "desirable" body vary historically. Moreover, a person's height, weight, and perceived attractiveness influence his or her annual income, health, likelihood of getting married, and much else. We explore the relationship between body characteristics and social status in the next section.

The relationship between the body and society is especially clear in the case of disability. The very definition of what constitutes a disability has varied over time and place. So have strategies for dealing with disabilities. In the following pages, we illustrate these variations. Among other things, we show that the dominant treatment tendency since the nineteenth century has involved the rehabilitation and integration of people with disabilities into "normal" society. Then, in the early twentieth century, some governments tried to eliminate people with disabilities altogether. Finally, in the late twentieth century, people with disabilities began to assert their dignity and normality. One consequence of this new attitude is a vigorous move toward self-help and the establishment of independent communities of people with disabilities.

In this chapter's final section, we turn to the problems of aging and death. We show that aging is not just a natural process of growth and decline. Age is one basis of social inequality. Thanks to improved social policy and medical advances, the social condition of the aged is much better than it was just half a century ago. However, older people face prejudice and discrimination. The systems for providing personal care and adequate pensions are in trouble. Poverty is a looming possibility for some and a bitter reality for others. We survey each of these issues and conclude by training our sociological eye on the ultimate social problems: dying and death.

## Summing Up

- Various aspects of the human body mean different things and have different consequences for different cultures, historical periods, and categories of people.
- For example, the definition of what constitutes a disability has varied over time and place, as have strategies for dealing with disabilities.
- Similarly, aging is not just a natural process of growth and decline, and age is one basis of social inequality.

# SOCIETY AND THE HUMAN BODY

## The Body and Social Status

### Height

In an experiment, four people of the same height and roughly similar appearance were introduced to a group of students. The first person was introduced as a fellow undergraduate, the second as a graduate student, the third as an assistant professor, and the fourth as a professor. Members of the group were asked to rank the four people in terms of their height. Despite the fact that all four were of equal stature, the students estimated that the professor was the tallest, the assistant professor next tallest, then the graduate student, and finally the undergraduate. Apparently believing that physical stature reflects social stature, the students correlated social status with height ("Short Guys Finish Last," 1995–96).

Is this perception accurate? Do tall people really tend to enjoy high social status? And why are some people tall in the first place? We can begin to answer these questions by first acknowledging that genes are an important determinant of any particular individual's height. However, the great majority of human *populations* are approximately the same genetically. A complex series of *social* factors determines the average height of most populations, whether the population consists of members of a country, a class, a racial or an ethnic group, and so on. Moreover, a complex series of social consequences flow from differences in height.

Figure 12.1 shows some of the main social causes and consequences of height. For purposes of illustration, consider the impact of family income on stature. Average family income is the single most important determinant of the quality of a person's diet, especially protein consumption. Higher family income translates into a higher-quality diet. In turn, the quality of diet during childhood strongly influences a person's stature. Thus, Japanese men were on average five centimetres (two inches) taller at the end of the twentieth century than they were at mid-century (French, 2001). Norwegian men were on average nearly eight centimetres (three inches) taller in 1984 than in 1761 (Floud, Wachter, and Gregory, 1990). North American–born children of immigrants are taller on average than their parents who

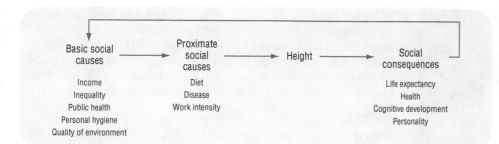

**FIGURE 12.1**
Selected Social Causes and
Consequences of Height in
Human Populations

Source: Adapted from Steckel,
1995: 1908.

were born abroad (Roberts, 1995). In all these cases, the main cause of growing stature is the same: A higher standard of living led to an improved diet that allowed the human body to come closer to realizing its full growth potential. The correlation between per capita family income and average height across many countries is very strong ($r = 0.82$ or higher; Steckel, 1995: 1912).

As we might expect, within countries there is also a correlation between stature and class position. Class differences in height are smaller than they were centuries ago. Even today, however, members of upper classes are on average taller than members of middle classes, who are in turn taller than members of working classes are. The Scandinavian countries are the exceptions that prove the rule. There are no differences in stature between classes in Scandinavia. That is because class inequality is less pronounced in Sweden, Norway, and the rest of Scandinavia than elsewhere (Floud, Wachter, and Gregory, 1990; Kingston, 1997).

The *consequences* of stature are important too. Scrutiny of many sources, ranging from U.S. Army records since the Civil War to all Norwegian X-ray records from the 1950s, reveals that, on average, tall people live longer than others do. In only three of the United States presidential elections held over the past century did the shorter candidate win ("Short Guys Finish Last," 1995–96). Tall people also earn more than others do and tend to reach the top of their profession more quickly (Kingston, 1997; McCulloch, 2003). One of the most thorough studies of the effect of height on income was recently conducted in Canada. Tom Perks (2005) found that an additional centimetre in height is associated with an additional $222 in annual income for men and an additional $57 for women. This means that over 10 years, a man who is 10 centimetres taller than another man but like him in all other relevant respects will earn $22 200 more on average. Remarkably, Perks also found that, in Canada, height has a bigger effect on income than whether one is an immigrant or a member of a visible minority group.

At least part of the reason that short people tend to be less successful in some ways than tall people are is that they experience subtle discrimination based on height. This argument may seem far-fetched. However, your own attitudes may help drive the point home. Is it important that you choose a spouse who is taller than you are? If you are a woman, there is a very good chance you will answer yes. Is it important that you choose a spouse who is shorter than you are? If you are a man, there is a very good chance you will answer yes. Why is this so? Practically speaking, it is unimportant whether the husband or the wife is taller. Yet the overwhelming majority of people believe that husbands should be taller than wives. They find it odd when a husband is shorter than his wife is or even when they are the same height. This attitude is widespread because, for most people, height is an indicator of status and most people believe that men should enjoy higher status than women do. You can extend this example to other kinds of relationships. Think about the leaders of your sports teams, friendship circles, college or university tutorials, families, and other groups to which you belong. Height will surely not be the only determinant of leadership, but you are likely to observe a tendency for leaders to be taller than followers are. This is so despite the fact that there is no practical reason that leaders need to be tall. Finally, consider where you sit in the status hierarchy based on height. Have you ever felt advantaged or disadvantaged because of your height?

### Weight

What is true for height is also true for body weight. Body weight influences status because of the cultural expectations we associate with it. Thus, one study of more than 10 000 young adults found that overweight women tend to complete four fewer months of school than do women who are not overweight. They are also 20 percent less likely to be married. An overweight woman's household is likely to earn nearly $8500 less per year than the household of a woman who is not overweight does. Overweight women are 10 percent more likely to live in poverty. The consequences of being overweight are less serious for men. Still, overweight men are 11 percent less likely to be married than men who are not overweight (Gortmaker et al., 1993; Averett and Korenman, 1996).

Interestingly, the negative effects of being overweight are evident even for women matched in terms of their social and economic backgrounds. This fact suggests the need to revise the simple, conventional view that poverty encourages obesity. It is certainly true that poor women have fewer opportunities and resources that would allow them to eat healthier diets, get more exercise, and bring down their weight. For example, if you live in a poor, high-crime neighbourhood, it is dangerous to go out for a speed walk and you may not be able to afford anything more nutritious than high-calorie fast food when you go out for a meal. However, the reverse is also true: Obesity in and of itself tends to make women poorer. This conclusion seems reasonable because, as noted, for women matched in terms of their social and economic backgrounds, being overweight still has negative effects on income. There is apparently a "reciprocal relationship" between obesity and social class, with each variable affecting the other (Gortmaker et al., 1993).

In preindustrial societies, people generally favoured well-rounded physiques because they signified wealth and prestige. Not surprisingly, beautiful women as depicted by the great artists of the past tend to be on the heavy side from our contemporary perspective.

In contrast, in our society, being well rounded usually signifies undesirability. Being overweight in Canada has become a source of negative stereotyping and even outright discrimination. Many of us think of overweight people as less attractive, industrious, and disciplined than thin people.

Yet the percentage of overweight people is big and growing in Canada, with men accounting for about two-thirds of the recent increase. The likelihood of being overweight increases with age and decreases with class and education (Godley and McLaren, 2010; Statistics Canada, 2002a, 2002b; see Figure 12.2 and Figure 12.3). Thus, a large and expanding number of Canadians live with a stigma that affects their life chances.

Bridgeman Art Library, London/SuperStock

Rubens's *The Toilette of Venus* (1613). Venus, the Roman goddess of beauty, as depicted by Peter Paul Rubens four centuries ago. Would Venus need a tummy tuck and a membership in a diet club to be considered beautiful today?

## Sociology of the Body

### The Body and Society

Our discussion of height and weight should make it clear that our bodies are not just biologically but also socially defined. Let us develop this point by considering how social forces influence the way we manipulate our body image. We then turn to an

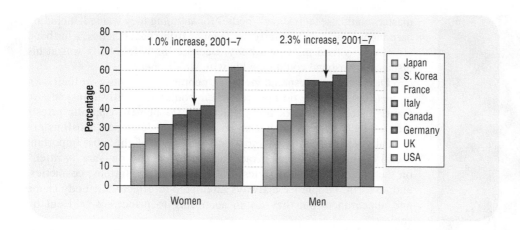

**FIGURE 12.2**

Percentage of Adults Who Are Overweight, Selected Countries, 2007

Note: Overweight adults have a BMI of 25 or higher (BMI = weight in kilograms divided by the square of height in metres).

Source: OECD. "Health: Key Tables from OECD." http://www.oecd-ilibrary.org/social-issues-migration-health/health-key-tables-from-oecd_20758480;jsessionid=1uk47wcovz5qu.delta (accessed 26 October 2010).

analysis of disability—how we define it and how people with and without disabilities deal with it.

In Canada and other highly developed countries, people tend to think they have rights over their own bodies. For instance, the feminist movement asserts the right of every woman to control her own reproductive functions through birth control (Gordon, 1990). Yet people have not always endorsed this view, and some Canadians still contest it. For instance, slaves' bodies were the property of their owners. In most slave societies,

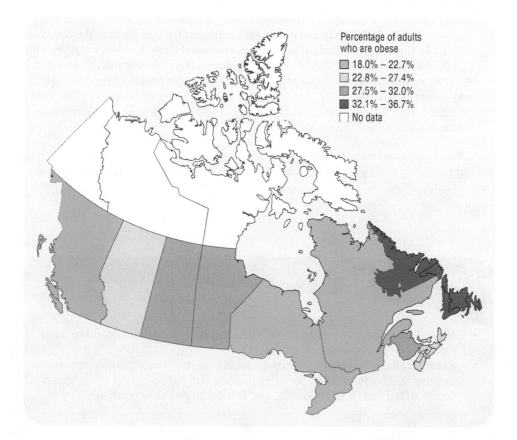

**FIGURE 12.3**

The Regional Distribution of Obesity in Canada, 2004

Note: Obese adults have a BMI of 30 or higher (BMI = weight in kilograms divided by the square of height in metres.)

Source: Body Mass Index (BMI). Health Canada, 2004. Reproduced with the permission of the Minister of Health, 2011.

Sinibaldi/Corbis

Many of the most important social distinctions—gender, race, age, tribe, and so forth— are "written" on the body by different styles of dress, jewellery, tattoos, cosmetics, and so on. People have always attempted to affect their body shape and appearance, but they do so according to principles laid out by society.

masters could use their slaves' bodies for anything they wanted, including hard labour and sex. Similarly, in deeply patriarchal societies, a husband effectively owned his wife's body. Because his wife's body was at his disposal, a husband could rape his wife with impunity.

Despite the widespread view that people have rights over their own bodies, most people do not treat their bodies in wildly idiosyncratic ways. Instead, norms of body practice influence us. Catholic priests are defined partly by sexual abstinence. Male Jews and Muslims are typically defined partly by circumcision. Many of the most important social distinctions—gender, race, age, tribe, and so on—are "written" on the body by different styles of dress, jewellery, tattoos, cosmetics, and so forth. People have always attempted to affect their body shape and appearance, but they do so according to principles laid out by society.

For social, economic, and technological reasons, enhancing body image to conform to prevailing norms became especially important in urban, industrial societies.

- *Socially*, urbanized societies present people with many more opportunities to meet and interact with strangers. This increases the need for the kinds of status cues and impression management techniques that can make social interaction easier (see Chapter 5, Social Interaction). Manipulating body image helps grease the wheels of social interaction in complex societies by making it clear to strangers exactly who you are.
- *Economically*, industrialized societies enable people to afford body enhancement. For example, peasants in preindustrial societies had no access to relatively inexpensive, mass-produced clothing and jewellery, something we take for granted.
- *Technologically*, we have created many new techniques for transfiguring the body (see Box 12.1). Consider something as basic as your teeth and gums. Until recently, the daily practice of brushing, much less of flossing, was uncommon. Two hundred years ago, a 40-year-old might boast a nice set of wooden dentures; poor people were often toothless and lacked false teeth. Today, dental hygiene, dentistry, and orthodontics allow many people to enjoy a set of straight, white teeth for a lifetime, with bridges, crowns, and implants indistinguishable from the real thing.

Thus, social, economic, and technological forces have transformed the way we manipulate our body image. As you will now see, they have also radically altered the way we deal with disability.

## Summing Up

- Many features of the human body, including height and weight, have social causes and consequences.
- Enhancing body image to conform to prevailing norms is especially important in urbanized, industrialized societies because it helps to grease the wheels of social interaction, it is affordable, and it is technologically feasible.

## BOX 12.1

# Sociology at the Movies

### NEVER LET ME GO

Anxiety about the relationship between technology and the human body has been growing at least since Mary Shelley published *Frankenstein* in 1818. Today, we face a new class of misgivings—and accompanying controversy—because it has become possible to grow human body parts from general-purpose stem cells. Almost all research in this area requires the removal of stem cells from an embryo, a procedure that destroys the embryo. Hence the controversy: Should we kill to prolong life?

On the horizon is an even more controversial procedure, first anticipated in Aldous Huxley's *Brave New World* (1932). In the novel, artificially cloned humans are given different aptitudes and then allocated to different social classes. Recently, some scientists, including Princeton University biologist Lee Silver and Nobel Prize–winning physicist Freeman Dyson, have applauded the idea of such genetically engineered social stratification (Brave, 2003).

*Never Let Me Go* is a masterfully directed and well acted movie that underscores some of genetic engineering's likely dangers.

Scene from *Never Let Me Go*

Kathy, Tommy, and Ruth are 11-year-old students at Hailsham Boarding School. They are nurtured to the very pinnacle of good health and meticulously socialized to take pride in their exalted life's purpose: donating their vital organs to grievously ill people. They undergo a series of operations beginning around the age of 28 and expect to "complete"—that is, die—shortly afterward. They are clones raised specifically for that end.

The problem is that they are also people. Kathy and Tommy fall in love as children, but Ruth intervenes to steal Tommy away from Ruth. As an adult who has already undergone two donor operations, Ruth (played by Keira Knightley) finally grows remorseful. She enables Kathy (Carey Mulligan) and Tommy (Andrew Garfield) to request a "deferral," a rumoured program that gives couples who are truly in love an opportunity to live together for a few years before they complete. However, in the end, we discover that the deferral program does not exist and, indeed, never existed; that Hailsham was a special school set up to discover whether clones have souls; and that Hailsham has now been shut down because the question of whether clones have souls has become irrelevant in a world where demand for healthy body parts far outstrips moral qualms. This is the cowardly new world toward which professors Silver and Dyson want to drive us.

# DISABILITY

## The Social Construction of Disability

Pity the poor lefty, for centuries considered inferior. About 400 years ago, the Catholic Church declared left-handed people servants of the Devil and burned some of them at the stake. Then it forced lefties to become right-handed in school. In Japan as recently as the early twentieth century, left-handedness in a wife was grounds for divorce. Natives in Papua New Guinea don't let their left thumbs touch their beer mugs because they believe that would poison the beer. Maori women in New Zealand weave ceremonial cloth with the right hand because they believe that using the left desecrates the cloth. Some African tribes along the Niger River do not allow women to prepare food with the left hand for fear of being poisoned. Almost universally, people have considered left-handedness a disability, so much so that the sentiment has been embedded in many languages. In Russian, to do something *na levo* means to do it under the table or illegally, but literally it means "on the left." In English, the word *left* derives from an Old English word that means "weak" or "worthless." Also in English, *gauche* means "ill-mannered"—but the French from which it is derived means "left." (In contrast, *adroit* means "proper" in English—but the French from which it is derived means "to the right.") In Latin, "right" is *dexter* (as in the English *dextrous*, a desirable attribute) while "left" is *sinister*, which of course means "evil" in English. *Linkisch* is German for "leftish"—and "awkward."

To us, negative attitudes toward left-handedness seem nonsensical. We don't think of left-handed people—roughly 10 percent of the population—as **impaired** or deficient in physical or mental capacity. Nor do we think of them as having a **disability** or being incapable of performing within the range of "normal" human activity. The fact that so many people once thought otherwise suggests that definitions of disability are not based on self-evident biological realities. Instead, they vary socially and historically. Note also that some people, but not others, consider a 1.5-metre-tall (4-foot-tall) person to have a disability, and that most people must be convinced by advertising that erectile dysfunction in a 75-year-old man is a disability. These examples suggest that definitions of disability differ across societies and historical periods, and that in any one time and place, people may disagree over these definitions.

## Rehabilitation and Elimination

Modern Western approaches to disability emerged in the nineteenth century. All scientists and reformers of the time viewed disability as a self-evident biological reality. Some scientists and reformers sought the **rehabilitation** of those with disabilities. Rehabilitation involves curing disabilities to the extent possible through medical and technological intervention. It also entails trying to improve the lives of people with disabilities by means of care, training, and education. Finally, it seeks to integrate people with disabilities into "normal" society (Stiker, 1999 [1982]; Terry and Urla, 1995). The desire for rehabilitation motivated the establishment of schools for the blind, the widespread use of prosthetics, the construction of wheelchair-accessible buildings, and so forth. It also prompted the passage of laws that benefit those with disabilities by mandating accessibility to buildings, public transportation, and jobs. These laws have done much to help integrate people with disabilities into "normal" society.

Other scientists and reformers took a different tack. They sought to eliminate disability altogether by killing people who had a disability or sterilizing them and preventing them from having children. The Nazis adopted this approach in Germany beginning in 1933. They engineered the sterilization and killing of the mentally "deficient" and the physically "deviant," including the blind and the deaf (Proctor, 1988).

One of the ugliest chapters in our history involves the government-funded, forced sterilization of Aboriginal North American women from the 1920s to the 1970s. The "disability" these women were alleged to have was that they were Aboriginal and were deemed by physicians to be having too many babies. Tubal ligations and hysterectomies were performed as a form of birth control on many thousands of Aboriginal North Americans, some of them minors, without their informed consent. In two cases, doctors told 15-year-old girls they were having their tonsils out and then proceeded to remove their ovaries. Tremendous damage had been inflicted on the Aboriginal North American population by the time such practices were outlawed. According to one estimate, in 1982, when 15 percent of white North American women of childbearing age had been sterilized for various reasons, the figure for Aboriginal North American women was about 40 percent (DeFine, 1997; England, n.d.; Johansen, 1998; *The Sterilization*, 1996).

**Impaired** people are considered deficient in physical or mental capacity.

A **disability** is a physical or mental problem that keeps people from performing within the range of "normal" human activity.

**Rehabilitation** involves curing disabilities to the extent possible through medical and technological intervention; trying to improve the lives of people with disabilities by means of care, training, and education; and integrating people with disabilities into society.

# Ableism

Perhaps a tenth of the world's people identify themselves as having a disability or are characterized as such by others (Priestly, 2001). Because the human environment is structured largely around the norms of those without disabilities, people with disabilities suffer many disadvantages. Their deprivations are still greater if they are seniors, women, or members of a lower class or a disadvantaged racial or ethnic group.

Specifically, people routinely stigmatize people with disabilities, negatively evaluating them because of a characteristic that supposedly sets them apart from others. People also routinely employ stereotypes when dealing with people with disabilities, expecting them to behave according to a rigid and often inaccurate view of how everyone with that disability acts. The resulting prejudice and discrimination against people with disabilities is called **ableism**. An historical example of ableism is the widespread belief among nineteenth-century Western educators that blind people are incapable of high-level or abstract thought. Because of this prejudice, the blind were systematically discouraged from pursuing intellectually challenging tasks and occupations. Similarly, an 1858 article in the *American Annals of the Deaf and Dumb* held that "the deaf and dumb are guided almost wholly by instinct and their animal passions. They have no more opportunity of cultivating the intellect and reasoning facilities than the savages of Patagonia or the North American Indians" (quoted in Groce, 1985: 102). Racists think of members of racial minorities as naturally and incurably inferior. Ableists think of people with disabilities in the same way. As the preceding quotation suggests, racists and ableists were often the same people.

Ableism involves more than active prejudice and discrimination. It also involves the largely unintended *neglect* of the conditions of people with disabilities. This point should be clear to anyone who has to get around in a wheelchair. Many buildings were constructed without the intention of discriminating against people in wheelchairs, yet they are extremely inhospitable to them. Impairment becomes disability when the human environment is constructed largely on the basis of ableism. Ableism exists through both intention and neglect.

**Ableism** is prejudice and discrimination against people who have disabilities.

## Challenging Ableism: The Normality of Disability

In 1927 science fiction writer H. G. Wells published a short story called "The Country of the Blind" (Wells, 1927). It provocatively reversed the old saying that "in the country of the blind, the one-eyed man is king." In the story, the protagonist, Nuñez, survives an avalanche high in the Andes. When he revives in a mountain valley, he discovers he is on the outskirts of an isolated village whose members are all blind because of a disease that struck 14 generations earlier. For them, words like *see*, *look*, and *blind* have no meaning.

Because he can see, Nuñez feels vastly superior to the villagers; he thinks he is their "Heaven-sent King and master." Over time, however, he realizes that his sight places him at a disadvantage vis-à-vis the villagers. Their senses of hearing and touch are more highly developed than his are, and they have designed their entire community for the benefit of people who cannot see. Nuñez stumbles where his hosts move gracefully and he constantly rants about seeing—which only proves to his hosts that he is out of touch with reality. The head of the village concludes that Nuñez is "an idiot. He has delusions; he can't do anything right." In this way, Nuñez's vision becomes a disability. He visits a doctor who concludes there is only one thing to do. Nuñez must be cured of his ailment. As the doctor says,

> Those queer things that are called eyes … are diseased … in such a way as to affect his brain. They are greatly distended, he has eyelashes, and his eyelids move, and consequently his brain is in a state of constant irritation and distraction.… I think I may say with reasonable

Lightscapes Photography, Inc./Corbis

The social environment turns an impairment into a disability. Architecture and urban planning that neglect some modes of mobility make life difficult for people who depend on wheelchairs.

certainty that, in order to cure him complete, all that we need to do is a simple and easy surgical operation—namely, to remove these irritant bodies.

Thus, Wells suggests that in the country of the blind, the man who sees must lose his vision or be regarded as a raving idiot.

Wells's tale is noteworthy because it makes blindness seem normal. Its depiction of the normality of blindness comes close to the way many people with disabilities today think of their disabilities—not as a form of deviance but as a different form of normality. As one blind woman wrote, "If I were to list adjectives to describe myself, blind would be only one of many, and not necessarily the first in significance. My blindness is as intrinsically a part of me as the shape of my hands or my predilection for salty snacks.... The most valuable insight I can offer is this: blindness is normal to me" (Kleege, 1999: 4).

The idea of the normality of disability has partly supplanted the rehabilitation ideal, which, as we saw, originated in the nineteenth century. Reformers without disabilities led the rehabilitation movement. They represented and assisted people with disabilities, who participated little in efforts to improve the conditions of their existence. This situation began to change in the 1960s. Inspired by other social movements of the era, people with disabilities began to organize themselves (Campbell and Oliver, 1996; Shapiro, 1993). The founding of the Disabled Peoples International in 1981 and inclusion of the rights of those with disabilities in the United Nations Universal Declaration of Human Rights in 1985 signified the growth—and growing legitimacy—of the new movement globally. Since the 1980s, people with disabilities have begun to assert their autonomy and the "dignity of difference" (Charlton, 1998; Oliver, 1996). Rather than requesting help from others, they insist on self-help. Rather than seeing disability as a personal tragedy, they see it as a social problem. Rather than regarding themselves as deviant, they think of themselves as inhabiting a different but quite normal world.

The deaf community typifies the new challenge to ableism. Increasingly, deaf people share a collective identity with other deaf people (Becker, 1980: 107). Members of the deaf community have a common language and culture, and they tend to marry other deaf people (Davis, 1995: 38). Rather than feeling humiliated by the seeming disadvantage of deafness, they take pride in their condition. Indeed, many people in the deaf community are eager to remain deaf even if medical treatment can "cure" them (Lane, 1992). As one deaf activist put it, "I'm happy with who I am ... I don't want to be 'fixed.' ... In our society everyone agrees that whites have an easier time than blacks. But do you think a black person would undergo operations to become white?" (quoted in Dolnick, 1993: 38).

## Summing Up

- Since the nineteenth century, movements to rehabilitate, eliminate, and normalize people with disabilities have emerged.
- Ableism—prejudice and discrimination against people who have disabilities—exists because of intention and neglect.

# AGING

## Sociology of Aging

Disability affects some people. Aging affects us all. Many people think of aging as a natural process that inevitably thwarts our best attempts to delay death. Sociologists, however, see aging in a more complex light. For them, aging is also a process of socialization or learning new roles appropriate to different stages of life (see Chapter 4, Socialization). The sociological nature of aging is also evident in the fact that its significance varies from one society to the next. That is, different societies attach different meanings to the progression of life through its various stages. Menopause, for example, occurs in all mature women. In Canada, we often see it as a major life event. Thus, the old euphemism for menopause was the rather dramatic expression "change of life." In contrast, menopause is a relatively minor matter in Japan. Moreover, while menopausal Canadian women frequently suffer hot flashes, menopausal Japanese women tend to complain mainly about stiff shoulders (Lock, 1993). In many Western countries, complaining about stiff shoulders is a classic symptom of having just given birth. As this example shows, the stages of life are not just natural processes but events deeply rooted in society and culture. As we will see, the same holds for death.

## Aging and the Life Course

All individuals pass through distinct stages of life, which, taken together, sociologists call the **life course**. These stages are often marked by **rites of passage**, or rituals signifying the transition from one life stage to another (Fried and Fried, 1980). Baptism, confirmation, the bar mitzvah and bat mitzvah, high school graduation, college or university convocation, the wedding ceremony, and the funeral are among the best-known rites of passage in Canada. Rituals do not mark all transitions in the life course, however. For example, in Canada people often complain about the "terrible twos," when toddlers defy parental demands in their attempt to gain autonomy. Similarly, when some Canadian men reach the age of about 40, they experience a "midlife crisis," in which they attempt to defy the passage of time and regain their youth. (It never works.)

Some stages of the life course are established not just by norms but also by law. For example, most societies have laws that stipulate the minimum age for smoking tobacco, drinking alcohol, driving a vehicle, and voting. Most societies have a legal retirement age. Moreover, the duration of each stage of life differs from one society and historical period to the next. For example, there are no universal rules about when a person becomes an adult. In preindustrial societies, adulthood arrived soon after puberty. In Japan, a person becomes an adult at 20. In Canada, adulthood arrives at 18 (the legal voting age and the legal drinking age in some provinces) or 19 (the legal drinking age in other provinces). Until the 1970s, the legal voting age was 21 and the legal drinking age ranged between 18 and 21.

Even the number of life stages varies historically and across societies. For instance, childhood was a brief stage of development in medieval Europe (Ariès, 1962 [1960]). In contrast, childhood is a prolonged stage of development in rich societies today, and adolescence is a new phase of development that was virtually unknown just a few hundred years ago (Gillis, 1981). Increased life expectancy and the need for a highly educated labour force made childhood and adolescence possible and necessary. (**Life expectancy** is the average age at death of the members of a population.)

Finally, although some life-course events are universal—birth, puberty, marriage, and death—not all cultures attach the same significance to them. Thus, ritual practices marking these events vary. For example, formal puberty rituals in many preindustrial societies are extremely important because they mark the transition to adult responsibilities. However, adult responsibilities do not immediately follow puberty in industrial and postindustrial societies because of the introduction of a prolonged period of childhood and adolescence. Therefore, formal puberty rituals are less important in such societies.

## Age Cohort

As you pass through the life course, you learn new patterns of behaviour that are common to people about the same age as you are. Sociologically speaking, a category of people born in the same range of years is called an **age cohort**. For example, all Canadians born between 1980 and 1989 form an age cohort. **Age roles** are patterns of behaviour that we expect of people in different age cohorts. Age roles form an important part of our sense of self and

The **life course** refers to the distinct phases of life through which people pass. These stages vary from one society and historical period to another.

**Rites of passage** are cultural ceremonies that mark the transition from one stage of life to another (e.g., baptisms, confirmations, weddings) or from life to death (funerals).

**Life expectancy** is the average age at death of the members of a population.

An **age cohort** is a category of people born in the same range of years.

**Age roles** are norms and expectations about the behaviour of people in different age cohorts.

others (Riley, Foner, and Waring, 1988). As we pass through the stages of the life course, we assume different age roles. To put it simply, a child is supposed to act like a child, an older person like an older person. We may find a 5-year-old dressed in a suit cute but look askance at a lone 50-year-old on a merry-go-round. "Act your age" is an expression that can be applied to people of all ages who do not conform to their age roles. Many age roles are informally known by character types, such as the "rebellious teenager" and "wise old woman." We formalize some age roles by law. For instance, the establishment of minimum ages for smoking, drinking, driving, and voting formalizes certain aspects of the adolescent and adult roles.

We find it natural that children in the same age cohort, such as preschoolers in a park, should play together or that people of similar age cluster together at parties. Conversely, many people find romance and marriage between people widely separated by age problematic and even repulsive.

Differences between age cohorts are sufficiently large in Canada that some sociologists regard youth culture as a distinct subculture. Adolescents and teenagers—divided though they may be by gender, class, race, and ethnicity—frequently share common interests in music, movies, and so forth (Allahar and Côté, 1994).

### Generation

A **generation** is an age group that has unique and formative historical experiences.

A **generation** is a special type of age cohort. Many people think of a generation as people born within a 15- to 30-year span. Sociologists, however, usually define generation more narrowly. From a sociological point of view, a generation comprises members of an age cohort who have unique and formative experiences during youth. Age cohorts are statistically convenient categories, but most members of a generation are conscious of belonging to a distinct age group. For example, "baby boomers" are North Americans who were born in the prosperous years from 1946 to 1964. Most of them came of age between the mid-1960s and the early 1970s. Common experiences that bind them include major historical events (the war in Vietnam, Trudeaumania, Canada's centenary, Expo '67) and popular music (the songs of the Beatles, the Rolling Stones, and the Guess Who). "Generation X" followed the baby boomers. Members of Generation X faced a period of slower economic growth and a job market glutted by the baby boomers. Consequently, many of them resented having to take so-called McJobs when they entered the labour force. Vancouver's Douglas Coupland, the novelist who invented the term Generation X, cuttingly defined a McJob as a "low pay, low-prestige, low-dignity, low-benefit, no-future job in the service sector. Frequently considered a satisfying career choice by people who have never held one" (Coupland, 1991: 5).

Tragedies can help to crystallize the feeling of being a member of a particular generation. For instance, when you are much older you will probably remember where you were when you heard about the attacks of September 11, 2001. Such memories may someday distinguish you from those who are too young to remember these tragic events. The outbreak of World War II may play a similar role in the memory of your grandparents.

The crystallization of a generational "we-feeling" among youth is a quite recent phenomenon. The very ideas of youth and adolescence gained currency only in the nineteenth century because of increased life expectancy, extended schooling, and other factors. Middle-class youth culture often challenged tradition and convention (Gillis, 1981). It was marked by a sense of adventure and rebellion, especially against parents, that manifested itself in political liberalism and cultural radicalism.

Finally, we note that generations sometimes play a major role in history. Revolutionary movements, whether in politics or the arts, are sometimes led by members of a young generation who aggressively displace members of an older generation (Eisenstadt, 1956; Mannheim, 1952).

Woodstock. A generation comprises members of an age cohort who have unique and formative experiences during their youth.

Erica Lansner/Getty Images

## Aging and Inequality

### Age Stratification

**Age stratification** refers to social inequality between age cohorts. It exists in all societies and we can observe it in everyday social interaction. For example, there is a clear status hierarchy in most high schools. On average, students in grade 12 enjoy higher status than those in grade 10 do, while students in grade 10 enjoy higher status than those in grade 9 do.

Age stratification is social inequality between age cohorts.

The very young are often at the bottom of the stratification system. Such age stratification is evident in rich countries today, where poverty is more widespread among children than among adults, and it was even more evident in preindustrial and early industrial societies. In some preindustrial societies, people occasionally killed infants so populations would not grow beyond the ability of the environment to support them. Facing poverty and famine, parents sometimes abandoned children. Many developing countries today are overflowing with orphans and street children. During the early stages of Western industrialization, adults brutally exploited children. The young chimney sweeps in *Mary Poppins* may look cute, but during the Industrial Revolution skinny "climbing boys" as young as four were valued in Britain because they could squeeze up crooked chimney flues no more than half a metre in diameter 12 hours a day. Space was tight, so they worked naked, and they rubbed their elbows, knees, noses, and other protrusions raw against the soot, which was often hot. The first description of job-related cancer appeared in an article published in 1775. "Soot-wart," as it was then known, killed chimney sweeps as young as eight (Nuland, 1993: 202–5).

### Gerontocracy

Some people believe that ancient China and other preindustrial societies were **gerontocracies**, or societies in which the oldest men ruled, earned the highest income, and enjoyed the most prestige. Even today, people in some industrialized countries pay more attention to age than North Americans do. In South Korean corporations, for instance, when a new manager starts work, everyone in the department who is older than the new manager may resign or be reassigned. Given the importance of age seniority in South Korea, it is considered difficult for a manager to hold authority over older employees. Older employees in turn find it demeaning to be managed by a younger boss (Lie, 1998).

A gerontocracy is a society ruled by older people.

Although some societies may approximate the gerontocratic model, its extent has been exaggerated. Powerful, wealthy, and prestigious leaders are often mature, but not the oldest, people in a society. Canada today is typical of most societies, past and present, in this regard. For example, total income rises with age, reaching its peak in the 45–54 age cohort, and then declines through later life (Statistics Canada, 2010k).

In general, true gerontocracy is rare. Like King Lear, seniors often give up power and become marginalized. Even in traditional societies that held seniors in high esteem, aging was not usually seen as an unambiguous good. After all, aging denotes physical and mental decline and the nearness of death. Ambivalence about aging—especially as people reach the oldest age cohorts—is a cultural universal. As one historian writes, "Youth has always and everywhere been preferred to old age. Since the dawn of history, old people have regretted [the loss of] their youth and young people have feared the onset of old age" (Minois, 1989 [1987]).

Just as true gerontocracy is uncommon, so is rule by youth. True, as noted previously, relatively young age cohorts sometimes supply most of a country's political leadership. This happened in revolutionary France in the late eighteenth century, revolutionary Russia in the early twentieth century, and revolutionary China in the mid-twentieth century. However, youthful ruling cadres may become gerontocracies in their own right, especially in non-democratic societies. This was the case with the Russian communist leadership in the 1980s and the Chinese communist leadership in the 1990s; the young generation that grabbed power half a century earlier still clung on as senility approached.

## Theories of Age Stratification

### The Functionalist View

How can we explain age stratification? *Functionalists* observe that in preindustrial societies, family, work, and community were tightly integrated (Parsons, 1942). People worked in and with their family, and the family was the lifeblood of the community. However, industrialization separated work from family. It also created distinct functions for different age cohorts. Thus, while traditional farming families lived and worked together on the farm, the heads of urban families work outside the home. Children worked for their parents in traditional farming families but in urban settings they attend schools. At the same time, industrialization raised the standard of living and created other conditions that led to increased life expectancy. The cohort of retired people thus grew. And so it came about that various age cohorts were differentiated in the course of industrialization.

At least in principle, social differentiation can exist without social stratification. But, according to the functionalists, age stratification did develop in this case because different age cohorts performed functions of differing value to society. For example, in preindustrial societies, older people were important as a storehouse of knowledge and wisdom. With industrialization, their function became less important and so their status declined. Age stratification, in the functionalist view, reflects the importance of each age cohort's current contribution to society, with children and seniors distinctly less important than adults employed in the paid labour force. Moreover, all societies follow much the same pattern. Their systems of age stratification "converge" under the force of industrialization.

### Conflict Theory

*Conflict theorists* agree with the functionalists that the needs of industrialization generated distinct categories of youth and seniors. They disagree, however, on two points. First, they dispute that age stratification reflects the functional importance of different age cohorts (Gillis, 1981). Instead, they say, age stratification stems from competition and conflict. Young people may participate in a revolutionary overthrow and seize power. Seniors may organize politically to decrease their disadvantages and increase their advantages in life.

The second criticism lodged by conflict theorists concerns the problem of convergence. Conflict theorists suggest political struggles can make a big difference in how much age stratification exists in a society. We saw, for example, that child poverty is higher in the United States than in other rich countries. That is because in other rich countries, particularly in Continental Western Europe, successful working-class political parties have struggled to implement more generous child welfare measures and employment policies that lower the poverty level. This suggests that the fortunes of age cohorts are shaped by other forms of inequality, such as class stratification (Gillis, 1981; Graff, 1995). Power and wealth do not necessarily correlate perfectly with the roles the functionalists regard as more or less important. Competition and conflict may redistribute power and wealth between age cohorts.

### Symbolic Interactionist Theory

*Symbolic interactionists* focus on the meanings people attach to age-based groups and age stratification. They stress that the way in which people understand aging is nearly always a matter of interpretation. Symbolic interactionists have done especially important research in community studies of seniors. They have also helped us to understand better the degree and nature of prejudice and discrimination against seniors. For example, one study examined how movies from the 1940s to the 1980s contributed to the negative stereotyping of older people, particularly women. Among other things, it found that young people were overrepresented numerically in the movies (as compared with their representation in the general population) and tended to be portrayed as leading active, vital lives. Older women were underrepresented numerically and tended to be portrayed as unattractive, unfriendly, and unintelligent (Brazzini, McIntosh, Smith, Cook, and Harris, 1997).

## Seniors

Canada's population, along with that of many other rich countries around the world, is greying. In 1901, only 5 percent of Canada's population was 65 or older and the median age of Canadians was just 22.7 years (Novak, 1997). In contrast, according to the 2006 census, the median age was 39.5 years, and 13.7 percent of the population was 65 or older (Statistics Canada, 2007a).

Another way of considering the greying of Canada is to examine **population pyramids**, graphs that show the percentage of the population in various age/sex cohorts (Figure 12.4 and Figure 12.5 on page 314). In 1901, Canada's population pyramid looked very much like a true pyramid. The base of the pyramid was wide, indicating that most people were younger, and the top was small, suggesting a small senior population. By 2050, however, Canada's population pyramid will look more like a T, indicating roughly the same percentage of people in all age cohorts except the oldest, which will be much more numerous. This change in population composition has wide-ranging implications for our social security system, housing, education, employment, and health care.

The number of seniors in Canada has increased for three main reasons. First, nearly a third of Canada's citizens (approximately 10 million people) were born during the 20-year "baby boom" after World War II. During that period, Canadian families averaged four children, resulting in more baby boomers per capita than in the United States, Australia, and New Zealand (Nikiforuk, 1999). Second, life expectancy has increased because of improvements in medical care, sanitation, nutrition, and housing. Third, Canada's current low birth rate contributes to a higher percentage of older people.

**Population pyramids** are graphs that show the percentage of the population in various age and sex cohorts.

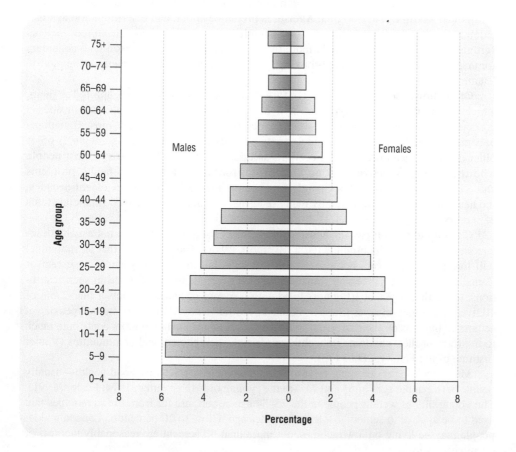

**FIGURE 12.4**
Population Pyramid, Canada, 1901

Source: McVey and Kalbach, 1995.

## FIGURE 12.5
Population Pyramid, Canada, 2050 (projected)

Source: U.S. Census Bureau, International Database.

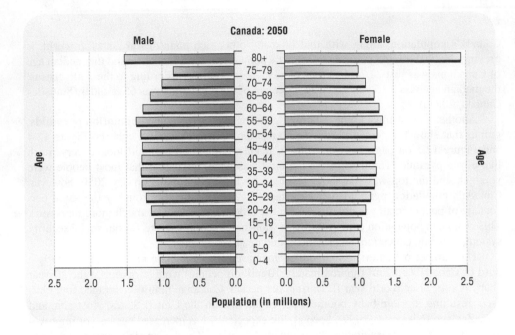

**Ageism** is prejudice and discrimination against older people.

## Ageism and the Decline of Old Stereotypes

Especially in a society that puts a premium on vitality and youth, such as Canada's, being older is still a social stigma. **Ageism** is prejudice about, and discrimination against, older people. Ageism is evident, for example, when older men are stereotyped as "grumpy." Ageism affects women more than men. Thus, the same person who considers some older men "distinguished-looking" may disparage older women as "haggard" (Banner, 1992).

Often, however, seniors do not conform to the negative stereotypes applied to them, which is why the old stereotypes are in decline. In Canada, 65 is sometimes considered the age at which people become seniors since 65 is the age at which most Canadians become eligible to receive Old Age Security benefits. But just because someone is 65 or older does not mean he or she is decrepit and dependent. On the contrary, most people who retire from an active working life are far from being a tangle of health problems and a burden on society. This change is due to the medical advances of recent decades, the healthier lifestyles followed by many older people, and the improved financial status of seniors.

Contrary to stereotypes, the housing arrangements of older people are not usually desolate and depressing (Hochschild, 1973; Myerhoff, 1978). The likelihood that an individual will live in a special-care home increases with age, but in 2001 only about 5 percent of Canadian men and 9 percent of Canadian women over the age of 65 lived in such institutions. More than 7 out of 10 seniors lived with a spouse or alone, and fewer than 2 out of 10 lived with other relatives (Statistics Canada, n.d.). Moreover, although stereotypes depict seniors as burdens on their families, evidence shows that Canada's seniors contribute much to the lives of their children, grandchildren, friends, neighbours, and communities (Vanier Institute of the Family, 2000: 172).

Many sociologists of aging refer to seniors who enjoy relatively good health—usually people between the ages of 65 and 74—as the "young old" (Neugarten, 1974; Laslett, 1991). The young old, as well as people in the 75–84 age cohort, are far from the stereotypes that used to be applied to seniors just a few decades ago. Close to 20 percent of Canada's older people may be living on low incomes, but more than 80 percent are reasonably well off or even well-to-do.

Consider these profiles of older Toronto-area women: Ruth Goldsmith, 76, enjoys financial stability. She exercises every morning (Aquafit, the treadmill, or yoga), meets friends for lunch, goes to the theatre and the symphony, travels to music festivals in Quebec, belongs to a book club, volunteers at the Older Women's Network, visits her sister in England annually, and is planning a trip to Israel. At 72, she learned how to use a computer. She dotes on her daughter and three grandchildren. Her friend, Margaret Hawthorn, 69, has a good pension from her years as a university librarian. She owns a car and a house and enjoys babysitting her grandson once a week. She also enjoys lawn bowling, swimming, and cycling, and has become fluent in Spanish. She travels extensively, sometimes off the beaten path; once she visited Baffin Island. She works for the NDP and is involved in a big garden restoration project. "I have to say that this is the best time—and I've had a reasonably good life," Hawthorn remarks. Nan Cooper, 67, has taken up painting in retirement and has rented an apartment in Italy so she can spend time visiting art galleries. Rosalie Brown, 73, loves dancing—square, ballroom, and line—and complains that she and her friend Margaret Hawthorn are so busy, they have to make appointments to see each other. "I feel I'm into maybe a bit too much," she says. She dates regularly and says it is as pleasurable as when she was younger. In a survey of 5000 older Canadians, two-thirds of respondents said they view retirement as an opportunity to start a new business and the same number said retirement freed them up to pursue a "dream job." Noticeably absent from this vibrant group are old people in rocking chairs eating cat food for supper (Galt, 2006; Kopun, 2006).

The active life of many seniors today is a far cry from traditional stereotypes.

## The "Old Old"

The situation is different for people 85 and older, whom sociologists refer to as the "old old." The rising number of old old concerns many people because the old old are most likely to suffer general physical decline and life-threatening diseases. Among seniors, the old old are also the most likely to face social isolation and poverty.

Significantly, the sex ratio (the number of men compared with the number of women) falls with age. In other words, because women live longer than men do on average, there are more women than men among seniors. This imbalance is most marked in the oldest age cohorts. Therefore, poverty and related problems among the oldest Canadians are in part a gender issue.

Economic inequality between older women and men is largely the result of women's lower earning power when they are younger. Women are entering the paid workforce in increasing numbers, but there are still more women than men who are homemakers and do not work for a wage. Therefore, fewer women than men receive employer pensions when they retire (Nelson and Robinson, 2002). Moreover, women who are in the paid labour force tend to earn less than men do. As a result, when they retire, their employer pensions are generally inferior. Consequently, the people most in need—older women—receive the fewest retirement benefits.

## The Power and Wealth of Seniors

Since the 1960s, Canadian seniors have benefited from rising incomes. In 1951 seniors earned on average about half that of Canadians of working age, but now the annual income of these two categories is close to the same (Statistics Canada, 1998b). Because of income security programs, such as the Guaranteed Income Supplement, the Old Age Security pension, and the Spouse's Allowance, Canadian seniors do not have to rely on welfare any more frequently than people in the general population do. The poverty rate for seniors is about the same as the poverty rate for non-seniors (National Council of Welfare, 1998a).

One reason for the improved economic security of seniors is that they are well organized politically. Their voter participation rate is above average, and they are overrepresented among those who hold positions of political, economic, and religious power. Many groups seek to improve the status of seniors. One of the earliest and most radical groups in North America was the Gray Panthers, founded in 1970, with 50 000 to 70 000 members. Much larger is CARP, Canada's Association for the Fifty-Plus, with about 370 000 members. CARP is a nonprofit association that does not accept funding from any government body. It speaks out on a wide range of issues important to those over 50.

Seniors' activism may have led to a redistribution of resources away from young people. For example, while educational funding has declined, funding has increased for medical research related to diseases that disproportionately affect older people. This redistribution of resources has led to the growth of the belief in some rich countries that seniors are a burden on the economy and especially on the nation's youth. Increasingly, young people in communities with a high proportion of wealthy retired people are expressing resentment (Peritz, 1999). In anticipation of government shortfalls, South Korea requires workers to save 35 percent of their income for retirement. In Japan, government benefits can be cancelled if redistribution of tax money is needed to ensure "equity between the generations" (Peterson, 1997). Whether Canadians are prepared to tolerate such tax burdens and cutbacks is questionable (see Box 12.2).

## BOX 12.2
## It's Your Choice

### A SOCIAL SECURITY CRISIS?

One of the greatest triumphs of public policy has been the development of the public health system, which has led to a substantial increase in life expectancy. Another major public policy achievement is social welfare, especially as it applies to seniors. The combination of social security, medicare, and other government programs goes a long way toward ensuring that seniors are not doomed to poverty and illness.

A longer and more secure lifespan is a wonderful thing. However, some scholars and policymakers worry that a major crisis is looming. Canada may not be able to afford government programs for seniors in the future because of the expected retirement of baby boomers, those born in the 20-year period after World War II. Many Canadians born in that period contribute to social security and other measures to support older people. As the baby boomers begin to retire from the active labour force, however, fewer Canadians will be contributing to government coffers.

Some scholars argue that economic growth and higher immigration could offset the expected decline in the active labour force. However, others argue that we need more concrete measures to deal with the expected crisis in government support for seniors. Some of the possible policy proposals include the following:

- increase national savings
- lower health care costs, especially the disproportionately higher burden of medical costs for seniors
- provide government support only to the truly needy, thereby eliminating or lowering social security and other federal benefits for the well-off

What do you think? Should Canadians worry about the expected crisis in social security and other government programs that support seniors? If you expect the potential crisis to erupt in your lifetime, what should you be doing now to avert the crisis? What are the advantages and disadvantages of each of the policy proposals listed above? What kind of lifestyle do you expect to lead when you are in your 60s, 70s, and 80s? Do you think you will be working full time, or will you be fully or partly retired?

## Summing Up

- The duration and number of life stages varies across societies and historical periods.
- The most powerful people in most societies are middle-aged, while the least powerful are children.
- Discrimination against seniors is a common problem.
- While functionalists hold that age stratification is based on the functional importance of different age groups, conflict theorists note that political struggles can substantially change the distribution of rewards among different age cohorts.
- The rapid aging of Canadian society has profound implications for Canada's health and social security systems.

# DEATH AND DYING

It may seem odd to say so, but the ultimate social problem everyone must face is his or her own demise. Why are death and dying *social* problems and not just religious, philosophical, and medical issues?

For one thing, attitudes toward death vary widely across time and place. So do the settings within which death typically takes place. Although individuals have always dreaded death, in most traditional societies, such as Europe until early modern times, most people accepted it (Ariès, 1982). That is partly because most people apparently believed in life after death, whether in the form of a continuation of life in Heaven or in cyclical rebirth. What also made death easier to accept is that the dying were not isolated from other people. They continued to interact with household members and neighbours, who offered them continuous emotional support. Finally, because the dying had previous experience giving emotional support to other dying people, they could more easily accept death as part of everyday life.

In contrast, we tend to separate dying and death from everyday life. Most terminally ill patients want to die peacefully and with dignity at home, surrounded by their loved ones. Yet about 80 percent of Canadians die in hospitals. Often, hospital deaths are sterile, noiseless, and lonely. Dying used to be public. It is now private. The frequent lack of social support makes dying a more frightening experience for many people (Elias, 1985 [1982]). In addition, our culture celebrates youth and denies death (Becker, 1973). We use diet, fashion, exercise, makeup, and surgery to prolong youth or at least the appearance of youth. This makes us less prepared for death than our ancestors were.

Our reluctance to accept death is evident from the many euphemisms we use as a means of distancing ourselves from it. People used to say that the dead had "entered the Pearly Gates" or had gone to "sing in God's heavenly choir." We are now more likely to say that the dead have "passed away" or "gone to meet their maker" in "a better place" or that they lie in "their final resting place." Sometimes we use humorous expressions as a distancing mechanism. We say that people have "croaked" or "kicked the bucket" or "cashed in their chips" or that they are now "pushing up daisies." These and other similar expressions allow us to separate ourselves symbolically from the horror of death.

Psychiatrist Elisabeth Kübler-Ross's analysis of the stages of dying also suggests how reluctant we are to accept death (Kübler-Ross, 1969). She based her analysis on interviews with patients who were told they have an incurable disease. At first, the patients went into *denial*, refusing to believe their death was imminent. Then they expressed *anger*, seeing their demise as unjust. *Negotiation* followed; they pled with God or with fate to delay their death. Then came *depression*, when they resigned themselves to their fate but became deeply despondent. Only then did the patients reach the stage of *acceptance*, when they put their affairs in order, expressed regret over not having done certain things when they had the chance, and perhaps spoke about going to Heaven.

## Euthanasia

The reluctance of many Canadians to accept death is evident in the debate over euthanasia, also known as mercy killing or assisted suicide (Rothman, 1991). Various medical technologies, including machines that are able to replace the functions of the heart and lungs, can prolong life beyond the point that was possible in the past. This raises the question of how to deal with people who are near death. In brief, is it humane or immoral to hasten the death of terminally ill patients?

**Euthanasia** is any "deliberate act undertaken by one person with the intention of ending the life of another person to relieve that person's suffering, where that act is the cause of death" (McTeer, 1999: 117). A narrower definition of euthanasia involves a doctor prescribing or administering medication or treatment that is *intended* to end a terminally ill patient's life. This form of euthanasia is sometimes referred to as *active euthanasia* inasmuch as it involves the commission of an act. So-called *passive euthanasia* involves intentionally withholding a life-saving medical procedure.

In Canada, assisting suicide or intentional killing, even in an attempt to end suffering, is a crime. In addition, doctors are legally prevented from withholding or withdrawing life-sustaining procedures. They are also legally obliged to ensure that patients whom they believe to be suicidal are prevented from harming themselves. Nevertheless, the reality of modern medicine is that doctors do practise passive euthanasia; not all of them, but rare is the doctor that has not, at the request of the patient, the patient's family, or on his or her own accord, decided to discontinue life-support. Studies also show that many doctors have acquiesced to life-ending drug dosages in cases of advanced terminal illness (Duhaime, 1997).

Many Canadians support a terminally ill person's right to die and believe that doctor-assisted suicide for terminally ill people should be legal. Just over three-quarters of Canadians believe that an individual who helps end the life of a loved one suffering from an incurable and extremely painful illness should not be prosecuted. However, almost 60 percent of Canadians oppose "mercy killing" by a parent of a child who has severe disabilities. Although 42 percent believe that access to euthanasia is necessary for those who are critically ill or have severe disabilities because current nursing-home and end-of-life care is inadequate, almost three-quarters agree that "if people with disabilities or those with chronic or terminal disease had access to adequate pain management and social services, there would be less demand for euthanasia" (Canada NewsWire, 2001).

Montreal physician Balfour Mount, who has been called Canada's father of palliative care, expressed a similar viewpoint when he noted that "our courts voted against euthanasia by the narrowest of margins, while … our governments have failed to give adequate support to palliative care" ("Poor Palliative Care," 2001). Mount warns that unless more palliative care is provided, the "appeal of [euthanasia and assisted suicide] as a 'compassionate' alternative to overcrowded clinical services, inadequate fiscal resources, and increasing family caregiver burden is unlikely to lessen."

Euthanasia is bound to become a major political issue in coming decades as medical technologies for prolonging life improve, the number of older people increases, and the cost of medical care skyrockets. Some people will uphold extending the lives of terminally ill patients by all means possible as an ethical imperative. Others will regard it as immoral because it increases suffering and siphons scarce resources from other pressing medical needs.

**Euthanasia** (also known as mercy killing and assisted suicide) involves a doctor prescribing or administering medication or treatment that is intended to end a terminally ill patient's life.

CP Photo Archive/Chuck Stoody

Sue Rodriguez, who suffered from amyotrophic lateral sclerosis (ALS; also known as Lou Gehrig's disease), launched a legal battle for the right to have a doctor help her die. She argued that the section of the *Criminal Code* that makes assisted suicide a criminal offence violates three rights guaranteed to all Canadians under the *Canadian Charter of Rights and Freedoms*: the right to life, liberty, and security of the person; the right not to be discriminated against on the basis of disability; and the right not to be subjected to cruel and unusual punishment. The Supreme Court of British Columbia dismissed her application. In 1993, the Supreme Court of Canada, in a 5–4 decision, dismissed her appeal.

## Summing Up

- Canadians tend to separate dying and death from everyday life, partly because they are reluctant to accept death as a natural part of life.
- Canadians' attitudes toward death are reflected in the debate over euthanasia, which is bound to become more heated as technology for prolonging life improves and becomes more expensive while the number of older adults soars.

# SUMMARY

1. The human body is a biological wonder. In what sense is it a sociological wonder too? The body's parts, its disabilities, its aging, and its death mean different things and have different consequences for different cultures, historical periods, and categories of people. The human body cannot be fully understood without appreciating its sociological dimension.

2. What is the connection between body type and social status? Because low status influences diet and other factors, it is associated with people of short stature and people who are overweight. In turn, people of short stature and people who are overweight tend to receive fewer social rewards because of their body type.

3. In what sense do people have rights over their own body? Most people believe they should and do have rights over their own body. Advances in medical technology and changing social norms encourage us to transform our bodies through surgery, prosthesis, and other means. However, we do not treat our bodies in idiosyncratic ways. Norms of body practice influence us.

4. Are disabilities defined similarly everywhere and at all times? Have disabilities always been handled in the same way? No. The definition of disability varies over time and place. For example, some people used to consider left-handedness and being Aboriginal as disabilities, but we do not share that view. As far as treatment is concerned, we also see much variation. People with disabilities have traditionally suffered much prejudice and discrimination, but attempts were made from the nineteenth century on to integrate and rehabilitate them. Some governments sought to eliminate people with disabilities from society in the twentieth century. Recently, people with disabilities have begun to organize themselves, assert the normality of disability, and form communities of those with disabilities.

5. What is sociological about the aging process? People attach different meanings to aging in different societies and historical periods. Thus, the stages of life vary in number and significance across societies.

6. Is there a positive correlation between age and status? Although it is true that the young have been, and still are, disadvantaged in many ways, it is rarely true that the eldest people in society are the best off. In most societies, including Canada, people of middle age have the most power and economic clout.

**7.** What are the main approaches to age stratification?
Functionalist theory emphasizes that industrialization led to the differentiation of age cohorts and the receipt of varying levels of reward by each age cohort based on its functional importance to society. This supposedly results in the convergence of age stratification systems in all industrialized societies. Conflict theory stresses the way competition and conflict can result in the redistribution of rewards between age cohorts and the divergence of age stratification systems. Symbolic interactionists focus not on these macrosociological issues but on the meanings people attach to different age cohorts.

**8.** How is Canada aging?
Canada's population is aging rapidly. Between 1901 and 2006 the median age of Canadians increased from 22.7 to 39.5 years, while the proportion of Canadians 65 or older increased from 5 percent to 13.7 percent. The age–sex distribution looked like a pyramid in 1901, but by 2050 all age–sex cohorts but one will be about the same size; only people 80 and over will form a disproportionately large part of the population. As the population ages, the ratio of men to women falls.

**9.** How are seniors faring economically in Canada?
Economically speaking, senior Canadians are faring reasonably well, partly because they have considerable political power. However, economic inequality exists between older women and men, largely because of women's lower earning power when they are younger; they have smaller pensions and fewer assets once they retire.

**10.** If seniors in Canada are doing reasonably well economically and politically, then does this mean that they don't face significant problems in our society?
Older Canadians face much prejudice and discrimination based on age because our society values youth and vitality and because some people think that seniors command a disproportionately large share of societal resources at the expense of young people.

**11.** What is sociological about death and dying?
Attitudes toward death vary widely across time and place, as do the settings within which death typically takes place. For example, many Canadians are reluctant to accept death, as is evident in the debate over euthanasia.

# KEY TERMS

ableism (p. 307)

age cohort (p. 309)

age roles (p. 309)

age stratification (p. 311)

ageism (p. 314)

disability (p. 306)

euthanasia (p. 318)

generation (p. 310)

gerontocracy (p. 311)

impaired (p. 306)

life course (p. 309)

life expectancy (p. 309)

population pyramids (p. 313)

rehabilitation (p. 306)

rite of passage (p. 309)

# WEB RESOURCES

## Companion Website for This Book

http://www.compass4e.nelson.com

Begin by clicking on the Student Resources section of the website. Next, select the chapter you are studying from the pull-down menu. From the Student Resources page you have easy access to additional Weblinks and other resources. The website also has many useful tips to aid you in your study of sociology, including practice tests for each chapter.

## InfoTrac® Search Terms

These search terms are provided to assist you in beginning to conduct research on this topic by visiting http://www.infotrac-college.com:

**age discrimination**
**disability**
**euthanasia**

# Chapter 39

## Be Thin: Contradictions Within the Social Constructions of Beauty and Happiness

SHARON E. ROBERTS

Many of us can identify with unreal expectations placed upon how our bodies look. To many, our bodies are to express our ascribed statuses. Men are expected to be masculine and, through their bodies, they are expected to be strong and physical. Women, on the other hand, are expected to be feminine and more subordinate, so, while many women are expected to be fit and thin, they are not to be too strong (i.e., masculine). This article looks not only at the expectations placed upon our bodies according to our ascribed genders, but at the complex processes that reproduce and replicate those expectations. This happens in ways that can be difficult to pinpoint.

Note: If you are struggling with any issues related to body image, please visit the National Eating Disorder Information Centre (http://www.nedic.ca), the Eating Disorder Foundation of Canada (http://www.edfofcanada.com), or talk to your doctor. As well, there are numerous treatment programs available in Canada (http://www.canadadrugrehab.ca/Eating-Disorder-Treatment.html).

1. What social expectations are placed upon women regarding their appearances? What expectations are placed upon men? What are the differences and similarities between the two?
2. How are these expectations articulated or expressed? Where do they come from?

"Thin" is a ubiquitous message in Western culture as a social construction of beauty and success. Phrases such as never being "too rich or too thin," a saying credited to Wallis Simpson, Duchess of Windsor, have laid the foundation for much of popular culture in the 20th and 21st centuries. The constructions of feminine and masculine ideals in our society mandate strong compliance to certain modes of physique. Women and men are overtly and covertly guided on how to become feminine and masculine beings: women are expected to be youthful, thin, and attractive (e.g., Stice et al. 2000), and males are expected to be muscular (e.g., Frederick et al. 2007). Adherence to these ideals has become an important part of the gendered identity, and the consequences for internalizing these gendered ideals can result in negative **body image** and the potential for eating disorders (e.g., Lawler & Nixon 2011; Stice et al. 2002).

Source: Roberts, Sharon. "Be Thin: Contradictions Within the Social Construction of Beauty and Happiness." Unpublished Manuscript, 2011. Reproduced with permission of the author.

**PART 15**

# BODY DISSATISFACTION AND EATING DISORDERS: MYTHS, FACTS, AND FIGURES

It should be no surprise that the rates of eating disorders (anorexia, bulimia, binge eating, and binge-eating related obesity) are increasing steadily in Canada. Berg et al. (2002) estimate the lifetime prevalence for women as 3.7 percent for anorexia and 4.2 percent for bulimia. Moreover, rates of young Canadians who are obese have doubled from 8.5 percent in 1978/79 to 20.5 percent in 2004 (Statistics Canada 2005), and binge eating disorder is present in a small but significant number of obesity cases— estimates range from 2–25 percent depending on the population studied (Yanovski 1999; 2003). Additionally, body image problems are rampant in our culture.

For example, Schur et al. (2000) examined young girls and boys' beliefs about their bodies, dieting, and dissatisfaction in a sample of children in grades three through six. They found that 50 percent of the 62 participants wanted to be thinner, 70 percent of the children knew about dieting from their families, and 16 percent of the children had already attempted dieting for weight loss. Clearly, our issues with food and dieting begin at an early age.

The common belief that eating disorders and poor body image are problems associated only with white, teenage girls is misguided. Gross and Rosen's (1988) study found evidence of bulimia in girls across all of the racial categories (Asian, Caucasian, Black, and Latina) in their sample (Asian and Caucasians had the highest percentages). Warren et al. (2010) studied Latina youth in the U.S. and found that Latina girls engaged in social comparison and were affected by the internalization of athletic appearance. They felt pressured by the thin ideal and, in some cases, possessed eating pathology. Hesse-Biber et al. (2010) studied African American women and found that those who subscribed more to the "white mainstream culture" were more dissatisfied with their bodies than other African American women who identified with other body types (e.g., fuller figure), and Harris (2006) concludes that "race/ethnic heritage and a high body mass index or heavy body do not necessarily shield African American college women from body dissatisfaction or prevent the development of eating disturbances. African American college women, similar to their European American peers, report dissatisfaction with their bodies and unfavourable appearance evaluations when body mass, preferred weight and weight discrepancy levels are perceived as high" (p. 46).

As such, eating disorders and negative body image are not necessarily restricted by race, nor do they have boundaries in age. Eating disorders commonly develop in the teen years; however, there are numerous cases of people who are in their 30s, 40s, 50s and older who develop eating disorders (e.g., Tolbin et al. 1995). Furthermore, Harriger et al. (2010) report that girls as young as three years old display evidence of internalizing the thin ideal, and children, both female and male, who are as young as seven years old have been diagnosed with anorexia and/ or bulimia and required hospitalization (e.g., Bryant-Waugh et al. 1996).

Males, too, are susceptible to eating disorders, body dissatisfaction, and negative body image problems. The male body has come under more media scrutiny in the past 20 years (Grogan, 2010), and there are implications for internalizing the "ideal" body type (thin with a muscular build) for men, too. With regard to body image, Peat et al. (2011) found that, compared to older men, younger adult men exhibit greater body dissatisfaction. Peplau et al. (2009) explored body image dissatisfaction in gay/straight men and women. Although few differences were found between lesbian and straight women, the researchers found that gay men were at an increased risk of experiencing body dissatisfaction than were heterosexual males. Blouin and Goldfield (1995) compared the self-reports of body image, steroid use, and eating attitudes of male runners, martial artists, and body builders. Body builders reported more desire to bulk up, internalized the thin ideal, had more bulimic tendencies, reported more perfectionism, and used more steroids than the other two categories of male athletes. They also found that steroid use was associated with bulimic tendencies. The authors conclude that male body builders are at a greater risk for body image disturbances and exhibit many of the pathologies associated with eating disordered patients. Overall, Hudson et al. (2007) report that, at the national level, lifetime prevalence estimates of anorexia, bulimia, and binge eating disorder for men are .3 percent, .5 percent, and 2.0 percent. Clearly, men and women of all ages and races need to be considered as we move forward with research on eating disorders, body dissatisfaction, and body image.

## THE ROLE OF MEDIA IN THE CONSTRUCTION OF GENDER AND BEAUTY

One of the main contributions to the construction of gender and physical expectation is media (Lawler & Nixon 2011). Brower and Leon (1999) cite estimates that people in America are exposed to 3000 advertisements daily. Thus, the influence of media, to some extent, is unavoidable. Individuals are inundated with images of the physically "ideal" person—models not only make the merchandise seem appealing, but they also provide an idealized image of what is seemingly a lifestyle choice. The good-looking woman who stands beside a sports car in an advertisement is selling to males a particular image of success—a sense of masculinity derived from wealth, consumerism, and heterosexuality. She is also portraying an "ideally attractive" construction for women, which is a pervasive image in Western culture. Fashion magazines boast thousands of pages containing pictures of thin women and toned men selling products and

services, and movies showcase thin and beautiful actors and actresses who make millions of dollars based on their looks. In essence, images teach us that to be thin is to be happy and wealthy. However, these messages of physical "perfection" and thinness are mixed with other media messages related to food, which is a consumer-based industry, too. Food companies market successfully to consumers by attaching their food products to emotions; advertisements have fused food with notions of family cohesion, rewards, financial success, status, celebration, happiness, release, and escape (see Helmer 1992, for a discussion of how McDonald's achieved this through advertising).

A review of late night television provides a good example of this cultural contradiction. Standard late night television hosts a plethora of fast-food commercials that entice the viewer to purchase "supersized" foods. Infomercials often showcase products that feature ways to consume more food, more quickly, and at a lower cost. Better, cheaper, and faster underlie the main sales pitch for products such as the "George Foreman" grill or the "Magic Bullet Blender," which claims to do "any job in 10 seconds … or less!" Often in the same timeslot on a different channel, other infomercials are focused on how to make consumers lose weight. These infomercials showcase products that are "guaranteed" to make the customer tone up, slim down, and hide "fat." Suzanne Somers' 1980s "ThighMaster," with the sales pitch "squeeze, squeeze your way to shapely thighs" netted a reported six million sales in Canada alone. Other products provide the consumer with "thin" by selling them an alternative to exercise. For example, "Spanx" provides a variety of "comfortable, slimming garments that minimize *figure flaws*" (emphasis added). It is worth noting that young, thin people regularly model these products.

The simultaneously contrasting messages in late night television are intense: eat more, be thin. This is symptomatic of a society where, for most people, food is a consumer choice; the economic

**PART 15**

and technological advances in Western culture have provided the environment that makes food readily available in mass quantities, and the competitive nature of the food industry results in companies vying for consumers' attention by making their products attractive. On the one hand, Westerners are encouraged to be indulgent in every way, including the consumption of food. Food is socially constructed as a symbol of success and wealth, a treat, a celebration, a release, and the advertisements offer justification and reason for indulgence (e.g., Xu & Schwarz 2009; Miao 2011). And thin, in Western culture, is constructed as attractive, sexually appealing, and morally good. These are seemingly incompatible messages. As such, advertising contributes to the problem of over consumption—a problem that is rectified by diet products—while reinforcing the "ideal image" of thin. It should be no surprise that the inherent contradictions in these messages can leave people feeling dissonant and conflicted—the result being the internal conflict that many experience as they consume food and then feel guilty about their food consumption (e.g., Miao 2011). These conditions can contribute to negative body image, body dissatisfaction, or purging behaviours (e.g., Lawler & Nixon 2011), and they can lead to feelings of being out of control (e.g., Berg et al. 2002). This may be exacerbated by individual circumstances, such as age, personal history, or genetic vulnerability.

## BODY DISSATISFACTION AND EATING DISORDERS: BEYOND MEDIA

It would be simplistic and naive to assess these complicated conditions—eating disorders—as being the result of media alone. There are numerous etiological factors to consider. For example, we know that trauma—particularly childhood sexual abuse—can have serious consequences for mental health, triggering over the

long-term eating disorders, depression, and other debilitating behaviour patterns (e.g., Schwartz & Cohen 1996; Berg et al. 2002; Briere & Scott 2007;); however, it is important to note that sexual abuse or assault is not a necessary condition for the onset of an eating disorder (Briere & Scott 2007). Studies have linked childhood trauma most commonly to bulimia (Ackard et al. 2001) as well as anorexia, and binge eating to the point of obesity (Gustafson & Sarwer 2004). In different studies, childhood sexual abuse has also been linked to objectified body consciousness as it relates to depression (theorized in Hyde et al. 2008) and poor body image and dieting in both girls and boys (Logio 2003).

In many cases of eating disorders, those who have experienced a loss of control in other aspects of life use the fixated, complete control over food as a (pathological) mechanism to gain control in their lives. In essence, in these cases, eating disorders are not actually about food at all but rather using food to deal with emotional turmoil. In the initial stages, people are often using power over eating to gain a sense of autonomy in their lives. Ironically, the eating disorder results in a total loss of control and autonomy over time (Berg et al. 2002).

Identity confusion (Erikson 1968) is often theorized to be another factor in eating disorders (e.g., Goodsitt 1985; Zerbe 1993; Berg et al. 2002; Wheeler et al. 2003; Algars et al. 2010), where "a defective sense of self is generally considered a hallmark of eating disorders" (Sigall & Pabst 2005, p. 96). Stein and Corte (2007) have linked disturbances in identity to eating disturbances. In the absence of autonomously acquired identity, whether it is a result of depression, trauma, or general struggles in the transition to adulthood, females are theorized to take on gender role ideologies that are present in media (e.g., Spence 1993). Mussap (2007), who studied gender role stress, concludes that for some women, "adopting the feminine gender role is akin to women internalizing the thin ideal" (p. 346). Thus, sociologists have argued that hyper-feminine ideologies can lead to increased body dissatisfaction and hence more negative self-appraisals. This is where the omnipresence of thin in media can be particularly influential and complicated by the pairing of food with emotion.

From biological and psychological perspectives, there are other etiological factors to consider. Research suggests that clinical patients who suffer with an eating disorder may also comorbidly present with an addictive personality. Davis and Claridge (1998) examined a clinical sample of individuals with anorexia and bulimia. They found that these patients scored high on an addiction scale and that excessive exercise and weight preoccupation were associated with addictive personality and obsessive compulsiveness. Other research (e.g., Brown et al. 2007) has focused on genetic (chromosomal) susceptibility to eating disorders and has found a link between genes and restrictive anorexia and bulimic anorexia. They argue that there may be a genetic susceptibility or predisposition to eating disorders. Brewerton (1995) reported that serotonin dysregulation can be a clinical feature of eating disorders, particularly with bulimia nervosa. Thus, in some cases, physicians may recommend medications, specifically serotonin reuptake inhibitors, to help treat symptoms. The evidence seems to indicate that these kinds of treatments, combined with nutritional and behavioural modification therapy, may be most useful in treating some eating disorders (e.g., Vaswani et al. 2003), although we clearly still have a long way to go in terms of successful treatment.

As such, eating disorders can be understood as the manifestation of serious social, medical, biological, and mental health problems. Research has also shown that comorbidities are common in people who have eating disorders: many people who live with eating disorders are also suffering from other concerning issues such as alcoholism and drug abuse (Piran & Gadella 2007), mental health comorbidities (Salbach-Andrae

et al. 2008), depression (e.g., Rodgers et al. 2010), and/or self-harming behaviours such as cutting (Hintikka et al. 2009). Bradford and Petrie (2008) found a reciprocal relationship between disordered eating and depressive affect, and Tiggerman and Kuring (2004) found that depression and eating disorders were predicted by body objectification.

The seriousness of these disorders cannot be overstated, as eating disorders have high mortality rates (e.g., James et al. 2010). Feingold and Mazzella (1998) state that destructive dieting, body image issues, and sub-clinical eating disorders affect the majority of American females. It is also important to note that it is incorrect to assume that a person must look emaciated to a) have an eating disorder, and b) be at any serious health risk. Bulimia and/or binge eating may result in very different body weights than does anorexia, but all of these disorders yield serious consequences for health and survival. We should never assume that because someone who purges is at a "normal" body weight (or purges and is overweight) that he or she is not at risk for serious medical complications such as electrolyte imbalance, heart arrhythmia leading to heart failure, organ failure, tears in the esophagus, or death. Thus, from a sociological perspective, the ubiquitous nature of thin in Western culture is cause for concern, as the consequences of the omnipresence of thin can be quite severe in terms of the potential for the internalization of the thin ideal (Grogan 2010) and the resulting manifestations—particularly in vulnerable populations.

## CONCLUSION

Eating disorders are extremely complicated conditions that culminate from any number of biological, psychological, and circumstantial factors that are often instigated and/or exacerbated by our social conditions. The mere existence of the "thin" and "beautiful" people in society is not the problem. The challenge relates to the lack of

**PART 15**

variation in this prototype and the constructed ideal physique—a challenge that most individuals will never physically be able to master. Humans come in all shapes and sizes, and the construction of feminine and masculine ideals in our society is, to some degree, at odds with most of our natural physiologies. For most people, it is a physiological impossibility to obtain the standards of beauty that are constructed as ideal, and for many who achieve them, it turns out to be grossly unhealthy. The range of healthy weights that physicians recommend does not necessarily fit in with the standards dictated by our media. The resulting focus on food is often a maladaptive attempt to deal with other personal issues. Unfortunately, a growing proportion of people are pathologically obsessed with forcing themselves to fit the media mold of "perfection." As noted, the role of culture and the resulting societal expectations and norms play a central role in the development and perpetuation of the serious problems discussed in this chapter.

## REFERENCES

Ackard, D., Neumark-Sztainer, D., Hannan, P., French, S., & Story, M. (2001). Binge and purge behavior among adolescents: Associations with sexual and physical abuse in a nationally representative sample: The Commonwealth Fund survey. *Child Abuse & Neglect*, 25, 6, 771–785.

Algars, M., Santtila, P., & Sandnabba, N. K. (2010). Conflicted gender identity, body dissatisfaction, and disordered eating in adult men and women. *Sex Roles: A Journal of Research*, 63(1–2), 118–125.

Berg, K., Hurley, D., McSherry, J., & Strange, N. (2002). *Eating disorders: A patient-centered approach.* Radcliff Medical Press Ltd: Abingdon, United Kingdom.

Blouin, A. & Goldfield, G. (1995). Body image and steroid use in male bodybuilders. *International Journal of Eating Disorders*, 18, 2, 159–165.

Bradford, J. & Petrie, T. (2008). Sociocultural factors and the development of disordered eating: a longitudinal analysis of competing hypotheses. *Journal of Counseling Psychology*, 55, 246–262.

Brewerton, T. (1995). Toward a unified theory of serotonin dysregulation in eating and related disorders. *Psychoneuroendocrinology*, 20, 6, 561–590.

Briere, J. & Scott, C. (2007). Assessment of trauma symptoms in eating disordered populations. *Eating Disorders*, 15, 347–358.

Brower, M. & Leon, W. (1999). *The consumer's guide to effective environmental choices: practical advice from the Union of Concerned Scientists.* New York: Three Rivers Press.

Brown, K, Bujac, S., Mann, D., Campbell, D., Stubbins, M., & Blundell, J. (2007). Further Evidence of Association of OPRD1 & HTR1D Polymorphisms with Susceptibility to Anorexia Nervosa. *Biological Psychiatry*, 61, 3, 367–373.

Bryant-Waugh, R., Cooper, P., Taylor, C. & Lask, B. (1996). The use of the eating disorder examination with children: A pilot study. *International Journal of Eating Disorders*, 19, 4, 391–397.

Davis, C. & Claridge, G. (1998). The eating disorders as addiction: A psychobiological perspective. *Addictive Behaviors*, 23, 4, 463–475.

Erikson, E. H. (1968). *Identity: Youth and crisis.* New York: Norton.

Feingold, A. & Mazzella, R. (1998). Gender differences in body image are increasing. *Psychological Science*, 9, 190–195.

Frederick, D., Buchanan, G., Sadehgi-Azur, L., Peplau, L., Haselton, M., & Berezovskaya, A. (2007). Desiring the muscular ideal: Men's body satisfaction in the United States, Ukraine, and Ghana. *Psychology of Men and Masculinity*, 8, 103–117.

Goodsitt, A. (1985). Self-psychology and the treatment of anorexia nervosa. In Garner and PE Garfinkel (eds) *Handbook of Psychotherapy of anorexia nervosa and bulimia.* Guilford Press, New York.

Grogan, S. (2010). Promoting positive body image in males and females: Contemporary issues and future directions. *Sex Roles*, 63(9–10), 757–765.

Gross, J., & Rosen, J. (1988). Bulimia in adolescents: Prevalence and psychosocial correlates. *International Journal of Eating Disorders*, 7, 1, 51–61.

Gustafson, T. & Sarwer, D. (2004). Childhood sexual abuse and obesity. *Obesity Reviews*, 5, 129–35.

Harriger, J., Calogero, R., Witherington, D., & Smith, J. (2010). Body size stereotyping and internalization of the thin ideal in preschool girls. *Sex Roles: A Journal of Research*, 63(9–10), 609–620.

Harris, S. (2006). Body image attitudes, physical attributes and disturbed eating among African American college women. *Race, Gender & Class*, 13, 1/2, 46–57.

Helmer, J. (1992). Love on a bun: How McDonald's won the burger wars. *Journal of Popular Culture,* 26, 2, 85–97.

Hesse-Biber, S., Livingstone, S., Ramirez, D., Barko, E. B., & Johnson, A. L. (2010). Racial identity and body image among black female college students attending predominately white colleges. *Sex Roles,* 63(9–10), 697–711.

Hintikka, J., Tolmunen, T., Rissanen, M., Honkalampi, K., Kylma, J., & Laukkanen, E. (2009). Mental disorders in self-cutting adolescents. *Journal of Adolescent Health,* 44, 464–467.

Hudson, J., Hiripi, E., Pope, H., & Kessier, R. (2007). The prevalence and correlates of eating disorders in the national comorbidity survey replication. *Biological Psychiatry,* 61, 3, 348–358.

Hyde, J., Mezulis, A., & Abramson, L. (2008). The ABC's of depression: Integrating affective, biological, and cognitive models to explain the emergence of the danger differences in depression. *Psychological Review,* 115, 2, 291–313.

James, A., Clacey. J., Seagroatt, V., & Goldacre, M. (2010). Adolescent inpatient psychiatric admission rates and subsequent one-year mortality in England: 1998–2004. *Journal of Child Psychology and Psychiatry,* 51, 12, 1395–1404.

Lawler, M., & Nixon, E. (2011). Body dissatisfaction among adolescent boys and girls: The effects of body mass, peer appearance culture and internalization of appearance ideals. *Journal of Youth and Adolescence,* 40(1), 59–71.

Logio, K. (2003). Gender, race, childhood abuse, and body image among adolescents. *Violence Against Women,* 9, 8, 931–954

Miao, L. (2011). Guilty pleasure or pleasure guilt? Affective experience of impulse buying hedonic-driven consumption. *Journal of Hospitality and Tourism Research,* 35, 1, 79–101.

Mussap, A. (2007). The relationship between feminine gender role stress and disordered eating symptomatology in women. *Stress and Health: Journal of the International Society for the Investigation of Stress,* 23, 5, 343–348.

Peat, C., Peverl, N., Ferraro, F., & Butler, M. (2011). Age and body image in caucasian men. *Psychology of Men and Masculinity,* 12, 2, 195–200.

Peplau, L., Frederick, D., Yee, C., Maisel, N., Lever, J., & Ghavami, N. (2009). Body image satisfaction in heterosexual, gay, and lesbian adults. *Archives of Sexual Behavior,* 38(5), 713–725.

Piran, N. & Gadalla, T. (2007). Eating disorders and substance abuse in Canadian women: a national study. *Addiction,* 102, 1, 105–113.

Rodgers, R., Paxton, S., & Chabrol, H. (2010). Depression as a moderator of sociocultural influences on eating disorder symptoms in adolescent females and males. *Journal of Youth and Adolescence,* 39(4), 393–402.

Salbach-Andrae, H., Lenz, K., Simmendinger, N., Klinkowski, N., Lehmkuhl, U., & Pfeiffer, E. (2008). Psychiatric comorbidities among female adolescents with anorexia nervosa. *Child Psychiatry and Human Development,* 39, 261–272.

Schur, E., Sanders, M., Steiner, H. (2000). Body dissatisfaction and dieting in young children. *International Journal of Eating Disorders,* 27 1, 74–82.

Schwartz, M. & Cohen, L. (1996). *Sexual abuse and eating disorders.* Philadelphia, PA: Brunner/Mazel.

Sigall, B. & Pabst, M. (2005). Gender literacy: enhancing female self-concept and contributing to the prevention of body dissatisfaction and eating disorders. *Social Sciences Information,* 44, 1, 85–111.

Spence, J. (1993). Gender-related traits and gender ideology: Evidence for a multifactorial theory. *Journal of Personality and Social Psychology,* 64, 4, 624–635.

Statistics Canada. (2005). Adult obesity in Canada. Measured height and weight. Downloaded (www.statscan.ca/english/research/82-620-MIE/2005001/articles/adults/aobesity.htm) on September 29, 2008.

Stein, K. & Corte, C. (2007) Identity impairment and eating disorders: Context and organization of the self-concept in women with anorexia nervosa and bulimia nervosa. *European Eating Disorders Review,* 15, 58–69.

Stice, E., Hayward, C., Cameron, R., Killen, J., & Taylor, C. (2000). Body image and eating related factors predict onset of depression in female adolescents. A longitudinal study. *Journal of Abnormal Psychology,* 109, 438–444.

Stice, E., Presnell, K., & Spangler, D. (2002). Risk factors for binge eating onset: A prospective investigation. *Health Psychology,* 21, 131–138.

Tiggerman, M. & Kuring, J. (2004). The role of body objectification in disordered eating and depressed mood. *British Journal of Clinical Psychology,* 43, 299–311.

Tolbin, D., Molteni, A., & Elin, E. (1995). Early trauma, dissociation, and late onset in the eating disorders. *International Journal of Eating Disorders,* 17, 3, 305–308.

Vaswani, M., Linda, F., Ramesh, S. (2003). Role of selective serotonin reuptake inhibitors in psychiatric disorders: A comprehensive review. *Progress in Neuro-Psychopharmacology and Biological Psychiatry,* 27, 1, 85–102.

**PART 15**

Warren, C., Schoen, A., & Schafer, K. (2010). Media Internalization and social comparison of eating pathology among Latino adolescents: The moderating effect of gender and generational status. *Sex Roles: A Journal of Research*, 63(9–10), 712–724.

Wheeler, H., Wintre, M., & Polivy, J. (2003). The association of low parent-adolescent reciprocity, a sense of incompetence, and identity confusion with disordered eating. *Journal of Adolescent Research*, 18, 4, 405–429.

Xu, J. & Schwarz, N. (2009). Do we really need to indulge? *Journal of Marketing Research*, 46, 25–36.

Yanovski, S.Z. (1999). Diagnosis and prevalence of eating disorders in obesity. In B. Guy-Grand & G. Ailhaud (Eds.), *Progress in obesity research* (pp. 229–236). London: Libby.

Yanovski, S. (2003). Binge eating disorder and obesity in 2003: Could treating an eating disorder have a positive effect on the obesity epidemic? *International Journal of Eating Disorders*, 34, S117–S120.

Zerbe, K. (1993). The body betrayed: women, eating disorders and treatment. *American Psychiatric Press*, Washington DC.

## Critical Thinking Questions

1. Our "culture of thin" is a relatively new phenomenon. Why do you think such a norm developed? What have been the consequences of this norm, besides the emergence of eating disorders?
2. Do men experience this type of pressure as well?

# Environment

# CHAPTER 16

# SOCIOLOGY AND THE ENVIRONMENT

**S. Harris Ali**
YORK UNIVERSITY

# INTRODUCTION

## THE EARTH IN DANGER

Sometimes small, seemingly trivial changes may make huge differences. For instance, very small changes in the temperature of our planet—just a few degrees—may suddenly trigger an avalanche of large-scale environmental changes with enormous consequences for life on Earth. This example highlights our vulnerability to "tipping points." A **tipping point** is a critical threshold (Gladwell, 2002). When a slow and gradual process reaches a tipping point, it will, with little or no warning, rapidly accelerate, causing dramatic changes. Current scientific evidence indicates that the world's ecological systems are coming dangerously close to just such a tipping point. When that tipping point is reached, Earth's environmental system will collapse. Our planet will no longer be able to provide the natural resources we depend on to survive.

Global climate change is one example of how environmental problems may develop incrementally and almost imperceptibly until a tipping point is reached. Scientists have found that intensified industrial activity over the last century has added huge amounts of carbon dioxide and other greenhouse gases to the atmosphere. These gases trap heat, gradually warming Earth. However, once we reach a critical temperature increase, global warming will occur far more rapidly. Accelerated warming will, in turn, lead to the rapid onset of many environmental changes that have serious consequences, including greater frequency of hurricanes and storms, record flooding, reduced biodiversity, extensive droughts, shrinking river flows, extensive bush fires, the diffusion of bacteria and viruses to new areas, the scarcity of many natural resources, and the creation of large numbers of environmental refugees and large weather-related insurance losses that will destabilize global financial markets.

Greater understanding of the role tipping points play in environmental problems has led to the realization that we need to act fast to prevent catastrophe. Sociologists can contribute to these efforts because many environmental problems originate in the relationship between nature and society. For example, the industrial and consumer activities that contribute to climate change are based on collective decisions about how we should structure social institutions and policies. We have the capacity to change them if we want.

In this chapter, I begin by examining how environmental issues and problems are linked to the way societies are organized. I then address some of the chief questions environmental sociologists investigate. First, how do members of society think, feel, and act in relation to environmental issues? Which social factors influence their thoughts, feelings, and actions? Second, how do different social groups affect various strategies for addressing environmental problems? Third, why are environmental risks unevenly distributed in society? What are the implications of the uneven distribution of risk for our health and well-being?

## INCORPORATING THE ENVIRONMENT INTO SOCIOLOGICAL ANALYSIS

Biology and geography were used in the nineteenth century to "explain" and thereby justify the superiority of certain classes, races, and civilizations. Sociology developed partly as a critique of conventional wisdom and an attempt to demonstrate the superiority of *social* explanations of such inequalities. Accordingly, sociologists were reluctant to consider the biophysical environment in their analyses until recently. The emergence of urgent environmental problems in the 1970s led them to reevaluate their bias. They came to appreciate that environmental problems have social *and* biophysical bases. Climate change is a case in point.

### Climate Change as a Sociological Issue

Climate change is partly the result of human intervention in nature, such as industrial and transportation activities that burn fossil fuels (oil, coal, natural gas, and so on) which, in turn, release greenhouse gases. Most societies have developed large-scale institutional structures and a whole way of life based on cars and factories that require fossil fuels to function. To a degree, we are locked in to a high-carbon society, and the coal, petroleum, and automobile industries have helped to keep things that way (Urry, 2011). These powerful players curry the favour of politicians, criticize the science that supports climate change, and lobby against environmentalists who demand new industrial practices and environmental policies. Not surprisingly, therefore, much of environmental sociology focuses on the relationships among industry, the state, and the environmental movement, including the role the mass media play in these relationships. To help understand these matters, it is useful to consider "the tragedy of the commons" (Hardin, 1968).

### The Tragedy of the Commons

The environmental commons consists of the natural resources that we share and depend on, such as the air, water, and soil. Tragedy arises when people try to maximize their personal economic gain by exploiting the commons. For example, industrial pollutants may enter the air and contaminate it. Currently, the cost of cleaning up the air falls not to the private company that caused the pollution but to the party responsible for taking care of the commons, namely the state (and, by extension, taxpayers and society at large). In this sense, the private company enjoys a "free ride." It profits from increased production but does not have to pay the costs associated with air pollution because all members of society share them. We refer to the pollution as an **externality** because its cost is externalized from the private company to the state and society. The tragedy of the commons grows when many companies engage in detrimental environmental pursuits. Motivated by profit, they all look for a free ride. If this practice is sufficiently widespread and enduring, the commons will be destroyed. Everyone will breathe foul air and pay the environmental and health consequences. Today, threats to the global commons are widespread.

## THE DEVELOPMENT OF ENVIRONMENTAL AWARENESS AND CONCERN

Although environmental issues have always existed, they did not become prominent until the 1970s. Until then, analysts emphasized protecting natural resources. They did not question the industrial processes that threatened them. Their outlook began to change when Rachel Carson published *Silent Spring* (1962). Carson documented how chemicals in the environment could transform a world full of life and the sounds of the wilderness into a world enshrouded in silence. She focused in particular on the effects of the pesticide DDT on the food chain. DDT was used indiscriminately after World War II. Its pervasiveness, combined with strong evidence of its dangers, made the silent spring scenario feasible and frightening. A movement sprang up to protect the environment from chemical contamination and demand more government regulation of industrial activity. In response, the chemical industry mobilized resources to counter the movement's claims. The confrontation became a dispute that politicians could not ignore.

In 1968, the environmental movement gained impetus when a group of European industrialists, business advisers, and civil servants known as the Club of Rome became convinced that governments' environmental policies were short-sighted and dangerous. They commissioned researchers to develop computer models to extrapolate the effects of continued industrialization, technological development, natural resource depletion, pollution, food production, and population growth to 2010 based on existing trends. Published in 1972, the Club of Rome report painted a picture of total societal collapse because of inadequate food, too much pollution, and insufficient natural resources (Meadows, Meadows, Randers, and Behrens, 1972). These findings reinforced the idea that industrial growth had to be curbed to prevent catastrophe.

In 1973, war broke out between Israel and its neighbouring Arab states. Because the West supported Israel, the Arab states stopped the flow of oil to the West, causing a crisis that drove home the environmental movement's message: many natural resources are in short supply. In the following years, government agencies in Canada and abroad established new environmental laws and agencies in response to this message.

During the 1980s, governments and societies grappled with two environmental problems of global proportions: ozone depletion and climate change. A decade earlier, scientists had predicted that chlorofluorocarbons (CFCs), a class of chemicals used as a refrigerant and a solvent for cleaning metals, could rapidly destroy Earth's ozone layer. The ozone layer filters out ultraviolet radiation from sunlight and thereby protects us from such ailments as skin cancer, immune system disorders, snow blindness, retinal damage, and cataracts. In 1985, scientists verified the earlier prediction. They found an enormous hole in the ozone layer over the Antarctic. Action was swift. Coordinated international efforts led to the banning of CFCs in 1987.

During the same period, some people raised concern about other chemicals arising from industrial activity, namely carbon dioxide and methane, and the ensuing problem of global climate change.

Policies to curb carbon dioxide production are contentious because they affect so many industries and consumers. Sharp conflict has erupted between climate change supporters and industry-led skeptics, each side arguing the scientific basis of their claims. The existence of benign chemical alternatives for CFCs allowed governments to take quick action to solve that problem, but no quick fix is available for the carbon dioxide issue. The pervasiveness of carbon dioxide, produced by burning wood, coal, and oil, complicates matters.

In light of the magnitude of environmental problems, the United Nations World Commission on Environment and Development published *Our Common Future* in 1987. It introduced the idea of **sustainable development.** As an industrial strategy, sustainable development recognizes the dual needs of protecting the environment and allowing economic growth. The idea was to adopt industrial strategies that meet the needs of the present generation without compromising the ability of future generations to meet their own needs. Many of the policies and actions that are needed to move sustainable development forward can happen only if there is "buy-in" from the public. For this reason, it is important to determine the degree to which environmental attitudes and behaviours are changing in the direction of environmental sustainability.

## ENVIRONMENTAL CONCERN

### Environmental Attitudes

According to sociologist Ulrich Beck's (1992) **risk society thesis,** in the optimistic decades immediately preceding World War II, the developing welfare states of the Western world were preoccupied with issues related to the distribution of social goods, including wealth, educational opportunities, consumer goods, income, and property. In contrast, over the last few decades, we have become preoccupied with issues related to the distribution of social "bads," chief among them the environmental risks and externalities produced by industry. For Beck, this switch has served as an impetus for individuals and institutions to start questioning the industrial basis of people's relationship to the environment. Previously, the environment was not an issue because any risks that were produced were simply dismissed as the "price of progress" and ignored. In the risk society, we ignore such issues as global warming and ozone depletion at our peril.

Figure 16.1 shows that, although environmental concern has been on the upswing in Canada in recent decades, it appears to follow an **economic contingency** logic (Buttel, 1975). Specifically, a larger proportion of the population considers environmental issues important during good economic times, while a smaller proportion considers environ-

**FIGURE 16.1**   ENVIRONMENTAL CONCERN IN CANADA (1972–1985) AND ONTARIO (1986–2009)

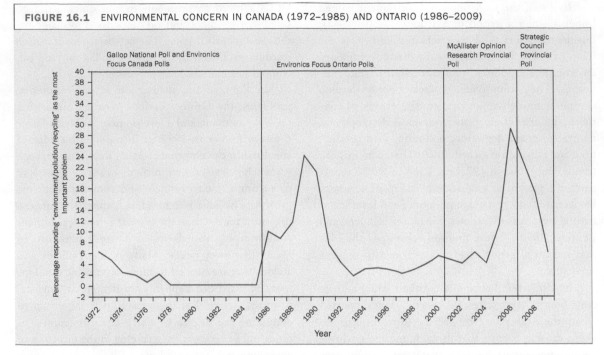

mental issues important during times of economic hardship. Thus, Figure 16.1 reveals a decline in environmental concern during the recessions in the early 1990s and around 2007. Still, many Canadians regard environmental problems as important even in the worst of economic times (see Figure 16.2). The realization persists that we need to confront environmental issues no matter what.

## Environmental Behaviour

Although surveys show that many people are sympathetic to environmental issues, they do not necessarily modify their behaviour accordingly. What accounts for inconsistency between environmental attitudes and behaviour? Sociologists have proposed several explanations.

Anthony Giddens (2009) argues that environmental issues are "back-of-the-mind" rather than "front-of-the-mind" issues because many environmental dangers, no matter how frightening they may appear, are not tangible, immediate, or visible in day-to-day life. Environmental issues are also kept on the back burner because of a psychological tendency known as **future discounting**. People find it difficult to give the same amount of consideration and thought to the future as they do to the present.

Present reality hits home more than future possibilities do. The future is therefore discounted. As such, a small reward offered now will normally be taken in preference to a much larger one offered at some undetermined point later. Future discounting has big implications for how people act in response to environmental problems. It means that many people are not inclined to change environmentally dangerous behaviour because of the current benefits they receive from it.

The inconsistency between environmental attitudes and behaviour is further complicated by the influence of "Jevon's paradox"—as we become more efficient in the use of a natural resource, the cost of using it falls and we then use more of it (Cato, 2011: 153). Environmental savings are thus soon lost. For instance, people may switch to low-energy light bulbs but they may soon realize that using them saves money, so they leave their lights on longer. The same may happen with the introduction of more fuel-efficient cars. People save money on gas by purchasing such vehicles, so they feel justified in going on more frequent or longer trips. Consequently, the rate of gas consumption remains high.

The **framing** of an environmental problem also influences the relationship between attitudes

**FIGURE 16.2    THE NEED TO FOCUS ON THE ENVIRONMENT**

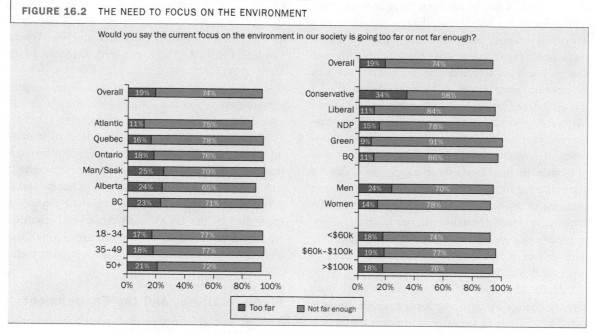

In December 2009, about three-quarters of the Canadian population felt that the current focus on the environment was not going far enough. Notice the variation among provinces and the political parties on this point. What do you think could account for this?

SOURCE: Harris/Decima. (2009). "In spite of recession, environment remains a high priority." On the World Wide Web at http://www.harrisdecima.com /sites/default/files/releases/2009/08/24/hd-2009-08-24-en275.pdf (retrieved 13 February 2012).

and behaviour. Framing refers to the way people interpret and give meaning to events and things in their social settings. When people enter a social setting, they frame it by asking themselves, in effect, "What's going on here?" (Goffman, 1974: 8). Framing renders what would otherwise be meaningless into something that we take into account when interacting. How something is framed therefore influences how people act. If people regard an environmental problem as significant, they may act on it. Otherwise they may not. For social constructionists, such considerations form the basis for analyzing environmental issues.

## THE SOCIAL CONSTRUCTION OF ENVIRONMENTAL ISSUES

How is a problem transformed from a nonissue to an issue that attracts public attention and political interest? The social constructionist perspective focuses on the stages in that process (Hannigan, 2006). In the first stage, people *assemble* a claim or complaint about an environmental problem they regard as undesirable. Scientists typically assemble

claims regarding environmental problems. Next, the claim must be brought to people's attention. Typically, the mass media serve as the platform for publicizing it. Popularizers, such as David Suzuki, and celebrities, such as Pamela Anderson, often play an important role in publicizing environmental claims because their fame allows them to grab the media spotlight. Environmental activists may also try to lure the mass media by drawing on dramatic visual images—for example, photographs of the clubbing of baby seals in Labrador. Coverage of high-profile events, such as the awarding of the 2007 Nobel Peace Prize to the Intergovernmental Panel on Climate Change and former U.S. vice-president Al Gore, serve much the same purpose.

## THE SOCIAL CONSTRUCTION OF CLIMATE CHANGE

People often contest claims about environmental problems, especially if the claims have wide-ranging political and economic implications. Consider climate change. Reducing the emission of greenhouse gases requires massive change in the way industry and government operate, as well as the lifestyles we will be able to pursue. Conflict has been fierce between those calling for action on climate change and those who deny its existence. Many of the latter have backing from powerful corporations. Evidence for climate change has been accumulating for some time. The Intergovernmental Panel on Climate Change (IPCC) was established by the United Nations and the World Meteorological Organization to collect and summarize relevant evidence. The IPCC consists of thousands of scientists who interpret tens of thousands of climate studies. Based on levels of carbon dioxide accumulating in tree rings, coral reefs, and ice core columns from the Arctic, the IPCC concluded that scientific evidence clearly indicates a dramatic rise in greenhouse gas since the time of industrialization. This in turn is linked to increased surface temperature (see Figure 16.3).

Much is at stake if actions are taken to curb climate change by reducing fossil fuel use. Because fossil-fuel-intensive industry represents the largest contributor to climate change, it has a particularly strong responsibility to curb fossil fuel extraction and use. Sociologists have found, however, that fossil-fuel-intensive industries have organized to discredit scientific research on climate change, sow doubt among the public by claiming that the research is erroneous or a hoax, and influence politicians to avoid passing meaningful environmental legislation.

Oil industry interests in particular have organized themselves covertly through front operations, such as the Global Climate Coalition and the World Climate Council (McCright and Dunlap, 2010; Urry, 2011).

The competing claims of those acknowledging climate change and the skeptics highlight the difference between popular and scientific truth (Derber, 2010). Popular truth refers to knowledge that most people in a society believe to be true. Scientific truth refers to knowledge established by scientific methods and on which the great majority of scientists agree. It is clear that the phenomenon of climate change, as confirmed by the IPCC, is an established scientific truth. Yet powerful corporate interests, by deliberately creating doubt, seek to influence popular truth, often through the mass media.

## Media, Culture, and the Environment

Popular culture plays an important role in influencing people's environmental attitudes and behaviours. In the decades following the energy crisis of the mid-1970s, depictions of a dark environmental future proliferated in Western popular culture. Such films as *Blade Runner*, *Total Recall*, and *The Day After Tomorrow* painted a picture of a time when Earth's environment is ruined. Misery, poverty, oppression, violence, disease, scarcity, and pollution

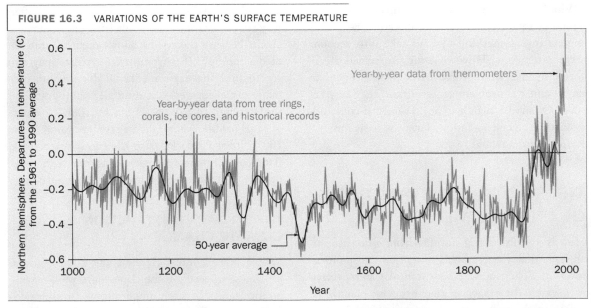

**FIGURE 16.3**   VARIATIONS OF THE EARTH'S SURFACE TEMPERATURE

SOURCE: Pearce, Fred, 2010. "Controversy behind climate science's 'hockey stick' graph." On the World Wide Web at http://www.guardian.co.uk /environment/2010/feb/02/hockey-stick-graph-climate-change (retrieved 11 February 2012). Copyright Guardian News & Media Ltd. 2010.

are everywhere. The popularity of such films raised environmental consciousness among the public (Buell, 2004). More recently, *Avatar*, the highest-grossing film ever, had a strong environmental theme. Set in 2154, the film tells the story of a powerful corporation mining a faraway planet for a valuable mineral. In the process, the corporation seeks to eradicate the indigenous people and the natural environment. Events now taking place in northern Alberta's tar sands region apparently inspired the movie.

The news media also play a significant role in framing environmental issues. They often cover environmental problems and issues precisely because the controversy associated with them is filled with dramatic moments. Environmental movements sometimes deliberately employ sensationalistic techniques to draw media attention (Hannigan, 2006). For instance, they may stage "morality plays" in which environmental group members present themselves as the idealistic and morally good protectors of the environment, challenging whalers, loggers, and nuclear operators who are depicted as villains in a David-versus-Goliath confrontation. For their part, journalists may themselves be involved in the framing process by covering environmental issues in ways they know will resonate with a larger audience. Thus, the coverage of an environmental issue might, for example, be framed in terms of health and safety, bureaucratic bungling, or good citizenship.

Greenpeace activists confronting whaling ships.
SOURCE: © Rex Weyler

# NATURAL RESOURCES

## NONRENEWABLE RESOURCES

We can classify natural resources according to their quantity and ability to regenerate. Nonrenewable resources are finite in quantity and therefore exhaustible since they can only be used once. Oil is an example. The finite quantity of nonrenewable resources has significant economic implications because resource scarcity results in high prices for the commodity in question (see Box 16.1). No big oil discoveries have been made since the 1970s; we have reached **peak oil** production and can expect only declining production in the future. We are now consuming four barrels of oil for every new barrel discovered (Urry, 2011: 78). Oil extraction has become problematic because sources that are more difficult and expensive to exploit must now be tapped. For instance, some analysts believe that, if we factor in externalities paid by taxpayers, the cost of extraction will soon be higher than the price we pay for oil from the Alberta tar sands. The technical difficulties involved in extracting oil from the tar sands means that tar sands oil generates three times the greenhouse gas emissions of normal oil extraction while consuming huge amounts of water and energy (Nikiforuk, 2010: 3).

Peak oil represents a sociological tipping point. Beyond the peak, our entire way of life will change. Resource and energy struggles will become a defining feature of our society. Experts predict that the full force of peak oil will be felt within a few years (Urry, 2011; see Box 16.2).

## RENEWABLE NATURAL RESOURCES

In contrast to fossil fuels, forests are renewable if we take care to ensure that new trees replace those that are harvested. In practice, renewal may not occur as quickly as needed. Some types of trees, such as those in the old growth forests of British Columbia, take centuries to grow. Similarly, overfishing may not allow fish stocks to replenish, as was the case with the cod fishery in Newfoundland in the early 1990s. The government had to impose a moratorium on cod fishing in 1992 to give the cod an opportunity to replenish, and only recently has hope been expressed that commercial fishing may soon resume. Some renewable natural resources—sunlight, gravity, wind power, and tidal wave power—are inexhaustible for all practical purposes. Such inexhaustible resources are widely considered to be critically important for sustainable development.

## BOX 16.1    BOOMTOWNS: THE CASE OF FORT McMURRAY

Boomtowns are predicated on the exploitation of natural resources. Since natural resources are usually located in remote and sparsely populated areas, their extraction requires people to migrate to the boomtown. The resulting population increase typically results in rapid and dramatic social change. For example, a greater number of salaried workers may lead to an infusion of money in the local economy, but this in turn may cause inflation in prices and rents. The existing community infrastructure may not be able to accommodate the rapidly increasing population, leading to a housing shortage and strain on the resources available for medical treatment, education, law enforcement, and public assistance. Increased rates of crime, divorce, suicide, alcoholism, and stress often follow (England and Albrecht, 1984; Freudenburg, 1984; Gramling and Brabant, 1986).

The transformation of Fort McMurray, Alberta, the heart of the province's booming tar sands industry, is a case in point (Nikiforuk, 2010):

- Fort McMurray's population growth has been 9 to 12 percent annually. About 100 000 people now live in the regional municipality.
- Nearly half the city's population comes from poor fishing communities in Newfoundland and Labrador. In total, about 340 000 people from the east coast have migrated to Alberta in the past few decades to supply labour power for the petroleum industry.

- Housing in Fort McMurray is scarce and expensive. The price of a single-family home climbed from $174 000 to more than $600 000 in a decade—twice the average price of a home in Canada.
- Inflation is rampant.
- It takes 40 minutes to order a cup of coffee at Tim Hortons. Lineups at the banks on payday can be 60-people deep.
- In summer, homeless Aboriginal peoples and drug addicts sleep under cars or in tents amid piles of garbage by the Syne, a small channel of water near downtown.

Fort McMurray
SOURCE: © Larry MacDougal/The Canadian Press.

SOURCES: Nikiforuk, Andrew. (2010). *Tar Sands: Dirty Oil and the Future of a Continent*. Vancouver: Greystone Books; http://homeprosgroup.com /fort-mcmurray (retrieved 20 February 2012).

## BOX 16.2    ENVIRONMENTAL MANAGEMENT ON EASTER ISLAND

Famous for its gigantic stone statues conspicuously sticking out from a dramatically desolate environmental wasteland, Easter Island is a 171-square-kilometre (66-square-mile) island in the South Pacific. Located 3700 kilometres (2300 miles) west of Chile, Easter Island is "the most remote habitable scrap of land in the world" (Diamond, 2011: 79). Because the island lacks significant natural resources, it is a mystery how nearly 400 statues, 4.5 to 21.3 metres (15 to 70 feet) high and weighing 9 to 245 metric tons (10 to 270 tons), could have been constructed or transported to the island.

However, archaeologists have found that the island was once thickly forested. Numerous tribes competed against one another to demonstrate their status by constructing and transporting bigger and bigger statues. Eventually, the competition required so much wood, rope, and food that everyone wound up losing. Natural resources became so badly depleted

that the island could no longer sustain human life. With nowhere to flee, the Easter Islanders died off.

Is the world today's Easter Island, a worst-case scenario of what lies ahead for the planet?

Easter Island
SOURCE: © iStockphoto/Thinkstock.

Canada is a country of vast natural resources but abundance may not translate into wealth for all. Why not? To answer this question, we must understand how profits generated from resource extraction are unequally distributed across society and why this is allowed to occur.

## THE RESOURCE CURSE

In Canada, natural resources are owned by the government. The government issues a licence for a private corporation to extract natural resources and is paid a royalty for this right. Usually, the royalty is a percentage of the revenue obtained through its use. In absolute terms, royalty rates for certain natural resources are very low. For example, at 39 percent of gross revenue, Alberta has one of the lowest royalty rates for oil extraction in the world (see Figure 16.4). Nevertheless, the amount of revenue generated from oil royalties enables Alberta to forgo imposing a provincial sales tax on its citizens and to collect income tax at a comparatively

low rate. In fact, the province collects more revenue from oil than it does from taxpayers. This situation has significant social and political consequences.

One consequence is that the public is less likely to scrutinize how the government spends public funds than would be the case if they were taxed at a higher rate. Taxation, it turns out, strengthens democracy. In turn, the government is less inclined to feel that it has to answer to the public. This is seen, for instance, in the Alberta government's failure to measure oil production data and report oil royalties accurately (Alberta Royalty Review Panel, 2007). At the same time, heavy dependence on resource royalties obliges the government to please the petroleum industry. For example, not wanting to bite the hand that feeds it, the government is disinclined to strictly regulate the environmental impact of the petroleum sector (Nikiforuk, 2010).

Such situations as those just described have led sociologists to conclude that ownership and licensing

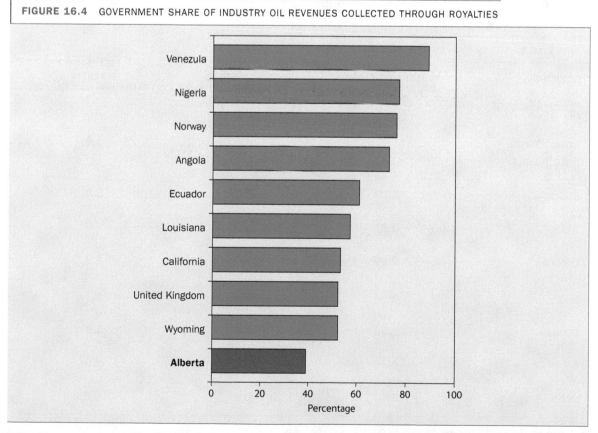

**FIGURE 16.4**   GOVERNMENT SHARE OF INDUSTRY OIL REVENUES COLLECTED THROUGH ROYALTIES

SOURCE: United States Government Accountability Office. Data supplied to the Alaska State Legislature, 2006. (GAO-07-676R).

arrangements used to govern natural resources in resource-rich countries amount to a **resource curse** that hampers democracy, increases corruption, and creates injustice (Friedman, 2006). In extreme cases, including those in Saudi Arabia and the other oil-rich Gulf states, autocratic government becomes firmly entrenched.

# ENVIRONMENTAL GOVERNANCE

Environmental governance refers to attempts by those in power to regulate and alleviate environmental problems (Davidson and Frickel, 2004). Students of environmental governance explore how environmental policies are developed and implemented, and how government interacts with industry, social movements, and consumers in addressing environmental issues.

The capacity of a state to regulate activities that have environmental consequences depends partly on its sovereign power, or its ability to rule without external interference. Many environmental threats are not confined to a particular locality or jurisdiction; they are international in scope. Cooperation among states is required to address them. For instance, the

need to regulate the emission of greenhouse gases on the part of each country led to heated disputes about sovereignty rights at the 1992 United Nations Conference on Environment and Development in Rio de Janeiro, the 1997 United Nations Framework Convention on Climate Change Conference in Kyoto, and the 2011 follow-up conference in Copenhagen. Some countries, including the United States, Canada, and Saudi Arabia, strongly oppose the imposition of regulations that would limit the extent to which their domestic industries are able emit greenhouse gases. Another example of this type of dispute occurred in 2008 when the Canadian government lobbied against proposed American legislation that would ban the United States from buying oil from the Alberta tar sands because extracting and refining it releases more pollutants than conventional petroleum production does. The Canadian lobby wanted to ensure a market for the oil despite its harsh environmental consequences (Nikiforuk, 2010).

As Table 16.1 and Figure 16.5 suggest, Canada has a poor record on the environmental front. The 1988 Canadian Environmental Protection Act could have been an important regulatory tool for the state.

**TABLE 16.1**  TOP CARBON DIOXIDE EMITTERS, 2011

| COUNTRY | PERCENT OF GLOBAL $CO_2$ EMISSIONS (A) | SHARE OF WORLD POPULATION (B) | INDEX OF IRRESPONSIBILITY (A/B) |
|---|---|---|---|
| China | 23.71 | 19.4 | 1.2 |
| United States | 17.91 | 4.6 | 3.9 |
| India | 5.47 | 17.1 | 0.3 |
| Russia | 5.28 | 2.1 | 2.5 |
| Japan | 3.77 | 1.9 | 2.0 |
| Germany | 2.59 | 1.2 | 2.2 |
| Iran | 1.84 | 1.1 | 1.7 |
| **Canada** | **1.80** | **0.5** | **3.6** |
| South Korea | 1.78 | 0.7 | 2.5 |
| United Kingdom | 1.61 | 0.9 | 1.8 |

SOURCE: Calculated from Germanwatch (2011: 2).

**FIGURE 16.5**   CANADA'S GREENHOUSE GAS EMISSIONS (1990–2007)

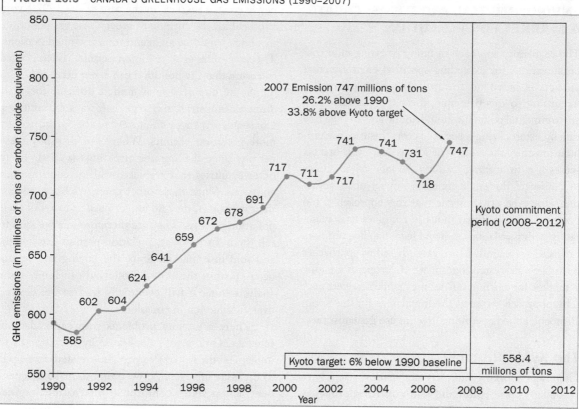

The greenhouse gas emission level that Canada committed itself to reach by 2012 under the Kyoto Agreement is 6 percent below the 1990 level. The graph shows that over the last two decades, the amount of greenhouse gas emissions has in fact increased dramatically.

SOURCE: Canada's 2007 Greenhouse Gas Inventory: A Summary of Trends (Environment Canada). Figure 1: Canada's GHG Emissions 1990–2007, on the World Wide Web at http://www.ec.gc.ca/ges-ghg/default.asp?lang=En&n=61B9E974-1 Environment Canada. Reproduced with the permission of the Minister of Public Works and Government Services, 2012.

However, because of consistent lobbying efforts by industry, the Act was revised in 1999 to emphasize the replacement of mandatory penalties with voluntary measures, self-regulation, and the establishment of regulations by nongovernmental bodies. An examination of investigations and inspections of possible Act violations from 1989 to 2008 found that the number of warnings increased but the number of persecutions declined (Girard, Day, and Snider, 2010). One factor accounting for this trend involves big budget cuts to Environment Canada over the years; warnings are cheaper and faster than investigations are.

## INDUSTRY, ECONOMY, AND THE ENVIRONMENT

From an environmental point of view, the material basis of our economy is organized in a linear fashion. This means that raw natural resources are first extracted from the earth, processed and refined into purer form, and used to manufacture commodities. The commodities are then transported to retailers, where consumers buy them. Once they no longer satisfy consumer needs, the commodities are discarded. Waste products end up in landfills.

Each stage of this linear economy—resource extraction, processing, commodity transport, wholesale and retail sale, consumption, and postconsumption—has its own environmental impacts. For example, with resource extraction, such materials as fossil fuels and iron ore are taken from the environment, but farmland or forested areas may be destroyed in the process. During other stages, environmental impacts usually take the form of solid, liquid, and gas emissions. Governments direct much regulatory attention to controlling or limiting these emissions. Clearly, the environment and the economy are intimately linked.

## THE BUSINESS SOLUTION TO ENVIRONMENTAL PROBLEMS: CREATE A MARKET FOR POLLUTION

The regulatory approach of fining or taxing industrial organizations for exceeding specified environmental impacts is based on the **polluter pays principle.** According to this principle, the party producing an environmental pollutant should not be able to get a free ride by externalizing associated costs. Instead, the polluter must pay the costs. The idea is that a fine or a tax serves as a disincentive, causing the industry to reduce or eliminate the environmental impact of its activities. However, critics argue that this approach is too coercive. They say that industry complies only reluctantly with regulations to avoid legal liability, taxation, or insurance claims. More recently, other approaches have been suggested, one of which proposes creating a market for buying and selling "pollution permits." This approach serves as the foundation for the Kyoto Protocol, aimed at curbing greenhouse gas emissions.

### The Kyoto Protocol

Generally speaking, industry and nation states have tended to oppose **command-and-control approaches** to regulating their activities for the purpose of environmental protection. Such approaches are based on the government issuing commands to industry to adopt environmentally protective practices and to control environmentally harmful emissions by adhering to certain regulations. One of the objections to this approach raised by industry is that it fails to give industry any room to adopt environmentally better practices on their own terms. That is, if industry is to implement changes to their practices, they want to do so according to their own schedule and capacity. In theory, marketable pollution permit schemes—also called "cap-and-trade"—allow such flexibility.

Here is how cap-and-trade works in principle: National or international governmental bodies set an absolute limit on the total amount of a certain pollutant that can be emitted. This limit (or cap) is to be reached by a certain date. For example, the target of the Kyoto Protocol was to reduce overall global emissions of greenhouse gases by at least 5.2 percent below 1990 levels by 2012 (Giddens, 2009: 186). To reach this cap, each country must cut emissions by a certain amount. As such, each country is allowed or permitted to pollute, but at a level significantly lower than before. The right to pollute must be purchased in the form of a permit from the national or international agency that runs the newly created market. In the case of the 1997 Kyoto Protocol for the curbing of greenhouse gas pollution, this body would be an agency of the United Nations. The total number of pollution permits issued is fixed to ensure that the pollution cap is not exceeded.

Some countries may find it difficult for their domestic industries to change their ways and emit less. Consequently, these countries will be forced to buy more pollution permits. Where can they buy these permits since the amount of permits is fixed? From other countries that are successful in reducing their emissions. Since these other countries have reduced their emissions, they no longer need as many of their pollution permits. They are therefore in a position to sell them. In this way, pollution permits are bought and sold in a market. Since the buying and selling occurs within the overall pollution cap limit, some analysts think it will eventually lead to the desired overall reduction in emissions.

There are many problems with cap-and-trade schemes. One is well illustrated by the attempt to implement the Kyoto Protocol. It is related once again to the issue of sovereignty—trying to make independent nation states conform to international agreements. There is no worldwide sovereign to impose sanctions if individual countries violate regulations or do not agree to participate in the scheme. Thus, in 2001, United States President Bush withdrew his country from the Kyoto Protocol by refusing to send it to the Senate for ratification ("Kyoto and Beyond," 2007). Other problems arise as differences within a nation state make it difficult to ratify the protocol. For example, in Canada, regional differences made it difficult to come to a consensus on the Kyoto Protocol. Given their province's reliance on oil and natural gas, politicians from Alberta strongly opposed it, while Quebec was a strong supporter since that province draws mainly on hydroelectric power. Manitoba supported it because of the potential devastation that global climate change may wreak on agriculture in that province (Mitchell, 2010: 4).

## MEASURING ECONOMIC VERSUS ENVIRONMENTAL PROGRESS

Concern about environmental protection and the economic interests of business and industry intersect in many ways, often to the detriment of the environment. Consider something as basic as how we measure the strength of the economy—by calculating gross national product (GNP). The GNP adds up the dollar value of all the goods and services produced in a country in a year. It does not distinguish economic activities that are bad for the environment from those that are benign. Let's say a mining operation produces a toxic liquid. A clean-up crew then collects the toxin and transports it to a landfill. The toxin leaks into groundwater and some of it enters a nearby community's water supply. Over the years, the cancer rate of residents and clean-up workers increases; the residents are consuming small quantities of the toxin and members of the clean-up crew were exposed to it when they collected it and took it to the landfill. Those afflicted require prolonged medical treatment and eventually die before they reach the average life expectancy for people in the country. All these activities add to the GNP, both the beneficial ones (producing a mineral and creating jobs) and the harmful ones (producing a toxin, exposing people to it, and causing the cancer rate to rise and people to die prematurely). In this manner, environmental destruction contributes to GNP. GNP figures suggest that the economy is growing stronger, but they give no indication of the environmental devastation that underlies development. Social scientists have proposed alternatives to the GNP that adjust for social and environmental costs, but to this point, they have not been influential in policymaking (Giddens, 2009).

Recently, the incorporation of the social and environmental aspects of economic activities has become a consideration for some businesses. This often takes the form of corporate social responsibility initiatives and eco-standards practices.

## CORPORATE SOCIAL RESPONSIBILITY AND ECO-STANDARDS

Increasing public concern about the environment has forced industry to make concessions. Today, for instance, some companies say they exercise "corporate social responsibility" by ensuring that their practices are ethically and environmentally sound and in the public interest. The problem is that such measures are voluntary, so they may not be effective. In some cases, companies even claim they are engaged in environmentally protective practices when they are not. They promote a "green" image merely as a public relations ploy to attract more business—a practice sometimes called "corporate greenwashing."

People would be able to identify instances of corporate greenwashing more easily if the environmental

practices of companies were made transparent to the public. One attempt to do this is with eco-standards and eco-labels. A company that conforms to established environmental standards for production and manufacturing would be able to apply for certification stating that its product or practice is environmentally friendly. The environmental standards themselves would be developed by another agency or sometimes by the government. An external auditor would ensure that the company complies with the standards and procedures, and issue a certificate on the basis of the assessment. The agency and auditor would therefore operate as watchdogs for the public, vouching for the company and ensuring it is not making false claims. The issued certificate could take different forms, such as the company or product being included in official green shopping guides or green mutual fund portfolios, or through the issuing of environmental stewardship certificates that can be displayed publicly in the storefront or factory. In addition, eco-labels could be displayed on products so consumers could see they conform to a standard before deciding whether to buy them.

The eco-standards approach has been used for a variety of products and processes, including organic food labelling, labelling of genetically modified food, energy efficiency certification, and marine certification and seafood labelling (to certify that only sustainable yields are being caught). But can these eco-labels be trusted? Toilet paper produced by J.D. Irving Limited of New Brunswick carries the Sustainable Forestry Limited (SFI) eco-label, yet investigation by CBC journalists found that forestry practices involved in manufacturing it violate important principles that the general population associates with sustainable forestry, including clear-cutting, herbicide use, lack of recycled material in the manufacturing process, and the replanting of just one tree species, which threatens the long-term survivability of the replanted forest ("Toilet Paper Chase," 2012). To address such false environmental claims, such groups as Greenpeace and CorpWatch have established websites and blogs to investigate and then inform the public of specific cases of greenwashing. This is just one sort of activity that environmental movement groups are involved with.

## THE ENVIRONMENTAL MOVEMENT

At the turn of the twentieth century, the increasingly pervasive impact of industrialization on forests gave rise to concerns about preserving the natural beauty of wilderness areas. Consequently, national parks, such as those at Niagara Falls, Ontario, and Banff, Alberta, were established to protect areas of natural beauty. (Another incentive for the national park system was the promotion of tourism and the Canadian National Railroad; Paehlke, 2009). At the time, the environmental movement consisted of nature-based groups, such as the Sierra Club and the National Audubon Society.

With the publication of *Silent Spring* in the 1960s, the first wave of the modern environmental movement was born. It focused on environmental threats to human health, and it took a somewhat anti-industrial perspective. By the mid-1980s, a second wave of environmentalism could be discerned. It was less apocalyptic and more pragmatic and professional in tone, more willing to work with business and government in dealing with issues such as acid rain. In Canada, business-government-environmentalist round tables were established. The shift from an adversarial to a cooperative stance may have reflected broader changes in society, including aging members in the first wave, who now had families to raise and mortgages to pay; a growing number of second-wave members who had graduated from university programs in environmental studies; and recognition by business and government that environmentalism was not just a passing fad (Paehlke, 2009).

By 2002, global climate change was at the top of the political agenda, signalling the rise of a third wave of environmentalism. Addressing climate change requires large-scale alterations in the way society is organized. For this reason, the issue subsumes other types of environmental issues, such as increasing energy efficiency in manufacturing, building design, and transportation; switching to renewable energy sources; significantly increasing the recycling and reuse of materials; and adopting more effective forest and other resource management strategies. This third wave of environmentalism was also characterized by the emergence of the federal Green Party. In every election since 2004, the Greens have been able to run a candidate in all federal ridings. So far, they have elected just one MP, but their presence on the national stage has forced the other political parties to give greater prominence to environmental issues—if only to prevent supporters from being attracted to the Green Party (Paehlke, 2009).

## SOCIAL BASE AND COMPOSITION

The social base of the environmental movement has shifted over time. During the early part of the twentieth century, the nature-orientated environmental movement consisted largely of the affluent. Modern environmental groups tend to draw disproportionately on the "new middle class" of young, well-educated people who often work in public, cultural, or social service occupations, including teachers, social workers, actors, journalists, artists, and academics—and their student apprentices (Brown, 2009). Such people may be attracted to the environmental movement for two reasons. First, they tend to have values that are incompatible with those of the business world and the idea of profit maximization at all cost. Second, they may be involved in jobs where they advocate for the rights of clients—such as a social worker involved in a campaign to improve environmental conditions in an inner-city community where she works. Both of these types of "new-middle-class" tendencies are in line with environmentally based values that call for social and political change to improve society (Kriesi, 1989).

The "new-middle-class" thesis only partly describes membership in Canada's Green Party (Camcastle, 2007). True, the Greens attract young, well-educated people—but an unusually large proportion of them are self-employed. Otherwise, the social profile of the Green Party is not hugely different from those voting for other parties. The Party itself has had some success with the electorate, indicating a small but broadening base of public support. In the 2011 election, the Greens won nearly 4 percent of the popular vote and well-known environmentalist and head of the Green Party

In the 2011 election, the Greens won nearly 4 percent of the popular vote.
SOURCE: © ZUMA Press/Newscom.

Elizabeth May became its first elected member of Parliament (Elections Canada, 2012).

Many issues that concern environmental activists are health related because they violate the core value of survival. Threats to health undoubtedly motivate some activists to become involved in health-related environment issues.

## THE ENVIRONMENT AND HEALTH

You are what you eat—and what you touch and breathe. If the air, water, food, and physical surroundings in which we carry on our daily activities are contaminated, we too become contaminated. Environmental and health issues are thus intimately connected. All human beings alive today have some level of **body burden**— the sum of dangerous chemicals that accumulate in the human body over a given period. Human decision making and the resulting organization of society shape the way chemicals enter the human body.

For example, in the mid-1960s, the Ontario Department of Lands and Forests (now the Ministry of Natural Resources) and private timber companies collaborated to spray the chemical Agent Orange on northern Ontario forests (Zlomislic, 2011). Agent Orange killed shrubs and birch, maple, and poplar tress so that profitable spruce trees would be free to grow without competition. We now know that Agent Orange causes cancer, but in the mid-1960s, workers involved in the spraying program, many of them university students, were unaware of the risks. They mixed chemicals with little protection and stood in fields holding red, helium-filled balloons on fishing lines while low-flying planes flew over them and sprayed the chemical. Decades later, these workers are experiencing serious health effects.

The Agent Orange case is one of acute exposure, that is, high-dose exposure in a short period. Other examples of acute exposure include explosions at chemical factories and industrial accidents. However, many environmental health risks are chronic, involving low-dose exposure over an extended period. One example involves bisphenol A, which is found in many clear, hard plastic products, such as CDs and DVDs, water and baby bottles, eyeglass lenses, and hockey helmet visors. It is also used in epoxy resins and the lining of tin cans containing food. It is one of the most common chemicals in the world (Smith and Lourie, 2009). Consequently, most people are in contact with bisphenol A every day for most of their lives.

With bisphenol A (and other chemicals that disrupt the body's hormonal system), low doses lead to potent health effects. Hence, low levels of such chemicals in the environment are of particular concern. Low levels of bisphenol A have been associated with a range of illnesses, including prostate and breast cancer, urogenital abnormalities in male babies, declining sperm quality in men, early onset of puberty in girls, insulin-resistant diabetes, obesity, and attention deficit hyperactivity disorder (Smith and Lourie, 2009). Because of such concerns, in 2008 Canada became the first country in the world to ban bisphenol A from baby bottles. There are, however, many other harmful chemicals that pervade the environment. How are these regulated? To address these questions we need to understand the process of risk management.

### RISK MANAGEMENT

Body burden is influenced by how a country regulates chemicals in the environment. The state does this through **risk management**—the process by which a regulatory agency establishes the levels of chemicals that are allowed to enter the environment. Risk management uses information from animal experiments to help determine safe levels of exposure. This technical information is combined with environmental information to come up with a specific regulation (Ali, 2008). However, the terms of the regulation are subject to political pressure. It may be that the strict regulation of a chemical emission will be costly to industry. Industry will therefore lobby for a laxer and less costly regulation. The environmental lobby, in contrast, may call for stricter regulation. As such, risk management is hardly a politically neutral, technical exercise.

In 2008, Canada became the first country in the world to ban bisphenol A from baby bottles.
SOURCE: © The New York Times/REDUX.

In North America, risk management works on the principle that a chemical is assumed to be harmless until it is proven dangerous. Until then, the chemical will still be produced and allowed to enter the environment. This pro-industry orientation has been challenged by environmentalists calling for the adoption of the precautionary principle.

## THE PRECAUTIONARY PRINCIPLE

The essence of the scientific method and the experimental approach is to establish the existence of cause-effect relationships. With respect to environmental health issues, this involves showing that exposure to a certain amount of a chemical in the environment (the cause) leads to a particular illness (the effect). In practice, causality is difficult to prove because environmental exposures take place while many compounding factors impinge on a given dose-response interaction. Laboratory experiments remove these confounding factors by manipulating the physical setting (see Chapter 20, Research Methods). However, researchers cannot remove compounding factors in the real world, where the cause of a disease may be due to many factors. Cancer, for instance, may result from several causes acting at different points in life, such as exposure to factory smoke during childhood, cigarette smoke during youth, and radon gas during adulthood. Ambiguity in what causes cancer exists; it may be one thing, or it may be several. Thus, the tobacco industry argued for decades that cigarette smoking might not be a cause of cancer because cigarette smokers tend to be overweight, have poor diets, live in polluted neighbourhoods, and so on—and all these factors are causes of cancer. (Only recently have researchers shown how exposure to tobacco smoke turns cells carcinogenic, thus silencing this particular line of defence.) Similarly, defenders of polluting industries have argued that just because a disease is found in laboratory animals exposed to a particular contaminant, this does not necessarily mean that it will lead to the disease in humans. In the end, polluting industries often argue that insufficient evidence proves conclusively the existence of a cause-effect relationship between a pollutant and a disease, so regulating or banning a pollutant is not justified. Chemicals are innocent until proven guilty beyond doubt in Canada and the United States.

In Western Europe, regulatory agencies take a different approach. They do not allow the introduction of a new chemical if statistical evidence shows a correlation between its use and a dangerous health effect. Underlying this approach is the precautionary principle—the view that, under conditions of uncertainty, it is better to err on the side of safety. Some researchers argue that the logic of the precautionary principle should be applied not just to the regulation of chemicals but also to other regulatory issues, including the use of genetically modified food, genetic engineering, nanotechnologies, global warming, and activities that lead to the loss of biodiversity (Raffensperger and Tickner, 1999).

Because of the inadequacies of risk management, environmental health risks persist. However, sociologists have found that these risks do not affect everyone in society equally. Some individuals and groups are disproportionately affected by these risks, depending on their race/ethnicity, social class, gender, and place of residence. In other words, the inequality exists in the distribution of risk. Certain organizations in the larger environmental movement have mobilized to address issues related to the unequal distribution of risk.

## ENVIRONMENTAL INEQUALITY

Race and ethnicity, social class, and gender all influence how environmental risks are distributed and experienced. Generally, people in subordinate positions are more exposed to environmental risk than are people in dominant positions. Recognition of this fact spurred the **environmental justice movement**. The initial impetus for the movement was the work of sociologist Robert Bullard (1993). Based on quantitative evidence and mapping, his research showed that toxic waste sites were located disproportionately in African American and Hispanic neighbourhoods in the United States. For example, about 60 percent of African Americans live near toxic waste sites.

Today, many workers, members of racial minority groups, and women have been drawn into environmental justice organizations. They tend to engage in local campaigns focusing on the survival needs of the poor, in contrast to some national and international environmental organizations that tend to engage in "full-stomach" environmentalism (dealing with nature preservation for enjoyment and enhancing the quality of life; see Guha and Martinez-Alier, 1998). As such, environmental justice organizations make a concerted effort to link occupational, community, economic, environmental, and social justice issues. They combat racism by asserting people's civil and human rights. They engage in activities aimed at eliminating the unequal enforcement of environmental, civil rights, and public health laws; the different degree of exposure of different races and classes to harmful chemicals in the home, school, neighbourhood and workplace; and discriminatory zoning and land-use practices.

## ENVIRONMENTAL JUSTICE AND CANADA'S FIRST NATIONS

Canadians do not have to deal with the historical legacy of slavery to the extent Americans do, which is why we have been less engaged in the struggle for human rights. Still, First Nations peoples in Canada face their own legacy of colonization and inequality (Agyeman, Haluza-DeLay, and O'Riley, 2009). For example, the rural area within the Sarnia-Windsor-London triangle of Southern Ontario hosts many harmful industries, including a regional landfill, numerous smaller landfills, a sewage treatment plant treating 15 million litres (4 million gallons) a day, and the country's largest concentration of heavy industry, much of it related to petrochemicals, called "Chemical Valley." It is also home to eight First Nations territories (Mascarenhas, 2009). From 1974 to 1986, this area experienced 32 major chemical spills and 300 smaller ones that poured about 9 metric tons (10 tons) of pollutants in the St. Clair River, which runs through the area (Walpole Island First Nation, n.d.). The waterways in the region are so polluted that they have been designated as "areas of concern" by the International Joint Commission (Environment Canada, 2010).

The Aamjiwnaang First Nations Reserve is located in Chemical Valley. Epidemiological studies of this community show that, over the past decade, a statistically significantly lower number of boys than girls have been born. The imbalance has been attributed to environmental endocrine disruptors present in the toxic chemicals emitted by area industry (Mackenzie, Lockridge, and Keith, 2005).

Many of the issues that environmental justice groups deal with in the United States relate to the urban setting. In contrast, the environmental justice issues many First Nations people face involve the distribution of environmental risks in more remote settings, such as mercury contamination in northern Ontario (Erikson, 1995), water quality problems on reserves (Indian and Northern Affairs Canada, 2003), contamination from radioactive materials from uranium mining at Great Bear Lake in the Northwest Territories (Blow, 1999), and chemical contamination in the Mohawk territory

A sign warning of toxic substances in Talfourd Creek on the Aamjiwnaang First Nation reserve near Sarnia, Ontario.
SOURCE: © AP Photo/Carlos Osorio.

of Akwesasne in eastern Ontario and western Quebec (Tarbell and Arquette, 2000).

Issues of environmental justice are even dealt with by those in some of the most remote parts of the country, such as Inuit in Nunavik. Since some dangerous chemicals found in the environment are fat soluble, they contribute to the body burden of women more than men. Mother's milk in particular is quite high in fat. Analysis of Inuit mothers' milk has shown that it contains five times as much polychlorinated biphenyl (PCB), a cancer-causing agent, than that of southern Canadian white women. In some cases, the concentration was even higher (Milly and Leiss, 1997). It is not permissible to feed cow's milk with this much PCB to infants.

PCB belongs to a set of chemicals known as persistent organic pollutants (POPs). POPs do not break down in the environment, even after centuries. They are produced for various industrial purposes in the southern areas of world. Over time, POPs are carried through wind currents to the northern regions, where they bioaccumulate in the fat of living things. Living things in the Arctic region are therefore threatened by environmental health risks they had no role in producing and from which they did not benefit. Such facts raise the issues of inequality and injustice.

## THE UNEQUAL BURDENS OF ENVIRONMENTAL INEQUALITY

Inequalitiy in the distribution of environmental health risks take various forms. For example, poorer neighbourhoods in Canadian cities contain a disproportionate amount of polluting industry. Thus, the North End of Hamilton, Ontario, is host to many heavy metal and chemical industries that pollute the local environment (Ali, 2002). North End residents have the lowest socioeconomic status in the city and are exposed to much higher levels of particulate air pollution than are residents of higher socioeconomic status neighbourhoods (Jerrett et al., 2001). True, the establishment of polluting and environmentally damaging industry in relatively poor parts of the city provides much-needed jobs. However, it also reflects the fact that powerful and wealthy people make decisions about where to place dirty industry, and they are in a position to avoid living nearby. This, too, is a form of environmental inequality.

The flow of waste from the northern to the southern hemisphere illustrates yet another form of environmental inequality. Increasingly, North America and Western Europe dump toxic waste, industrial pollution, and discarded consumer goods in the southern hemisphere in exchange for fees and jobs (Faber, 2009). The countries of the southern hemisphere have weaker environmental regulations than those in the north do, and they often lack the expertise to evaluate and manage the risks of the hazardous waste they accept. In the end, we apply two standards of environmental health and safety—a relatively high standard for those in the north and a relatively low standard for those in the south, implying that human life in one region is worth less than that in the other. As a former World Bank's chief economist once wrote in a leaked memo, "I think the economic logic behind dumping a load of toxic waste in the lowest wage country is impeccable and we should face up to that. ... I've always thought that under-populated countries in Africa are vastly under-polluted" (Rich, 1994: 248).

As the world's second biggest exporter of asbestos, a mineral known for its fire-resistant properties, Canada upholds the double standard. For decades, we have known that asbestos causes serious lung-related ailments including mesothelioma, a rare form of cancer. Consequently, many countries have banned the import and export of the substance. Yet Canada refuses to list asbestos as a hazardous product and sends large quantities of it from Quebec to India, Pakistan, and China ("Canada Wins Battle," 2011).

Today, the problem of environmental inequality because of the trade in toxic waste is intensified because of the proliferation of computers. Soldered circuit boards contain various toxic heavy metals, while cathode ray tubes components release toxic compounds when burned—which happens when incineration is used as a waste disposal method. Computers quickly become obsolete and we tend to discard them quickly. Consequently, mountains of toxic "e-waste" accumulate and are shipped to developing nations, such as China, India, and Pakistan. There, the material is reused, recycled, or incinerated under largely unregulated conditions, endangering the environment and the lives of electronic waste workers (Markoff, 2002).

## CLIMATE CHANGE AND INEQUALITY

Environmental inequality is also evident in the unequal burden created by climate change. Many analysts argue that climate change will have the greatest effect on those least responsible for causing the problem. One study based on an ecological mapping of climate change effects around the world found that countries producing the least amount of greenhouse gas per capita tend to be the most vulnerable to climate change (Shingler, 2011). For example, rising sea levels caused by climate change will entirely submerge South Pacific island nations, such as the Solomon Islands, Tongo, and Tuvalu. Furthermore, such poor nations have inadequate technical, financial, and administrative capacity, putting them at a disadvantage in international negotiations related to the regulation of climate change. Similar arguments have been made in international discussions on sustainable development. Developing nations argue that it is unfair to impose strict regulations on their greenhouse gas emissions because that would unjustly limit their industrial development—a limitation not faced by nations in the northern hemisphere when they underwent industrialization. The charge of the developing nations is that the countries of the northern hemisphere engaged in unrestricted industrialization using fossil fuels, induced climate change, and now want to penalize the countries of the southern hemisphere as they attempt to industrialize. As seen in Table 16.2, data support the claims made by developing nations concerning relative resource consumption and environmental impact.

Finally, environmental inequality has a generational component. Decisions made by the present generation that result in environmental degradation may jeopardize the survival chances of the unborn. The rights of the unborn deserve to be considered by today's decision makers and the world's citizenry, including you and me.

**TABLE 16.2**  AVERAGE CARBON DIOXIDE EMISSIONS AND RESOURCE CONSUMPTION IN CANADA, THE UNITED STATES, INDIA, AND THE WORLD

| CONSUMPTION PER PERSON IN 1991 | CANADA | UNITED STATES | INDIA | WORLD |
|---|---|---|---|---|
| $CO_2$ emission (in tons per year) | 15.2 | 19.5 | 0.81 | 4.2 |
| Purchasing power (in US$) | 19 320 | 22 130 | 1150 | 3800 |
| Motor vehicles per 100 persons | 46 | 57 | 0.2 | 10 |
| Paper consumption (in kilograms/year) | 247 | 317 | 2 | 44 |
| Fossil energy use (in gigajoules/years) | 234–250 | 287 | 5 | 56 |
| Fresh water withdrawal (in $m^3$/year) | 1688 | 1868 | 612 | 644 |

Note the dramatic differences in the consumption of resources and the production of carbon dioxide between Canada and the United States compared with India and the world.

SOURCE: Wackernagel, Mathias and William E. Rees. (1996). *Our Ecological Footprint: Reducing Human Impact on the Earth*. Gabriola Island, BC: New Society Publishers, p. 85.

# SUMMARY

1. Sociologists recognize that environmental problems have a biophysical basis. They consider the role of social and material factors in their analyses of environmental issues.

2. The origin of many environmental problems may be understood in terms of the tragedy of the commons. The central feature of this tragedy is that since environmental commons, such as air and water, are used by all members of society, the ownership and use of these resources are not clearly defined or delimited. Consequently, private corporations will try to maximize the economic benefits they receive from exploiting the commons, knowing that the environmental consequences of their actions will be shared by all, potentially leading to the destruction of the commons.

3. Public awareness of environmental issues increased from the 1960s onward, with the unfolding of a sequence of influential events, including the publication of *Silent Spring* and the *Limits to Growth Report*, the establishment of the environmental movement, and the oil crisis of 1973. In the 1980s, the identification of two global environmental problems further reinforced the public's environmental concern: ozone depletion and global climate change. During that period, the influential notion of sustainable development was proposed by the international community as a way to manage environmental impacts without derailing economic growth. From the 1990s onward, several high-profile international conferences were held to coordinate efforts to combat global environmental problems.

4. The social constructionist perspective analyzes how environmental issues garner public attention. It focuses on the claims-making process and how the interactions among various individuals and institutions, such as industry and government representatives, environmental movement activists, scientists, and the mass media are able to promote certain claims over others. Popular culture also plays an important role in the social construction process.

5. Members of the new middle class, particularly young, highly educated individuals involved in service and cultural occupations, are disproportionately attracted to the environmental movement. However, support for the Green Party is more broadly based.

6. The attempt by nation-states (or other jurisdictions) to alleviate environmental problems is generally referred to as environmental governance. The international nature of many environmental

problems makes environmental governance efforts of individual nation-states and jurisdictions difficult. This is because each nation-state has sovereign powers and cannot impose its will on other nation-states without violating the other's sovereignty rights.

7. State environmental governance initiatives may be directed at private industries. Traditionally in Canada, under the Canadian Environmental Protection Act, the government has pursued a top-down, "command-and-control" approach to regulating the environmental impact of manufacturing and production. This approach has been resisted by industry. Consequently, voluntary self-regulatory mechanisms have been introduced, including the establishment of a market for pollution permits.

8. A healthy biophysical environment helps ensure good human health, while a chemically contaminated environment means that human beings are exposed to illness-causing chemicals. To minimize or eliminate exposure to toxic chemicals, the precautionary principle has been favoured in Western Europe. According to this principle, a chemical should be banned if there is even the suspicion that it can cause illness.

9. The regulation of toxic chemicals occurs through risk management, which involves interpreting technical information from animal tests. Political and economic interests influence risk management. For example, to carry on business, industry tends to argue for more lenient regulatory standards for the chemical by-products they produce while environmental activists demand more stringent standards.

10. Inequality arises from the unequal distribution of environmental risks. Relatively low status groups tend to shoulder a disproportionate share of environmental risks. As this fact came to be more widely recognized, environmental justice groups emerged to address issues related to environmental inequality. First Nations communities face particularly difficult conditions stemming from government and industrial policies that do not sufficiently consider issues of environmental inequality and injustice.

## QUESTIONS TO CONSIDER

1. Sociologist Ulrich Beck (1995: 140) writes that "the environmental problem is by no means a problem [only] of our surroundings. It is a crisis of industrial society itself, reaching deeply into the foundations of institutions; risks are produced industrially, externalized economically, legitimized scientifically, and minimized politically." Take an example of any environmental problem and construct an argument that supports or challenges the above statement.

2. Select an environmental issue and explain how it is socially constructed. Consider the different claims made by government officials, environmental movement actors, scientists, and industry officials. How did media coverage of the environmental issue you selected represent the various claims expressed? Was equal coverage given to all involved?

3. Search the Web to analyze the controversies that arose at the International Climate Summit held in Copenhagen in December 2009. What sort of issues arose and how can they be understood sociologically in terms of such concepts as the tragedy of the commons, sovereignty rights, environmental inequality and injustice, power relations, economic contingency, and framing? What were some of the reasons that the Canadian government gave for not agreeing on the protocol that the international community put forward as necessary for combating global climate change?

## GLOSSARY

**Body burden** (p. 409) refers to the sum of all foreign chemicals that accumulate in the human body over a given period.

The **command-and-control approach** (p. 406) to environmental management is the top-down government strategy of issuing regulations to control the environmental impact of industry.

The **economic contingency** (p. 397) thesis holds that public environmental concern depends on the state of the economy. In good economic times, more attention will be given to environmental issues, while in bad times, environmental concern will lessen.

The **environmental justice movement** (p. 410) seeks to address issues associated with the unequal distribution of environmental risks caused by discrimination.

An **externality** (p. 396) is an environmental impact that is produced by one party (such as an industry) that does not take responsibility for the consequences of the environmental impact. Rather, the consequences are addressed by another party, such as the state or the general public, which bears the cost of addressing the environmental impact.

**Framing** (p. 399) refers to the process of how events and issues are interpreted based on how they are presented.

**Future discounting** (p. 398) refers to the psychological tendency to forgo future benefits in favour of immediate benefits.

**Peak oil** (p. 401) is the tipping point at which new oil reserves can no longer be found, thus forcing society to rely on depleting reserves.

The **polluter pays principle** (p. 406) addresses the externality problem by charging fines or taxes to force a corporation or country that causes pollution to pay the cost of environmental cleanup and protection.

A **resource curse** (p. 404) arises in regions where valuable natural resources are especially abundant. Such abundance discourages democracy because privately owned natural resource industries provide government with most of its revenue, allowing them to exert excessive political influence and rendering

government insufficiently politically accountable to taxpayers.

**Risk management** (p. 409) is the process of establishing regulations for protecting the environment and health. Risk management is not a narrow, technical field so much as a political process.

The **risk society thesis** (p. 397) is that contemporary societies have become preoccupied with issues related to the distribution of social "bads," chief among them the environmental risks and externalities produced by industry.

**Sustainable development** (p. 397) is an industrialization strategy that attempts to address economic, social, and environmental concerns in a balanced way, by meeting the needs of the present generation without jeopardizing the ability of future generations to meet their needs.

A **tipping point** (p. 395) is a threshold beyond which a system unexpectedly, rapidly, and dramatically changes.

## SUGGESTED READING

Hannigan, John. 2006. *Environmental Sociology*, 2nd ed. New York: Routledge. A definitive overview of the field.

Kolbert, Elizabeth. 2006. *Field Notes from a Catastrophe: Man, Nature and Climate Change.* London: Bloomsbury. An exceptionally clear and balanced analysis of the problem of climate change.

Nikiforuk, Andrew. 2010. *Tar Sands: Dirty Oil and the Future of a Continent.* Vancouver: GreystoneBooks. A comprehensive analysis of one of Canada's most pressing environmental issues.

# Religion

# CHAPTER 13

# RELIGION

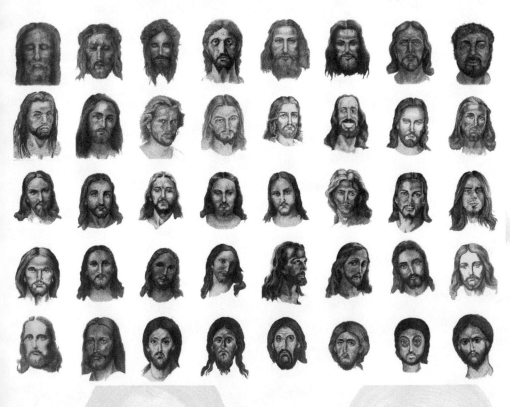

**REGINALD W. BIBBY**
UNIVERSITY OF LETHBRIDGE

SOURCE: © Morgan Danveau

# INTRODUCTION

Religion is very much alive today. In recent years, religion has received worldwide attention in such varied developments as the death of Pope John Paul II, the phenomenal sales of Dan Brown's *The Da Vinci Code*, and the exposure given to the so-called atheist books of such authors as Richard Dawkins and the late Christopher Hitchens. Religion's presence and importance is blatant in the conflict, terrorism, and peacemaking efforts in the Middle East. In 2006 it was centre stage in the clash of values and perhaps even civilizations as European countries and their leaders experienced the protests and threats of Muslims for allowing their newspapers to publish cartoon depictions of Muhammad (Ghafour, 2006). Even more daunting in light of September 11, 2001, was the 1998 directive of "fundamentalist"/"extremist" Osama bin Laden that "in compliance with God's order ... every Muslim who believes in God and wishes to be rewarded" is to "kill the Americans and plunder their money wherever and whenever they find it"—thinking that, in turn, has been widely condemned by most Muslim leaders.

In North America, religion's presence is also readily evident in the God-laced responses to such militancy on the part of U.S. political leaders, whose supporters frequently include large numbers of the so-called Christian Right. Apart from its links to global issues, religion in the United States is pervasive. Attendance at services is extremely high and the majority of people say that religion is very important to them. The organizational health of American religion can be seen in the emergence of a growing number of very large and influential "megachurches," such as Joel Osteen's much-publicized Lakewood Church that occupies a 16 000-seat former basketball arena in Houston. Far from having only a local focus, many function as religious multinational corporations—spreading the message of "how to do ministry" to other parts of the world, including Canada. Spirituality has joined religion in going public and become part of pop culture, read about in books, such as Rhonda Byrne's *The Secret* and Eckhart Tolle's *A New Earth*, and talked about on *Oprah*.

In Canada, beyond such media offerings, the reality of religion is readily apparent in the tendency of the vast majority of people to continue to identify with a religious tradition; in the growing numbers of individuals identifying with faiths that include Islam, Hinduism, Sikhism, and Buddhism; in the widespread interest in spirituality; in debates about same-sex marriage and polygamy; in the efforts of Catholics and mainline Protestants to resolve problems relating to the legacy of residential schools; in the imminent prime minister of the day ending his 2006 election victory speech with the words "God bless Canada," and in the national publicity given to Toronto's Catholic Archbishop being elevated to the status of Cardinal in early 2012.

Many early social scientists were convinced that religion's days were numbered, that it would be just a short time before it was discarded in favour of science. Through the 1990s, the widespread consensus was that religion's influence was declining and that Canadians and people in most other technologically advanced countries were leaving religion behind—although the United States stood out as a puzzling anomaly.

We now know that such observers were wrong. In the early decades of the twenty-first century, religion lives on, embraced by large numbers of people in virtually all cultures, however "advanced" or "nonadvanced." Moreover, interest in religion and spirituality is actually on the upswing in many parts of the world, including North America, Russia, and Asia. In many Islamic countries, it is not clear that the importance of religion has ever been in doubt. Today, religion is frequently associated with conflict and division. But it also continues to bring meaning, sustenance, and hope to billions of people.

I begin the chapter by taking a brief look at what some of the early and influential social scientists had to say about religion, and then discuss how sociologists go about studying religion in both its individual and group forms. After clarifying what sociologists mean by religion, I look at "how much of it" we have in Canada and proceed to examine its sources and consequences—what kinds of factors contribute to people being religious and the influence that religion has on both individuals and societies. In concluding the chapter, I reflect on the kinds of religious developments we can expect in the future.

I'll be giving particular attention to Canada, in large part because I have spent much of my life examining religious developments here and have some fairly unique research findings I can tell you about. However, while focusing on Canada, I will keep my eyes on the rest of the world, starting with the United States.

Contrary to the opinion of some people, religious belief is not disappearing in Canada. In fact, in urban areas most people have many options for worship.
SOURCE: © Dick Hemingway.

## SOCIOLOGY AND RELIGION

A number of years ago, an American evangelist who was holding services in Edmonton was asked by a fairly strident television interviewer, "How do you know there is a God?" The evangelist immediately responded, "Because I talked to Him five minutes ago." It was an interesting claim but one that a sociologist is not in a position to verify. A basic rule of science is that "what counts" as real is what we can detect through our senses—what we refer to as "empirical" knowledge. In contrast, proponents of religion have traditionally asserted that the world we know through the senses is only part of a greater reality that, because of the limitations of sense perception, can only be known through faith.

In principle, science and religion are compatible. Science limits itself to what is perceivable, and religion maintains that reality includes the nonperceivable. Conflict between the two should only arise when one oversteps its boundaries and invades the other's territory.

Still, for the most part, science is in the driver's seat. As Émile Durkheim (1965 [1912]: 479) pointed out many years ago, religion "can affirm nothing that [science] denies, deny nothing that it affirms." Try though it might, religion cannot overrule science in refuting basic evolutionary claims or dismissing sound medical diagnoses. At the same time, since science is limited to conclusions about the observable, it too can only go so far. Sociologists cannot address the evangelist's claim that he had actually spoken to God, any more than it can evaluate the claim that a person whose cancer has gone into remission was healed by God.

Sociology consequently suffers from one serious methodological limitation in studying religion: It cannot probe the supernatural claims that religion so often is about. Sociologists nonetheless can offer considerable insight into "the observable part" of religion. For example, they can examine the following:

- Who tends to think they have experienced God
- Who believes in life after death and what individuals think will happen when they die
- The extent to which people have spiritual needs, and what they mean by "spirituality"
- How many and what kinds of people are involved in religious groups
- The impact that religious involvement has on individuals and societies

In short, sociologists cannot address everything when it comes to religion; but they can address much, without getting caught up in the issue of religion's ultimate truth or falsity. Max Weber summed up the focus of sociological explorations into religion this way: "The essence of religion," he wrote, is not the concern of sociologists, since "we make it our task to study the conditions and effects of a particular type of social behaviour" (1963 [1922]: 1). For our purposes, whether or not religious ideas are true is not as important as the fact they are *believed* to be true. As W. I. Thomas and Dorothy Swaine Thomas noted in their classic theorem, if we define things as real, they are real in their consequences (Thomas and Znaniecki, 1918: 79). The very fact that religious ideas are held means they potentially can have an important impact on individuals and social life.

## THEORETICAL TRADITIONS

Three early theorists—Karl Marx, Émile Durkheim, and Max Weber—have had a strong influence on the sociology of religion.

## MARX AND CONFLICT

Karl Marx grew up in a Jewish environment but came to believe that religion is a human creation. Using the language of the day, Marx (1970 [1843]: 131) wrote, "Man makes religion; religion does not make man." He argued that man has "found only his own reflection in the fantastic reality of heaven, where he sought a supernatural being," and that being religious characterized "the self-consciousness and self-esteem of a man who has either not yet gained himself or has lost himself again."

It has been argued that we can resolve undesirable conditions by either changing them or reinterpreting them. Peasants, slaves, and the marginalized in our day theoretically can rise up and revolt; they also can minimize the importance of "this world" by looking heavenward, singing spirituals, and dreaming of walking streets of gold after they die. According to Marx, religion constitutes the latter response, resulting in people who are economically and politically deprived redefining reality, rather than changing their oppressive conditions. Religion, Marx wrote, soothes the disadvantaged like a narcotic—functioning as "the opium of the people" (Marx, 1970 [1843]: 131), in the process blinding them to the inequalities at hand and bottling up their creative energies. So it is that some observers today would argue that many socially and financially deprived individuals who are unable or unwilling to play an active role in altering social conditions or even their own lives substitute religious status for social status. A taxi driver by day is the head of a temple committee by night; the housekeeper in the hotel during the week is the star soloist in the church choir on the weekend. Religious status supplants social status; the next world supplants this world.

But Marx did not see such a redefining of reality as a chance happening. On the contrary, he maintained that those who hold power encourage religious belief among the masses as a subtle tool in the process of exploiting and subjugating them. Aligned with the interests of the dominant few, religion serves to hold in check the potentially explosive tensions of a society. Consistent with his thinking, respected social historian H. Richard Niebuhr (1957 [1929]: 51) has been among those who have claimed, for example, that a widely held belief among nineteenth-century American slave owners was that religion helped African Americans to become "better" slaves. He cites one advocate of "negro missions" who asserted that "slaves well-instructed in the Christian faith were less likely to develop revolutionary inclinations than the half-educated, such as [revolt leader] Nat Turner."

Historically, said Marx, society and religion were so intertwined that attacks on feudalism, for example, were attacks on the church, while revolutionary social and political doctrines were simultaneously viewed as theological heresies (Marx and Engels, 1964: 132). We might argue that we see similar fusion between politics and religion today, not only in theocracies, such as Iran, but also in such a country as the United States, where the dominant religion, according to some observers, is "the American Way of Life," supported by the country's primary religious groups. We'll return to this issue shortly.

For Marx (1970 [1843]: 131), religion was an inadequate salve for a sick society—"the sigh of the oppressed creature, the heart of a heartless world and the soul of soulless conditions." When the sickness was remedied, there would be no need for the salve. Using another metaphor, Marx (1970 [1843]: 132) wrote that his criticism of religion was an attempt to remove "the imaginary flowers from the chain, not so that man shall bear the chain without fantasy or consultation, but so that he shall cast off the chain and gather the living flowers." Freed from the panacea of religion, individuals would be able "to think, act, and fashion their reality with illusions lost and reason regained" (Marx, 1970 [1843]: 132).

If you are someone who is personally religious, you understandably are not particularly excited to have Marx suggest that you may well be disadvantaged in some way and need to open your eyes and give your energies to changing your current situation. But before you reject his thinking altogether, it is worth noting that, at minimum, Marx seems to offer considerable insight, even today, into why some people join extreme religious groups that downplay the importance of this life—encouraging them to give up what possessions they have and, in some instances, give up their lives as well.

## DURKHEIM AND COLLECTIVITY

Émile Durkheim was the son of a rabbi but was raised in a Catholic educational tradition. He himself was an atheist and an anti-cleric, who believed that a scientific understanding of society has the potential to raise the quality of social life.

In his classic work *The Elementary Forms of the Religious Life* (1965 [1912]), Durkheim argued that religion's origin is social. People who live in a community come to share common sentiments, and as a result a **collective conscience** is formed. When they gather together, they have a feeling of being in the presence of something beyond themselves that is experienced by each member, yet is greater than the sum of their individual consciences. The feeling is not unlike "the electricity in the air" we experience at an exciting playoff hockey game or a big rock concert, where that feeling "out there" seems to transcend the sum of individual emotions. Durkheim maintained that the experience is so vivid that people have felt the need to label it. In reality, Durkheim asserted, "God" is the group experiencing itself. The experience *is* real, he argues; it's just that it isn't what those involved think it is.

Once people experience such an alleged supernatural reality, they proceed to designate some related objects as **sacred** and others as **profane.** Christians have accorded special status to the cross, the Bible, and holy water, in contrast to almost everything else. Symbols of the sacred are many and diverse: Jews have assigned sacred status to the Torah and Star of David, Muslims to the Qur'an and the Saudi Arabian city of Mecca, Hindus to the Vedas and the sacred syllable "Aum"(or "Om"). In Durkheim's view, religious beliefs articulate the nature of the sacred and its symbols, and religious rites provide guidelines as to how people should act in the presence of the sacred. So it is that Muslims, for example, are expected to pray at specific times five times a day, facing Mecca,

In Durkheim's view, religious rites provide guidelines as to how people should act in the presence of the sacred. Muslims, for example, are expected to pray at specific times five times a day, facing Mecca, and to make a pilgrimage to Mecca at least once in their lifetimes.
SOURCE: © Shutterstock.

and to make a pilgrimage to Mecca at least once in their lifetimes; Hindus offer daily devotional prayers in the morning and evening, sometimes accompanied by ritual bathing. Sikhs, when they enter their temples, must cover their heads and remove their shoes, and, where the opportunity is provided, wash their hands and feet.

Because all groups feel the need to uphold and reaffirm their collective sentiments, people come together as what he refers to as a "church." According to Durkheim (1965 [1912]: 62–63), "the idea of religion is inseparable from that of the Church," since it is "an eminently collective thing." Even when religion seems to be entirely a matter of individual conscience, it still is nourished by social sources. Besides meeting needs at the individual level, he claimed, religion creates and reinforces social solidarity. Collective life is consequently both *the source* and *the product* of religion. Accordingly, Durkheim (1965 [1912]: 62) defined religion as "a unified system of beliefs and practices relative to sacred things ... which unite into one single moral community called a Church, all those who adhere to them."

Durkheim (1965 [1912]: 475–76) observed that "we are going through a stage of transition and moral mediocrity. The great things of the past which filled our fathers with enthusiasm do not excite the same ardour in us." He added poetically, "The gods are growing old or are already dead, and others are not yet born." But despite the problems of traditional Catholicism in particular, Durkheim didn't believe that religion would disappear: "There are no gospels which are immortal, but neither is there any reason for believing that humanity is incapable of inventing new ones." The dominant groups and forms of expression might change, but the social sources that give rise to religion obviously will remain and, with them, religion. Durkheim also contended that there would always be a place for religious explanations. The reason? Science is fragmentary and incomplete, advancing too slowly—life cannot wait. Religion will therefore continue to have an important "gap-filling" role.

Durkheim's legacy has been important. You don't have to agree with his assertion that the gods are socially created to realize that God and ethical conceptions, for example, frequently reflect social and individual characteristics. In fact, an age-old concern among people valuing faith has been the inclination of humans to create the gods in their own images. What's more, Durkheim's acknowledgment that

science moves too slowly for many of us anticipated the ongoing "market" for alternative explanations on the part of religious leaders and just about anyone else, including—to use just one illustration—psychics. The vast market for explanations of the unknown is evident from the fact that in 2012, Google listed more than 20 million entries for "psychics."

## WEBER AND IDEAS

Max Weber was born in Germany. His grandparents were Protestants who had been refugees from Catholic persecution and eventually became successful in business. He was interested in religion from an early age but never shared the deep commitment of his Calvinist mother. His background was reflected in one of his most important works.

Weber's interest in the origin and nature of modern capitalism led him into extensive debate with Marx's ideas and stimulated much of his work in the sociology of religion. Unlike Marx and Durkheim, Weber had little interest in the question of whether religion is ultimately true or false. Rather, he maintained that religion, in addition to having a supernatural component, is largely oriented toward this world. As a result, religious ideas and behaviour should frequently be evident in everyday conduct. In *The Protestant Ethic and the Spirit of Capitalism* (1958 [1904–05]), for example, Weber examined the possibility that the moral tone that characterizes capitalism in the Western world—the *Protestant ethic*—can be traced back to the influence of the Protestant Reformation. His hope was that his work would contribute "to the understanding of the manner in which ideas become effective forces in history" (Weber, 1958 [1904–05]: 90).

Weber took the position that ideas, regardless of whether they are objectively true or false, represent a person's definition of reality and therefore have the potential to influence behaviour. Accordingly, he emphasized the need to interpret action by understanding the motives of the actor (a method he called *Verstehen*, or understanding). To achieve such awareness, he said, researchers should place themselves in the roles of those being studied.

Weber understood the need to study diverse societies, present and past, to examine culture's influence on religion. He therefore embarked on comparative and historical studies of religion and its relationship to social and economic life in China, India, and ancient Israel. A compilation of his writings,

*Sociology of Religion* (1963 [1922]), illustrates the way that Weber approached religion. He noted that god-conceptions are strongly related to the economic, social, and political conditions in which people live. The gods of light and warmth and of rain and Earth have been closely related to practical economic needs; heavenly gods that rule the celestial order have been related to the more abstract problems of death and fate. In political conquest, the gods of the conquered are fused with the gods of the conqueror and reappear with revised characteristics. Furthermore, the growth of **monotheism** (belief in one god) is related to goals of political unification.

Beyond the social sources of the gods, Weber dealt with such major themes as the relationship between religion and social class, and the nature of religious organizations. He reflected on religious leadership and the important process whereby a personal following is transformed into a permanent congregation, which he referred to as "routinization." He noted that different groups in society vary in their inclination to be religious: Peasants are religious when they are threatened; the nobility find religion beneath their honour; the middle class sees religion largely in ethical terms; the working class supplants religion with other ideologies.

Over the years I have found that students, whether religious or otherwise, appreciate the way in which Weber attempted to take religion seriously and not become embroiled in attacking it or dismissing it. His approach has become fairly typical in the contemporary study of religion. Still, along with Weber, some of the ideas of Marx and Durkheim have remained insightful.

## THE NATURE OF RELIGION

Are you religious? If you are like many Canadians, you may promptly say, "Yes" or "No, I'm not," perhaps adding, "I'm not religious but I am spiritual." The term *religion* is widely used, but obviously people have different ideas in mind when they use it. Up to now, I have been assuming that we have a consensual understanding of what we mean by "religion." But before we go much further, and particularly before we look at research on religion, we need to clarify what we actually mean by the term.

"Religion" can be a blurry concept. Many people use it in a functional sense: What people value most becomes their religion—money, career, family, sports. A young boy allegedly told a Canadian

religious doorknocker, "My mother is RC; my dad is NHL." The problem with such functional definitions of religion, sociologist Peter Berger (1974: 129) once observed, is that they become like grey cats on a dark night. If religion is everything, then it is nothing.

In a pioneering work published some five decades ago, Charles Glock and Rodney Stark (1965) offered some thoughts that continue to be helpful. They pointed out that, in defining religion for social scientific purposes, we should begin by recognizing that humans develop systems of meaning to interpret the world. Some systems—commonly referred to as "religions," including Christianity, Judaism, and Islam—have a supernatural referent. Others, such as a science-based system (scientism) or political "isms" (communism, fascism), do not. The latter systems, they suggested, might be viewed as human-centred or **humanist perspectives,** in contrast to *religious perspectives*, which are succinctly referred to here as **religions.**

The two types of perspectives differ on one critical point: Religion is concerned with discovering life's meaning, and humanist perspectives are concerned with making life meaningful. Humanist Bertrand Russell stated the difference well: "I do not think that life in general has any purpose. It just happened. But individual human beings have purposes" (in Cogley, 1968: 171). Religious perspectives suggest that our existence has meaning, preceding that which we, as humans, decide to give it. In contrast, humanist perspectives assume that life has no "ultimate meaning" and therefore focus on giving it meaning.

The dichotomy is not perfect; some would say that such criteria might lead us to see Buddhism, for example, as a humanist perspective. Here I would simply defer to commonly understood thinking and place Buddhism in its familiar religion category for the sake of communication. However, for the most part, I think the religious perspectives/humanist perspectives approach is helpful.

### PERSONAL RELIGIOSITY

Now that I've clarified things a bit, let's go back to the pointed question: How religious are you? And to be less pointed, how religious are Canadians as a whole? Sociologists have not believed that the answers are arbitrary or simply subjective. They have given much effort to finding ways of defining and measuring what they have called **personal religiosity.**

Much of the early research used one of three basic indicators to determine the religiosity of a person.

All three assumed group involvement: identification, membership, and attendance. In surveys, people were asked questions, such as "What is your religious preference?" "Do you belong to a congregation?" and "How often do you attend religious services?" People who indicated that they had a religious preference, belonged to a local group, or attended services with regularity were viewed as religious.

However, as you know well, simply knowing that someone is "Protestant" or "Hindu," "Jewish" or "Mennonite," tells us very little about a person's actual commitment to his or her faith. Similarly, people might be group members, but members may be active or inactive, committed or uncommitted. And service attendance, although measuring participation in a group, excludes people who could be very committed yet, for such reasons as age, health, work schedule, and geographical location, are not overly active in a religious organization.

Since the mid-1960s, social scientists have responded to the limitations of these three measures by viewing religious commitment as having a variety of dimensions. In one of the more helpful frameworks

devised, Stark and Glock (1968) suggested that the religions of the world typically expect their most devoted followers to hold key beliefs, engage in certain practices, have supernatural experiences, and be aware of the central tenets of their faiths. Stark and Glock refer to these belief, practice, experience, and knowledge components of commitment as **dimensions of religiosity.** It is not enough to believe *or* practise *or* experience *or* know; all four traits are expected of the committed.

My ongoing Project Canada national surveys, which to date span 1975 through 2005, provide comprehensive data on personal religiosity in this country. The surveys have found that Canadians continue to exhibit relatively high levels of religious belief, practice, experience, and knowledge (see Table 13.1). Indeed, some eight in ten say they believe in God, close to seven in ten maintain there is life after death, six in ten acknowledge that they pray privately at least once a month, and about five in ten think they have experienced the presence of God. Almost half also exhibit some basic knowledge of Islam, Judaism, and Christianity. On the surface,

**TABLE 13.1**  RELIGIOUS COMMITMENT ALONG FOUR DIMENSIONS, CANADA, 2005 (IN PERCENTAGE)

| DIMENSION | RESPONSE | PERCENTAGE |
|---|---|---|
| Believe in God | Yes, I definitely do | 49 |
| | Yes, I think so | 33 |
| | No, I don't think so | 11 |
| | No, I definitely do not | 7 |
| Believe in life after death | Yes, I definitely do | 36 |
| | Yes, I think so | 31 |
| | No, I don't think so | 21 |
| | No, I definitely do not | 12 |
| Practise private prayer | Daily | 27 |
| | Several times a week | 11 |
| | About once a week | 7 |
| | Once or more times a month | 8 |
| | Hardly ever/never | 47 |
| Experience God | Yes, I definitely have | 26 |
| | Yes, I think so | 23 |
| | No, I don't think I have | 30 |
| | No, I definitely have not | 21 |
| Knowledge | The name of the sacred book of Islam (Qur'an) | 53 |
| | The first book in the Old Testament (Genesis) | 47 |
| | Who denied Jesus three times? (Peter) | 41 |

SOURCE: Derived from Reginald W. Bibby, *Project Canada 2005 National Survey.*

then, early twenty-first century Canadians seem to be a fairly religious people.

However, the surveys have also found that although around 50 percent claim to be committed to Christianity or another religion, less than half of the committed demonstrate the belief, practice, experience, and knowledge characteristics that Stark and Glock (1968) saw as central to commitment. Among the other 50 percent of Canadians, about three in ten indicate that they are interested in but not committed to any religion, and the remaining two in ten simply say that they are not religious (Bibby, 2004a). According to the 2005 Project Canada survey, 25 percent of Canadians say that religion is "very important" to them, with most having fairly conventional ideas of religion in mind. Regional variations are striking, with the levels ranging from a high of about 40 percent in the Atlantic region, through around 30 percent to 35 percent in Ontario and the three Prairie provinces, to lows of 15 percent in British Columbia and 10 percent in Quebec.

An interesting footnote is worth pondering: Pollsters are continually reminding us that Americans are more religious than Canadians are (Kiefer, 2004; Ray, 2003; Winseman, 2004). However, New Brunswick sociologist Samuel Reimer (2003) has been arguing for some time now that we must not overlook an important qualitative difference in religious belief and commitment in the two countries. Reimer maintains that it is easier to be highly committed in the American religious environment than it is in Canada since, in his words, higher levels of religiosity in the United States have "more to do with cultural supports for religiosity than with deeper religious conviction." Since it is more difficult to be religiously committed in Canada, religious devotion, among Canadians, he argues, "is more likely to be based on conviction."

## COLLECTIVE RELIGIOSITY

How many times have you heard people say, "I don't have to go to church to be religious"? Increasingly the generalization has been expanded to include temples and synagogues as well. It may be a common argument, but it doesn't have much sociological support.

Most social scientists, beginning with Durkheim, have maintained that personal religiosity is highly dependent on **collective religiosity,** or group support of some kind. Such dependence is not unique to religion. It stems from a basic fact of life: The ideas we hold tend to come from our interaction with other people. However creative we might like to think we are, the fact is that most of the ideas we have in our heads right now can be traced back to the people with whom we have been in contact—family, friends, teachers, authors, journalists, and any number of other so-called experts. Moreover, if we are to retain those ideas, they have to be continually endorsed by at least a few other people whose opinions we value. Ideas are sustained by relationships.

Consequently, it is not surprising that researchers find that evangelicals, for example, one of the most numerically vibrant "religious families" in the country, have learned that they need to "grow their own and keep their own." They have more children than members of most other groups do, provide them with positive church-life experiences from the time they hit the church nursery, make sure they have youth-friendly programs when they are teens, and encourage them to marry each other—or if worst comes to worst, marry an outsider and bring the partner into the group—and then continue to be part of young adult and adult activities. To fail at any of those three crucial points in the biography of their daughters and sons is to run the risk of seeing them abandon evangelical faith. People cannot hold ideas or commitment for long without a measure of social support.

Seem like a strong claim? Try it on your own biography.

## The Church-Sect Typology

Those who have examined religious groups in predominantly Christian settings have recognized two major kinds of organizations. First, there are numerically dominant groupings—the Roman Catholic Church in medieval Europe, the Church of England, the so-called mainline denominations in Canada and the United States (Anglican, United, Presbyterian, Lutheran), and so on. Second, smaller groups have broken away from the dominant bodies. For example, in the sixteenth century, Protestant groups, including the Church of England, broke away from the Roman Catholic Church; but Methodists in turn broke away from the Church of England, and the Salvation Army emerged as a breakaway group from the Methodists. Today, additional emerging groups include an array of Baptist and Pentecostal denominations and nondenominational "grassroots" congregations that are found in virtually every North American city.

From this pattern of dominant groups and breakaway groups, sociologists who try to make sense of religious groups developed an analytical scheme known as the **church-sect typology.** This framework attempted to describe the central characteristics of these two types of organizations, as well as account for the origin and development of sects.

In perhaps its earliest formulation, Max Weber distinguished church from sect primarily on the basis of theology (churches emphasize works, sects stress faith) and relationship to society (for churches, accommodation; for sects, separation). Weber noted the irony in the sect's development: Initially a spinoff from an established church, the sect gradually evolves into a church itself (Gerth and Mills, 1958). The sect at first is characterized by spontaneity and enthusiasm. In time, however, these traits give way to routinization and institutionalization.

Although the church-sect typology has been used extensively, alternative ways of understanding religious groups have become increasingly popular.

## Organizational Approaches

In sociological terms, religious organizations are no different from other social organizations. Therefore, there has been a growing tendency to analyze religious groups by making use of the same frameworks we use in studying social organizations in general.

Led by the work of respected American sociologist Rodney Stark and his associates (Finke and Stark, 1992; Stark and Bainbridge, 1985; Stark and Finke, 2000), a market model for understanding religion has become prominent in recent years. Religious groups are seen as "firms" or "companies" competing for "market share."

- Seen through such eyes, the Roman Catholic, Anglican, and Eastern Orthodox churches are part of multinational corporations; so is the Salvation Army.
- A number of groups, including the United Church and the Pentecostal Assemblies of Canada, are companies that are "Canadian-owned and -operated."
- Many smaller evangelical Protestant denominations have been "branch plant" operations of American groups—not unlike "Ford Canada" or "Wal-Mart Canada"—that, over the years, have become increasingly autonomous. Some other groups, including Presbyterians and some Lutherans and Baptists, have similarly evolved from overseas operations.
- Despite the fact that Jews, Muslims, Hindus, Sikhs, and Buddhists all have worldwide roots

and ongoing ties with those roots, none have developed official international or national structures that oversee their Canadian businesses. They have lobby groups and other organizations that address some common interests. But their "business outlets" are typically highly autonomous, with their synagogues, mosques, and temples owned and operated by their local congregations.
- Similarly, large numbers of other religious firms operate as privately owned companies. They are started by religious entrepreneurs who are convinced that a market exists for their particular product. The early days are often modest, with operations launched in homes, schools, and warehouses. Some are successful; many are not.

Apart from provocative marketing language and corporate analogies, a general organizational approach to religious groups sheds new light on basic features of religious groups, including (1) the nature and the sources of their members, (2) their formal and informal goals, (3) the norms and roles that are established to accomplish their purposes, (4) the sanctions that are used to ensure that norms are followed and roles are played, and (5) the degree of success that groups experience in pursuing their goals. Let me briefly illustrate.

**Membership**  When studying the membership of religious groups, it readily becomes apparent that the vast majority of those involved are following in parental footsteps. Canadian census data show that when two parents have the same faith, 95 percent of their children are also raised in that faith. As a result, new additions to almost any given congregation are primarily active members who are on the move geographically. These include people coming to Canada from other countries. For example, during the 1980s and 1990s immigrants contributed most of the growth to Hindu, Sikh, Muslim, and Buddhist groups. Given the extensive worldwide growth of Roman Catholicism, Pentecostalism, and Islam, "immigration pipelines" are going to favour those traditions in the immediate future (Allen, 2009). Conversely, the "pipelines" have narrowed for members of the United and Presbyterian Churches (Bibby, 2011a: 30–31).

Congregations frequently compete with one another for members and staff, especially in urban areas where some "outlets" are larger and more affluent than others are. The more attractive congregations typically have the resources to search farther for their leaders and hold them longer.

During the 1980s and 1990s, immigrants contributed most of the growth to Hindu, Sikh, Muslim, and Buddhist groups in Canada. SOURCE: © iStockphoto.com/David P. Lewis.

They also have better physical facilities. It's not just a Protestant or Catholic phenomenon: Muslims, Hindus, Sikhs, Buddhists, and Jews typically define their meeting places as important centres for social activity. Consequently, groups tend to build structures as lavish as their resources will permit. In recent years, a number of Protestant "megachurches" have come into being in Canada and the United States. They typically have seating for one thousand to four thousand people, are serviced by many full-time staff members, and have annual budgets in the millions of dollars. They are found in major cities, such as Toronto, Montreal, Winnipeg, Edmonton, Calgary, and Vancouver. But they also are appearing in smaller communities, such as Abbotsford, Red Deer, and St. Catharines. They typically co-opt technology and culture. PowerPoint and worship bands, cellphones and texting are part of services, with Starbucks coffee commonly found both outside and inside sanctuaries. These megachurches make it difficult for other congregations to compete. Catholics are showing signs of following suit, recognizing that one way of dealing with the priest shortage and the need for specialized ministries is to have larger, regional parishes.

Congregations, like secular businesses, also expand their services and personnel in keeping with their economic means. Some of the megachurches, for example, offer many of the typical worship and educational opportunities of more traditional, older groups. But they also have extensive programs aimed at children, teenagers, young adults, and seniors. The programs range from small but sophisticated groups studying in homes ("cell groups"), through well-developed music and drama programs, to multimedia education, entertainment, and elaborate Web activities that often include podcasts. A room in one well-known British Columbia megachurch resembles a 1950s diner—complete with a car front, jukeboxes, booths, and stools. As the church's head youth minister told me, "The young people love this room; but the seniors love it too."

An obvious point of tension involves maintaining integrity while providing products that attract customers.

**Goals** The conscious and unconscious goals of local religious groups vary by congregation and members. Like the goals of other social groupings, these conscious and unconscious goals commonly appear to be in conflict. For years observers have noted that the formal goals derived from religious doctrine, such as spiritual growth, frequently exist in tension with "survival goals" relating to numerical growth that translate into necessary human and financial resources (Metz, 1967).

Similarly, congregations frequently have difficulty in reconciling their pastoral or "comfort" function with their prophetical or "challenge" function (Glock, Ringer, and Babbie, 1967). For example, the national leadership of the United Church of Canada viewed itself as prophetic in its call during the mid-1980s to allow gays and lesbians to be eligible for ordination as ministers. In taking such a controversial position, the denomination lost a sizable number of dissenting members and, in some cases, entire congregations (O'Toole et al., 1993). Prophecy has its organizational price.

There is an additional point of tension: how to satisfy the needs of the existing clientele while reaching out to new people who are not involved yet have important needs themselves. For example, as the twenty-first century began, the most divisive issue in U.S. Protestant congregations was whether church music should be traditional and oriented toward *insiders* or contemporary and aimed at *outsiders*. It is a dilemma that congregations of virtually all religious stripes are not particularly adept at resolving, with obvious negative implications for growth.

**Norms, Roles, and Sanctions** If groups, like companies, are to achieve their official and unofficial goals, they have to be able to establish norms for what has to be done and assign roles for their members to play. An examination of congregational roles reveals that most groups in Canada—led by Catholics, evangelicals, Muslims, Hindus, and Sikhs—often have a human resource problem for two main reasons. The first is that they are top-heavy with men and often inadequately tap the resources of women, a reality that has been variously met with acquiescence, resistance, and a measure of change (Nason-Clark, 1993; Nesbitt, 1997; Speaker-Yuan, 2005; Stackhouse, 2005). The second problem is that groups typically rely on volunteers to carry out key roles. These are the same people who congregational leaders have to work hard to recruit and retain—people on whom they depend for involvement and financial support. They are not hired and they can't exactly be fired. It adds up to a situation in which religious groups are frequently fragile and inefficient companies (Bibby, 1993; Brannon, 1971; Monahan, 1999).

**Success**   In their studies of religion in Canada, researchers have tended to emphasize "the numerical bottom lines" of religious groups and to focus on such indicators of success as attendance, membership, and finances.

Through the early 1990s, the research news was not particularly good for organized religion. Overall, attendance and membership were down, with some groups feeling great hardship as a result of inadequate finances. The mainline Protestant groups—the United, Anglican, Presbyterian, and Lutheran churches—were the most severely hit, along with Roman Catholics in Quebec. Despite some attendance and membership losses, the Roman Catholic Church outside Quebec appeared to be relatively healthy. And although their numbers were not as large as many people think, conservative Protestant groups were at least able to hold their own and grow modestly—a significant accomplishment, given that they have represented only about 8 percent of the population since 1871 and could have readily been absorbed by larger competitors. Other faith groups, such as Hindus, Muslims, Sikhs, Jews, and Buddhists, were having a difficult time growing, primarily because they were having considerable difficulty holding on to their offspring, who all too frequently were marrying Catholics, Protestants, and people with no religion (Brym, Shaffir, and Weinfeld, 2010).

The size of a group is largely a function of immigration, birth, and mortality factors. What was disconcerting for religious leaders in Canada through the early 1990s was that most groups were top-heavy with older people, and many did not seem able to replace them with comparable numbers of younger people. As a result, it was estimated that, by 2015, weekly attendance would drop dramatically for mainline Protestants and Quebec Catholics, decline

Religious groups are increasingly recognizing the importance of connecting with culture. Here Toronto Roman Catholic Archbishop Thomas Collins wears a Maple Leafs sweater in St. Peter's Square at the Vatican in February 2012, during the week when he was elevated to Cardinal.
SOURCE: Emanuel Pires/Archdiocese of Toronto.

slightly for "Other World Faith" groups, and remain fairly stable for conservative Protestants and Roman Catholics elsewhere in Canada (Bibby 1993: 103ff). There was a very real possibility that the dominant players on the Canadian religious scene would be Roman Catholics and evangelical Protestants.

Such projections are proving accurate. However, as we will see shortly, there is good reason to believe that the "old story" of *secularization* needs to be replaced by a "new story" of polarization. **Religious polarization** refers to the growing tendency of some people in a given setting to embrace religion and the tendency of others to reject it. A solid and growing core of Canadians are choosing to live life without religion. Simultaneously, a solid and durable core continues to see faith as important. The ongoing significance of religion for many people appears to reflect the efforts of groups to be more effective in addressing the needs and interests of children, teenagers, and young adults.

## The Canadian Situation

Affiliation with religious groups has been widespread in Canada since the founding of this country. Close ties have always been apparent between Canadians of British descent and the Church of England, Methodism, and Presbyterianism; between the French and the Roman Catholic Church; and between other ethnic groups and the churches of their homelands (see, for example, Bramadat and Seljak, 2008). As noted earlier, Islam, Hindu, Sikh, and Buddhist growth in recent years has been directly related to immigration from Asia.

In the 2001 census, 84 percent of Canadians indicated that they have a religious preference. Nationally, Catholics compose 45 percent of the population; Protestants, 29 percent; and unspecified Christians, 3 percent. Seven percent consist of those with other religious preferences, and 16 percent have no specified religion (Table 13.2). A 2010 update offered by Statistics Canada's *General Social Survey* (GSS) of more than 15 000 people found the preference level remained high but had slipped a bit to 76 percent, with Catholics and Protestants composing 67 percent of the national population.

Such data suggest that it is an exaggeration to think of Canada as a highly diversified religious mosaic. As Statistics Canada (2003: 5) noted in releasing the 2001 census findings, Canada is "still predominantly Roman Catholic and Protestant." It's true that Muslim, Hindu, Sikh, and Buddhist populations all doubled in size between 1991 and 2001, and they have added diversity and vitality to the Canadian religious scene. Yet, measured against the

Canadian population, their numbers are still relatively small. It is also premature to assume that their numbers will continue to grow, given the tendency of many of their offspring to socialize with and marry people outside their groups—a reality and challenge well known, for example, to Canada's Jewish community. Christian groups not only continue to hold a large monopoly but are frequently the primary beneficiaries of such intermarital "religious defection" (Bibby, 2002: 82–85). Time will fill out the story.

The Christian faith also continues to be pervasive in the United States, where surveys show that about 85 percent of Americans identify with Christian groups (Gallup, 2012). However, the numerically dominant groups in the United States are not the same as those in Canada. While one in two Canadians is Catholic, the same is true of only one in four Americans. Furthermore, just one in ten Canadians identifies with conservative Protestant (evangelical) groups, in contrast to more than three in ten Americans. A tipoff on the difference is that some

**TABLE 13.2**   RELIGIOUS IDENTIFICATION, CANADA AND THE PROVINCES AND TERRITORIES, 2001 (IN PERCENTAGE)

| | CANADA | BC | AB | SK | MB | ON | QC | NB | NS | PE | NL | YT | NT | NU |
|---|---|---|---|---|---|---|---|---|---|---|---|---|---|---|
| **Catholic** | 45 | 19 | 28 | 33 | 29 | 37 | 84 | 54 | 37 | 48 | 37 | 22 | 46 | 24 |
| Roman | 43 | 18 | 26 | 31 | 27 | 34 | 83 | 54 | 37 | 47 | 37 | 22 | 46 | 23 |
| Eastern Orthodox | 2 | 1 | 2 | 2 | 2 | 2 | 1 | <1 | <1 | <1 | <1 | <1 | <1 | <1 |
| **Protestant** | 29 | 32 | 39 | 48 | 45 | 35 | 5 | 37 | 49 | 43 | 60 | 34 | 31 | 67 |
| United | 10 | 9 | 14 | 20 | 16 | 12 | <1 | 10 | 16 | 20 | 17 | 9 | 6 | 1 |
| Anglican | 7 | 8 | 6 | 7 | 8 | 9 | 1 | 8 | 13 | 5 | 26 | 15 | 15 | 58 |
| Presbyterian | 1 | 1 | 1 | <1 | <1 | 3 | <1 | 1 | 3 | 6 | <1 | 1 | 1 | <1 |
| Lutheran | 2 | 3 | 5 | 8 | 5 | 2 | <1 | <1 | 1 | <1 | <1 | 2 | 1 | <1 |
| Baptist | 3 | 3 | 3 | 2 | 2 | 3 | <1 | 11 | 11 | 5 | <1 | 4 | 2 | <1 |
| Pentecostal | 1 | 1 | 1 | 2 | 2 | 1 | <1 | 3 | 1 | 1 | 7 | 2 | 3 | 4 |
| Other | 8 | 7 | 9 | 9 | 12 | 5 | 3 | 4 | 4 | 6 | 10 | 1 | 3 | 4 |
| **Christian: Other** | 3 | 5 | 4 | 3 | 4 | 3 | 1 | 1 | 1 | 2 | 1 | 4 | 3 | 3 |
| **Other faiths** | 7 | 8 | 6 | <1 | 3 | 9 | 4 | <1 | <1 | <1 | <1 | 1 | 2 | <1 |
| Jewish | 1 | <1 | <1 | <1 | 1 | 2 | 1 | <1 | <1 | <1 | <1 | <1 | <1 | <1 |
| Muslim | 2 | 2 | 2 | <1 | <1 | 3 | 2 | <1 | <1 | <1 | <1 | <1 | <1 | <1 |
| Hindu | 1 | <1 | <1 | <1 | <1 | 2 | <1 | <1 | <1 | <1 | <1 | <1 | <1 | <1 |
| Buddhist | 1 | 2 | 1 | <1 | <1 | 1 | 1 | <1 | <1 | <1 | <1 | <1 | <1 | <1 |
| Sikh | <1 | 4 | <1 | <1 | <1 | <1 | <1 | <1 | <1 | <1 | <1 | <1 | <1 | <1 |
| Other | <1 | <1 | <1 | <1 | <1 | <1 | <1 | <1 | <1 | <1 | <1 | <1 | <1 | <1 |
| **No religion** | 16 | 36 | 23 | 16 | 19 | 16 | 6 | 8 | 12 | 6 | 2 | 39 | 18 | 6 |

SOURCE: Adapted from Statistics Canada. (2003). "Religions in Canada," Analysis Series, 2001 Census. Catalogue no. 96F0030XIE2002015.

40 percent of Americans claim that they are "born again" (Gallup, 2012); the term itself is not even particularly common in Canadian religious group circles, even among many of today's evangelicals. In fact, 31 percent of Canadians in our 2005 survey told us that if they were in the presence of someone they didn't know who was "born again," their immediate reaction would be to feel uncomfortable. They'd better not wander too far into the United States.

When Canadians are asked about actual *membership* in religious groups, as opposed to mere affiliation or identification, more people—about 30 percent—claim to belong to churches than to any other single voluntary group. About one in four attends services at least once a month, and roughly the same proportion of parents with school-age children expose their children to Sunday schools or similar kinds of religious instruction on a fairly frequent basis.

However, between approximately the 1940s and 2000, church attendance in Canada declined sharply, documented by Gallup poll findings summarized in Figure 13.1. Gallup had been asking Canadians if they attended a service "in the last seven days"—the phrasing of the inquiry adds sporadic attendees to those who claim they attend every week. Using such a measure, Gallup found that Protestant weekly attendance dropped from around 60 percent to about 30 percent between the 1940s and mid-1970s, rebounding to around 40 percent by the mid-1990s. The decline in Roman Catholic attendance appears to have started around 1965, dropping from roughly 85 percent to 40 percent by the late 1990s—led by low church-going in

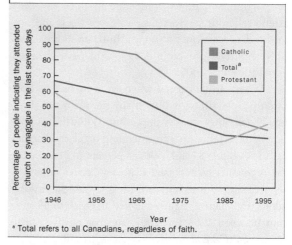

FIGURE 13.1  ATTENDANCE AT RELIGIOUS SERVICES, CANADA, 1946–2001

ᵃ Total refers to all Canadians, regardless of faith.

SOURCE: Gallup Canada, Inc., surveys, 1946–1995. Gallup's national figure for 2001 is 31 percent, for 2010 26 percent; no Protestant-Catholic breakdowns are available (Bibby, 2011a).

Quebec (for details, see Eagle, 2011; Bibby, 2011b). No such dramatic decline in attendance has taken place in the United States: Weekly attendance has remained remarkably steady at just over 40 percent dating back to the late 1930s when polling began (Newport, 2010; Newport, Moore, and Saad, 1999).

On the surface, evidence suggests that attendance has levelled off in Canada (Figure 13.2). In 1984, 23 percent of the country's 15- to 19-year-olds were attending services weekly. By 1992, the figure had dropped to 18 percent. Surprisingly, teenage

FIGURE 13.2  ATTENDANCE IN CANADA, 1975–2010

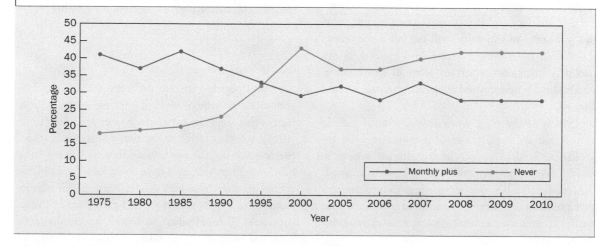

SOURCES: Reginald W. Bibby, *Project Canada Surveys*, 1975–1980; *General Social Surveys*, Statistics Canada, 1985–2010.

attendance rebounded to 21 percent in 2000, where it remains today (Bibby, 2009). Close to the same proportion of adults—some one in five—say they attend religious services close to every week, and one in three, at least once a month. Both levels are down only slightly from around 1990 and have changed very little since 2005.

What can be missed when we look only at how often people attend is how many people never show up. The findings are very important. While the proportion of teenagers who were attending regularly changed little between 1984 and 2008 (23 percent to 21 percent), the segment who reported that they "never" attended services almost doubled, from 28 to 47 percent. Among adults, the "never" figure doubled from 20 to 40 percent between 1985 and 2007, and has changed little since then (*General Social Survey*, 1985, 2010).

These attendance patterns point to an intriguing emerging religious situation in Canada: polarization. A fairly stable and durable segment of the population, comprised of both younger and older people, continue to value faith. However, for another growing segment, faith is unimportant. A significant proportion—like undecided voters—constitute something of an ambivalent middle who, in the longer run, "are up for grabs" (Bibby, 2011a: 51ff). Polarization, rather than secularization, captures the reality of these three important population components in Canada and elsewhere.

## THE SOURCES OF RELIGION

More than a few religious leaders over the years who have seen their best efforts to involve people come up empty have murmured, "There is only so much we can do." It's an insightful lament. The best programs and ministries in the world will not hit a responsive chord with everybody. Personal and societal factors also play critically important roles in determining who embraces religion and religious groups, and who does not.

Much of the early work in the scientific study of religion by people like Durkheim focused on preliterate cultures in which religion was pervasive. Everyone was religious, or so it seemed. Consequently, it's not surprising that observers gave considerable attention to the origin of religion itself, rather than examining variations in religious commitment.

However, individual differences in religion's importance in contemporary societies have called for explanations as to why some people are religious and others are not. The explanations tend to focus either on individuals or on social structure.

## INDIVIDUAL-CENTRED EXPLANATIONS

At least three dominant "person-centred" explanations of religious commitment have emerged. See to what extent you see yourself and others in what the experts have had to say.

### Reflection

The desire to comprehend reality is widespread among humans. In reflecting on the meaning of existence, people have commonly concluded that life has a supernatural, "transempirical" dimension. As Weber (1963 [1922]: 117) put it, religion is the product of an "inner compulsion to understand the world as a meaningful cosmos and take up a position toward it."

There is little doubt that Canadians, like people elsewhere, reflect on life's so-called big questions. Some 80 percent say they think about such issues as the origin and purpose of life, the meaning of suffering, and what happens after we die. Such questions take on particular urgency when people have to come to grips with such events as the attacks on September 11, 2001, or a devastating tsunami—or have to deal with the suicide of a friend or the loss of a parent. Still, although such times of reflection may provide religious groups with an opportunity to respond, reflection in itself does not usually lead to religious commitment and involvement. Fewer than one in three Canadians who often raises these meaning questions gives evidence of being religiously committed.

### Socialization

A second person-centred explanation sees religious commitment as the product of learning—socialization factors that were the focus of Chapter 3. Freud (1962 [1928]) went so far as to say that religion is learned pretty much like the multiplication table. He may not have been exaggerating. I have never forgotten a high-school teacher who had played for the Edmonton Eskimos telling us that if we had grown up in India, we would all be Hindus. As Durkheim emphasized, personal religiosity has social origins and, consequently, will strongly reflect the social environments from which we come, beginning with our family.

Why is an Iraqi a Muslim, a Londoner Church of England, a Ute (as in Utah) a Mormon, a Quebecker a Catholic? The answers are obvious. What is less clear is why some of those four people take their religion more seriously than the others do. To address the question, we probably would start by looking at the commitment level of their parents. Beyond family, we would expect that individuals who are devout have been exposed to additional social sources that are positive toward religion—friends, an ethnic group, an institution, a community or region, perhaps an entire society. Religion is very much a learned phenomenon.

Accommodation to social pressures, notably those of primary groups, seems to be a related source of religious group involvement. For example, one marriage partner may become more active in response to the hopes and expectations of the other, friends in response to friends, parents in response to having young children, children in response to their parents. As John McEnroe of tennis fame once put it, "I can go to church once in a while, just for Mom." In small communities where religion is pervasive and normative, accommodation would be expected to be an important source of religious involvement.

It's important to keep in mind that socialization appears to be a *necessary* but not a *sufficient* cause of religiosity. That is to say, to the extent that Canadians are currently involved in religious groups, most had parents who also were involved. However, the fact that Canadians had parents who were involved does not ensure that their sons and daughters will follow suit. Although about eight in ten of today's weekly attendees had parents who attended weekly, only about three in ten Canadians whose fathers or mothers attended weekly have followed their example.

With a decreasing number of parents actively involved in religious groups in recent decades, fewer have been passing the experience of organized religion on to their children. For example, in 1975, some 35 percent of Canadians with school-age children claimed that they and their children were attending services on a regular basis. By 2000, that figure had dropped to around 20 percent. Such a pattern, if it had continued, obviously would have had devastating numerical consequences for organized religion. But as of 2005, it had increased to 23 percent. The fact that the pro-religious proportion of parents remains fairly stable points to religion continuing to be important for a significant core of people, at the same time as it is becoming less salient for others.

One of the strongest predictors of adult religiosity is childhood religious practice. When parents participate in religious observance with their children, the early socialization experience is often imprinted for life.

SOURCE: © iStockphoto.com/Sean Locke.

If religious involvement and commitment are to last a lifetime, they need to receive ongoing social support. Our surveys have found that the commitment level of a partner is strongly related both to personal involvement and to the importance placed on religion. In more than seven in ten cases, if one partner is a weekly attendee, so is the other. In fewer than three in ten cases does a person attend weekly or view religion as "very important" if the partner does not.

## Deprivation

A third person-centred explanation of religious commitment is that the devout are drawn primarily from the ranks of society's deprived or disadvantaged. Religion provides them with compensation, sometimes in this life, sometimes later. The roots of such thinking, of course, are found in the work of Marx and Freud.

The deprivation argument was developed more fully by Glock and Stark (1965), whose work has been influential. They maintained that five types of deprivation are predominant in the rise and development of religious and secular movements: economic, social, organismic (that is, physical or mental), psychic, and ethical. The first three types of deprivation are self-explanatory. Psychic deprivation refers to the lack of a meaningful system of values, and ethical deprivation refers to having values that are in conflict with those dominant in a society.

Research in the 1970s and 1980s using objective indicators, such as income, health, and social relationships, did not find deprivation to be a particularly good predictor of broad religious participation in either the United States (Roof and Hoge, 1980) or Canada (Hobart, 1974). The learning perspective seems to have had far more applicability.

Since 2000, suicide bombing has received considerable world attention. Because such attacks are often religiously inspired, and because they are so violent, you might expect the attackers to be driven by extreme deprivation. And, in fact, some observers initially hypothesized that suicide bombers must be poor, unemployed, uneducated, unmarried, socially marginal young adults with little to lose. Analysts assumed that people with such characteristics could be relatively easily convinced to exchange their lives of suffering in the here-and-now for promises of glory and martyrdom in the hereafter.

Research has demonstrated, however, that the deprivation argument does not hold in the case of suicide bombers. Sociologists Robert Brym of the University of Toronto and Bader Araj of Birzeit University in Palestine note in their study of suicide bombings in Israel, the West Bank, and Gaza from 2000 to 2005 that suicide bombers typically come from working-class and middle-class backgrounds, and they are generally better educated than the populations from which they are drawn. For example, the suicide bombers who were responsible for the attacks of September 11, 2001, were all well-educated, middle-class men (Brym and Araj, 2006). Studies of extreme forms of religious participation thus lead us to the same conclusion as studies of general populations: Deprivation does not appear to be systematically associated with religious commitment. This leads us to look for additional explanations of religious commitment.

## STRUCTURE-CENTRED EXPLANATIONS

Suicide bombers hardly exist in social isolation. On the contrary, they typically are members of political and military groups found in the Middle East and, in the case of the Tamil Tigers, Sri Lanka. The groups to which they belong in turn are committed to getting rid of occupying forces, overthrowing existing regimes in their own countries or, in the case of a group like Hamas—the largest Palestinian resistance movement—obliterating Israel and creating an Islamic theocracy. Structural conditions clearly play an important role in such "religio-political" organizations coming into being and in individuals being recruited as members.

Such realities remind us that, in addition to personal characteristics of the reflection, socialization, and deprivation variety, religious commitment is strongly influenced by the broader national, regional, and group contexts in which people find themselves. You might immediately think of a theocracy, such as Iran, where the president and legislature are subject to clerical supervision. However, in virtually every society, Canada included, history and culture combine to create milieux that, to varying degrees, do or do not support religion.

Those proclivities often vary not only along national lines but also by the region in which people live and the groups of which they are a part. Historically, Canada's "Bible Belt" has been viewed as Alberta, when by every conceivable measure it probably has actually been the Atlantic region (Bibby, 1987; Hiller, 1976). Regardless, to grow up in either of these two regions results in being exposed to environments that are far more "pro-religious" than people experience in a province like British Columbia. Social environments are important determinants of religious commitment and involvement.

Two early prominent Canadian sociologists, S. D. Clark (1948) and W. E. Mann (1962) argued that, historically, the emergence of sect-like groups, such as indigenous Baptists and Pentecostals, in Canada was tied to the existence of unstable conditions, which were produced by such factors as immigration and economic depression. With industrialization and increased prosperity and stability, some of these smaller, independent evangelical groups evolved into denominations—a process referred to as **denominationalism.**

A further example of the impact of societal factors on religion can be found in Quebec. Much of the drop-off in Roman Catholic attendance between 1965 and 1980 was related to the accelerated modernization of Quebec, including the Church's relinquishing of much of its important role in education and social services to the provincial government (Beyer, 1993, 1997; Rouleau, 1977).

NEL

The climate that present-day societies provide for religion is the subject of considerable debate. Some observers maintain that increasing industrialization and postindustrialization contribute to a decline in the pervasiveness and importance of religion. This widely held **secularization thesis** has been prominent in the social sciences, largely because of the influence of Durkheim, Marx, and Freud. It's a framework that seems particularly appropriate to developments in much of Protestant Europe. It also is the dominant explanatory framework the media and Statistics Canada use in making sense of religious developments in Canada (see, for example, Catto, 2003; Statistics Canada, 2004a, 2004b; Valpy and Friesen, 2010).

But there is also another take on religious developments—what we might call the **persistence thesis.** Proponents of this position, among them Daniel Bell (1977) and Rodney Stark and William Bainbridge (1985), claim that religion—traditional or otherwise—persists in industrial and postindustrial or postmodern societies, continuing to address questions of meaning and purpose, and responding to widespread interest in spirituality. Stark maintains that some religious groups or companies will fail, but because of ongoing market demand, new ones will emerge to pick up the slack. What is in doubt is not the persistence of religion, only the identity of the key players.

In Canada, we can readily explore the relationship between religious involvement and commitment and some of the correlates of social and cultural change, such as age, urbanization, education, and employment status. If the secularization thesis is correct, we would expect religiosity to be pretty low for everyone by this point in our history, particularly so for Canadians who are younger, are living in larger communities, are well educated, and are part of the paid work force. Conversely, if the persistence thesis is correct, we would expect some variations in these anticipated patterns.

Here are the main findings:

- Differences in religious group involvement are readily apparent, with attendance lowest among people under 35, somewhat higher for those 35 to 54, and highest among Canadians 55 and older (Table 13.3). There is also some support for the idea that secularization is most advanced in those parts of Canada that were first to experience extensive economic development—central Canada and the west coast.

- Religious participation varies little by community size, education, gender, and employment status. However, full-time employment is associated with a noticeable decline in attendance for women, presumably related to time pressures. The post-1950s increase in dual-employed parents may, in fact, be largely responsible for the decline in mainline Protestant and Catholic attendance in Canada in the last half of the twentieth century (Bibby, 2011a: 262. Robert Putnam (2000: 195) makes a similar point with respect to the impact on service attendance in the United States, while Callum Brown (2009) has drawn attention to the same pattern in Britain. Religious groups needed to adapt by providing "ministries" that responded to changing family life. Few have.

- It is intriguing to note that, while just fewer than one in three Canadians currently attends services monthly or more, one in two people across the country says that he or she engages in personal religious practices or spiritual activities at least once a month, while two in three tell Statistics Canada that their religious or spiritual beliefs are either very important" or "somewhat important" to how they live their lives. While there are some variations by age, region, and gender, differences are minor by community size, education, and employment. A majority of Canadians in every demographic and social category, for example, report that their religious or spiritual beliefs have significantly influenced how they live.

Such findings about the ongoing personal importance of religion and/or spirituality are consistent with what observers from Durkheim to Stark have expected. Many Canadians are religious and spiritual, many are spiritual but not religious, but only a minority appears to be *neither* religious *nor* spiritual (Bibby, 2011a: 124–26. The data also point to the fact that an extensive market for religion and spirituality persists.

## THE CONSEQUENCES OF RELIGION

In today's increasingly pragmatic world, Canadians face what seem like unlimited choices and limited resources. We need to sort out what is worth our time and what is not. Religion gets no exemption from such selective consumption.

**TABLE 13.3**   SERVICE ATTENDANCE, PERSONAL PRACTICES, AND THE IMPORTANCE OF RELIGION AND SPIRITUALITY BY SOCIAL CHANGE CORRELATES, CANADIAN ADULTS, 2010 (IN PERCENTAGES)

| | SERVICE ATTENDANCE MONTHLY-PLUS | PERSONAL RELIGIOUS PRACTICES OR SPIRITUAL ACTIVITIES MONTHLY-PLUS | RELIGIOUS OR SPIRITUAL BELIEFS VERY OR SOMEWHAT IMPORTANT TO HOW YOU LIVE YOUR LIFE |
|---|---|---|---|
| **Nationally** | 28 | 51 | 66 |
| **Age** | | | |
| 55 and over | 37 | 61 | 78 |
| 35–54 | 25 | 50 | 66 |
| 18–34 | 22 | 41 | 53 |
| **Community Size** | | | |
| Larger urban centres | 24 | 48 | 62 |
| Rural areas | 25 | 49 | 65 |
| **Region** | | | |
| Atlantic | 33 | 54 | 71 |
| Prairies | 33 | 55 | 72 |
| Ontario | 31 | 54 | 69 |
| British Columbia | 25 | 47 | 64 |
| Quebec | 20 | 44 | 56 |
| **Education** | | | |
| High school or less | 29 | 52 | 67 |
| Some postsecondary | 26 | 49 | 65 |
| Degree or more | 31 | 52 | 66 |
| **Gender and Paid Employment (under 65, non-students)** | | | |
| Female | 27 | 56 | 69 |
|   Not employed outside the home | 33 | 62 | 74 |
|   Employed outside the home | 24 | 53 | 68 |
| Male | 23 | 40 | 57 |
|   Not employed outside the home | 25 | 41 | 57 |
|   Employed outside the home | 22 | 39 | 56 |
|   Not employed outside the home (male and female) | 32 | 58 | 71 |
|   Employed outside the home (male and female) | 23 | 46 | 62 |
| Women (all) | 24 | 53 | 68 |
| Men (all) | 22 | 39 | 56 |

SOURCE: Derived from Statistics Canada, *General Social Survey*, 2010.

Gone is the day when religious leaders could expect people to become involved in their groups because it's "their duty." Our 2005 national survey found that 61 percent of Canadians believed that their parents "felt they were supposed to go to church." Eighty-seven percent of respondents maintained that, today, "people who attend religious services should not go because they feel they have to but because they find it to be worthwhile."

Is religion "worthwhile"? On balance, does it enhance personal and social life?

## PERSONAL CONSEQUENCES

Research findings on religion and what we might refer to generally as "mental health" are contradictory. Important early work carried out by social psychologist Milton Rokeach (1965: 2) led him to conclude, "We have found that

Canadians of every social and demographic stripe tend to acknowledge that they have spiritual needs.
SOURCE: © Shutterstock.

people with formal religious affiliation are more anxious [than others are]. Believers, compared with non-believers, complain more often of working under great tension, sleeping fitfully, and similar symptoms." Yet research dating back to the 1970s has consistently found a negative relationship between religious commitment and *anomie*—valuelessness and rootlessness (Lee and Clyde, 1974). Over the years a number of researchers have argued that involvement in groups, such as sects and cults, has contributed to upward mobility, providing an improved self-image and hope in the face of economic and social deprivation (e.g., Johnson, 1961; Whyte, 1966). During the 1970s and 1980s, considerable literature emerged warning against the psychological and emotional damage that could be inflicted by the alleged "brainwashing" of cults (Dawson, 2006: 95ff).

Gale Frankel and W. E. Hewitt (1994) of the University of Western Ontario are among the researchers who have found a positive relationship between religious group involvement and good mental health. Research into the "Toronto Blessing" congregation has even maintained that physical healing sometimes occurs (Poloma, 1997; Poloma and Hoelter, 1998). National denominational surveys that I have carried out for the United Church of Canada and the evangelical Christian and Missionary Alliance document a fairly predictable conclusion: People who are highly involved in established religious groups claim that their involvement significantly enriches their lives (Bibby, 2012; in the United States, Newport, 2007).

What seems apparent from all this is that some forms of religiosity are connected with well-being, while others are not.

My own analyses of our survey data dating back to 2000 suggest that, overall, Canadians who exhibit religious commitment are slightly more inclined than others to claim a high level of happiness; to find life exciting; to express a high level of satisfaction with family, friends, and leisure activities (Bibby, 2004a: 128–29, 2011a: 98ff; Figure 13.3). However, when the impact of other factors, such as age, education, community size, and region, is taken into account, the apparent modest influence of commitment typically disappears or at least has to be qualified. For example, Gee and Veevers (1990) found that religious involvement and life satisfaction were positively related nationally, but not in British Columbia.

In short, religious commitment by itself appears to have a fairly limited influence on valued personal characteristics. Moreover, it is often less important than such variables as age, education, or employment in predicting personal well-being.

An important word of caution: this "no difference" finding does not mean that faith is not adding something to the lives of people who value faith. Rather, in light of the high levels of happiness and contentment reported by Canadians generally, it suggests that large numbers of other people are finding alternative pathways to personal well-being. Religion is having an impact—but not necessarily a unique impact.

## INTERPERSONAL CONSEQUENCES

One of the first attempts to examine the relationship between religious commitment and compassion was carried out by Clifford Kirkpatrick in Minnesota in 1949. He found that religiously committed people

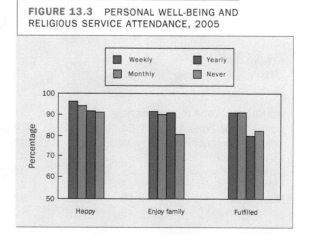

**FIGURE 13.3**   PERSONAL WELL-BEING AND RELIGIOUS SERVICE ATTENDANCE, 2005

SOURCE: Reginald W. Bibby, *Project Canada 2005*.

were somewhat less humanitarian in their outlook than were others.

Some 20 years later, Rokeach (1969), drawing on U.S. national data, observed that religious commitment was *negatively* related to social compassion; in the case of Roman Catholics, no relationship—positive or negative—existed. Rokeach concluded that "the results seem compatible with the hypothesis that religious values serve more as standards for condemning others ... than as standards to judge oneself by or to guide one's own conduct" (Rokeach, 1969: 35).

These findings have not gone unchallenged. Research conducted on specific religious groups and in certain locales has found a positive relationship between commitment and compassion. In a more immediate relational sense, Wilcox (1998) has found that, although conservative Protestant parents are more likely than others are to use corporal punishment in disciplining their children, they also are more likely than other parents were to praise and hug their children. Extensive research on religion and racial prejudice, such as Smith's (1999) look at anti-Semitism and "the Religious Right," has yielded contradictory results.

However, some three decades ago, Richard Gorsuch and Daniel Aleshire claimed to have found the key reason for the discrepancies. Church members often appear to be more prejudiced than those who have never joined a church. But, they say, it is not because of religious involvement. On the contrary, when involvement level is taken into account, the people who turn out to be the most prejudiced are the "marginally involved" members. Gorsuch and Aleshire concluded, "The highly committed religious person is—along with the nonreligious person— one of the least prejudiced members of our society" (Gorsuch and Aleshire, 1974: 287). If this is the case, then, as with personal characteristics, religion may be making a difference interpersonally—but it is not a unique difference.

Ongoing analyses of Project Canada data have found that religiously committed people in this country do not differ significantly from others with respect to their interpersonal relationship attitudes (Bibby, 1987, 1995, 2004a). They hold a similar view of people, claim a comparable level of compassion, and appear to be no more or less tolerant of deviants, members of minority groups, and people of other religious faiths than are other Canadians. Furthermore, in contrast to the findings of Rokeach and Stark and Glock, no noteworthy differences appear in the interpersonal attitudes held by Roman Catholics and Protestants.

There is, however, one area in which religion still appears to speak with a fairly loud if not unique voice—the area of personal morality, notably sexuality. With few exceptions and with varying degrees of explicitness, religious groups tend to oppose "moral innovation." Examples include opposition to changing sexual standards, legal abortion, and distribution of pornographic materials (see Table 13.4).

That said, there is considerable variation in the position that religious groups take on many sex-related

**TABLE 13.4** PERCENTAGE OF CANADIANS OPPOSED TO SELECTED ISSUES BY SERVICE ATTENDANCE AND GROUP IDENTIFICATION, 2005

| | PRE-MARITAL SEX | EXTRA-MARITAL SEX | HOMO-SEXUALITY | SAME-SEX MARRIAGE | ABORTION: RAPE | ABORTION: CHILD UNWANTED | DISTRIBUTION OF PORNOGRAPHY |
|---|---|---|---|---|---|---|---|
| **ATTENDANCE** | | | | | | | |
| Weekly | 60 | 96 | 75 | 62 | 45 | 79 | 69 |
| Less than weekly | 7 | 82 | 25 | 20 | 4 | 36 | 31 |
| **RELIGIOUS GROUP IDENTIFICATION** | | | | | | | |
| Conservative Protestants | 64 | 98 | 74 | 64 | 41 | 82 | 69 |
| Christian Unspecified | 30 | 92 | 45 | 44 | 28 | 65 | 44 |
| RC: Outside Quebec | 25 | 91 | 47 | 37 | 25 | 62 | 47 |
| Other World Faiths | 21 | 86 | 38 | 33 | 12 | 46 | 39 |
| Mainline Protestants | 13 | 89 | 35 | 28 | 6 | 40 | 43 |
| RC: Quebec | 10 | 78 | 33 | 22 | 6 | 40 | 35 |
| No Religion | 3 | 73 | 10 | 7 | 1 | 19 | 17 |

SOURCE: Derived from Reginald W. Bibby, *Project Canada 2005 National Survey.*

issues, as well as in the inclination of average people who identify with those groups to "follow the party line." Generally speaking, evangelical Protestants are the most likely to be opposed to changes in the sexual realm, Quebec Catholics—despite the official position of their Church—the most receptive, with their openness exceeded only by Canadians with no religion.

But this just in. Two recent analyses that I have carried out on adults and teens show that there is a consistent, positive relationship between holding clear-cut belief in God and endorsing interpersonal values that make for civility—such traits as honesty, concern for others, politeness, and the like. Canadians who "definitely believe in God" consistently differ from atheists (Bibby, 2009, 2011a; see Table 13.5). That's not to say that theists necessarily come through behaviourally, or that there is no social compassion, for example, among atheists. The findings do suggest, however, that belief in God is one, if only one, potential source of civility. To the extent that that is the case, there could be some significant social value in people believing in God. Recent atheist media blitzes in Canada and elsewhere—using such catch lines as, "There's probably no god. Now stop worrying and enjoy your life"—may, in the end, have limited interpersonal payoffs.

## SOCIETAL CONSEQUENCES

I've looked at some personal and interpersonal consequences of religious involvement and commitment.

---

**TABLE 13.5**  VALUES OF THEIST AND ATHEIST TEENS, PERCENTAGE INDICATING "VERY IMPORTANT"

|  | NATIONALLY | THEISTS | ATHEISTS |
|---|---|---|---|
| Trust | 84 | 88 | 78 |
| Honesty | 81 | 86 | 75 |
| Concern for others | 65 | 72 | 54 |
| Politeness | 64 | 71 | 57 |
| Forgiveness | 60 | 72 | 44 |
| Working hard | 55 | 61 | 49 |
| Patience | 44 | 55 | 35 |

SOURCE: Bibby, Reginald W. (2009). *The Emerging Millennials*. Lethbridge, AB: Project Canada Books.

---

But what about the net consequences for societies more generally? On balance, is religion a plus or a minus—or simply irrelevant?

A cursory look at the historical evidence in Canada provides mixed reviews. Many would argue that religion has played and continues to play an important role in helping immigrants adjust to life in Canada, providing resources in the form of both personal faith and social support. Others would quickly add that many religious groups, notably the United, Anglican, and Roman Catholic churches, along with the Jewish community, have played important roles in helping to establish a just society, where diversity and inclusiveness today are valued on a level matched by few countries anywhere in the world. In addition, the claim can be made that religious groups are among the few organizations in Canada that explicitly attempt to instill morality, ethics, and compassion, thereby making an important contribution to civility.

Those things said, you hardly need me to remind you that other views of religious groups are not so charitable. For example,

- In the course of taking their place in the country, a number of Christian groups were anything but just and compassionate in their treatment of Aboriginal peoples, including their complicity with government goals in running residential schools.
- The "Quiet Revolution" in Quebec in the 1960s that saw the province take over many services from the Catholic Church was not accompanied by an overt revolt. However, covertly, large numbers of Catholics had found the Church to be highly oppressive and began to stay away (Graham, 1990: 114ff).
- A variety of highly publicized sexual abuse cases that spanned the country—from the Mount Cashel orphanage in Newfoundland and Labrador, through the "Orphans of Duplessis" in Quebec and the Christian Brothers in Ontario, to the Catholic Diocese in Prince Rupert, B.C.—left many Canadians stunned and disenchanted with organized religion (see Bibby, 1993: 68ff).
- Catholics, Jews, and Muslims, along with smaller religious bodies, including Mennonites, Hutterites, Jehovah's Witnesses, Scientologists, and Doukhobors, have been on the receiving end of hostility and discrimination at various points in our nation's history.

Clearly the evidence to date is mixed. Religion adds to the quality of life in the country and sometimes subtracts. What does seem to contribute to a fairly unique religious situation in Canada is the entrenchment of pluralism. Religious groups here have to play by the rules of diversity, being respectful of one another—not making excessive claims of uniqueness, not being overly aggressive in raiding each other's ranks, not being exploitive of vulnerable categories, such as immigrants, children, and seniors. And they have to respect individual rights, in keeping with the Charter of Rights.

So contained, religious organizations that might otherwise have a detrimental effect on collective life in Canada are kept in check. We have no effective "Moral Majority," as the United States does. The same-sex marriage issue was not allowed to become an unrestrained and uncivil debate, and if someone tested the boundaries—as one Alberta bishop was tempted to do on occasion—public opinion tended to result in public relations retreats. This is not a country where Christians can call other people "heathen," but they also cannot be ridiculed as "bigoted Bible-thumpers." This is not a country where Muslims can call for the heads and hands of artists who draw caricatures of Mohammed, but it also is not a place where artists can insult and incite Muslims. Some groups don't always like the rules, but that's the way the religion game is played in Canada. So contained, religion—it seems to me—is positioned to contribute positively to our individual and collective life (Box 13.1).

More than half a century ago, Peter Berger (1961) noted that Durkheim's assertion that religion functions primarily to integrate societies seems to offer a good description of religion in the United States. Religion, or at least the mainline segment of organized Christianity that historically has embraced the largest number of members, has tended to endorse American culture rather than to challenge it, to endorse the status quo rather than call for social transformation. So intense has been the bond between religion and American life that for some time observers such as Robert Bellah (1967) have described the phenomenon as American **civil religion.** In an influential book, *Protestant, Catholic, Jew,* Will Herberg (1960: 75) put it this way:

> Americans, by and large, do have their "common religion" and that "religion" is the system familiarly known as the American Way of Life. ... By every realistic criterion the American Way of Life is the operative faith of the American people. ... To be a Protestant, a Catholic, or a Jew are today the alternative ways of being an American.

Canada, committed as it is to diversity and a downplaying of overt nationalism—except for the occasional international hockey championship—has no such civil religion. As the University of Regina's William Stahl (1986: 16) has colourfully put it, "Other than a few bands and firecrackers, Confederation was not attended by much emotional outpouring." And religious groups have done little to add fervour to our rather lifeless expressions of nationalism. Still, Harold Fallding (1978) reminds us that, historically, "Canadian Protestant churches have reflected the British position of legitimizing authority through supporting government, offering prayers, for example, for its success in securing order and justice." The fusion of Catholicism with life in Quebec, Anglicanism with the status quo in southern Ontario, and conservative Protestantism with political and social life in Alberta are obvious examples.

On occasion, of course, religion has challenged North American culture. The civil rights movement in the United States received much of its leadership and impetus from African American evangelical churches. American Catholic bishops and the National Council of Churches have frequently spoken out against perceived injustices, including poverty, racism, and war. Jerry Falwell's "Moral Majority," which peaked in the 1980s, contributed to a very vocal "Christian Right," committed to altering the nature of American life by influencing the country's major institutions.

In Canada, religious groups have had and continue to have the freedom to address governments. To varying degrees they have availed themselves of the opportunity—and responsibility. Protestant churches, for example, have received mixed reviews for their concern about the plight of Jews during World War II; some churches and individuals were silent, while others were not (Davies and Nefsky, 1997). In the 1940s, a radical effort was made by the Roman Catholic Church to support striking workers, a preview of the ongoing inclination of the Canadian Conference of Catholic Bishops to support average Canadians and to be vocal in criticizing the profit orientation of the nation's economy. Protestant groups, often led by the United Church, along with a growing number of ecumenical consortia and initiatives, and, more recently, evangelical churches, have been making concerted efforts to bring about

## BOX 13.1 WHY THE GLOBAL RAGE HASN'T ENGULFED CANADA: MULTICULTURALISM AND MEDIA LIKELY MUTED PROTESTS

Why haven't Muslims in Canada taken to the streets in large numbers to protest against cartoons of the Prophet Mohammed? It's not because everyone in Canada is so nice to each other, say Canadian Muslim leaders and Islamic scholars. It's because Canada's multiculturalism is complex.

They say Muslim immigration into Canada has been different. So has Muslim integration into Canadian society. And so has the political action of Canadian Muslim organizations around the highly sensitive issue of Islamic religious fundamentalism.

The difference is illustrated by events in France in 2004 and Canada in 2005, said Tarek Fatah, a leader of the Muslim Canadian Congress.

In France, few if any representative voices within the French Muslim community were heard in the news media speaking in favour of a law banning conspicuous religious symbols, such as the traditional Muslim head scarf, in public schools.

This was the case even though a significant percentage of French Muslims had no problem accepting the law within the cultural context of French secular society.

The powerful Muslim opposition that was heard, Mr. Fatah said, came from "the mosque structure" but "the mobilization of moderate Muslim voices never happened."

In contrast, in Canada in 2005, the news media pointedly reported that the most vociferous opposition to an Ontario law permitting Islamic religious tribunals to arbitrate family and marital disputes came from Muslim organizations themselves.

In Mr. Fatah's view, the mainstream Muslim community in Canada has recognized the need to take what he calls "ownership of the word Muslim." It has become actively involved in Canadian political life and not marginalized as is the case in many Western countries.

"It's a shift, for Canadian Muslims, that has not happened anywhere else."

Mohamed Elmasry, president of the Canadian Islamic Congress, said violent demonstrations simply aren't a fit with the Canadian Muslim community—which, because of Canada's immigration requirements, he said, is the most highly educated Muslim community in the world.

"They would find legal and peaceful means of protest far more productive," said the imam and professor at the University of Waterloo. "With demonstrations, you cannot have full control over who does what."

His organization, the largest Muslim umbrella group in Canada, has actively discouraged demonstrations over the cartoons and has spoken publicly against the violent protests—as has the Muslim Canadian Congress.

Earle Waugh, a University of Alberta Islamic scholar, said most Muslim immigrants to Canada do not feel sidelined, a factor significantly fuelling the protests in European countries.

"There is no sympathy within the Canadian Muslim community for a radical approach," he said. "No sympathy for the fundamentalists."

Canada has had no legacy of Muslim colonies like that of the British and French, and no history of migrant Muslim guest workers like that of Germany.

SOURCE: Michael Valpy, 2006, "Why the Global Rage Hasn't Engulfed Canada: Multiculturalism and Media Likely Muted Protests," *Globe and Mail* 8 February, p. A14. Reprinted with permission from *The Globe and Mail*.

social change (Crysdale, 1961; Lewis, 1993; Stiller, 1997). Religious coalitions, such as the national Citizens for Public Justice and, in Ontario, the broad-based Interfaith Social Assistance Reform Coalition (ISARC), have been among those calling for greater and more effective attention being directed toward social programs, the environment, and Aboriginal issues.

It is important to note that locally, nationally, and globally, religion clearly has the potential both to bring people together and to tear them apart. Religion's role in contributing to conflict, past and present, is well known. Globally, what seems like never-ending conflict in the Middle East and elsewhere provides further contemporary examples of religion playing a role in contributing to divisiveness. At times I—along with many others—wonder about the long-term outcome of what seems to be a deepening chasm between the West and the Muslim world.

Yet in the aftermath of both the September 11, 2001, attacks and the fury over the publishing of the Mohammed caricatures in 2006, significant numbers of Muslim leaders were among the first to decry violence and bloodshed, and to call on people worldwide to find peaceful means of resolving their differences. Therein lies the paradox of religion: It can both enrich and destroy social life.

# THE FUTURE OF RELIGION

One thing is certain: Religion is not going to disappear. Proponents of the secularization thesis expected religion to be replaced by science and reason as societies evolved. Opponents of the secularization thesis countered that humans have needs, notably the need to come to grips with death, that only religion can satisfy. It is noteworthy that one unique contribution religion brings to the Canadian religious and spiritual marketplace is hope in the face of death (Bibby, 2011a: 174–76). Consequently, even if secularization leads to the demise of some religious groups, new providers are bound to appear. Ironically, rather than signalling the end of religion, secularization stimulates innovation (Stark and Bainbridge, 1985).

Emerging religious forms will include sects— groups that break away from established religions, and new religious movements (**cults**) with origins outside of older religions. From this point of view, shifts in the overall "religious economy" over time involve "the rising and falling fortunes of religious firms, not the rise and fall of religion per se" (Finke and Stark, 1992: 275).

As we glance around the globe, there is no need to spend time debating religion's future with the wise social scientists of old. Religion is simply everywhere (see, for example, Cox, 2009; Allen, 2009; Mead, 2010; Reynolds, 2011; Thomas, 2010; Table 13.6).

In Canada, there are signs that a modest rise in religious involvement is taking place that will continue in the immediate future. However, it is due not so much to the arrival of new religions as it is to the rejuvenation of the older, well-established ones.

Census and survey data reveal that fairly small numbers of Canadians have opted for new religious groups in recent decades. The proportion of Canadians who identified with such groups as Jehovah's Witnesses and Mormons has never been more than one-half of 1 percent. In a country of some 35 million people, newer, sect-like groups remain on the margins of the Canadian religious scene.

Further, we now know that relatively few people have been switching from one group to another—apart from a fair amount of movement *within* conservative Protestantism, where people who are Pentecostal move to a Baptist church, for example. The amount of "inter-family" switching—such as Roman Catholics becoming Protestants, or Jews or Muslims opting for Catholicism—has been grossly exaggerated.

## TABLE 13.6   THE WORLD'S 16 LARGEST RELIGIONS

| RELIGION | NUMBER OF ADHERENTS WORLDWIDE |
|---|---|
| 1. Christianity | 2.1 billion |
| 2. Islam | 1.5 billion |
| 3. Hinduism | 900 million |
| 4. Chinese folk | 395 million |
| 5. Buddhism | 375 million |
| 6. Sikhism | 23 million |
| 7. Juche | 19 million |
| 8. Spiritism | 15 million |
| 9. Judaism | 14 million |
| 10. Falun Gong | 10 million |
| 11. Bahái | 7 million |
| 12. Cao Dai | 5 million |
| 13. Confucianism | 5 million |
| 14. New Age | 5 million |
| 15. Jainism | 4 million |
| 16. Shinto | 4 million |
| No Religion, secular | 1.1 billion |

SOURCE: Bibby, Reginald W. (2011a). *Beyond the Gods & Back: Religion's Rise and Demise and Why It Matters.* Lethbridge, AB: Project Canada Books, p. 201. Drawn from www.adherents.com 2010 and www.religion-facts.com 2010.

A big surprise? Despite the fact that the proportion of Canadians who say they have "no religion" increased from 4 percent in 1971 to 16 percent in 2001, most haven't really been dropping out permanently. The majority of people in this category are young and single. About one-third have come from mainline Protestant homes, another one-third from Catholic homes; only about one in three have parents who also have no religion. As they get a bit older, marry, have children, and want religious weddings, baptisms, and the like, lo and behold, many proceed to tell pollsters that they are "Catholic" or "United" or "Jewish"—again. Using the panel component of our national surveys, we have found that, within five years, one in three people who said he or she had "no religion" proceeds to have one; within ten years that figure jumps to two in three. The "no religion" category is a temporary residence for most people—sort of like living in an apartment before moving into a house (Bibby, 2004b: 29–51).

We consequently have a situation in which Canada's established religious groups find themselves with lots of "affiliates" who identify with the group and aren't about to turn elsewhere. I'm not talking only about adults. Our national surveys of teenagers between the ages of 15 and 19 have found that the country's "emerging generation" closely resembles adults when it comes to current service attendance levels. About 90 percent of teens claim the same group affiliation as their parents, and only about 2 percent indicate any strong interest in new religions. Their belief, practice, experience, and knowledge levels, while typically lower than those of adults, are appreciable and, in at least some instances, can be expected to rise as teens move into their 20s and beyond. Some three in ten say religious involvement is important to them and their level of enjoyment of religious groups is on par with that of adults. In addition, more than half acknowledge that they have spiritual needs (see Table 13.7).

So let's add all this up: Canadians are not doing much switching or dropping out. The overwhelming majority continue to hold beliefs, engage in practices, experience the gods, and express spiritual needs. Perhaps they just aren't interested in organized religion? Not so. Our surveys over the past few decades have been documenting a consistent finding: More than one in two people who attend services less than once a month say they are receptive to greater involvement if it is worthwhile for themselves or their families (Figure 13.4). What do these people see as "worthwhile?" Having their spiritual needs met, getting some insight into how they might have better relationships with partners and children and friends, and maybe finding some emotional resources to help them cope with the needs they face in living everyday life. Likewise, about 40 percent of seldom-attending teens say they are open to greater involvement—"if I found it to be worthwhile" (Bibby, 2009, 2011a, 2012). In short, many people in Canada haven't given up on religion—and haven't even given up on religious groups. However, in the midst of living lives that are full, where time and other resources are often being severely stretched, they have to find significance in religious participation. Otherwise, why bother? The research suggests that, to the

**TABLE 13.7**  A PROFILE OF RELIGION AND SPIRITUALITY IN CANADA: TEENAGERS AND ADULTS (IN PERCENTAGE)

|  | ADULTS | TEENAGERS |
| --- | --- | --- |
| **Beliefs** | | |
| God | 82 | 67 |
| Atheism | 7 | 16 |
| Life after death | 67 | 75 |
| Spirit world contact | 46 | 46 |
| **Practice (weekly)** | | |
| Pray privately | 45 | 30 |
| Attend religious services | 25 | 21 |
| Read the Bible/ other scriptures | 19 | 9 |
| **Experience** | | |
| Have experienced God | 49 | 39 |
| **Knowledge** | | |
| Denier of Jesus | 41 | 23 |
| Sacred book of Islam | 53 | 30 |
| **Religious Involvement** | | |
| Is important | 53 | 30 |
| Is enjoyed | 25 | 26 |
| **Spirituality** | | |
| Have spiritual needs | 72 | 54 |

SOURCES: Bibby (2006, 2009).

**FIGURE 13.4**  RECEPTIVITY TO GREATER INVOLVEMENT IN RELIGIOUS GROUPS BY AGE COHORT, PROTESTANTS AND CATHOLICS ATTENDING LESS THAN ONCE A MONTH, 2005

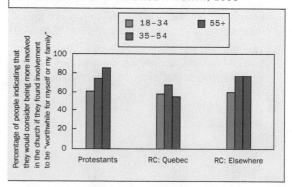

SOURCE: Bibby (2006: p. 202).

extent that groups literally find "their affiliates" and succeed in touching their lives in significant ways, many will become involved. There's no doubt that the proportion of Canadians who are tuning out of religion has been increasing in recent decades. They may compose about one-third of the population. But another one-third or so continue to value faith. The remaining one-third are "religiously undecided"; they haven't dropped out and occasionally drop in.

Assuming that the need for religion will persist for large numbers of people, the three central academic questions that need to be answered are (1) Which "religious companies" will be the most prominent? (2) How effective will be they be in responding to Canadians? (3) To what extent will the population tend to gravitate toward the religious and nonreligious ends of "the polarization continuum."

## SUMMARY

1. Sociology uses the scientific method to study religion. Religion explores reality beyond what can be known empirically.

2. The sociology of religion has been strongly influenced by the theoretical contributions of Marx, who stressed the compensatory role of religion in the face of economic deprivation; Durkheim, who emphasized both the social origin of religion and its important social cohesive function; and Weber, who gave considerable attention to the relationship between ideas and behaviour.

3. Religion can be defined as a system of meaning with a supernatural referent used to interpret the world. Humanist perspectives make no such use of the supernatural realm, attempting instead to make life meaningful.

4. Personal religious commitment increasingly has come to be seen as having many facets or dimensions. Four such dimensions are commonly noted: belief, practice, experience, and knowledge. Personal commitment is created and sustained by collective religiosity. In Canada, religious polarization has been increasing in recent decades, resulting in solid cores of people both valuing religion and rejecting it—trends with critical implications for commitment at the individual level.

5. Variations in the levels of individual commitment that characterize complex societies have led to explanations that emphasize individual and

structural factors. Reflection, socialization, and deprivation have been prominent among the individual explanations, while the dominant structural assertion has been the secularization thesis.

6. Religion appears to be, at best, one of many paths leading to valued characteristics, such as personal happiness and compassion. Although religion can be socially disruptive, Canada's emphasis on social and cultural diversity functions to put limits on how religion can be expressed, thereby optimizing the possibility of religions contributing positively to social and collective life.

7. Although proponents of secularization saw religion as being replaced by science and reason, it is now apparent that religion continues to be important throughout the world, including Canada. Its future is not in doubt.

8. The search for alleged religious switchers and drop-outs in Canada reveals that few have turned elsewhere or permanently opted for "no religion." Most still identify with the country's established groups.

9. Canadians young and old, in large numbers, continue to hold religious beliefs, claim religious experiences, and express spiritual needs. Many also say they are receptive to greater involvement with religious groups.

10. The inclination for Canadians to embrace religion or reject it will depend largely on how religious groups respond to ongoing interests and needs.

# QUESTIONS TO CONSIDER

1. Which of the three key theorists do you find to be the most helpful in understanding religion: Durkheim, Marx, or Weber?

2. What does it mean to be religious?

3. Do you see yourself as (a) religious and spiritual, (b) spiritual but not religious, (c) religious but not spiritual, or (d) neither religious nor spiritual?

4. What kinds of people do you find are interested in (a) spirituality and (b) organized religion? Do you think there are any noticeable differences by age?

5. Does religion make any difference in the lives of the people you know? How would Canadian society be different if organized religion disappeared?

6. Do you think it is true that secularization stimulates religious innovation—that the decline of old groups provides the opportunity for new groups to surface and prosper?

7. Imagine that you are serving as a consultant to a major Canadian religious group. What might you suggest it consider doing to (a) keep the people it has and (b) gain the interest of people who are not actively involved?

# GLOSSARY

The **church-sect typology** (p. 319) is a framework, originating with Weber, in which religious organizations are studied in terms of ideal-type characteristics. (churches emphasize works and stress accommodation to society, while sects stress faith and separation from society).

**Civil religion** (p. 332) refers to the tendency for nationalistic emphases to be nurtured by a society's religions, so that a culture takes on many religious-like characteristics. The term is most often used with respect to the United States.

**Collective conscience** (p. 314) is Durkheim's term referring to awareness that a group is more than the sum of its individual members and the belief that such awareness is experienced as the supernatural.

**Collective religiosity** (p. 318) is religious commitment as manifested in and through religious groups; it is key to the creation and sustenance of personal religiosity.

**Cults** (p. 334) are religious groups that have their origins outside older religions. Sects, in contrast, are groups that have broken away from established religions.

**Denominationalism** (p. 326) refers to the tendency for a wide variety of Protestant religious groups to come into being, seemingly reflecting variations not only in theology but also—and perhaps primarily—in social characteristics.

**Dimensions of religiosity** (p. 317) are the various facets of religious commitment, including belief, experience, practice, and knowledge.

**Humanist perspectives** (p. 316) are systems of meaning that do not have a supernatural referent and that are used to interpret the world.

**Monotheism** (p. 316) refers to belief in one god.

The **persistence thesis** (p. 327) is the assertion that religion will continue to have a significant place in the modern world because it has never actually declined or because people continue to have interests and needs that only religion can satisfy.

**Personal religiosity** (p. 316) refers to the level of religious commitment characterizing an individual.

**Profane** See Sacred and profane.

**Religions** (p. 316) are systems of meaning for interpreting the world that have a supernatural referent.

**Religious polarization** (p. 321) refers to the growing tendency of some people in a given setting to embrace religion and the tendency of others to reject it.

**Sacred and profane** (p. 314) are the two categories by which Durkheim claimed all things are classified; the sacred represents those things that are deemed to warrant profound respect, and the profane encompasses essentially everything else.

The **secularization thesis** (p. 327) holds that religion as it has been traditionally known is continually declining, resulting in a loss of religious authority, societally and individually, as well as changes in religious organizations themselves.

# SUGGESTED READING

Beaman, Lori G., ed. (2012). *Religion and Canadian Society* (2nd ed.). Toronto: Canadian Scholars Press. A collection of valuable, wide-ranging articles on religion in Canada by many of the country's top thinkers in sociology and religious studies.

Bibby, Reginald W. (2011). *Beyond the Gods & Back: Religion's Demise and Rise and Why It Matters.* Lethbridge, AB: Project Canada Books. This work draws on the author's extensive surveys and newly available international data in maintaining that the current religious situation in Canada is characterized by polarization. It features an examination of the implications for personal and social life, and religion's future.

Bramadat, Paul and David Seljak, eds. (2008). *Christianity and Ethnicity in Canada.* Toronto: University of Toronto Press. A superb reader by leading Canadian scholars examining the relationships between religious and ethnic identity in nine major religious traditions. Complements their earlier reader (2004), *Religion and Ethnicity in Canada,* Toronto: University of Toronto Press.

Brym, Robert J., William Shaffir, and Morton Weinfeld, eds. 2010. *The Jews in Canada* (Toronto: Oxford University Press).

Christiano, Kevin J., William H. Swatos, Jr., and Peter Kivisto. (2008). *Sociology of Religion: Contemporary Developments*, 2nd ed. Walnut Creek, CA: AltaMira Press. An excellent overview of theory, methods, and up-to-date findings on religion and society from an American point of view.

Clark, S. D. (1948). *Church and Sect in Canada.* Toronto: University of Toronto Press. This Canadian classic examines the social factors contributing to the rise of different types of religious groups in this country.

Dawson, Lorne L. (2006). *Comprehending Cults: The Sociology of New Religious Movements*, 2nd ed. Toronto: Oxford University Press. A succinct overview of cults that have emerged from the 1970s onward, dealing with such issues as why cults emerge, who joins, and their social significance.

Noll, Mark. (2007). *What Happened to Christian Canada?* Vancouver: Regent College Publishing. This is a short but detailed and invaluable essay in which a renowned American historian examines religious change in Canada since the 1950s and contrasts the religious histories of Canada and the United States.

# Chapter 26

## Religion: The Comeback

REGINALD BIBBY

In his article, Bibby argues that some religions survive because they successfully compete with others that decline. He does not think that religion is doomed, rather he argues that religion is about to make a "comeback." Bibby uses a framework to study religions as "firms" that compete in a market for "customers" who become their believers. In order to be competitive, a particular religion must be appealing and offer something different and enticing to potential members, while retaining current participants. Consider this analogy as you go through the reading and decide whether it is a useful way to understand the reality of religions today.

1. How are religious groups currently evolving in Canada?
2. How does the situation in Canada regarding religious groups compare worldwide?

Prophecy is not exactly a social science virtue.

. . .

It's not that we never try. When it comes to religion, we have had a good share of would-be social prophets. People like Auguste Comte (1798–1857), Karl Marx (1818–1883), and Sigmund Freud (1856–1939) saw religion's disappearance as inevitable. Comte said scientific thought would replace religious thinking, Marx felt the resolving of social and economic inequities would eliminate the need for religion as a pain-killing drug, and Freud maintained that science and personal resolve would combine to allow us to abandon our child-like fantasies about a father-like God and a future existence in heaven.

There obviously is much data that point to the fact that such thinkers were too quick to write off religion. In settings where religion is currently flourishing, a measure of **secularization** undoubtedly will take place. The historical precedents of Europe and North America suggest such a trend will be closely associated with heightened levels of development.

But in other places where polarization is prominent, or where secularity is pronounced, comebacks are in the works.

. . .

## THE CANADIAN SITUATION

As we look at Canada, some general observations about the immediate future of some of the groups can be made with a high level of confidence.

*Roman Catholics.* Make no mistake about it—this is the big player in Canada. The 2001 census revealed that close to 13 million Canadians (43%) viewed themselves as Catholic—about 7 million outside Quebec (23%), 6 million in Quebec (20%). The median age of Catholics is 37.8, about the same as the Canadian population as a whole.

Source: Bibby, Reginald. *Beyond the Gods and Back: Religion's Demise and Rise and Why it Matters.* Lethbridge: Project Canada Books, 2011. Reprinted with permission of Project Canada Books.

As the Roman Catholic Church goes, so goes organized religion in the nation. Other groups may get much of the ink. Some might even believe they are the key to the country's religious health. But at the end of the day, Catholics rule. Don't fear for their future. Besides, this is not just a big regional or national company. This is a vast and powerful multinational corporation.

Seen in such perspective, the Catholic Church in Quebec is "merely" a problem spot on the Catholic global map. Yes, the provincial government plays no religious favourites.[1] Yes, Catholics have become selective consumers. But the research to date is definitive: most people in the province remain Catholic and are not going anywhere. Lack of commitment understandably troubles leaders. But widespread defection is not on the horizon. Religion à la carte, Catholic-style, rules in Quebec.

Elsewhere, Catholicism's vitality is fueled in part by new arrivals from other countries. But let's not minimize the importance of faith for earlier generations of people who were raised in Canadian Catholic homes.

The time is come to quit belittling the health of Canadian Catholicism. Large numbers may show up only occasionally for seasonal services, for rights of passage, or because they think they are overdue to share in a Mass. But they still show up. And they are still Catholic.

Large numbers also are open to greater involvement if they find it to be worthwhile. The challenge lies with the supplier. If the Catholic Church comes through, who knows what could happen?

*Mainline Protestants.* As I look at the four primary "firms" in this grouping—the United, Anglican, Lutheran, and Presbyterians churches. . . .

. . .

In short, the demographics have not been good. Limited growth through immigration, migration, and birth, coupled with mortality, add up to an obvious result: zero or negative growth. Given their global nature, Anglicans have the potential to be helped considerably by immigration. But to date their potential global gains have been neutralized considerably by divisive homosexuality and gender issues.

There is an additional problem. To the extent Stark and others are right in maintaining people will be drawn to groups which address questions that "only the gods can answer," it's not clear that Mainline Protestants have particularly strong ultimate answer "product lines." Tom Harpur doesn't mince his words. In the case of life after death, he says that many groups simply "avoid the topic completely."[2] And he's not talking about the evangelicals.

Unlike Catholics, for example, who give a fair amount of attention to things like heaven and the importance of "last rites" so that people are ready for life after death, the United Church—for example—rightly or wrongly is seen by many as focusing almost exclusively on life. Perhaps Anglicans, Presbyterians, and Lutherans are different.[3]

Beyond tirelessly debating the reasons for the decline, the bottom line is that Mainline numbers are down, with significant resource implications: good ministry is all the more difficult to accomplish.[4] Still, Diana Butler Bass could be right: it may yet be possible for Mainline churches to be renewed "by weaving personal spiritual quests" with a primary strength—"their more traditional forms of religious life."[5] David Harris, editor of the *Presbyterian Record*, comments that "the church desperately needs to find a way to move forward." But he cautions that flexibility and creativity can be hard to come by. In the words of one former moderator, "Zacchaeus was not a Presbyterian."[6]

*Conservative Protestants.* The "evangelicals," as they are commonly known collectively, are characterized by considerable vitality. Their major demographic accomplishment has been their ability to sustain a market share of approximately 8% (7% Baptist) from the first census in 1871 through to the present day.

Religious intermarriage alone should have decimated the Conservative Protestants. Yet,

PART 10

because of factors that include immigration, their emphasis on tight-knit communities and strong youth and family ministries, they have been able to sustain their market share. The thesis of Mainline Protestant executive Dean Kelley, put forth in the early 1970s, also knows increasing support. In his book, *Why Conservative Churches Are Growing*, Kelley maintained that two key factors of central importance were (1) the demands that evangelicals placed on their members, in the form of expectations such as participation, tithing, and lifestyles and (2) the provision of answers to ultimate questions, including life after death.[7]

My examination of Calgary evangelical church growth dating back to the late-1960s shows that, contrary to popular myth, Conservative Protestants know only modest growth through the recruitment of outsiders. Their numerical stability and growth are tied primarily to their ability to retain their own people—their children and their geographically-mobile members.[8]

To the extent they are outsiders, the key factor is relationships: they tend to either befriend or marry them.

. . .

Somewhat paradoxically, while Conservative Protestants tend to stay with their "Believers' Church" denominations, they move fairly freely between individual evangelical groups.[9] As a result, no single denomination in this "family" makes up even 3% of the Canadian population, nowhere near the 7% who identified themselves as "Baptist" when the first census was conducted in 1871. Many prefer to go simply by "Christian."[10]

Evangelicals, who typically are younger than Mainline Protestants, will continue to be a smaller player on the Canadian religious scene. But their steady market share of 8% is finally about to increase. Why? The explosive growth of evangelicals in many parts of the world will result in an increasingly robust immigration pipeline—and an increasingly multicultural church. . . .

*Other Faith Entries.* As people came to Canada from an array of countries, they brought other religions besides Christianity to Canada. At the time of Confederation, Jews made up about one-tenth of one percent of the population. With the arrival of increasing numbers of people from countries other than Europe and the United States, additional faiths also took root.

Through about 1981, the number of people identifying with faiths other than Christianity remained very small. Much of the difficulty such groups had, of course, was tied to the fact that they had difficulty holding on to their children: many married Protestants and Catholics.

The net result was that, by 1981, less than 3% of Canadians indicated they were either Jewish, Muslim, Buddhist, Hindu, or Sikh. Another 1% were either Jehovah's Witnesses or Mormons.

As we have seen, over the past three decades or so, immigration has seen the percentage of people who identify with the other major world religions double to about 6%. The largest of these is Islam at 2%.

The historical track records of the number of these faiths—Judaism, Buddhism, Hinduism, and Sikhism, along with the Latter Day Saints and Jehovah's Witnesses—suggest that they will continue to be part of the Canadian religious scene. But like the four Mainline Protestant groups, they will not be among the major religious firms.

Islam is another story. There already are more Muslims in Canada than Presbyterians, Pentecostals, and Jews, for example. They may well be on the verge of attaining the proverbial "critical mass"—such as the evangelicals have experienced—where their numbers reach a point where they are able to cut down on losses through intermarriage. Moreover, Islam obviously is a very powerful multinational religion. In light of the diverse number of countries in which it is prominent, the immigration pipeline that has been such a critically important component of religious group growth over the years will contain to produce new people for some time to come.

**TABLE 26.1**  CANADA'S 16 LARGEST RELIGIOUS GROUPS

| | | NUMBERS | % | MEDIAN AGE |
|---|---|---|---|---|
| 1. | Roman Catholic | 12,793,125 | 44 | 37.8 |
| 2. | United Church | 2,839,125 | 12 | 44.1 |
| 3. | Anglican | 2,035,500 | 8 | 43.8 |
| 4. | Christian *(unspecified)* | 780,450 | 3 | 30.2 |
| 5. | Baptist | 729,475 | 3 | 39.3 |
| 6. | Eastern Orthodox | 606,620 | 2 | 40.1 |
| 7. | Lutheran | 606,590 | 2 | 43.3 |
| 8. | Muslim | 579,640 | 2 | 28.1 |
| 9. | Protestant *(unspecified)* | 549,205 | 2 | 40.4 |
| 10. | Presbyterian | 409,830 | 1 | 46.0 |
| 11. | Pentecostal | 369,475 | 1 | 33.5 |
| 12. | Jewish | 329,995 | 1 | 41.5 |
| 13. | Buddhist | 300,345 | 1 | 38.0 |
| 14. | Hindu | 297,200 | 1 | 31.9 |
| 15. | Sikh | 278,410 | <1 | 29.7 |
| 16. | Greek Orthodox | 215,175 | <1 | 46.1 |
| | *No Religion* | *4,796,325* | *16* | *31.1* |

SOURCE: Statistics Canada, 2001 Census.

In addition, a relatively high birth rate and an emphasis on the retention of children will further contribute to Islam's viability. It is worth noting that the median age of Muslims as of the 2001 census was 28.1. Some additions through proselytism—or what many social scientists call "switching"—also can be expected.

Finally, the two traits that observers such as Kelley and Stark see as essential to success—an emphasis on demands and rewards, as well as the ability to speak to ultimate questions—are major features of Islam.

In short, as we look to the future of religion in Canada, we can anticipate that the Roman Catholic Church will continue to be the dominant player. Other key market members will be the Conservative Protestants and Muslims.

The marketplace will not lack for other players, both old and new. But those groups will have to work hard just to retain—let alone expand—their market shares.

## THE GLOBAL SITUATION

As with Canada, there are and will continue to be people all over the world who are not in the market for religion, old or new. But they will be in the minority.

At this point in history, some 6 billion of the planet's 7 billion people are identifying with a religion. They are led by Christians (2.1 billion), Muslims (1.5 million) and Hindus (900 million).

Like the auto multinationals, including Toyota, GM, Volkswagen, Ford, and Hyundai, these religious powerhouses will continue to lead the way as the most prominent religious "suppliers" on earth.

To the extent that markets in any country become open to their presence and that of other smaller suppliers—in part because their existing clienteles simply move to new places—religions will make national inroads.

Collectively, the religious companies have been performing very well of late. In the words of Harvey Cox, "Instead of disappearing, religion is now exhibiting new vitality all around the world."[11]

*Christianity's Growth.* In recent years Christianity has experienced more worldwide growth than any religion. Such a reality of the faith's global health will come as news to many people. After all, as Philip Yancey noted recently, it's not making the headlines of CNN.[12] *Globe and Mail* columnist

**PART 10**

Neil Reynolds similarly wrote in early 2010, "You could call it the greatest story never told."[13]

Reynolds drew on two prominent observers of the global religious scene, U.S. political scientist Walter Russell Mead and British scholar Scott M. Thomas. Their thoughts are worth retrieving in detail.[14]

The flamboyant Mead has noted that Christianity is now "on its biggest roll" in its 2000-year history.[15] It is both the world's largest faith and the world's fastest growing faith. Its absolute numbers and market share are at all-time highs. In the last fifty years, Mead says, "It has surpassed Islam as the most popular religion in sub-Saharan Africa and as the leading Abrahamic religion in China." The Christian faith, he asserts, "claims almost twice as many adherents as Islam worldwide."[16] By 2050, the worldwide Christian population could top three billion.

- Roman Catholic commentator John Allen would note that, between 1950 and 2000, the number of Catholics worldwide grew from just under 500 million to over one billion. The church suffered serious losses in the global North (Europe and North America), but grew dramatically in the global South (Africa, Asia, and Latin America).[17]
- In a country like Russia, Orthodox Christianity is enjoying a revival after seventy years of communist suppression.[18]
- But of particular significance, Pentecostals have experienced the fastest growth of any religious movement in history, says Mead, "from zero to something like half a billion members in the last 100 years." Growth has been pronounced in Africa, Asia, and Latin America.[19]

Thomas likewise maintains that "around the world, religion is on the rise, and notes that, "the most dramatic religious explosion is the spread of evangelical Protestantism, led by Pentecostalism." After Catholics, he says, Pentecostals represent the largest single group of Christians worldwide.[20] It typically crosses class lines.

What perhaps is startling to learn is not only that evangelicals now number close to 700 million people worldwide; it's that they have achieved strategic masses in such places as China, Indonesia, India, Nigeria, the Philippines, South Africa, and Brazil.

For example, it is estimated that, by 2050, there could be 220 million Christians in China—about 15% of the population.[21]

In many instances, Thomas notes, Christianity is "returning to its roots by becoming a post-Western religion dominated by the peoples, cultures, and countries of the global South."[22] While having a strong personal focus, it also has become increasingly politically active, especially in Latin America.[23]

These expansion patterns, of course, have not been without conflict. Thomas points out that "three countries with substantial Muslim communities—India, Indonesia, and Nigeria—also have large Pentecostal populations and sizable minorities of Christians more broadly." Tensions have been rising, resulting in violence such as the conflict in Nigeria in 2010 that left over 500 people dead.[24]

In addition, competition with Catholicism in various parts of the world is frequently intense. John Allen writes that as "Pentecostals march across the planet," they have been "siphoning off significant numbers of Catholics." He notes that "the Catholic Church is itself being 'Pentecostalized' through the Charismatic movement.[25]

A massive shift in population growth from the developed countries of the North to the developing countries of the global South will result in a changing global religious landscape. Thomas points out that the developed countries of the North accounted for 32% of the world's population in 1900 and 18% in 2000. By 2050, that figure will drop to just 10%.[26] "A new kind of world is in the making," he says, "and the people, states, and religious communities that compose the global South are making it."[27]

In the case of Roman Catholics, Allen notes that the church was dominated in the last century by the global North. Today, two in three Catholics are found in Africa, Asia, and Latin America.[28] One obvious result? An unprecedented number of Catholic leaders are coming from all over the world[29]—often, in the Canadian instance, to a parish near you.

Mead and Thomas both draw attention to the fact that the rise in evangelical Christianity in particular can be expected to bring with it a concomitant increase in Protestant ideals, such as the work ethic, entrepreneurial aspirations, and personal freedom.[30] Thomas sees global Christianity as becoming more conservative than European Christianity, but more liberal than the Catholic model which, in some Latin American settings, will be replaced by evangelicalism. Sometimes it will be a hybrid with Catholicism, sometimes not.[31]

In addition, both Mead and Thomas maintain that the spread of evangelical Christianity will have important social consequences. Globally, "Evangelicals will be a major religious, social, and political force in the coming century," Thomas writes.[32] In China, for example, he maintains that the government tacitly allows the established religions of Christianity and neo-Confucianism "to operate relatively freely, believing that they can promote social harmony amid rapid social changes." He suggests that if Christianity achieves the culture permeation in China that it knows in South Korea—at around 25%—it could fundamentally alter China's political fabric.[33]

*Islamic Growth.* Observers maintain that Islam also is experiencing a revival that extends well beyond the more extreme Islamic fundamentalist movements. As we have seen with the global Gallup data, large proportions of people in predominantly Muslim countries are saying that religion is an important part of their daily lives. In reminding readers that Islamic renewal is extending far beyond the Arab world, Thomas writes that "more Muslim women are wearing the veil, more Muslim men are growing beards, and more Muslims are attending mosques more often."[34]

- Russia now has more Muslims and any other country in Europe.
- Northwestern China "is home to over 20 million Muslims and is now in the grip of an Islamic reawakening."[35] Many young Chinese Muslims are studying across the Middle East.
- Sheer numbers alone mean that Christian-Islam relations will, in John Allen's words, "be a major driver of world history in the twenty-first century."[36]

One cannot underestimate the role that the Internet is playing in connecting Christians, Muslims, and people of many other faiths who, because of geographical separation, were isolated religious diasporas.

Yet, ironically, notes Thomas, globalization in general simultaneously contributes to "a more unified and yet more fragmented world."[37]

## ASSESSMENT

Obviously the receptivity levels to religion vary considerably around the world. In Stark's parlance, settings are variously religiously "regulated" and "deregulated." They have open as well as closed markets, robust competition as well as long-standing monopolies.

But because of both (1) the ongoing demand and (2) the ongoing availability of global suppliers, one thing is clear: religion will persist as far as the social scientific eye can see, individually and organizationally.

The scope of the market for religion is so vast that, apart from the gods, entrepreneurial human beings would find its potential too great to ignore.

Religions, major and minor, well-established and freshly minted, will continue to be at work, attempting to increase their local, national, and global market shares.

Individuals will continue to explore the options, and will usually opt for one—or more. After all, for some, religion enriches life. For all, it offers market entries when it comes to death.

PART 10

And as for the gods, if they actually exist and people ignore them for very long, they can be expected to shake things up from time to time.

## NOTES

1. deSouza, Father Raymond J. (2010, December 30). "Quebec worships the idol of secularism." *National Post*.

2. Harpur, Tom. (1991). *Life after death*. Toronto: McClelland and Stewart.

3. Nicolisi, Gary. (2010, November 1). "Guest reflections: What happens when we die?" *AnglicanJournal.com*.

4. Bagnell, Kenneth. (2010). "Secular shift." *The United Church Observer*. January.

5. Butler Bass, Diana. (2006) *Christianity for the rest of us*. New York: HarperOne.

6. Harris, David. (2009, October 1). "Start something unthinkable: The church needs to be flexible." *Presbyterian Record*.

7. Kelley, Dean. (1972). *Why conservative churches are growing*. New York: Harper and Row.

8. Bibby, Reginald W. and Brinkerhoff, Merlin B. (1973). "The circulation of the saints: A study of people who join conservative churches." *Journal for the Scientific Study of Religion* 12: 273-83; and Bibby, Reginald. (2003). "The circulation of the saints: One final look at how conservative protestant churches grow." Presented at the annual meeting of the Pacific Sociological Association, San Diego, April.

9. Bibby, Reginald W. and Brinkerhoff, Merlin B. (1973). "The circulation of the saints: A study of people who join conservative churches." *Journal for the Scientific Study of Religion* 12: 273-83; and Bibby, Reginald. (2003). "The circulation of the saints: One final look at how conservative protestant churches grow." Presented at the annual meeting of the Pacific Sociological Association, San Diego, April.

10. Clarke, Brian and Macdonald, Stuart. (2007). "Simply christian: Canada's newest major religious denomination." *Toronto Journal of Theology* 23(2): 109-25.

11. Cox, Harvey. (2009). The future of faith. New York: HaperOne.

12. Yancy, Philip. (2010) *What good is God?* New York: FaithWords/Hatchett Book Group. 4

13. Reynolds, Neil. (2011, January 10). "The globalization of God in the 21st century." *Globe and Mail*.

14. Mead, Walter Russell. (2010, May 28). "Pentecostal power." A blog in *The American Interest*.

15. Mead, Walter Russell. (2010, May 28). "Pentecostal power." A blog in *The American Interest*.

16. Mead, Walter Russell. (2010, May 28). "Pentecostal power." A blog in *The American Interest*.

17. Allen, John L., Jr. (2009). *The future church*. New York: Doubleday. 20.

18. Thomas, Scott M. (2010). "A globalized god." *Foreign Affairs*, November/December 89: 93–101.

19. Mead, Walter Russell. (2010, May 28). "Pentecostal power." A blog in *The American Interest*.

20. Thomas, Scott M. (2010). "A globalized god." *Foreign Affairs*, November/December 89: 93–101.

21. Thomas, Scott M. (2010). "A globalized god." *Foreign Affairs*, November/December 89: 93–101.

22. Thomas, Scott M. (2010). "A globalized god." *Foreign Affairs*, November/December 89: 93–101.

23. Thomas, Scott M. (2010). "A globalized god." *Foreign Affairs*, November/December 89: 93–101.

24. Thomas, Scott M. (2010). "A globalized god." *Foreign Affairs*, November/December 89: 93–101.

25. Allen, John L., Jr. (2009) *The future church*. New York: Doubleday.

26. Thomas, Scott M. (2010). "A globalized god." *Foreign Affairs*, November/December 89: 93–101.

27. Thomas, Scott M. (2010). "A globalized god." *Foreign Affairs*, November/December 89: 93–101.

28. Allen, John L., Jr. (2009) *The future church*. New York: Doubleday.

29. Allen, John L., Jr. (2009) *The future church*. New York: Doubleday.

30. Mead, Walter Russell. (2010, May 28). "Pentecostal power." A blog in *The American Interest*.

31. Brinkerhoff, Merlin B. and Reginald Bibby. (1985). "Circulation of the saints in South America." *Journal for the Scientific Study of Religion* 24: 253–262.

32. Thomas, Scott M. (2010). "A globalized god." *Foreign Affairs*, November/December 89: 93–101.

33. Thomas, Scott M. (2010). "A globalized god." *Foreign Affairs*, November/December 89: 93–101.

34. Thomas, Scott M. (2010). "A globalized god." *Foreign Affairs,* November/December 89: 93–101.

35. Thomas, Scott M. (2010). "A globalized god." *Foreign Affairs,* November/December 89: 93–101.

36. Allen, John L., Jr. (2009) *The future church.* New York: Doubleday.

37. Thomas, Scott M. (2010). "A globalized god." *Foreign Affairs,* November/December 89: 93–101.

## Critical Thinking Questions

1. Why has organized religion persisted?
2. Will religious groups be maintained in the future in Canada?

**PART 10**

# Education

# CHAPTER

# 17

# Education

## IN THIS CHAPTER, YOU WILL LEARN THAT

- A complete system of schools, from elementary to post-graduate, is the prerequisite of industrial society and is found in all rich societies. Consequently, national wealth and national education levels are strongly related.

- School systems carry out two tasks: homogenizing and sorting. Students are made similar by indoctrination into a common cultural system but are also steered into different social classes.

- Mass education, once established, brings about nearly universal literacy and numeracy. Mass education makes large populations linguistically and culturally uniform, providing the basis for nationalism.

- Functionalists believe that education fosters meritocracy. Conflict theorists argue that the high cost of education favours the wealthy and that schools inevitably favour students whose parents are highly educated.

- Inside schools, inequalities are reproduced by a hidden curriculum that values middle-class manners and attitudes, testing and tracking that segregate students by class background, and self-fulfilling prophecies of poor performance by lower-class students.

- Women now exceed men in years of completed schooling. However, men remain more likely to complete programs that lead to high pay.

Janaka Dharmasena/Shutterstock

# THE RIOT IN ST. LÉONARD

On the night of September 10, 1969, a confrontation that had long been brewing in the Montreal suburb of St. Léonard boiled over. A march organized by the French unilinguist *Ligue pour l'intégration scolaire* paraded through a predominantly Italian neighbourhood. Despite pleas for calm from leaders on both sides, many people turned out to march while others, hostile to the marchers' cause, showed up to line the route. Scuffles broke out and a full-scale brawl ensued. Roughly a thousand people participated. Police read the Riot Act and made about 50 arrests.

Commentators of all political persuasions deplored the violence, but today the St. Léonard riot is recognized as a turning point in Quebec history. It culminated in Bill 101, the law making French the language of public administration, imposing French language tests for admission to the professions, requiring most businesses with more than 50 employees to operate mainly in French, and requiring collective agreements to be drafted in French. Bill 101 also ensured that in Quebec children of immigrants are required to receive primary and secondary schooling in French.

A year before the street violence erupted, the language of instruction in public schools emerged as a hotly contested issue. Political commentators raised concerns that French was in demographic decline and that francophones were at risk of becoming a minority in the province's biggest city, Montreal. They noted that in 1963, the St. Léonard school board had responded to an influx of new residents of Italian descent by establishing the option of bilingual education. Soon, more than 90 percent of children with neither English nor French background ("allophones") were enrolling in the bilingual track and, of those, 85 percent continued to English secondary schools. The public school system was contributing heavily to the Anglicization of Montreal.

Brian Summers/First Light

In 1968, the St. Léonard school board eliminated bilingual programs, setting off a cycle of protests and counter-protests. Allophone parents, mainly of Italian descent and forming 30 percent of the community, withdrew children from the public schools and organized their own "basement schools" in English. Meanwhile, francophone unilinguists mobilized and were able to dominate school board elections and win a referendum requiring a unilingual school system. Elites tried but failed to find a middle ground. Ultimately, in 1976, the Parti Québécois won their first election, Bill 101 was enacted, and immigrants' children were restricted to French schools by law.

It is hardly surprising that schooling in Quebec has evoked sharp controversy. Schools are hugely important institutions. They teach students a common culture that forms a framework for social life. They shape work, politics, and much else. Moreover, which children have access to which schools is the starting point for sorting children into adult jobs and social classes. Not surprisingly, therefore, fierce conflicts often arise around such educational issues as who can or must go to what kinds of schools and what will be taught.

Schools are important and sometimes controversial because they endow young people with the key capacities of communication, coordination, and economic productivity. Schools accomplish two main tasks: homogenizing and sorting. They create homogeneity out of diversity by instructing all students in uniform curriculum, and they sort students into paths that terminate in different social classes. Homogeneity is achieved by enforcing common standards that serve as a cultural common denominator. Sorting favours students who develop the greatest facility in the common culture while confining those of lesser skills to subordinate work roles and lower ranks in the class structure.

Homogenizing and sorting are organized at primary, secondary, and postsecondary levels, and, within those levels, in public and private institutions. Individuals typically move

NEL

in a regulated way from one educational site to the next. Curricula are adapted to what has been taught earlier, often in other places, and to prepare students for subsequent studies.

To fully understand education, we must grasp its broader implications. For example, mass schooling is a relatively recent development that is closely tied to industrialism and to maintaining a modern, productive economy. However, industrialism needs interchangeable workers who can move among ever-changing, technically sophisticated production facilities. Potential workers have to be culturally homogenized so they have similar outlooks and a common language, but some of them have to be identified as able and willing to receive specialized training to carry out technically demanding tasks.

Although the number of years people devote to education has steadily risen, more education is easier to obtain if you are born in a rich country and into a prosperous family. In turn, more education ensures better treatment in labour markets, such as lower rates of unemployment and higher earnings. Thus, education turns students into citizens by giving them a common outlook but it also reproduces the class structure and the structure of global inequality.

## Summing Up

- Schools perform two main functions: they homogenize young people by socializing them into a shared culture and they sort young people into different levels of certification and, ultimately, different social classes.

## MASS EDUCATION: AN OVERVIEW

The education system has displaced organized religion as the main purveyor of formal knowledge, and it is second in importance only to the family as an agent of socialization (see Chapter 4, Socialization). By the time you finished high school, you had spent nearly 13 000 hours in a classroom.

Three hundred years ago, only a small minority of people learned to read and write. A century ago most people in the world never attended school. As late as 1950, only about 10 percent of the world's countries boasted systems of compulsory mass education (Meyer, Ramirez, and Soysal, 1992). Even today, many countries in Africa have literacy rates below 50 percent, while in nations like India and Egypt a third of the population is illiterate.

In contrast, Canada has just over 16 000 elementary and secondary schools employing nearly 276 000 teachers, who educate 5.3 million children. (Elementary schools are primary schools, high schools are secondary schools, and colleges and universities are postsecondary institutions.) In 2008–9, university enrolment stood at 1.11 million (Human Resources and Skills Development Canada [HRSDC], 2011b). The proportion of people between the ages of 25 and 64 with a college or university degree is higher in Canada than in any other country at 49 percent (Japan is in second place at 43 percent, the United States third at 41 percent; HRSDC, 2011b). Enrolment rates are more than 95 percent for five-year-olds and remain at about that level through the mandatory schooling age of 16–18 years. Since 1990, the proportion of Canadians over the age of 14 with trade or college certification or a university degree has increased from about 30 percent to over 50 percent (HRSDC, 2011b). Clearly, in Canada education is a way of life.

Universal mass education is a recent phenomenon and is limited to relatively wealthy countries (see Figure 17.1 on page 434). Around 1900, Canada and the United States were the first countries to approach universal educational participation by young people. Societies that today are highly advanced in terms of economy and technology, such as Japan, Italy, and England, lagged far behind.

**FIGURE 17.1**

Elementary School Enrolments per 1000 Children Aged 5–14 for Various Countries, 1870–1930

Source: Peter H. Lindert, *Growing Public: Social Spending and Economic Growth since the Eighteenth Century* (Cambridge, UK, New York: 2004), pp. 91–93. Reprinted with the permission of Cambridge University Press.

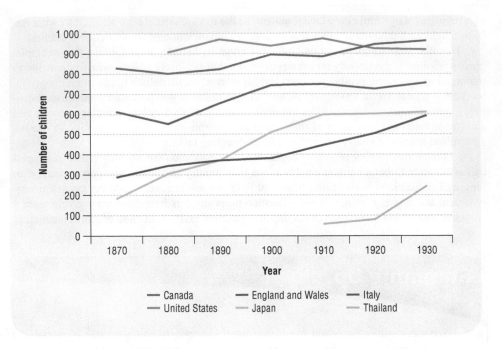

For most of history, families were chiefly responsible for socializing the young and training them to perform adult roles. Thus, in preindustrial Europe, the vast majority of children learned to work as adults by observing and helping their elders in the largely agricultural economy. Only a small urban minority had much use for skills like reading and arithmetic. The literate and numerate few were typically trained in religious institutions. In fact, before the rise of Protestantism, priests held a virtual monopoly on literacy. The Catholic Church's authority depended on the *in*ability of ordinary people to read the Bible. It even went so far as to persecute people who made the Bible available in local languages. William Tyndale, whose English translation became the standard King James Bible, was burned at the stake for his efforts in 1536.

## Uniform Socialization

Creating systems of education with sufficient resources to include all children was a social change of breathtaking scope. Training in families had been decentralized, unorganized, and uneven in quality. Religious training was never widely available and tended to set people apart from the surrounding community. Replacing these forms of instruction with a centralized and rationalized system created strong pressures toward uniformity and standardization. Diversity among families, regions, and religious traditions gradually gave way to homogenized indoctrination into a common culture.

Canada was something of an exception because, in the nineteenth century, the provinces recognized separate school systems for Catholics and Protestants. However, lack of recognition of distinct religious tracks by postsecondary institutions pressured secondary schools to cover the same topics in the same fashion in preparing their students for more advanced training. As a result, students today can travel thousands of kilometres for higher education and experience no more discontinuity than do those who attend the nearest school.

Surrendering children to state control was not universally popular, especially at first. Some students preferred skipping class to sitting in school, and special police (truant officers) were charged with tracking down absentees, who were then punished. Effective mass education was achieved only through laws that made attendance compulsory. All Canadian provinces and territories now require parents to ensure their children are educated up to a certain age. Although more than 5 percent of families send children to private schools, and about 80 000 children are home-schooled (Fraser Institute, 2007), some 94 percent of families surrender their children to public schooling (Statistics Canada, 2001a). Although some children resist schooling's forced drill toward cultural ideals that are at odds with their other experiences, they are in a small minority.

## Rising Levels of Education

Making education available to everyone, whether they liked it or not, was only a starting point. The amount of education that people receive has risen steadily, and this trend shows no sign of abating. In 1951, fewer than 1 in 50 Canadians had completed a university degree. Completing university allowed a person entry into a narrow elite. Today, nearly 1 in 5 Canadians over age 14 has a university degree, and over half have postsecondary education. In 50 years, a rarity became common (Table 17.1).

Canadians' growing commitment to higher education is illustrated by Table 17.1. Since 1990, the percentage of those without a high school diploma almost halved (from 38 to 20 percent), while those with a university degree nearly doubled (from 11 to 21 percent). Widespread growth in postsecondary education reflects the recognition that education is the most viable option for improving employment opportunities.

Sociologists distinguish *educational attainment* from *educational achievement*. **Educational achievement** is the knowledge or skills that an individual acquires. Achievement refers to mastery of educational content and, in principle, is reflected in grades. We say "in principle" because the validity of grades is a matter of debate (see Box 17.1 on page 436) **Educational attainment** reflects participation in educational programs and is measured by the number of years of schooling completed or, for higher levels, certificates and degrees earned. In theory, educational attainment and achievement are directly related. More time in educational institutions leads to more knowledge and skills. In practice, the connection is looser, since educational exposure affects students differently. Nonetheless, educational exposure is necessary, so who continues schooling and who does not raises important issues that we address below. In principle, selection might depend only on individual educational achievements. In practice, non-academic factors, including family background, play a large role in determining who completes an advanced education.

**Educational achievement** is the learning of valuable skills and knowledge.

**Educational attainment** is the number of years of schooling successfully completed or, for higher learning, the degrees or certificates earned.

## Individual Advantages and Disadvantages

Higher educational attainment helps people get jobs and earn more. Figure 17.2 on page 437 illustrates how education level influenced rates of unemployment in Canada in 2009. Lower rates of unemployment were associated with more education. People who did not finish high school had an unemployment rate three times as high as did people with a university degree.

Education also increases earnings. As Figure 17.3 on page 437 shows, the odds of earning high pay steadily improve as educational attainment increases. In 2009, people with a certificate less than a bachelor's degree earned $30 116, those with a university degree averaged $58 767, while those with more than a bachelor's degree earned $69 230 (Statistics Canada, 2009c). The pattern is far from rigid—people with every level of education are found at each level of earnings. However, more education and better earnings tend to go together.

**TABLE 17.1**

Population Ages 14 and over, by Highest Level of Educational Attainment, Canada, 2010 (in percent)

Source: HRSDC calculations based on Statistics Canada. Labour force survey estimates (LFS), by educational attainment, sex and age group, annual (CANSIM Table 282-0004). Ottawa: Statistics Canada, 2011. Retrieved April 29, 2011 (http://www4.hrsdc.gc.ca/ .3ndic.1t.4r@-eng.jsp?iid=29).

| | |
|---|---|
| Without high school diploma | 20 |
| High school diploma | 20 |
| Some postsecondary | 8 |
| College or trade certification | 31 |
| University degree | 21 |

# Social Policy: What Do You Think?

## IS GRADE INFLATION HARMFUL?

In schools and universities, grades are the principal indicator of educational achievement. Grades are supposed to reflect what students know. But do they? We can test the validity of school grades by comparing the grades teachers assign to standardized examination results. When this comparison was completed in New Brunswick and Newfoundland and Labrador, the results revealed substantial grade inflation (Laurie, 2007). In math, for example, the average standardized exam score was 60 percent,

while school grades in math averaged 74 percent.

Two sociologists (Côté and Allahar, 2007) report that grade inflation is a clear trend in Canadian universities. By their estimate, under half of undergraduate students received grades of A or B in the 1970s. Today, comparable figures range between 60 and 80 percent, depending on the institution and course. In the early 1980s, about 40 percent of students applying to Ontario's universities had A averages; now over 60 percent do.

Some commentators attribute grade inflation to an attitude of entitlement among the current generation of students (Laurie, 2007; Tylee, 2005). Many in this generation attended elementary schools with "no-fail" policies and now consider high grades a right. Failure is not considered a possible outcome, and Cs are no longer considered average. In a recent survey of first-year university students, 70 percent rated themselves as above average (a statistical impossibility; Côté and Allahar, 2007). Students now come

to university with the orientation of consumers who expect to receive good grades in exchange for paying tuition.

Educational institutions are agents of socialization. Setting expectations is an important part of this process. Grade inflation promotes lowered expectations. If high grades are easily awarded, good students are not challenged to strive for excellence. Likewise, grade inflation gives weaker students a false sense of their competence, which does little to encourage them to improve. Schools and universities that participate in grade inflation are shifting their mandate from the promotion of excellence to keeping more students in the education system for a longer time.

What do you think? Did you have to work hard in school to get good grades? Do your university courses challenge you to achieve excellence? Does paying tuition give students a right to high grades or even passing grades? What consequences does grade inflation in the educational system have for the economy? Why do you think grade inflation has taken place?

In the next section, we examine how mass education arose. We then examine theories that connect the rise of mass education to industrialization, arguing that education provides a basis for collective and individual wealth and motivates widespread loyalty to culture and society. We will see how education reproduces class inequality. We conclude by reviewing a series of recent developments and future challenges for Canada's system of mass schooling.

## The Rise of Mass Schooling

What accounts for the spread of mass schooling? Sociologists usually highlight four factors: the development of the printing press that led to inexpensive book production, the Protestant Reformation, the spread of democracy, and industrialism. Let us consider each of these factors in turn.

First, the printing press: In 1436, Johannes Gutenberg introduced the printing press with movable type in Europe. The effect was revolutionary. Books were expensive when scribes were the only source of new copies. The printing press led to a dramatic fall in book prices and an explosion of supply. Many of the new printed books were in the vernacular—languages used every day by common folk—and not in the Latin that only scholars understood. Literacy spread beyond elite circles, first in cities and eventually into rural areas, as inexpensive books fostered demand for schools to teach children the useful art of reading (Eisenstein, 1983).

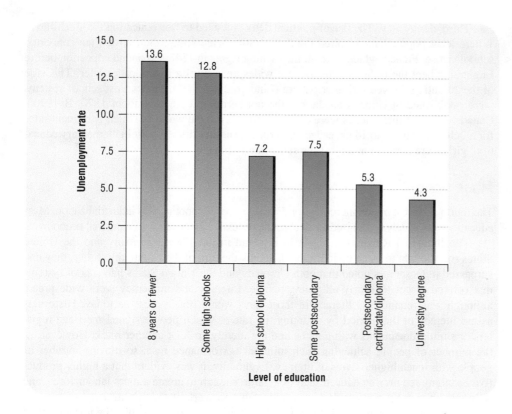

**FIGURE 17.2**

Unemployment Rate by Highest Level of Education Completed, Canada, 2008–9 (in percent)

Source: Statistics Canada, 2008–09, Labour Force Survey. "Unemployment Rate and Employment Rate, by Education Level". Retrieved March 20, 2011 (http://www.rhdcc-hrsdc.gc.ca/eng/employment/ei/reports/eimar_2009/annex/ann ex1_5.shtml).

Second, Protestantism: The Catholic Church relied on priests to convey dogma to believers. The education of priests was a primary motivation for the foundation of European universities in the Middles Ages. However, in the early sixteenth century, Martin Luther, a German monk, began to criticize the Catholic Church. Protestantism grew out of his criticisms. The Protestants believed that the Bible alone, and not Church doctrine, should guide Christians. They expected Christians to have more direct contact with the word of God than was allowed by the Catholic Church. Accordingly, Protestants needed to be able to read the scriptures for themselves. The rise of Protestantism was thus a spur to popular literacy.

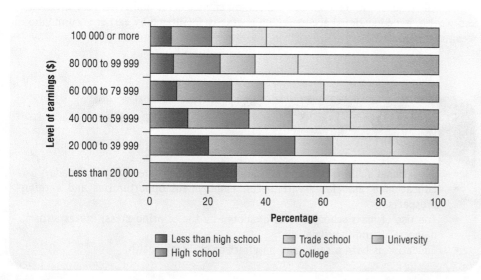

**FIGURE 17.3**

Earnings by Amount of Education, Canada, 2006

Source: Created from analysis of Statistics Canada 2006 Census, public use microdata files, May 3, 2011.

Third, democracy: The rise of political democracy led to free education for all children. Where local populations acquired the democratic means to tax themselves, tax-supported schools arose. France, which gave all men voting rights in 1848, expanded education before England, where the right to vote was not widespread until a few decades later. This side of the Atlantic followed a similar pattern (Lindert, 2004: 107). The earliest school systems were established in Upper Canada and the northern United States about 1870. By 1900, Canada and the United States were the first countries in the world in which enrolment rates for all children ages 5 to 14 exceeded 90 percent. Another first: at least in elementary education, girls were enrolled at almost the same rate as boys were.

## Mass Schooling and National Wealth

The fourth and most important reason for the rise of mass schooling was industrialization. Mass education was widely recognized as an absolute necessity for creating an industrial economy.

The Industrial Revolution began in England in the 1780s. Germany and the United States soon sought to catch up to England, and by the turn of the twentieth century, they had surpassed it. Observers noted that both Germany and the United States had school systems that offered places to nearly all young people. Literacy and numeracy were widespread, although what counted as literacy in those days would not impress us today. Historians assess literacy of that period by counting the rate at which people signed marriage registers or similar documents with a name and not merely an X or another mark. However, as the number of people achieving such minimal performance rose, so did the number of people with much higher levels of literacy. Eventually, it was evident that a highly productive economy requires an education system large enough to create a mass labour force, and rich enough to train and employ researchers able to work at the cutting edge of modern science. Democratic countries led the way, but communist countries, like the former Soviet Union, also invested heavily in education to foster economic development.

Today, investment in education is acknowledged as an important step in achieving great national wealth. However, the connection between education and wealth is by no means automatic. Some countries educate a relatively small proportion or a relatively large proportion of their population given their level of wealth (United Nations, 2005).

Education is not only a *source* of wealth; it is also a *product* of wealth. After all, education is expensive. Raising education levels for entire populations requires overcoming a vicious cycle: A significant fraction of a country's population must invest a great deal of time and money to become educated before there are enough teachers to instruct nearly everyone. This time and money must somehow be saved from the pressures of producing enough to supply necessities, like food and shelter. What is true for individuals is also true for societies: Education enhances the ability to generate earnings and wealth, but educational accumulation is greatly facilitated by earlier accumulation of wealth (see Box 17.2).

## Summing Up

- Educational achievement and educational attainment are rising in Canada.
- Education is associated with better employment opportunities and earning prospects.
- The rise of mass schooling was promoted by the printing press, Protestantism, democracy, and industrialism.
- Education is both a cause and an effect of national wealth.

# Social Policy: What Do You Think?

## ARE VIRTUAL CLASSROOMS NEXT?

Because education is so expensive, governments, universities, and public school boards are always looking for ways to cut costs. In recent years, online courses have become increasingly popular in Canada and elsewhere. They maximize revenue by accommodating more students than can be fit into a classroom and they minimize the cost of overhead (building construction and maintenance) and labour (instructors' salaries). Are virtual classrooms—online courses without instructors—next?

You can imagine Naomi Baptiste's surprise when she arrived at her pre-calculus class at North Miami Beach Senior High School in September 2010 and found a bank of computers instead of a teacher (Herrera, 2011). Naomi is one of 7000 students in Miami-Dade public schools who were enrolled in classes without teachers in the academic year 2010–11. Only a classroom "facilitator" was available to make sure students progressed and to deal with technical issues.

While virtual classrooms save money, quality of learning is a separate issue. Alix Braun, a sophomore at Miami Beach High taking Advanced Placement macroeconomics in a virtual classroom, said, "none of [my classmates] want to be there." According to Chris Kirchner, an English teacher at Coral Reef Senior High School in Miami, "the way our state is dealing with class size is nearly criminal" (quoted in Herrera, 2011).

Virtual classrooms (sometimes blended with intermittent, real classroom instruction) are spreading to K–8 public schools in Florida and to public schools in other states, such as Illinois and Nebraska. Can Canada be far behind? What kinds of students are most likely to be required to take classes in virtual classrooms? How will the spread of virtual classrooms likely affect social stratification?

# THE FUNCTIONS OF EDUCATION

## Latent Functions

Schools do not merely carry out training; they also concentrate young people for extended periods in common locations. In children's early years, the law requires attendance. In more advanced programs, economic incentives and family pressures encourage student attendance. Certain latent or unintended consequences arise from segregating people by age and forcing them to spend much of their time together.

One result is that schools encourage the development of a separate youth culture that can conflict with parents' values (Coleman, 1961). When students are asked to rank the popularity of fellow students, rankings don't centre on academic achievement. Instead, they signify athletic and social success. Many students who are low on such peer rankings find the youth culture of school alienating.

Role conflict occurs when a person's situation presents incompatible demands. One result of role conflict is alienation or disconnection from others, as Lance Roberts recalls from his own high school experience. "I attended high school in the 1960s and, besides girls, had two major interests—grades and basketball. These interests were connected since, if your grades were poor, you were ineligible to play on the varsity basketball team. In my school, unacceptable grades were below 45 percent. For students on athletic teams, unacceptable grades were circled in red on your report card. Three red circles and you were off the team.

Schools concentrate young people into a small number of places for extended periods of time. This has unintended consequences, such as encouraging the growth of a separate youth culture.

**Assortative mating** occurs when marriage partners are selected so that spouses are similar on various criteria of social rank.

"During basketball season, our team practised three times a day. Report cards were distributed just before lunch, so at the noon practice, the locker room was full of inquiries and boasts about red circles. Statements like 'How many did you get?' and 'I was damn lucky, I thought Mr. Charles would give me a third one for sure' filled the room. Since our top three players were routinely in danger of ineligibility, their opinions set the standard. The norm was clear: Getting red circles was acceptable (even preferable), as long as you remained eligible to play.

"In my first year on the team, a teammate asked, 'Hey, how many red circles?' My report of 'none' was greeted with mean-spirited laughter from several players and endless chiding, bordering on harassment. As an impressionable adolescent who desperately wanted my teammates to accept me, the chastisement hurt.

"When I mentioned this situation at dinner that evening, my parents gave a united, emphatic reply: 'Anything less than your best school performance is unacceptable.' This external demand reinforced the lesson I took away from my just-completed summer job as a labourer. Educational achievement was important to my family and me.

"Nonetheless, I found the conflicting expectations of parents and teammates stressful. In class and out, I was awash with anxiety. I obsessed over the red-circle issue. I withdrew and felt lonely, isolated, and powerless. I dreaded going to practice for fear of hearing my new nickname, 'Egghead.' My performance both on the court and in class suffered. The coach inquired about what was troubling me, but I was too embarrassed to tell my story.

"On the next round of report cards, my grades dropped—but not nearly enough to qualify for membership in the red-circle club. Lower grades produced a predictable response from my parents, and I was still stuck with an outsider stigma by key teammates. I was irritable and felt overwhelmed and sad. Role conflict generated debilitating stress.

"The conclusion of the basketball season brought relief. However, my experience was so stressful I decided not to play basketball the following year. I matured during my season off and returned to the courts in my final year of high school, but not without lasting memories of what role conflict can do."

Encouraging the development of a separate youth culture is only one of the latent functions performed by schools. At higher levels, educational institutions also serve as a "marriage market" that brings potential mates together. Students in educational institutions often share common social class and related background characteristics. Moreover, since many students postpone mate selection until they complete their education, potential mates often share similar educational qualifications. In these ways, educational settings encourage the choice of partners who share social origins and destinations (Rytina, Blau, Blum, and Schwartz, 1988). The result is **assortative mating**—choosing a mate who is similar to oneself on various ranking criteria.

Schools also perform other unintended functions. For example, in the early years they provide the custodial service of keeping children under close surveillance for much of the day and freeing parents to work. University and college attendance postpones full-time labour force participation, which helps restrict job competition and support wage levels (Bowles and Gintis, 1976). Through their encouragement of critical, independent thinking, educational institutions can also become "schools of dissent" that challenge authoritarian regimes and promote social change (Brower, 1975; Freire, 1972).

## Manifest Functions: The Logic of Industrialism

The characteristics of institutions in preindustrial societies vary widely. Functionalists argue that industrialism causes convergence among societies, dictating that social institutions develop according to a common pattern. Said differently, social institutions must perform certain common, manifest (or intended) functions to make industrialism possible. In particular, industrialism requires the widespread application of science and technology in the economy, making work more specialized and technical, and changing working conditions (Kerr, Dunlop, Harbison, and Myers, 1960: 36). The education system mirrors these trends.

## Cultural Homogeneity and Solidarity

Durkheim saw people as continuously torn between egoistic needs and moral impulses, with schools enhancing the moral side by working to create cultural uniformity and social solidarity. By instilling a sense of authority, discipline, and morality in children, schools make society cohesive (Durkheim, 1956, 1961 [1925]).

Contemporary sociologists acknowledge Durkheim's argument and broaden it. They point to a variety of manifest functions schools perform that are aimed at creating solidarity through cultural homogeneity. For example, Canadian schools teach students civic responsibility, pride in their nation, respect for the law, and to think of democracy as the best form of government and capitalism as the best type of economic system (Callahan, 1962). Schools also transmit shared knowledge and culture between generations, thereby fostering a common cultural identity.

## Common School Standards

The uniformity of much industrial work requires an education system that teaches workers common standards. Staffing schools to meet this goal was a huge challenge. A large number of student teachers had to be taught the same outlook and skills. Language was a problem too because, until recently, substantial variations in language and dialect existed within small areas. Creating cultural conformity required designating certain conventions of grammar, spelling, and pronunciation as correct and imposing these conventions on teacher-candidates and certification centres. A demanding and expensive system had to be created in which a privileged few were recruited to elite institutions, socialized to the new standards, and then sent back to peripheral regions to impose the uniform standards on students. By this means, the language conventions at such university centres as Oxford and the Sorbonne were established as the cultural ideal against which student performances were judged.

## National Solidarity

Before the rise of public education, an individual identified with the idiosyncratic worldview of his or her local community. As public education grew, mass socialization shifted to a common set of cultural beliefs, norms, and values directed by a central state. In this way, public education promoted membership in a national community composed of individuals who were mostly strangers but who felt connected because of a shared culture. They became part of an "imagined community" known as the nation.

The loyalties of imagined communities were centred on states because only states could afford the enormous expense of mass education. States provided classrooms with flags, rituals, patriotic songs, and historical myths, along with adults who supplied enthusiastic leadership. Legal requirements meant participation was not a matter of choice. Upper Canada led the world in not only providing universal education but requiring it. In 1871, Ontario pioneered compulsory education by fining parents whose children ages 7 to 12 did not attend school for at least four months each year. Since then, all provinces and territories have gradually tightened such requirements; most now require that students stay in school until they turn 16. Tightening requirements had the desired effect of increasing the number of years children spent in school and, subsequently, reducing unemployment rates (Oreopoulos, 2005). Such benefits soften the harsh realities of required participation imposed on those who unwillingly participate in state-sponsored public schooling.

Functionalists are correct in saying that mass education offers many people a ticket to economic, social, and cultural success. They also have a point when they argue that mass education socializes students into a common culture that enhances economic development.

Nonetheless, the functionalist view of education is one-sided. While education can produce these positive individual and social outcomes, it does not do so for everyone. Institutionalized education also produces division and disadvantage, as you will now learn.

## Summing Up

- Education performs latent functions, including the creation of a separate youth culture and a marriage market.
- The manifest functions of mass education include promoting cultural uniformity and national solidarity. Common school standards also prepare students for participation in an industrial economy.

# SORTING INTO CLASSES AND HIERARCHIES: CONFLICT PERSPECTIVES

A **meritocracy** is a social hierarchy in which rank corresponds to individual capacities fairly tested against a common standard.

Functionalists argue that modern educational institutions provide all students with equal opportunity to excel. In this view, differences in ability, motivation, and effort allow some students to perform better than others do. Those who learn poorly get inferior jobs, but that's the nature of a **meritocracy**—a social hierarchy in which rank is allocated by tests of individual merit. In a meritocracy, some children are born to lower-ranked families but if they perform well in school they can expect upward mobility. Likewise, some children are born to higher-ranked families but if they perform poorly in school they can expect downward mobility (Bell, 1973).

Conflict theorists challenge the functionalist assumption that educational attainment and subsequent social ranking are regulated by performance based on individual merit. They identify other factors that contribute to educational and economic success, and we survey several of them here. We also examine several prominent features of primary and secondary schooling that tend to preserve the stratification system. We begin by first examining how higher education and advanced degrees are forms of privilege that are less accessible to those with lower-class backgrounds.

## Economic Barriers to Higher Education

It might be possible to create an education system in which academic performance is the sole criterion for allocating people to the stratification system. However, few academic programs admit only qualified people and supply all who do qualify with funding to meet all expenses. In most cases, higher education in Canada and elsewhere requires students and their families to shoulder significant financial burdens. Tuition fees are rising. On average, Canadian full-time undergraduates paid $5138 in tuition fees in 2010–11, up from $1185 in 1988–89. Taking inflation into account, this represents a 164 percent increase. During the 1990s, undergraduate tuition increased at an annual average rate of nearly 10 percent, and since 2000 it has increased at an annual average rate of nearly 4 percent (Statistics Canada, 2009k). Moreover, tuition is only part of the cost of a year at school, particularly for those who leave home to pursue their studies.

Social class origin strongly affects how much formal education people attain (Goldthorpe and Breen, 1997). Many countries, Canada among them, have greatly expanded postsecondary education in the past 50 or 60 years. Expansion has lessened class effects, but it has not eliminated them.

How exactly does family income affect postsecondary participation rates? The evidence shows a clear social gradient in which postsecondary education increases at every step of the family income ladder. While access to postsecondary education is much less restricted by family income in Canada than it is in the United States, substantial social inequality remains. About a third of students from families in the bottom quarter of the income distribution attend postsecondary institutions, while about half from families in the top quarter do (Belley, Frenette, and Lochner, 2010; Statistics Canada, 2007). In addition, while the average student loan on completion of university was $16 341 in 2008–9 ($10 085 on completion of college), students from less affluent families have to borrow more money to complete their education, so they face a significantly weightier economic burden when they graduate (HRSDC, 2011a).

## Credentialism and Professionalization

Because postsecondary education is a valuable asset that children from richer families are more likely to obtain, education becomes a tool for **social exclusion**—setting up boundaries so that certain social opportunities and positions are not open to all (Parkin, 1979). Exclusion occurs when some groups have more resources than others do, allowing them to obtain educational credentials that allow them to amass still more privileges. Note that social exclusion takes place even if advanced education does not lead to useful knowledge or genuine skills; esoteric skills, such as knowledge of classical music or fine art, may still be used to distinguish insiders from outsiders.

**Credential inflation** takes place when qualifying for specific jobs requires more and more certificates and degrees over time. Because certificates and degrees are expensive, credential inflation contributes to social exclusion. Credential inflation occurs in part because the technical knowledge required for jobs has increased. For example, because aircraft engines and avionics systems are more complex than they were, say, 75 years ago, working as an airplane mechanic today requires more expertise. Certification ensures that the airplane mechanic can meet the high technical demands of the job. However, in many jobs there is a poor fit between credentials and responsibilities. On-the-job training, not a diploma or a degree, often gives people the skills they need to get the job done. Nonetheless, credential inflation takes place partly because employers find it a convenient sorting mechanism. For example, an employer may assume that a university graduate has certain manners, attitudes, and tastes that will be useful in a high-profile managerial position. The effect is to exclude people from less advantaged families from such positions, while favouring individuals from families and groups with the advantages that facilitate education (Collins, 1979).

Credential inflation is fuelled by **professionalization**, which occurs when members of an occupation insist that people earn certain credentials to enter the occupation. Professionalization ensures the maintenance of standards. It also keeps earnings high. After all, if "too many" people enter a given profession, the cost of services offered by that profession is bound to fall. This helps explain why, on average, physicians earn more than university professors who have Ph.D.s. The Canadian Medical Association is a powerful organization that regulates and effectively limits entry into the medical professions (see Chapter 19, Health and Medicine). Canadian professors have never been in a position to form such a powerful organization. Because professionalism promotes high standards and high earnings, it has spread widely.

## Cultural Capital

French sociologist Pierre Bourdieu wrote extensively about the role of education in maintaining social inequality. His central theme grew out of an analogy with the theories of Karl Marx. Marx had emphasized the role of economic capital—ownership of the physical means of producing wealth—in sustaining inequality. Bourdieu argued that education was central to the creation and transmission of **cultural capital**—learning and skills that ensured superior positions in productive activity (Bourdieu, 1998b; Bourdieu and Passeron, 1979).

**Social exclusion** is achieved by creating barriers that restrict certain opportunities or positions to members of one group.

**Credential inflation** occurs when it takes ever more certificates or degrees to qualify for a particular job.

**Professionalization** occurs to the degree that certain levels and types of schooling are established as criteria for gaining access to an occupation.

**Cultural capital** is the stock of learning and skills that increases the chance of securing a superior job.

**TABLE 17.2**

Rates of Participation in Postsecondary Education by Highest Level of Parental Education for Canadians Ages 24–26, 2007

Source: Adapted from Statistics Canada PISA Data, "Participation in Post-Secondary Education." Retrieved March 17, 2011 (http://www.pisa.gc.ca/eng/participation.shtml).

**Pedagogic violence** is Bourdieu's term for the application by teachers of punishments intended to discourage deviation from the dominant culture.

| | Participation rate in . . . | |
| Parental Education | College | University |
|---|---|---|
| Less than high school | 43 | 32 |
| High school | 40 | 37 |
| Some postsecondary | 35 | 43 |
| Postsecondary graduate | 28 | 60 |

Cultural capital is expensive and difficult to acquire. Bourdieu emphasized that learning in school involves **pedagogic violence**, the application by teachers of punishments intended to discourage deviation from the dominant culture. Teachers routinely insist that there is one "correct" way to speak, spell, or do arithmetic. They lay down intricate rules, and individuals must learn to follow them with little pause for reflection or judgment. Such learning involves long periods of disciplinary pressure.

For Bourdieu, much of what schools teach is how to evaluate people. Tastes in books, music, food, and clothing come to reflect level of schooling. The books or music that people discuss signals their place in the class structure.

Although schools pressure all students to internalize shared cultural standards, students are not equally receptive. The cultural standard designated as correct or proper in schools matches what families practise at home *to varying degrees*. If your parents are university professors, from your earliest babbling you will be imitating the speech patterns of the dominant cultural group. Families from less advantaged countries or regions enjoy the least overlap with the ideal. If your parents come from rural Newfoundland or Bangladesh, and especially if they lack a higher education, teachers are likely to spend a lot of time correcting your English. Children from such families often struggle to meet teachers' standards.

When teachers evaluate performance, they inevitably reward students who are close to the standards of the dominant culture. Although some students from all backgrounds succeed, a student's stock of cultural capital—of disciplined familiarity with the dominant culture—will influence how hard or easy success is. Advantaged children will find rewards easier to achieve. Children from families with less cultural capital will be punished more and will tend to experience school as less pleasant.

A key part of Bourdieu's argument is readily confirmed. Table 17.2 above shows how much growing up with parents who are highly educated enhances one's educational attainment. University attendance is nearly twice as common among students whose parents have a postsecondary degree as among those whose parents did not graduate from high school.

## Summing Up

- Families with few financial resources experience restricted access to higher education.
- Through credentialism and professionalism, education acts as a mechanism of social exclusion.
- Limited cultural capital restricts higher educational achievement.

# REPRODUCING INEQUALITY: THE CONTRIBUTION OF SYMBOLIC INTERACTIONISM

Most sociologists find the conflict perspective on education more credible than the functionalist view. Based on the evidence, they believe that the benefits of education are unequally distributed and tend to **reproduce the existing stratification system** (Jencks et al., 1972).

Factors other than class matter too. Students with higher grades are more likely to advance to higher education. Parental encouragement plays a role, as does support from peers and teachers. However, research consistently finds that such social supports are part of how class advantage is transmitted; it is the wealthier students with more highly educated parents who are likely to enjoy more parental, peer, and teacher support. Furthermore, family income and parental education contribute to educational attainment over and above any influence they exert on academic performance and social support, insofar as they provide students with cultural capital that assists their advancement (Lambert, Zeman, Allen, and Bussière, 2004).

Why do schools fail to overcome class differences? Symbolic interactionists emphasize three social mechanisms that operate to reproduce inequality: the hidden curriculum, testing and tracking, and self-fulfilling prophecies.

> The **reproduction of the existing stratification system** refers to social processes that ensure that offspring enter a rank or class similar or identical to that of their parents.

## The Hidden Curriculum

Apart from academic and vocational subjects, students learn a **hidden curriculum** in school (Snyder, 1971; see Chapter 4, Socialization). Teachers and school administrators never state that understanding it contributes powerfully to educational achievement, and they never teach it formally, but "getting it" is central to success.

The content of the hidden curriculum centres on obedience to authority and conformity to cultural norms. Teachers expect students to accept the curriculum, institutional routines, and grading system without question. Students who comply do well; those who do not are headed for trouble. Success stories are most common among middle- and upper-class children who are well-endowed with cultural capital and whose socialization at home has cultivated the hidden curriculum's standards of dress, speech, motivation, and deferred gratification.

Staying in school requires accepting the terms of the hidden curriculum and feeling positively involved. Researchers at Statistics Canada explored this phenomenon by developing measures of academic and social involvement. Social involvement included not feeling like an outsider and believing that people cared what a student said. Academic involvement consisted of liking teachers, not skipping classes, and regarding class content as "not useless." Chances of continuing to higher education were twice as high for students who reported social acceptance or positive attitudes toward the formal organization, authority, and procedures of the school (Shaienks and Gluszynski, 2007).

> The **hidden curriculum** in school teaches obedience to authority and conformity to cultural norms.

## Testing and Tracking

Most schools in Canada are composed of children from various socioeconomic, racial, and ethnic backgrounds. Apart from the hidden curriculum, testing and tracking maintain these social inequalities in schools. IQ tests sort students, who are then channelled into high-ability (enriched), middle-ability, and low-ability (special needs) classrooms based on test scores. Often, the results are classrooms that are stratified by socioeconomic status, race, and ethnicity, much like the larger society. For example, Toronto Board of Education research showed that while 20 percent of black students were enrolled in low-level academic programming, only 10 percent of white students and 3 percent of Asian students were similarly streamed (Henry, Tator, Mattis, and Rees, 2000: 239).

Nobody denies that students vary in their abilities and that high-ability students require special challenges to reach their full potential. Nor does anyone deny that underprivileged students tend to score low on IQ tests. The controversial question is whether IQ is mainly genetic or social in origin. If IQ is genetic in origin, then it cannot be changed, so improving the quality of schooling for the underprivileged is arguably a waste of money (Herrnstein and Murray, 1994). If IQ is social in origin, IQ tests and tracking only reinforce social differences that could otherwise be reduced by changing the social circumstances of students.

Most sociologists believe that IQ reflects social standing in great part. That is because all that IQ tests can ever measure is acquired proficiency with a cultural system. How much exposure a person has had to whatever examiners count as correct will play a large role in testing. Even the most able Canadian children would perform abysmally if tested in Mongolian. IQ test results turn on a combination of two factors: (1) how effectively an individual absorbs what his or her environment offers, and (2) how closely his or her environment reflects what the test includes.

Most sociologists believe that members of underprivileged groups tend to score low on IQ tests because they do not have the training and the cultural background needed to score high (Fischer et al., 1996). To support their argument, they point to cases in which changing social circumstances result in changes in IQ scores. For instance, in the first decades of the twentieth century, most Jewish immigrants to North America tested well below average on IQ tests. This was sometimes used as an argument against Jewish immigration (Gould, 1996; Steinberg, 1989). Today, most North American Jews test above average in IQ. Since the genetic makeup of Jews has not changed in the past century, why the change in IQ scores? Sociologists point to upward mobility. During the twentieth century, most Jewish immigrants worked hard and moved up the stratification system. As their fortunes improved, they made sure their children had the skills and the cultural resources needed to do well in school. Average IQ scores rose as the social standing of Jews improved.

Consider also the "Flynn effect," named after political scientist James R. Flynn, who first pointed it out (Flynn, 1987). Flynn showed that average IQ scores increase over time on every major test, in every age range, and in every industrialized country (Neisser, 1997: 2). He observed increases of as much as 21 points in only 30 years. Typical improvements in test performance were large. For example, differences between children and their grandparents were far greater than differences observed across race and class divides in contemporary societies. This evidence suggests that IQ tests do not provide a fixed measuring rod that captures innate abilities or, for that matter, any sort of trait fixed by genetic endowment. It therefore makes sense to invest a lot in the early education of the underprivileged (see Box 17.3).

## Self-Fulfilling Prophecies

A third social mechanism that operates in schools to reproduce inequality is the self-fulfilling prophecy. A self-fulfilling prophecy is an expectation that helps to cause what it predicts. In a classic study, Ray Rist (1970) revealed how a self-fulfilling prophecy can influence a person's life chances. He found that after just eight days of observing students in a kindergarten classroom, and without giving a formal intelligence test, the teacher felt she could confidently assign the children to one of three tables. She assigned "fast learners" to Table 1, closest to her own desk and "slow learners" to Table 3, at the back of the class. Students she judged to be "average" were seated at Table 2, in the middle of the classroom. On what basis did she make these distinctions? Probing the issue, Rist found that the key variable distinguishing the students was social class. Children at

Canada was one of the first countries in the world to link its student body to the Internet. By 1997, almost all Canadian schools had Internet access through the SchoolNet electronic network.

PhotoDisk/Getty Images

# It's Your Choice

## IS SCHOOL ENOUGH?

Native Child and Family Services

Sociologists began to understand how little schools could do on their own to encourage upward mobility and end poverty in the 1960s, when sociologist James Coleman and his colleagues conducted a monumental study of academic performance (Coleman et al., 1966). What they found was that differences in the quality of schools—measured by assessment of such factors as school facilities and curriculum—accounted at most for about a third of the variation in students' academic performance. At least two-thirds of the variation in academic performance was due to inequalities imposed on children by their homes, neighbourhoods, and peers. Forty years later, little research contradicts Coleman's finding.

Various social commentators have argued that if we are to improve the success of disadvantaged students, we must develop policies aimed at improving the social environment of young, disadvantaged children *before* they enter the formal education system (Hertzman, 2000). Compensatory education programs for preschool children were largely developed in the United States and attempt to meet the needs of children who are socially and economically disadvantaged. In Canada, such programs have also been aimed at "children with special needs" and "at-risk children"—those who, because of one or more factors in their background, are believed to face a heightened risk of poor academic

performance or social adjustment. Although the traditional focus of early childhood education has been on children's social and emotional development, at least some of these compensatory education programs focus on children's intellectual development.

Survey research shows that household income is associated with developmental maturity and future success at school (Doherty, 1997). In addition, as family income decreases, the likelihood that children will experience a host of other problems that will negatively influence their school performance increases. For example, poor health, hyperactivity, and delayed vocabulary development are all higher among children in low-income families than among children in middle- and high-income families (Ross, 1998). Children who score low on school readiness are also more likely to have mothers with low levels of education and to be living in neighbourhoods that their mothers characterize as unsafe or as lacking in social cohesiveness (Health Canada, 1999b: 79).

Some observers believe that early developmental programs can decrease the chances of developmental problems in children and enhance their school performance. For example, Head Start programs are based on the belief that to assist children, the entire family must be helped. They provide access to food

banks, nutrition programs, literacy programs, parental support groups, and parenting courses. Promoting child readiness for school is also a key element of Head Start. Evaluations of Head Start programs in Canada report such benefits as more students completing school with better grades, requiring fewer medical and mental health services, and being less exposed to violent and alcoholic parents (Government of Canada, 2001). Head Start programs have been identified as particularly important in increasing the educational success of Aboriginal students.

While the cost of providing early childhood intervention programs is substantial, investments made in the critical early years of a child's life benefit not only Canada's children but the economy as well. One study reports that "every dollar spent in early intervention can save seven dollars in future expenditures in health and social spending" (Health Canada, 1999b: 88).

Do you believe that early childhood intervention programs are useful in improving the educational success of children? If not, why not? If so, do you feel that attendance in these programs should be compulsory? Should parents who refuse to send their children to such programs be penalized? What background factors should be used to select children and their families for inclusion in such programs?

## BOX 17.4
# Sociology at the Movies

### THE GREAT DEBATERS

The Civil War (1861–65) outlawed slavery in the United States, but legal and violent resistance against black rights persisted for more than a century. For example, in 1866 an amendment to the Texas Constitution stipulated that all taxes paid by blacks had to be used to maintain black schools, and that it was the duty of the legislature to "encourage colored schools" ("Jim Crow Laws: Texas," 2008). In this segregationist atmosphere, the Methodist Church founded Wiley College in the northeast corner of Texas in 1873 "for the purpose of allowing Negro youth the opportunity to pursue higher learning in the arts, sciences and other professions" (Wiley College, 2007).

In 1923, Wiley hired Melvin Tolson to teach speech and English. He proceeded to build up the college debating team to the point where they challenged and beat the mighty University of Southern California for the 1935 national debating championship. The victory shocked and scandalized much of the country's white population even as it instilled pride in African Americans, provided them with a shining model of academic achievement, and motivated black youth to strive for new heights. No self-fulfilling prophecy condemning black students to academic mediocrity operated at Wiley. To the contrary, Tolson worked his students hard, demanded excellence, and expected the best from them. Supported by the black community, they rose to his challenge.

*The Great Debaters* shows why the 1935 victory was so difficult.

*Everett Collection/CP Picture Archive*

English professor Melvin B. Tolson led the Wiley College debate team to a national championship against the University of Southern California (portrayed as Harvard in *The Great Debaters*) in 1935.

Tolson (played by Denzel Washington) is harassed by the local sheriff, who brands him a troublemaker for trying to unionize local black and white sharecroppers. On one out-of-town road trip, Tolson and his debating team come across a white mob that has just lynched a black man and set his body on fire. They barely escape with their lives. The pervasive racism of the times might discourage and immobilize lesser people, but it steels Tolson and his debaters, who feel compelled to show the world what blacks are capable of achieving even in the most inhospitable circumstances.

The successes of historically black colleges raise an important policy issue that is being debated in Canada's big cities today. Can segregated black public schools benefit black youth and should they be funded out of general tax revenue? Critics of separate black public schools argue that Canadian multiculturalism seeks to teach tolerance and respect for all cultures, and that separate public schools for any minority group would therefore be a step backward. Arguably, however, integrated public schools are still the home of self-fulfilling prophecies that make it difficult for black students to excel. Their curricula do little if anything to instil pride in the achievements of the black community. As a result, some black public school students dangerously identify academic excellence with "acting white," thus helping to condemn themselves to mediocre academic achievement and restricted social mobility. From this point of view, the achievements of historically black colleges like Wiley should be taken as a model of what is possible when black students are academically challenged and nourished in a non-threatening environment.

Table 1 were overwhelmingly middle class, while those assigned to Tables 2 and 3 were more likely to come from poorer homes. The assignment of these children was consequential because the children at Table 1 received more attention, were treated better, and, as the year progressed, came to see themselves as superior to the other children. In contrast, the other students tended to be ignored by the teacher and were referred to by the Table 1 children as "dumb." Unsurprisingly, they did not fare well. The following year, the grade 1 teacher took note of what the children had accomplished in kindergarten. The Table 1 children once again assigned to places in the classroom that marked them as superior.

Rist's findings suggest that, rather than valuing all students equally and treating them as if they have equally good prospects, teachers may suspect that disadvantaged students and students who are members of some minority groups are intellectually inferior. In turn, these students may come to feel rejected by teachers, other classmates, and the curriculum. Students from minority groups may also be disadvantaged by overt racism and discrimination. In response, students presumed to be inferior and marginalized in the classroom often cluster together out of resentment and in defiance of authority. Some of them eventually reject academic achievement as a goal. Discipline problems, ranging from apathy to disruptive and illegal behaviour, can result. Consistent with this argument, the dropout rate for Aboriginals (22.6 percent) is about three times as high as it is for non-Aboriginals (HRSDC, 2011b). In contrast, research shows that challenging lower-class students and those from minority groups, giving them emotional support and encouragement, giving greater recognition in the curriculum to the accomplishments of the groups from which they originate, creating an environment in which they can relax and achieve—all these strategies explode the self-fulfilling prophecy and improve academic performance (see Box 17.4).

In sum, schools reproduce the stratification system because of the hidden curriculum, IQ testing and tracking, and the self-fulfilling prophecy that disadvantaged and minority students are bound to do poorly. These social mechanisms increase the chance that students who are socially marginal and already disadvantaged will earn low grades and wind up with jobs near the bottom of the occupational structure.

## Summing Up

- The hidden curriculum operates to restrict the educational success of less advantaged students.
- The cultural bias in IQ testing and associated tracking disadvantages underprivileged students.
- Self-fulfilling prophecies contribute to academic success and failure.

# PROSPECTS AND CHALLENGES FOR EDUCATION IN CANADA

## Gender Differences: A Feminist Perspective

With every passing decade, Canadians spend more time in school, and with every passing decade, women's level of education increases relative to men's. Women currently receive more than 60 percent of university degrees awarded annually (Statistics Canada, 2010l). There are about 20 percent more Canadian women than men over the age of 14 with at least a bachelor's degree. Women still lag behind men in medicine and dentistry, and among people with master's degrees and Ph.D.s, but they are catching up (Table 17.3 on page 450). With women obtaining more degrees annually, it will not be long before university-educated women will be more numerous than university-educated men.

**TABLE 17.3**

Highest University Degree Obtained, for Population Age 15+, by Sex, Canada, 2006

Source: Statistics Canada, 2007, "Highest Certificate, Diploma or Degree (14), Age Groups (10A) and Sex (3) for the Population 15 Years and Over of Canada, Provinces, Territories, Census Metropolitan Areas and Census Agglomerations, 2006 Census—20% Sample Data." Retrieved March 5, 2011 (http://www12.statcan.ca/english/census06/data/topics/RetrieveProductTable.cfm?Temporal=2006&PID=93609&GID=837928&METH=1&APATH=3&PTYPE=88971&THEME=75&AID=&FREE=0&FOCUS=&VID=0&GC=99&GK=NA&RL=0&d1=1).

| | Women | Men | Ratio of Women to Men |
|---|---|---|---|
| Bachelor's degree | 1 603 040 | 1 378 425 | 1.2 |
| University certificate or diploma above bachelor level | 269 480 | 224 060 | 1.2 |
| Degree in medicine, dentistry, etc. | 54 705 | 82 145 | 0.7 |
| Master's degree | 402 910 | 464 065 | 0.9 |
| Ph.D. | 55 850 | 121 090 | 0.5 |

However, as feminists note, these figures mask the ways in which greater female participation in postsecondary education still conforms to traditional gender divisions. Figure 17.4 shows the distribution of university degrees by gender and academic field in Canada. Women outnumber men overall, but men predominate in business and management, architecture and engineering, physical and life sciences, math, computer and life sciences, and agricultural and related sciences. Differences between women and men are narrowing, but a strong tendency still exists for women to be concentrated in less scientifically oriented fields that pay less, notably the field of education.

## Participation and Aboriginal Background

Barriers to education other than gender are also substantial. For example, Canadians with Aboriginal backgrounds lag behind other Canadians. Thus, 34 percent of Aboriginal people do not have a high school diploma, compared with 15 percent of non-Aboriginals. Only 8 percent of Aboriginal people receive university degrees, while 23 percent of non-Aboriginals do (Statistics Canada, 2008d). Despite gains in recent years, equal educational achievement among Aboriginal people is a long way off.

## International Competition

Although access to higher education in Canada remains uneven, the Canadian accomplishment in higher education is impressive when compared with that of other countries. Figure 17.5 shows rankings of countries in the rate of education for working-age

**FIGURE 17.4**

University Degrees by Field of Study and Gender, Canada, 2006 (in '000s)

Source: Statistics Canada, 2007, "Major Field of Study—Classification of Instructional Programs, 2000 (13), Highest Postsecondary Certificate, Diploma or Degree (12), Age Groups (10A) and Sex (3) for the Population 15 Years and Over with Postsecondary Studies." Retrieved March 15, 2011 (http://www12.statcan.ca/english/census06/data/topics/ListProducts.cfm?Temporal=2006&APATH=3&THEME=75&FREE=0&GRP=1).

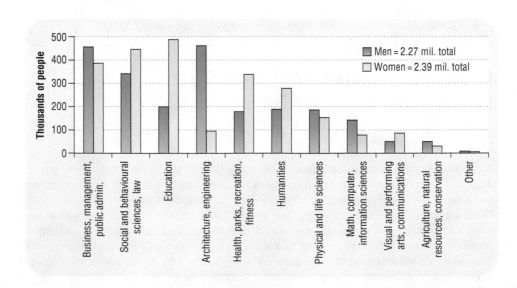

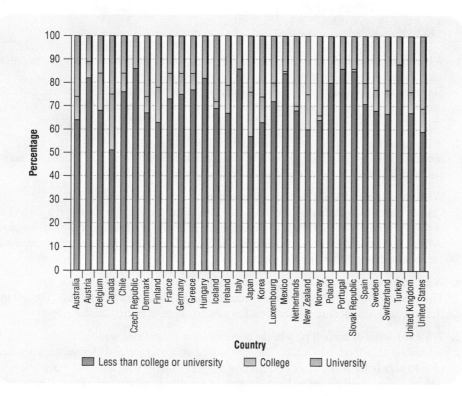

**FIGURE 17.5**

Educational Attainment of Adult Population (25–64), Selected Countries, in Percent, 2008

Source: Measured by the OECD, Various Countries, 2008; OECD, 2010

adults in 2008. Canada had the highest percentage of adults with postsecondary education. Still, several other countries have a higher rate of *university* graduation. Some relative latecomers, like South Korea, are making up ground by providing today's youth with many more years in school than earlier generations received. Canada's century-long place at the head of the class may give way before too long to such a newcomer.

In the 1990s, some observers raised doubts about the quality of Canada's education system. Suspicions grew that students were not applying themselves and learning enough, and that curricula and requirements had become lax. Critics were in for a surprise. The Organisation for Economic Co-operation and Development (OECD) organized a Programme for International Student Assessment (PISA) to assess the academic performance of 15-year-olds. Thirty-one countries were included and great care was taken to ensure that comparisons would be valid. When the first results came in, in 2001, Canadian students placed second in reading, sixth in mathematics, and fifth in science. These results placed Canada among a select group of countries that performed well on all three measures. The 2009 PISA results included 65 countries. These were the top five overall: (1) South Korea, (2) Finland, (3) Japan, (4) Canada, (5) New Zealand (Fleischman, Hopstock, Pelczar, and Shelley, 2010: 8–9, 18, 24). This ranking is a remarkable showing of which all Canadians should be proud.

## Summing Up

- Women perform better than men do in higher education, even though they are underrepresented in higher paying professions.
- Limited Aboriginal educational achievement continues to contribute significantly to social inequality in Canada.
- Canada is among the top performers in international achievement assessments.

# SUMMARY

1. What kind of societies provide education for all and specialized training for large minorities?
   Societies that have achieved industrialism, and the wealth industrialism brings, provide complete systems of schooling that take in nearly all children and allow many of them to remain in school for many years.

2. What manifest functions are performed by school systems?
   Schools homogenize future citizens by indoctrination into a common culture. Schools also sort and steer students to different class positions as adults.

3. What latent functions are carried out by schools?
   Latent functions include the creation of a youth culture, a marriage market, a custodial and surveillance system for children, a means of maintaining wage levels by keeping college and university students temporarily out of the job market, and occasionally a "school of dissent" that opposes authorities.

4. What factors account for the rise of mass, compulsory education?
   The spread of mass, compulsory education was encouraged by the Protestant Reformation, democratic revolutions, the modern state, and industrialization.

5. What role does education play in the accumulation of national wealth?
   Education is a form of wealth. The amount of education that different societies are able to supply for their future citizens corresponds closely with national income levels. Although nearly all countries have systems of mass, compulsory education, illiteracy is still widespread in poor countries.

6. What are the results of education according to functionalists?
   Functionalists argue that education is critically important for industrialization. They also argue that education ensures meritocracy.

7. What consequences of education do conflict theorists identify?
   Conflict theorists argue that education intensifies nationalism. They also argue that success at school is easier for privileged people, so education perpetuates privilege.

8. What is credential inflation and how does it relate to professionalization?
   Credential inflation (the need for more certification and diplomas to qualify for a given job) has been fuelled by the increasing technical requirements of many jobs. It has also been encouraged by the ability of people in certain occupations to exercise control over their occupations (professionalization). Credential inflation is thus a means of excluding people from the professions to maintain high standards and income levels.

9. What is cultural capital and how does it influence schooling?
   Parents who are advantaged are more likely to have acquired larger stocks of scarce, valued skills—that is, cultural capital. In turn, their children find it easier to win rewards at school by repeating what is familiar from their home life. Children from less advantaged families may have to unlearn family practices, such as vocabulary, grammar, or pronunciation, that are stigmatized as culturally inferior. This makes schooling less pleasant, which in turn is a major factor in the decision to forgo further education.

10. What are some interaction processes in school that tend to reinforce class differences among students?
    Positive and negative expectations by teachers result in self-fulfilling prophecies that favour students from privileged backgrounds and discourage students from less privileged origins. A hidden curriculum encourages teachers to reward conformity to middle-class values and standards.

11. What do feminists say about the fact that women are more numerous than men among university graduates?

Feminist scholars point out that the rising levels of female participation in postsecondary and graduate training are largely confined to a narrow range of academic fields and thereby tend to perpetuate occupational segregation by gender.

12. What do standardized tests measure and what are their effects?

Standardized tests are supposed to measure innate ability (IQ tests) or mathematical and reasoning abilities related to performance in college or university. To some extent, they do. Thus, to a degree, they help to sort students by ability and aid in the creation of a meritocracy. However, they also measure students' preparedness to learn and thrive in school, and preparedness is strongly related to background factors, such as a family's class position. Therefore, standardized tests also help to reproduce existing social inequalities.

## KEY TERMS

**assortative mating (p. 440)**

**credential inflation (p. 443)**

**cultural capital (p. 443)**

**educational achievement (p. 435)**

**educational attainment (p. 435)**

**hidden curriculum (p. 445)**

**meritocracy (p. 442)**

**pedagogic violence (p. 444)**

**professionalization (p. 443)**

**reproduction of the existing stratification system (p. 445)**

**social exclusion (p. 443)**

## WEB RESOURCES

### Companion Website for This Book

http://www.compass4e.nelson.com

Begin by clicking on the Student Resources section of the website. Next, select the chapter you are studying from the pull-down menu. From the Student Resources page you have easy access to additional Weblinks and other resources. The website also has many useful tips to aid you in your study of sociology, including practice tests for each chapter.

### InfoTrac® Search Terms

These search terms are provided to assist you in beginning to conduct research on this topic by visiting http://www.infotrac-college.com:

**educational achievement**
**educational attainment**
**globalization**
**multiculturalism**

# 25

# Learning the Student Role
## Kindergarten as Academic Boot Camp

HARRY L. GRACEY

*Schools are agents of socialization, preparing students for life in society. In preparing children, they teach expectations and demand conformity to society's norms. They help teach children the attitudes and behaviors appropriate to the society. Gracey points out that this process of teaching children to "fit in" begins early. His focus is the routines children in kindergarten are expected to follow.*

*As you read the article, think about the following questions:*

1. *What are key elements of the learning experience of kindergarteners?*
2. *How does the kindergarten routine encourage conformity and help prepare children for later life?*
3. *What might happen in later schooling and life if children do not receive this early childhood socialization?*
4. *How did your schooling prepare you for what you are doing and plan to do?*

GLOSSARY **Educational institution/system** The structure in society that provides systematic socialization of young. **Student role** Behavior and attitudes regarded by educators as appropriate to children in schools.

Education must be considered one of the major institutions of social life today. Along with the family and organized religion, however, it is a "secondary institution," one in which people are prepared for life in society as it is presently organized. The main dimensions of modern life, that is, the nature of society as a whole, is determined principally by the "Primary institutions," which today are the economy, the political system, and the military establishment. Education has been defined by sociologists, classical and contemporary, as an institution which serves society by socializing people into it through a formalized, standardized procedure. At the beginning of this century Emile Durkheim told student teachers at the University of Paris that education "consists of a methodical socialization of the younger generation." He went on to add:

> It is the influence exercised by adult generations on those that are not ready for social life. Its object is to arouse and to

Source: In Dennis Wrong and Harry L. Gracey (eds.), *Readings in Introductory Sociology*. New York: Macmillan, 1967. Reprinted with permission.

187

develop in the child a certain number of physical, intellectual, and moral states that are demanded of him by the political society as a whole and by the special milieu for which he is specifically destined.... To the egotistic and asocial being that has just been born, [society] must, as rapidly as possible, add another, capable of leading a moral and social life. Such is the work of education.[1]

The education process, Durkheim said, "is above all the means by which society perpetually recreates the conditions of its very existence."[2] The contemporary educational sociologist, Wilbur Brookover, offers a similar formulation in his recent textbook definition of education:

> Actually, therefore, in the broadest sense education is synonymous with socialization. It includes any social behavior that assists in the induction of the child into membership in the society or any behavior by which the society perpetuates itself through the next generation.[3]

The educational institution is, then, one of the ways in which society is perpetuated through the systematic socialization of the young, while the nature of the society which is being perpetuated—its organization and operation, its values, beliefs, and ways of living—are determined by the primary institutions. The educational system, like other secondary institutions, *serves* the society which is *created* by the operation of the economy, the political system, and the military establishment.

Schools, the social organizations of the educational institution, are today for the most part large bureaucracies run by specially trained and certified people. There are few places left in modern societies where formal teaching and learning is carried on in small, isolated groups, like the rural, one-room schoolhouses of the last century. Schools are large, formal organizations which tend to be parts of larger organizations, local community School Districts. These School Districts are bureaucratically organized and their operations are supervised by state and local governments. In this context, as Brookover says:

> The term education is used ... to refer to a system of schools, in which specifically designated persons are expected to teach children and youth certain types of acceptable behavior. The school system becomes a ... unit in the total social structure and is recognized by the members of the society as a separate social institution. Within this structure a portion of the total socialization process occurs.[4]

Education is the part of the socialization process which takes place in the schools; and these are, more and more today, bureaucracies within bureaucracies.

Kindergarten is generally conceived by educators as a year of preparation for school. It is thought of as a year in which small children, five or six years old, are prepared socially and emotionally for the academic learning which will take place over the next twelve years. It is expected that a foundation of behavior and attitudes will be laid in kindergarten on which the children can acquire the skills and knowledge they will be taught in the grades. A booklet prepared for parents by the staff of a suburban New York school system says that the kindergarten experience will stimulate the child's desire to learn and cultivate the skills he will need for learning in the rest of his school career. It claims that the child will find opportunities for physical growth, for satisfying his "need for self-expression," acquire some knowledge, and provide opportunities for creative activity. It concludes, "The most important benefit that your five-year-old will receive from kindergarten is the opportunity to live and grow happily and purposefully with others in a small society." The kindergarten teachers in one of the elementary schools in this community, one we shall call the Wilbur Wright School, said their goals were to see that the children "grew" in all ways: physically, of course, emotionally, socially, and academically. They said they wanted children to like school as a result of their kindergarten experiences and that they wanted them to learn to get along with others.

None of these goals, however, is unique to kindergarten; each of them is held to some extent by teachers in the other six grades at Wright School. And growth would occur, but differently, even if the child did not attend school. The children already know how to get along with others, in their families and their play groups. The unique job of the kindergarten in the educational division of labor seems rather to be teaching children the student role. The student role is the repertoire of behavior and attitudes regarded by educators as appropriate to children in school. Observation in the kindergartens of the Wilbur Wright School revealed a great variety of activities through which children are shown and then drilled in the behavior and attitudes defined as appropriate for school and thereby induced to learn the role of student. Observations of the kindergartens and interviews with the teachers both pointed to the teaching and learning of classroom routines as the main element of the student role. The teachers expended most of their efforts, for the first half of the year at least, in training the children to follow the routines which teachers created. The children were, in a very real sense, *drilled* in tasks and activities created by the teachers for their own purposes and beginning and ending quite arbitrarily (from the child's point of view) at the command of the teacher. One teacher remarked that she hated September, because during the first month "everything has to be done rigidly, and repeatedly, until they know exactly what they're supposed to do." However, "by January," she said, "they know exactly what to do [during the day] and I don't have to be after them all the time." Classroom routines were introduced gradually from the beginning of the year in all the kindergartens, and the children were drilled in them as long as was necessary to achieve regular compliance. By the end of the school year, the successful kindergarten teacher has a well-organized group of children. They follow classroom routines automatically, having learned all the command signals and the expected responses to them. They have, in our terms, learned the student role. The following observation shows one such classroom operating at optimum organization on an afternoon late in May. It is

the class of an experienced and respected kindergarten teacher.

## AN AFTERNOON IN KINDERGARTEN

At about 12:20 in the afternoon on a day in the last week of May, Edith Kerr leaves the teachers' room where she has been having lunch and walks to her classroom at the far end of the primary wing of Wright School. A group of five- and six-year-olds peers at her through the glass doors leading from the hall cloakroom to the play area outside. Entering her room, she straightens some material in the "book corner" of the room, arranges music on the piano, takes colored paper from her closet and places it on one of the shelves under the window. Her room is divided into a number of activity areas through the arrangement of furniture and play equipment. Two easels and a paint table near the door create a kind of passageway inside the room. A wedge-shaped area just inside the front door is made into a teacher's area by the placing of "her" things there: her desk, file, and piano. To the left is the book corner, marked off from the rest of the room by a puppet stage and a movable chalkboard. In it are a display rack of picture books, a record player, and a stack of children's records. To the right of the entrance are the sink and clean-up area. Four large round tables with six chairs at each for the children are placed near the walls about halfway down the length of the room, two on each side, leaving a large open area in the center for group games, block building, and toy truck driving. Windows stretch down the length of both walls, starting about three feet from the floor and extending almost to the high ceilings. Under the windows are long shelves on which are kept all the toys, games, blocks, paper, paints, and other equipment of the kindergarten. The left rear corner of the room is a play store with shelves, merchandise, and cash register; the right rear corner is a play kitchen with stove, sink, ironing board, and bassinette with baby dolls in it. This area is partly shielded from the rest of the room by a large standing display rack for posters and children's art work. A sandbox is found against the back wall between these two areas. The room is light, brightly colored and filled with things adults feel five- and six-year-olds will find interesting and pleasing.

At 12:25 Edith opens the outside door and admits the waiting children. They hang their sweaters on hooks outside the door and then go to the center of the room and arrange themselves in a semi-circle on the floor, facing the teacher's chair, which she has placed in the center of the floor. Edith follows them in and sits in her chair checking attendance while waiting for the bell to ring. When she has finished attendance, which she takes by sight, she asks the children what the date is, what day and month it is, how many children are enrolled in the class, how many are present, and how many are absent.

The bell rings at 12:30 and the teacher puts away her attendance book. She introduces a visitor, who is sitting against the wall taking notes, as someone who wants to learn about schools and children. She then goes to the back of the room and takes down a large chart labeled "Helping Hands." Bringing it to the center of the room, she tells the children it is time to change jobs. Each child is assigned some task on the chart by placing his name, lettered on a paper "hand," next to a picture signifying the task—e.g., a broom, a blackboard, a milk bottle, a flag, and a Bible. She asks the children who wants each of the jobs and rearranges their "hands" accordingly. Returning to her chair, Edith announces, "One person should tell us what happened to Mark." A girl raises her hand, and when called on says, "Mark fell and hit his head and had to go to the hospital." The teacher adds that Mark's mother had written saying he was in the hospital.

During this time the children have been interacting among themselves, in their semi-circle. Children have whispered to their neighbors, poked one another, made general comments to the group, waved to friends on the other side of the circle. None of this has been disruptive, and the teacher has ignored it for the most part. The children seem

to know just how much of each kind of interaction is permitted—they may greet in a soft voice someone who sits next to them, for example, but may not shout greetings to a friend who sits across the circle, so they confine themselves to waving and remain well within understood limits.

At 12:35 two children arrive. Edith asks them why they are late and then sends them to join the circle on the floor. The other children vie with each other to tell the newcomers what happened to Mark. When this leads to a general disorder Edith asks, "Who has serious time?" The children become quiet and a girl raises her hand. Edith nods and the child gets a Bible and hands it to Edith. She reads the Twenty-third Psalm while the children sit quietly. Edith helps the child in charge begin reciting the Lord's Prayer; the other children follow along for the first unit of sounds, and then trail off as Edith finishes for them. Everyone stands and faces the American flag hung to the right of the door. Edith leads the pledge to the flag, with the children again following the familiar sounds as far as they remember them. Edith then asks the girl in charge what song she wants and the child replies, "My Country." Edith goes to the piano and plays "America," singing as the children follow her words.

Edith returns to her chair in the center of the room and the children sit again in the semi-circle on the floor. It is 12:40 when she tells the children, "Let's have boys' sharing time first." She calls the name of the first boy sitting on the end of the circle, and he comes up to her with a toy helicopter. He turns and holds it up for the other children to see. He says, "It's a helicopter." Edith asks, "What is it used for?" and he replies, "For the army. Carry men. For the war." Other children join in, "For shooting submarines." "To bring back men from space when they are in the ocean." Edith sends the boy back to the circle and asks the next boy if he has something. He replies "No" and she passes on to the next. He says "Yes" and brings a bird's nest to her. He holds it for the class to see, and the teacher asks, "What kind of bird made the nest?" The boy replies, "My friend says a rain bird made it." Edith asks what the nest is made of and different children reply, "mud," "leaves," and "sticks." There is also a bit of moss woven into the nest, and Edith tries to describe it to the children. They, however, are more interested in seeing if anything is inside it, and Edith lets the boy carry it around the semi-circle showing the children its insides. Edith tells the children of some baby robins in a nest in her yard, and some of the children tell about baby birds they have seen. Some children are asking about a small object in the nest which they say looks like an egg, but all have seen the nest now and Edith calls on the next boy. A number of children say, "I know what Michael has, but I'm not telling." Michael brings a book to the teacher and then goes back to his place in the circle of children. Edith reads the last page of the book to the class. Some children tell of books which they have at home. Edith calls the next boy, and three children call out, "I know what David has." "He always has the same thing." "It's a bang-bang." David goes to his table and gets a box which he brings to Edith. He opens it and shows the teacher a scale-model of an old-fashioned dueling pistol. When David does not turn around to the class, Edith tells him, "Show it to the children" and he does. One child says, "Mr. Johnson [the principal] said no guns." Edith replies, "Yes, how many of you know that?" Most of the children in the circle raise their hands. She continues, "That you aren't supposed to bring guns to school?" She calls the next boy on the circle and he brings two large toy soldiers to her which the children enthusiastically identify as being from "Babes in Toyland." The next boy brings an American flag to Edith and shows it to the class. She asks him what the stars and stripes stand for and admonishes him to treat it carefully. "Why should you treat it carefully?" she asks the boy. "Because it's our flag," he replies. She congratulates him, saying, "That's right."

"Show and Tell" lasted twenty minutes and during the last ten one girl in particular announced that she knew what each child called upon had to show. Edith asked her to be quiet each time she spoke out, but she was not content, continuing to offer her comment at each "show." Four children from other classes had come into the room to bring

something from another teacher or to ask for something from Edith. Those with requests were asked to return later if the item wasn't readily available.

Edith now asks if any of the children told their mothers about their trip to the local zoo the previous day. Many children raise their hands. As Edith calls on them, they tell what they liked in the zoo. Some children cannot wait to be called on, and they call out things to the teacher, who asks them to be quiet. After a few of the animals are mentioned, one child says, "I liked the spooky house," and the others chime in to agree with him, some pantomiming fear and horror. Edith is puzzled, and asks what this was. When half the children try to tell her at once, she raises her hand for quiet, then calls on individual children. One says, "The house with nobody in it"; another, "The dark little house." Edith asks where it was in the zoo, but the children cannot describe its location in any way which she can understand. Edith makes some jokes but they involve adult abstractions which the children cannot grasp. The children have become quite noisy now, speaking out to make both relevant and irrelevant comments, and three little girls have become particularly assertive.

Edith gets up from her seat at 1:10 and goes to the book corner, where she puts a record on the player. As it begins a story about the trip to the zoo, she returns to the circle and asks the children to go sit at the tables. She divides them among the tables in such a way as to indicate that they don't have regular seats. When the children are all seated at the four tables, five or six to a table, the teacher asks, "Who wants to be the first one?" One of the noisy girls comes to the center of the room. The voice on the record is giving directions for imitating an ostrich and the girl follows them, walking around the center of the room holding her ankles with her hands. Edith replays the record, and all the children, table by table, imitate ostriches down the center of the room and back. Edith removes her shoes and shows that she can be an ostrich too. This is apparently a familiar game, for a number of children are calling out, "Can we have the crab?" Edith asks one of the children to do a crab "so we can all remember how," and then plays the part of the record with music for imitating crabs by. The children from the first table line up across the room, hands and feet on the floor and faces pointing toward the ceiling. After they have "walked" down the room and back in this posture they sit at their table and the children of the next table play "crab." The children love this; they run from their tables, dance about on the floor waiting for their turns and are generally exuberant. Children ask for the "inch worm," and the game is played again with the children squirming down the floor. As a conclusion Edith shows them a new animal imitation, the "lame dog." The children all hobble down the floor on three "legs," table by table to the accompaniment of the record.

At 1:30 Edith has the children line up in the center of the room: she says, "Table one, line up in front of me," and children ask, "What are we going to do?" Then she moves a few steps to the side and says, "Table two over here; line up next to table one," and more children ask, "What for?" She does this for table three and table four, and each time the children ask, "Why, what are we going to do?" When the children are lined up in four lines of five each, spaced so that they are not touching one another, Edith puts on a new record and leads the class in calisthenics, to the accompaniment of the record. The children just jump around every which way in their places instead of doing the exercises, and by the time the record is finished, Edith, the only one following it, seems exhausted. She is apparently adopting the President's new "Physical Fitness" program for her classroom.

At 1:35 Edith pulls her chair to the easels and calls the children to sit on the floor in front of her, table by table. When they are all seated she asks, "What are you going to do for worktime today?" Different children raise their hands and tell Edith what they are going to draw. Most are going to make pictures of animals they saw in the zoo. Edith asks if they want to make pictures to send to Mark in the hospital, and the children agree to this. Edith gives drawing paper to the children, calling them to her one by one. After getting a piece of paper, the children go to the crayon box on the

righthand shelves, select a number of colors, and go to the tables, where they begin drawing. Edith is again trying to quiet the perpetually talking girls. She keeps two of them standing by her so they won't disrupt the others. She asks them, "Why do you feel you have to talk all the time?" and then scolds them for not listening to her. Then she sends them to their tables to draw.

Most of the children are drawing at their tables, sitting or kneeling in their chairs. They are all working very industriously and, engrossed in their work, very quietly. Three girls have chosen to paint at the easels, and having donned their smocks, they are busily mixing colors and intently applying them to their pictures. If the children at the tables are primitives and neo-realists in their animal depictions, these girls at the easels are the class abstract-expressionists, with their broad-stroked, colorful paintings.

Edith asks of the children generally, "What color should I make the cover of Mark's book?" Brown and green are suggested by some children "because Mark likes them." The other children are puzzled as to just what is going on and ask, "What book?" or "What does she mean?" Edith explains what she thought was clear to them already, that they are all going to put their pictures together in a "book" to be sent to Mark. She goes to a small table in the play-kitchen corner and tells the children to bring her their pictures when they are finished and she will write their message for Mark on them.

By 1:50 most children have finished their pictures and given them to Edith. She talks with some of them as she ties the bundle of pictures together—answering questions, listening, carrying on conversations. The children are playing in various parts of the room with toys, games, and blocks which they have taken off the shelves. They also move from table to table examining each other's pictures, offering compliments and suggestions. Three girls at the table are cutting up colored paper for a collage. Another girl is walking about the room in a pair of high heels with a woman's purse over her arm. Three boys are playing in the center of the room with the large block set, with which they are building walk-ways and walking on them.

Edith is very much concerned about their safety and comes over a number of times to fuss over them. Two or three other boys are pushing trucks around the center of the room, and mild altercations occur when they drive through the block constructions. Some boys and girls are playing at the toy store, two girls are serving "tea" in the play kitchen and one is washing a doll baby. Two boys have elected to clean the room, and with large sponges they wash the movable blackboard, the puppet stage, and then begin on the tables. They run into resistance from the children who are working with construction toys on the tables and do not want to dismantle their structures. The class is like a room full of bees, each intent on pursuing some activity, occasionally bumping into one another, but just veering off in another direction without serious altercation. At 2:05 the custodian arrives pushing a cart loaded with half-pint milk containers. He places a tray of cartons on the counter next to the sink, then leaves. His coming and going is unnoticed in the room (as, incidentally, is the presence of the observer, who is completely ignored by the children for the entire afternoon).

At 2:15 Edith walks to the entrance of the room, switches off the lights, and sits at the piano and plays. The children begin spontaneously singing the song, which is "Clean up, clean up. Everybody clean up." Edith walks around the room supervising the clean-up. Some children put their toys, the blocks, puzzles, games, and so on back on their shelves under the windows. The children making a collage keep right on working. A child from another class comes in to borrow the 45-rpm adapter for the record player. At more urging from Edith the rest of the children shelve their toys and work. The children are sitting around their tables now, and Edith asks, "What record would you like to hear while you have your milk?" There is some confusion and no general consensus, so Edith drops the subject and begins to call the children, table by table, to come get their milk. "Table one," she says, and the five children come to the sink, wash their hands and dry them, pick up a carton of milk and a straw, and take it back to their table. Two talking girls wander about the

room interfering with the children getting their milk and Edith calls out to them to "settle down." As the children sit, many of them call out to Edith the name of the record they want to hear. When all the children are seated at tables with milk, Edith plays one of these records called "Bozo and the Birds" and shows the children pictures in a book which go with the record. The record recites, and the book shows the adventures of a clown, Bozo, as he walks through a woods meeting many different kinds of birds who, of course, display the characteristics of many kinds of people or, more accurately, different stereotypes. As children finish their milk, they take blankets or pads from the shelves under the windows and lie on them in the center of the room, where Edith sits on her chair showing the pictures. By 2:30 half the class is lying on the floor on their blankets, the record is still playing, and the teacher is turning the pages of the book. The child who came in previously returns the 45-rpm adapter, and one of the kindergartners tells Edith what the boy's name is and where he lives.

The record ends at 2:40. Edith says, "Children, down on your blankets." All the class is lying on blankets now. Edith refuses to answer the various questions individual children put to her because, she tells them, "It's rest time now." Instead she talks very softly about what they will do tomorrow. They are going to work with clay, she says. The children lie quietly and listen. One of the boys raises his hand and when called on tells Edith, "The animals in the zoo looked so hungry yesterday." Edith asks the children what they think about this and a number try to volunteer opinions, but Edith accepts only those offered in a "rest-time tone," that is, softly and quietly. After a brief discussion of animal feeding, Edith calls the names of the two children on milk detail and has them collect empty milk cartons from the tables and return them to the tray. She asks the two children on clean-up detail to clean up the room. Then she gets up from her chair and goes to the door to turn on the lights. At this signal, the children all get up from the floor and return their blankets and pads to the shelf. It is raining (the reason for no outside play this afternoon) and cars driven by mothers clog the school drive and line up along the street. One of the talkative little girls comes over to Edith and pointing out the window says, "Mrs. Kerr, see my mother in the new Cadillac?"

At 2:50 Edith sits at the piano and plays. The children sit on the floor in the center of the room and sing. They have a repertoire of songs about animals, including one in which each child sings a refrain alone. They know these by heart and sing along through the ringing of the 2:55 bell. When the song is finished, Edith gets up and coming to the group says, "Okay, rhyming words to get your coats today." The children raise their hands and as Edith calls on them, they tell her two rhyming words, after which they are allowed to go into the hall to get their coats and sweaters. They return to the room with these and sit at their tables. At 2:59 Edith says, "When you have your coats on, you may line up at the door." Half of the children go to the door and stand in a long line. When the three o'clock bell rings, Edith returns to the piano and plays. The children sing a song called "Goodbye," after which Edith sends them out.

## TRAINING FOR LEARNING AND FOR LIFE

The day in kindergarten at Wright School illustrates both the content of the student role as it has been learned by these children and the processes by which the teacher has brought about this learning, or "taught" them the student role. The children have learned to go through routines and to follow orders with unquestioning obedience, even when these make no sense to them. They have been disciplined to do as they are told by an authoritative person without significant protest. Edith has developed this discipline in the children by creating and enforcing a rigid social structure in the classroom through which she effectively controls the behavior of most of the children for most of the school day. The "living with others in a small society" which the school pamphlet tells parents is the

most important thing the children will learn in kindergarten can be seen now in its operational meaning, which is learning to live by the routines imposed by the school. This learning appears to be the principal content of the student role.

Children who submit to school-imposed discipline and come to identify with it, so that being a "good student" comes to be an important part of their developing identities, *become* the good students by the school's definitions. Those who submit to the routines of the school but do not come to identify with them will be adequate students who find the more important part of their identities elsewhere, such as in the play group outside school. Children who refuse to submit to the school routines are rebels, who become known as "bad students" and often "problem children" in the school, for they do not learn the academic curriculum and their behavior is often disruptive in the classroom. Today schools engage clinical psychologists in part to help teachers deal with such children.

In looking at Edith's kindergarten at Wright School, it is interesting to ask how the children learn this role of student—come to accept school-imposed routines—and what, exactly, it involves in terms of behavior and attitudes. The most prominent features of the classroom are its physical and social structures. The room is carefully furnished and arranged in ways adults feel will interest children. The play store and play kitchen in the back of the room, for example, imply that children are interested in mimicking these activities of the adult world. The only space left for the children to create something of their own is the empty center of the room, and the materials at their disposal are the blocks, whose use causes anxiety on the part of the teacher. The room, being carefully organized physically by the adults, leaves little room for the creation of physical organization on the part of the children.

The social structure created by Edith is a far more powerful and subtle force for fitting the children to the student role. This structure is established by the very rigid and tightly controlled set of rituals and routines through which the children are put during the day. There is first the rigid "locating procedure" in which the children are asked to find themselves in terms of the month, date, day of the week, and the number of the class who are present and absent. This puts them solidly in the real world as defined by adults. The day is then divided into six periods whose activities are for the most part determined by the teacher. In Edith's kindergarten the children went through Serious Time, which opens the school day, Sharing Time, Play Time (which in clear weather would be spent outside), Work Time, Clean-up Time, after which they have their milk, and Rest Time after which they go home. The teacher has programmed activities for each of these Times.

Occasionally the class is allowed limited discretion to choose between proffered activities, such as stories or records, but original ideas for activities are never solicited from them. Opportunity for free individual action is open only once in the day, during the part of Work Time left after the general class assignment has been completed (on the day reported the class assignment was drawing animal pictures for the absent Mark). Spontaneous interests or observations from the children are never developed by the teacher. It seems that her schedule just does not allow room for developing such unplanned events. During Sharing Time, for example, the child who brought a bird's nest told Edith, in reply to her question of what kind of bird made it, "My friend says it's a rain bird." Edith does not think to ask about this bird, probably because the answer is "childish," that is, not given in accepted adult categories of birds. The children then express great interest in an object in the nest, but the teacher ignores this interest, probably because the object is uninteresting to her. The soldiers from "Babes in Toyland" strike a responsive note in the children, but this is not used for a discussion of any kind. The soldiers are treated in the same way as objects which bring little interest from the children. Finally, at the end of Sharing Time the child-world of perception literally erupts in the class with the recollection of "the spooky house" at the zoo. Apparently this made more of an impression on the children than did any of the animals, but Edith is unable to make any sense of it for herself. The tightly imposed order of the class begins to

break down as the children discover a universe of discourse of their own and begin talking excitedly with one another. The teacher is effectively excluded from this child's world of perception and for a moment she fails to dominate the classroom situation. She reasserts control, however, by taking the children to the next activity she has planned for the day. It seems never to have occurred to Edith that there might be a meaningful learning experience for the children in re-creating the "spooky house" in the classroom. It seems fair to say that this would have offered an exercise in spontaneous self-expression and an opportunity for real creativity on the part of the children. Instead, they are taken through a canned animal imitation procedure, an activity which they apparently enjoy, but which is also imposed upon them rather than created by them.

While children's perceptions of the world and opportunities for genuine spontaneity and creativity are being systematically eliminated from the kindergarten, unquestioned obedience to authority and rote learning of meaningless material are being encouraged. When the children are called to line up in the center of the room they ask "Why?" and "What for?" as they are in the very process of complying. They have learned to go smoothly through a programmed day, regardless of whether parts of the program make any sense to them or not. Here the student role involves what might be called "doing what you're told and never mind why." Activities which might "make sense" to the children are effectively ruled out, and they are forced or induced to participate in activities which may be "senseless," such as calisthenics.

At the same time the children are being taught by rote meaningless sounds in the ritual oaths and songs, such as the Lord's Prayer, the Pledge to the Flag, and "America." As they go through the grades children learn more and more of the sounds of these ritual oaths, but the fact that they have often learned meaningless sounds rather than meaningful statements is shown when they are asked to write these out in the sixth grade; they write them as groups of sounds rather than as a series of words, according to the sixth grade teachers at Wright

School. Probably much learning in the elementary grades is of this character, that is, having no intrinsic meaning to the children, but rather being tasks inexplicably required of them by authoritative adults. Listening to sixth-grade children read social studies reports, for example, in which they have copied material from encyclopedias about a particular country, an observer often gets the feeling that he is watching an activity which has no intrinsic meaning for the child. The child who reads, "Switzerland grows wheat and cows and grass and makes a lot of cheese" knows the dictionary meaning of each of these words but may very well have no conception at all of this "thing" called Switzerland. He is simply carrying out a task assigned by the teacher *because* it is assigned, and this may be its only "meaning" for him.

Another type of learning which takes place in kindergarten is seen in children who take advantage of the "holes" in the adult social structure to create activities of their own, during Work Time or out-of-doors during Play Time. Here the children are learning to carve out a small world of their own within the world created by adults. They very quickly learn that if they keep within permissible limits of noise and action they can play much as they please. Small groups of children formed during the year in Edith's kindergarten who played together at these times, developing semi-independent little groups in which they created their own worlds in the interstices of the adult-imposed physical and social world. These groups remind the sociological observer very much of the so-called "informal groups" which adults develop in factories and offices of large bureaucracies.[5] Here, too, within authoritatively imposed social organizations people find "holes" to create little subworlds which support informal, friendly, unofficial behavior. Forming and participating in such groups seems to be as much part of the student role as it is of the role of bureaucrat.

The kindergarten has been conceived of here as the year in which children are prepared for their schooling by learning the role of student. In the classrooms of the rest of the school grades, the children will be asked to submit to systems and routines imposed by the teachers and the curriculum. The days will be much like those of kindergarten, except that academic subjects will be substituted for the activities of the kindergarten. Once out of the school system, young adults will more than likely find themselves working in large-scale bureaucratic organizations, perhaps on the assembly line in the factory, perhaps in the paper routines of the white collar occupations, where they will be required to submit to rigid routines imposed by "the company" which may make little sense to them. Those who can operate well in this situation will be successful bureaucratic functionaries. Kindergarten, therefore, can be seen as preparing children not only for participation in the bureaucratic organization of large modern school systems, but also for the large-scale occupational bureaucracies of modern society.

## NOTES

1. Emile Durkheim, *Sociology and Education* (New York: The Free Press, 1956), pp. 71–72.

2. *Ibid.*, p. 123.

3. Wilbur Brookover, *The Sociology of Education* (New York: American Book Company, 1957), p. 4.

4. *Ibid.*, p. 6.

5. See, for example, Peter M. Blau, *Bureaucracy in Modern Society* (New York: Random House, 1956), Chapter 3.

# Family

The following is a brief excerpt from an article entitled "Out Family Values" by Prof. James Miller from the University of Western Ontario:

*The family I live in as a father is also the family I live out in as a gay man. I call it an "out family" for three reasons: its openness to homosexual membership; its opposition to heterosexist conformity (the prejudicial assumption of heterosexuality as normal and proper); and its overtness within the contemporary lesbian and gay movement.*

*Mine is a family that opens out, steps out, and stands out. It opens out to people traditionally excluded from the charmed circle of Home; it steps out beyond the polite and policed borders of the Normal; and it stands out as a clear new possibility on the horizon of what used to be called—in the heady days following Pierre Trudeau's decriminalization of homosexuality in Canada (1969)—the Just Society. Against the drone of current conservative rhetoric urging decent citizens to protect "family values" from homefront activists like me, I shall try to spell out here the distinctive qualities that my family has discovered in itself to meet the challenges of living in a pervasively homophobic culture that would rather we closed down, stepped in, and stood back . . .*

*When I first came out to my children in January of 1990, they immediately wanted to know whether they were gay, too. Not necessarily, I told them, trying to allay their time-honoured fears without compromising my newfound sense of pride. Yet was I not outing them by outing myself? For better or worse, I realized my uncloseted gayness was bound to be socially projected onto all who lived with me. Whatever my children's sexual orientations might be, their close association with me would effectively gay them in the eyes of straight society and queer their cultural outlook. So look out, I warned them, the World likes to see things straight.*

*They have taken my warning to heart by setting the record straight about me and them ("Our Dad's gay, but we're probably not") for any curious soul who comes into our domestic space . . . An out family must learn to speak about itself in unaccustomed ways, develop its own outlandish frontier lingo, for its members are always proudly, if at times also painfully, aware of their strategic positioning outside the normative vision of heterosexual monogamy. . . . My out family bravely resists the exclusionary pressures of heterosexist institutions and their defenders simply by existing as such,*

© LWA-Dann Tardif/Corbis

*by brazenly occupying hallowed spaces like "family rooms" and "family cottages" and even "family restaurants" where we're not supposed to exist. (2003:104)*

Fifty years ago, the majority of Canadian families consisted of two adults in a permanent union that produced three to five children. Other kinds of families were the exception. Today, when we think of families, we think of diversity and change, and exceptions are the rule. The experiences of the family in the above narrative certainly are not unique. Other variations on what has been described as a "traditional" family are also common. Separation and divorce, remarriage, and blended or reconstituted families are a reality for many Canadians. Regardless of the form it takes, family life continues to be a source of great personal satisfaction and happiness.

In this chapter, we will examine the diversity and complexity of families and intimate relationships. Pressing social issues, such as same-sex marriage, divorce, child care, and new reproductive technologies, will be used as examples of how families and intimate relationships continue to change. Before reading on, test your knowledge about the changing family by taking the quiz in Box 13.1 on page 371.

(*Source:* From Lynn, Marion. *Voices: Essays on Canadian Families*, 2nd edition. Copyright © 2003 Nelson Education Ltd. Reproduced by permission. www.cengage.com/permissions.)

## Critical Thinking Questions

1. It has been suggested that variations of the "traditional" family are common today. Identify some of these alternative family forms.

2. James Miller "came out" to his children in 1990. Do you think childen of gay parents would have a similar experience today? What changes have occurred in the past 20 years that might make this experience easier for both parent and child?

3. Which, if any, heterosexist institutions continue to place exclusionary pressures on families with gay parents today?

---

| CHAPTER FOCUS QUESTION | How is social change affecting the Canadian family? |

## Learning Objectives
### AFTER READING THIS CHAPTER, YOU SHOULD BE ABLE TO

**LO-1** Explain why it is difficult to define family.

**LO-2** Understand the key assumptions of functionalist, conflict, feminist, symbolic interactionist, and postmodernist perspectives on families.

**LO-3** Understand the various options available to Canadian families in establishing families.

**LO-4** Describe the challenges facing families today.

**LO-5** Identify the primary problems facing Canadian families today.

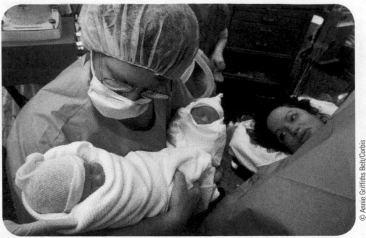

Despite the idealized image of "the family," North American families have undergone many changes in the past century, as exemplified by the increase in the number of families using assisted reproductive technologies to start a family.

## LO-1    DEFINING FAMILY

What is a family? Although we all have a family of some form or another and we all understand the concept of family, it is not an easy word to define. More than ever, this term means different things to different people. As the nature of family life and work has changed in high-, middle-, and low-income nations, the issue of what constitutes a family has been widely debated. For example, Hutterite families in Canada live in communal situations in which children from about the age of three spend most of their days in school. The children also eat their meals in a communal dining hall, away from their parents. In this case, the community is the family, as opposed to a traditional nuclear family.

Some Aboriginal families in Canada also tend to have a much broader idea of family membership. Children are often cared for by relatives in the extended family. A social worker may define a family as consisting of parents and children only. Some Aboriginal parents may be perceived as neglecting their children when the parents feel they are safe and well cared for by "their family"—that is, by uncles, grandparents, siblings, or other relatives (Vanier Institute of the Family, 2009a).

Similarly, gay men and lesbians often form unique families. Many gay men and lesbians have **families we choose**—social arrangements that include intimate relationships between couples and close familial relationships with other couples, as well as with other adults and children (Ambert, 2005).

In a society as diverse as Canada, talking about "a family" as though a single type of family exists or ever did exist is inaccurate. In reality, different groups will define their family lives in unique ways, depending on a number of factors, such as their socioeconomic background, immigrant status, religious beliefs, or cultural practices and traditions (Baker, 2009).

For many years, a standard sociological definition of family has been a group of people who are related to one another by bonds of blood, marriage, or adoption and who live together,

**families we choose**
Social arrangements that include intimate relationships between couples and close familial relationships with other couples, as well as with other adults and children.

form an economic unit, and bear and raise children (Benokraitis, 2005). Many people believe that this definition should not be expanded—that social approval should not be extended to other relationships simply because the persons in those relationships wish to be considered a family. Others, however, challenge this definition because it simply does not match the reality of family life in contemporary society. Today's families include many types of living arrangements and relationships, including single-parent households, unmarried couples, lesbian and gay couples, and multiple generations (such as grandparents, parents, and children) living in the same household. To accurately reflect these changes in family life, we need an encompassing definition of what constitutes a family. Accordingly, we will define a **family** as a relationship in which people live together with commitment, form an economic unit and care for any young, and consider their identity to be significantly attached to the group. Sexual expression and parent–children relationships are a part of most, but not all, family relationships (based on Benokraitis, 2005; Lamanna and Riedmann, 2011).

In our study of families, we will use our sociological imaginations to see how our personal experiences are related to the larger happenings in our society. At the microlevel, each of us has our own "biography," based on our experience within a family; at the macrolevel, our families are embedded in a specific social context that has a major impact on them (Aulette, 1994). We will examine the institution of the family at both of these levels, beginning with family structure and characteristics.

> **family** A relationship in which people live together with commitment, form an economic unit and care for any young, and consider their identity to be significantly attached to the group.

## Family Structure and Characteristics

In preindustrial societies, the primary form of social organization is through kinship ties. **Kinship** refers to a social network of people based on common ancestry, marriage, or adoption. Through kinship networks, people cooperate so that they can acquire the basic necessities of life, including food and shelter. Kinship systems can also serve as a means by which property is transferred, goods are produced and distributed, and power is allocated.

> **kinship** A social network of people based on common ancestry, marriage, or adoption.

In industrialized societies, other social institutions fulfill some of the functions previously taken care of by the kinship network. For example, political systems provide structures of social control and authority, and economic systems are responsible for the production and distribution of goods and services. Consequently, families in industrialized societies serve fewer and more specialized purposes than do families in preindustrial societies. Contemporary families are primarily responsible for regulating sexual activity, socializing children, and providing affection and companionship for family members.

| BOX 13.1 | SOCIOLOGY AND EVERYDAY LIFE |
| --- | --- |

### How Much Do You Know About the Changing Family in Canada?

| True | False | |
| --- | --- | --- |
| T | F | 1. Today, people in Canada are more inclined to get married than at any time in history. |
| T | F | 2. Men are as likely as women to be single parents. |
| T | F | 3. One out of every two marriages ends in divorce. |
| T | F | 4. Age of first marriage has increased significantly in the past 40 years for both men and women. |
| T | F | 5. In recent years, the number of extended families where members live together in the same home has decreased. |

For answers to the quiz about the changing family in Canada, go to **www.nelson.com/ sociologyinourtimes6e.**

**FAMILIES OF ORIENTATION AND PROCREATION**   During our lifetime, many of us will be members of two different types of families—a family of orientation and a family of procreation. The **family of orientation** is the family into which a person is born and in which early socialization usually takes place. Although most people are related to members of their family of orientation by blood ties, those who are adopted have a legal tie that is patterned after a blood relationship. The **family of procreation** is the family that a person forms by having or adopting children (Benokraitis, 2005). Both legal and blood ties are found in most families of procreation. The relationship between a husband and wife is based on legal ties; however, the relationship between a parent and child may be based on either blood ties or legal ties, depending on whether the child has been adopted or is by marriage (Aulette, 1994).

Although many young people leave their families of orientation as they reach adulthood, finish school, and/or get married, recent studies have found that many people maintain family ties across generations, particularly as older persons have remained actively involved in relationships with their adult children.

**EXTENDED AND NUCLEAR FAMILIES**   Sociologists distinguish between extended and nuclear families based on the number of generations that live within a household. An **extended family** is a family unit composed of relatives in addition to parents and children who live in the same household. These families often include grandparents, uncles, aunts, or other relatives who live in close proximity to the parents and children, making it possible for family members to share resources (see Box 13.2). In horticultural and agricultural societies, extended families are extremely important; having a large number of family members participate in food production may be essential for survival. Today, extended families are becoming more common across North America and Britain. This trend is related to an increase in the number of families caring for aging seniors in their homes, an increase in the number of grandparents with children and grandchildren living with them for economic reasons, and an increase in immigration from countries where extended family living is the norm (Milan, Keown, and Robles Urquijo, 2011).

**family of orientation**
The family into which a person is born and in which early socialization usually takes place.

**family of procreation**
The family that a person forms by having or adopting children.

**extended family** A family unit composed of relatives in addition to parents and children who live in the same household.

BOX 13.2   **SOCIOLOGY IN GLOBAL PERSPECTIVE**

## Buffering Financial Hardship: Extended Families in the Global Economy

- Day after day, Nang Pajik sews collars on workshirts at a factory in Vientiane, Laos, so that she can send money home to her six brothers and sisters and her extended family in her home village (Bradsher, 2006).
- Odilon Hernandez bought a television and several appliances from La Curacao, a Los Angeles store, for his parents in Puebla, Mexico. La Curacao delivers items directly to the extended families of U.S. immigrant workers from the store's warehouse in Mexico, which was set up for that purpose (Associated Press, 2006).
- A United Kingdom building society estimates that the number of homes containing three generations of a family will triple in England during the next 20 years. The causes are rising levels of debt and the high cost of property. According to a Skipton Building Society

spokesperson, "These issues are likely to get worse and so combining incomes and sharing mortgage repayments may well be the only alternative for some families." (BBC News, 2004)

Although many people think of the extended family as primarily a thing of the past, current evidence suggests that the extended family is far from becoming obsolete. What unique benefits do extended families offer? The answer is quite simple: Extended families offer a financial safety net that is unavailable in the typical nuclear family. For many families in the United Kingdom, purchasing a house is a possibility only if multiple generations combine their incomes and share their living expenses and mortgage payments. However, as the cost of child care rises in the United Kingdom, extended family residential patterns are important not only for house purchases but also for child care because expenditures are greatly reduced when grandparents serve as live-in childminders (BBC News, 2004).

In low-income and immigrant families, the extended family is particularly important: Pooling resources often means economic survival for the family. In the poorest of nations, such as Laos, some family members remain in the home village to tend the family's rice plot while other members migrate to the city to earn money that can be shared with relatives at home.

To people in high-income nations, the thought of earning wages of $50 a month for factory work is unheard of. For individuals with few educational opportunities or little experience using machines, however, moving from a village to the city to work in a factory constitutes a major economic improvement (even if it is only temporary) in the standard of living for their entire family.

The stories above could be repeated in many nations. In Africa, for example, extended family systems help buffer inequality through the exchanges of resources and fostering of children across nuclear family units. At this time, it does not appear that globalization or greater exposure to other cultural norms of family life will change this pattern significantly. The African HIV/AIDS epidemic has left many children dependent on relatives for their survival. Like children, many older adults benefit from extended family patterns. In a study of elderly Asians living in Britain, researchers found that the grandmothers in their study had better mental health—were "better adjusted"—when they resided in an extended family rather than in a nuclear family (Guglani, Coleman, and Sonuga-Barke, 2000).

What conclusions might we draw from this brief look at extended families in the global economy? Apparently, extended families meet specific needs that are not easily met by nuclear families, and current evidence suggests that extended family patterns are not likely to disappear in the near future. Do you or does someone you know live in an extended family? What are the strengths and limitations of this arrangement?

© Jack Dempsey/A² Images

In the global economy, many immigrant workers regularly send portions of their paycheques to relatives living in their country of origin. What other important functions do extended family patterns serve in the 21st century?

A **nuclear family** is a family composed of one or two parents and their dependent children, all of whom live apart from other relatives. A traditional definition specifies that a nuclear family is made up of a "couple" and their dependent children; however, this definition became outdated as a significant shift occurred in the family structure. For the first time ever, there are more families without children than families with children. As shown in the Census Profile, in 2006 about 41 percent of all households were composed of couples with children under the age of 18, while 43 percent of couples did not have children living at home. This latter group consisted of childless couples and empty nesters, or couples whose children no longer lived at home (Statistics Canada, 2007c).

Nuclear families are smaller than they were 20 years ago; whereas the average family size in 1971 was 3.7 persons, in 2006 it was 2.5 persons. This decrease has been largely attributed to decisions to postpone or forgo childbearing and to increases in separation and divorce rates (Milan, Keown, and Robles Urquijo, 2011).

> **nuclear family** A family made up of one or two parents and their dependent children, all of whom live apart from other relatives.

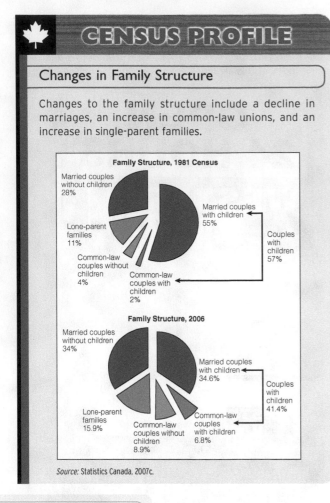

### Changes in Family Structure

Changes to the family structure include a decline in marriages, an increase in common-law unions, and an increase in single-parent families.

**Family Structure, 1981 Census**

- Married couples without children 28%
- Married couples with children 55%
- Lone-parent families 11%
- Common-law couples without children 4%
- Common-law couples with children 2%
- Couples with children 57%

**Family Structure, 2006**

- Married couples without children 34%
- Married couples with children 34.6%
- Lone-parent families 15.9%
- Common-law couples without children 8.9%
- Common-law couples with children 6.8%
- Couples with children 41.4%

*Source:* Statistics Canada, 2007c.

**marriage** A legally recognized and/or socially approved arrangement between two or more individuals that carries certain rights and obligations and usually involves sexual activity.

**monogamy** marriage to one person at a time.

**polygamy** The practice of having more than one spouse at a time.

**polygyny** The concurrent marriage of one man with two or more women.

**polyandry** The concurrent marriage of one woman with two or more men.

## Marriage Patterns

Across cultures, families are characterized by different forms of marriage. **Marriage** is a legally recognized and/or socially approved arrangement between two or more individuals that carries certain rights and obligations and usually involves sexual activity. In Canada, the only legally sanctioned form of marriage is **monogamy**—marriage to one person at a time. For some people, marriage is a lifelong commitment that ends only with the death of a partner.

Members of some religious groups believe that marriage is "forever"; if one spouse dies, the surviving spouse is precluded from marrying anyone else. For others, marriage is a commitment of indefinite duration. Through a pattern of marriage, divorce, and remarriage, some people practise *serial monogamy*—a succession of marriages in which a person has several spouses over a lifetime but is legally married to only one person at a time.

**Polygamy** refers to the concurrent marriage of a person of one sex with two or more members of the opposite sex. The most prevalent form of polygamy is **polygyny**—the concurrent marriage of one man with two or more women. Polygyny has been practised in a number of Islamic societies, including in some regions of contemporary Africa and southern Russia. The reality television show *Sister Wives*, which documents the life of polygamist family which includes a husband with four wives and 17 children certainly challenges traditional notions of family. How many wives and children might a polygynist have at one time? Some analysts believe that the practice of polygamy contributes to the likelihood that families will live in poverty (Chipungu, 1999).

The second type of polygamy is **polyandry**—the concurrent marriage of one woman with two or more men. Polyandry is rare; when it does occur, it is typically found in societies where men greatly outnumber women because of high rates of female infanticide or where marriages are arranged between two brothers and one woman (fraternal polyandry). According to recent research, polyandry is never the only form of marriage in a society: Whenever polyandry occurs, polygyny co-occurs (Trevithick, 1997). Although Tibetans are the most frequently studied population where polyandry exists, anthropologists have also identified the Sherpas, Paharis, Sinhalese, and various African groups as sometimes practising polyandry (Trevithick, 1997). An anthropological study of Nyinba, an ethnically Tibetan population living in northwestern Nepal, found that fraternal polyandry (two brothers sharing the same wife) is the normative form of marriage and that the practice continues to be highly valued culturally (Levine and Silk, 1997).

## Patterns of Descent and Inheritance

Even though a variety of marital patterns exist across cultures, virtually all forms of marriage establish a system of descent so that kinship can be determined and inheritance rights established. In preindustrial societies, kinship is usually traced through one parent (unilineally). The most common pattern of unilineal descent is **patrilineal descent**—a system of tracing descent through the father's side of the family. Patrilineal systems are set up in such a manner that a legitimate son inherits his father's property and sometimes his position upon the father's death. In nations such as India, where boys are seen as permanent patrilineal family members and girls are seen only as temporary family members, girls tend to be considered more expendable than boys (O'Connell, 1994).

Even with the less common pattern of **matrilineal descent**—a system of tracing descent through the mother's side of the family—women may not control property. However, inheritance of property and position is usually traced from the maternal uncle (mother's brother) to his nephew (mother's son). In some cases, mothers may pass on their property to daughters.

By contrast, in industrial societies, kinship is usually traced through both parents (bilineally). The most common form is **bilateral descent**—a system of tracing descent through both the mother's and father's sides of the family. This pattern is used in Canada for the purpose of determining kinship and inheritance rights; however, children typically take the father's last name.

## Power and Authority in Families

Descent and inheritance rights are intricately linked with patterns of power and authority in families. A **patriarchal family** is a family structure in which authority is held by the eldest male (usually the father). The male authority figure acts as head of the household and holds power and authority over the women and children as well as over other males. A **matriarchal family** is a family structure in which authority is held by the eldest female (usually the mother). In this case, the female authority figure acts as head of the household. Although there has been a great deal of discussion about matriarchal societies, scholars have found no historical evidence to indicate that true matriarchies ever existed.

The most prevalent pattern of power and authority in families is patriarchy—a hierarchical system of social organization in which cultural, political, and economic structures are controlled by men. Across cultures, men are the primary (and often sole) decision makers regarding domestic, economic, and social concerns facing the family. The existence of patriarchy may give men a sense of power over their own lives, but it also can create an atmosphere in which some men feel greater freedom to abuse women and children (O'Connell, 1994). According to some feminist scholars and journalists, hostility and violence perpetrated by men against women and children are the results of patriarchal attitudes, economic hardship, rigid gender roles, and societal acceptance of aggression (Johnson and Dawson, 2011). Moreover, some economists believe that the patriarchal family structure (along with prevailing market conditions and public policy) limits people's choices in employment. According to this view, the patriarchal family structure has remained largely unchanged in this country, even as familial responsibilities in the paid labour market have undergone dramatic transformation. In the post-industrial age, for example, gender-specific roles may have been reduced; however, women's choices remain limited by the patriarchal tradition in which women do most of the unpaid labour, particularly in the family. Despite dramatic increases in the number of women in the paid workforce, there has been little movement toward gender equity, which would equalize women's opportunities (Lindsay, 2008).

An **egalitarian family** is a family structure in which both partners share power and authority equally. In egalitarian families, issues of power and authority may be frequently negotiated as the roles and responsibilities within the relationship change over time. Recently, a trend toward more egalitarian relationships has been evident in a number of countries as women have sought changes in their legal status and greater educational and employment opportunities. Some degree of economic independence makes it possible for women to delay marriage or to terminate a problematic marriage (Ward, 2005). However, one study of the effects of egalitarian values on the allocation and performance of domestic tasks in the family found that changes were relatively slow in coming. According to the study, fathers were more likely to share domestic tasks in nonconventional families where members held more egalitarian values. Similarly, children's gender-role stereotyping was more closely linked to their parents' egalitarian values and nonconventional lifestyles than to the domestic tasks they were assigned (Marshall, 2011).

**patrilineal descent**
A system of tracing descent through the father's side of the family.

**matrilineal descent** A system of tracing descent through the mother's side of the family.

**bilateral descent**
A system of tracing descent through both the mother's and father's sides of the family.

**patriarchal family**
A family structure in which authority is held by the eldest male (usually the father).

**matriarchal family**
A family structure in which authority is held by the eldest female (usually the mother).

**egalitarian family**
A family structure in which both partners share power and authority equally.

While the relationship between husband and wife is based on legal ties, relationships between parents and children may be established either by blood ties or by legal ties.

## LO-2   THEORETICAL PERSPECTIVES ON FAMILIES

**sociology of family**
The subdiscipline of sociology that attempts to describe and explain patterns of family life and variations in family structure.

The **sociology of family** is the subdiscipline of sociology that attempts to describe and explain patterns of family life and variations in family structure. Functionalist perspectives emphasize the functions that families perform at the macrolevel of society, while conflict and feminist perspectives focus on families as a primary source of social inequality. By contrast, symbolic interactionists examine microlevel interactions that are integral to the roles of different family members. Finally, postmodern theorists emphasize the fact that families today are diverse and variable.

### Functionalist Perspectives

Functionalists emphasize the importance of the family in maintaining the stability of society and the well-being of individuals. According to Émile Durkheim, marriage is a microcosmic replica of the larger society; both marriage and society involve a mental and moral fusion of physically distinct individuals (Lehmann, 1994). Durkheim also believed that a division of labour contributed to greater efficiency in all areas of life—including marriages and families—even though he acknowledged that this division imposed significant limitations on some people.

Talcott Parsons was a key figure in developing a functionalist model of the family. According to Parsons (1955), the husband/father fulfills the *instrumental role* (meeting the family's economic needs, making important decisions, and providing leadership), while the wife/mother fulfills the *expressive role* (running the household, caring for children, and meeting the emotional needs of family members).

Contemporary functionalist perspectives on families derive their foundation from Durkheim and Parsons. Division of labour makes it possible for families to fulfill a number of functions that no other institution can perform as effectively. In advanced industrial societies, families serve four key functions:

1. *Sexual regulation.* Families are expected to regulate the sexual activity of their members and thus control reproduction so that it occurs within specific boundaries. At the macrolevel, incest taboos prohibit sexual contact or marriage between certain relatives. For example, virtually all societies prohibit sexual relations between parents and their children and between brothers and sisters.

2. *Socialization.* Parents and other relatives are responsible for teaching children the necessary knowledge and skills to survive. The smallness and intimacy of families makes them best suited for providing children with the initial learning experiences they need.

3. *Economic and psychological support.* Families are responsible for providing economic and psychological support for members. In preindustrial societies, families are economic production units; in industrial societies, the economic security of families is tied to the workplace and to macrolevel economic systems. In recent years, psychological support and emotional security have been increasingly important functions of the family.

4. *Provision of social status.* Families confer social status and reputation on their members. These statuses include the ascribed statuses with which individuals are born, such as race and ethnicity, nationality, social class, and sometimes religious affiliation. One of the most significant and compelling forms of social placement is the family's class position and the opportunities (or lack thereof) resulting from that position. Examples of class-related opportunities include access to quality health care, higher education, and a safe place to live.

## Conflict Perspectives

Both conflict and feminist analysts view functionalist perspectives on the role of the family in society as idealized and inadequate. Rather than operating harmoniously and for the benefit of all members, families are sources of social inequality and conflict over values, goals, and access to resources and power (Benokraitis, 2005).

In his classic work *The Origin of the Family, Private Property and the State* (1972/1884), Friedrich Engels argued that the family in a capitalist society is an exploitive social institution that oppresses women. According to some conflict theorists, families in capitalist economies are similar to workers in a factory. Women are dominated by men in the home in the same manner that workers are dominated by capitalists and managers in factories (Engels, 1970/1884). Although childbearing and care for family members in the home contribute to capitalism, these activities also reinforce the subordination of women through unpaid (and often devalued) labour. Engels predicted that the oppression of women would end when women moved out of the private sphere of the home and into the paid workforce. As discussed in Chapter 11, women's oppression has not disappeared as a result of the dramatic increases in the number of women in the paid workforce.

Other conflict analysts are concerned with the effect that class conflict has on the family. The exploitation of the lower classes by the upper classes contributes to family problems, such as high rates of divorce and overall family instability.

## Feminist Perspectives

The contributions of feminist theorists have resulted in radical changes in the sociological study of families. Feminist theorists have been primarily responsible for redefining the concept of the family by focusing on the diversity of family arrangements. Some feminist scholars reject the "monolithic model of the family" (Eichler, 1981:368), which idealizes one family form—the family with a male breadwinner and stay-at-home wife and children—as the normal household arrangement. Feminist theorists argue that limiting our concept of family to this traditional

Functionalist theorists believe that families serve a variety of important functions that no other social institution can adequately fulfill. In contrast, conflict and feminist analysts believe that the functionalist perspective is idealistic and inadequate for explaining problems in contemporary families.

form means ignoring or undervaluing diverse family forms, such as single-parent families, childless families, gay or lesbian families, and stepfamilies. Roles within the family are viewed by feminist theorists as primarily socially constructed rather than biologically determined (Smith, 1974). Feminist scholars have challenged a number of common assumptions about family life and the roles women fulfill within families. For example, they question whether all "real" women want to be mothers and whether the inequality between traditional husbands and wives is "natural" (Mandell and Duffy, 2005).

Feminist perspectives on inequality focus on patriarchy. From this viewpoint, men's domination over women existed long before private ownership of property and capitalism (Mann, 1994). Women's subordination is rooted in patriarchy and men's control over women's labour power (Hartmann, 1981). The division of labour by gender, both within the larger society and within households, is a fundamental focus of feminist analysis (Luxton and Corman, 2001, cited in Ambert, 2006a:21). Although the division of labour may appear to be an equal pooling of contributions within the family unit, feminist scholars view women as giving much but receiving less in return. According to sociologist Patricia Mann, "Male power in our society is expressed in economic terms even if it does not originate in property relations; women's activities in the home have been undervalued at the same time as their labor has been controlled by men" (1994:42).

Many women resist male domination. Women can control their reproductive capabilities through contraception and other means, and they can take control of their labour power from their husbands by working for wages outside the home (Mann, 1994). However, men may be reluctant to relinquish their status as family breadwinner. Why? Although only 15 percent of families in Canada are supported solely by a male breadwinner, many men continue to construct their ideal of masculinity around this cultural value.

Feminist perspectives on families also draw attention to the problems of dominance and subordination inherent in relationships. Specifically, feminist theorists have acknowledged what has been described as the "dark side of the family," focusing research efforts on issues such as child abuse, wife abuse, and violence against the elderly (Ambert, 2001; Johnson and Dawson, 2011; Smith, 1985). The idea that family relations, including wife abuse and child abuse, are private, personal matters has been challenged by feminists and successfully brought into the public domain of social policy and legislative changes. As a result, feminist analysis of families is viewed not only as a theoretical perspective, but also as a broad movement for social change (Johnson and Dawson, 2011).

## Symbolic Interactionist Perspectives

Early symbolic interactionists, such as Charles Horton Cooley and George Herbert Mead, provided key insights on the roles we play as family members and how we modify or adapt our roles to the expectations of others—especially significant others, such as parents, grandparents, siblings, and other relatives. How does the family influence the individual's self-concept and identity? Contemporary symbolic interactionist perspectives examine the roles of husbands, wives, and children as they act out their own parts and react to the actions of others. From such a perspective, what people think, as well as what they say and do, is very important in understanding family dynamics.

According to sociologists Peter Berger and Hansfried Kellner (1964), interaction between marital partners contributes to a shared reality. Although newlyweds bring separate identities to a marriage, over time they construct a shared reality as a couple. In the process, the partners redefine their past identities to be consistent with new realities. Development of a shared reality is a continuous process, taking place not only in the family but also in any group in which the couple participates together. Divorce is the reverse of this process; couples may start with a shared reality and, in the process of uncoupling, gradually develop separate realities (Vaughan, 1985).

Symbolic interactionists explain family relationships in terms of the subjective meanings and everyday interpretations people give to their lives. Sociologist Jessie Bernard (1982/1973) pointed out that women and men experience marriage differently and that a marriage contains two marriages: "his marriage" and "her marriage." While a husband may see his marriage positively, his wife may feel less positive about her marriage, and vice versa. Researchers have found that husbands and wives may give very different accounts of the same event and their two "realities" frequently do not coincide (Safilios-Rothschild, 1969).

Other symbolic interactionists have examined ways in which individuals communicate with one another and interpret these interactions. According to Lenore Walker (1979), females are socialized to be passive and males are socialized to be aggressive long before they take on the adult roles of battered and batterer. However, even women who have not been socialized by their parents to be helpless and passive may be socialized into this behaviour by abusive husbands. Three factors contribute to the acceptance of the roles of batterer and battered: (1) low self-esteem on the part of both people involved, (2) a limited range of behaviours (he only knows how to be jealous and possessive; she only knows how to be dependent and eager to make everyone happy), and (3) a belief by both in stereotypic gender roles (she should be feminine and pampered; he should be aggressive and dominant). Other analysts suggest that this pattern is changing as more women are gaining paid employment and becoming less dependent on their husbands or male companions for economic support.

## Postmodern Perspectives

Although postmodern theorists disparage the idea that a universal theory can be developed to explain social life, a postmodern perspective might provide insights on questions such as this: How is family life different in the Information Age? Social scientist David Elkind (1995) describes the postmodern family as *permeable*—capable of being diffused or invaded in such a manner that an entity's original purpose is modified or changed. According to Elkind, if the nuclear family is a reflection of the age of modernity, the permeable family reflects the postmodern assumptions of difference, particularity, and irregularity.

Difference is evident in the fact that the nuclear family is now only one of many family forms. Similarly, under modernity, the idea of romantic love has given way to the idea of consensual love: Individuals agree to have sexual relations with others they have no intention of marrying or, if they marry, do not necessarily see the marriage as having permanence. Maternal love has also been transformed into shared parenting, which includes not only mothers and fathers but also caregivers, who may be either relatives or nonrelatives (Elkind, 1995).

Urbanity is another characteristic of the postmodern family. The boundaries between the public sphere (the workplace) and the private sphere (the home) are becoming more open and flexible. As a result, family life may be negatively affected by the decreasing distinction between what is work time and what is family time. As more people are becoming connected "24/7" (24 hours a day, seven days a week), the boss who before would not have called at 11:30 p.m. or when an employee was on vacation may send an email or text asking for an immediate response to some question that has arisen while the person is away with family members.

Social theorist Jean Baudrillard's idea that the simulation of reality may come to be viewed as "reality" by some people can be applied to family interactions in the Information Age. Does the ability to contact someone anywhere and any time of the day or night provide greater happiness and stability in families? Or is "reach out and touch someone" merely an ideology promulgated by the consumer society? Journalists have written about the experience of watching a family gathering at an amusement park, restaurant, mall, or other location, only to see family members pick up their cellphones to receive or make calls to individuals not present, rather than spending "face time" with those family members who are present.

The Concept Snapshot on the next page summarizes these sociological perspectives on the family. Taken together, these perspectives on the social institution of families help us understand both the good and bad sides of familial relationships. Now we shift our focus to love, marriage, intimate relationships, and family issues in Canada.

## CONCEPT SNAPSHOT

**FUNCTIONALIST PERSPECTIVES**

Key thinker: Talcott Parsons

In modern societies, families serve the functions of sexual regulation, socialization, economic and psychological support, and provision of social status.

**CONFLICT PERSPECTIVES**

Key thinker: Friedrich Engels

Families both mirror and help perpetuate social inequalities based on class and gender.

**FEMINIST PERSPECTIVES**

Key thinkers: Nancy Mandell, Ann Duffy

Women's subordination is rooted in patriarchy and men's control over women's labour power.

**SYMBOLIC INTERACTIONIST PERSPECTIVES**

Key thinker: Jessie Bernard

Family dynamics, including communication patterns and the subjective meanings that people assign to events, mean that interactions within families create a shared reality.

**POSTMODERN PERSPECTIVES**

Key thinker: David Elkind

In postmodern societies, families are diverse and fragmented. Boundaries between the workplace and home are also blurred.

## LO-3   ESTABLISHING FAMILIES

### Cohabitation

**cohabitation** The sharing of a household by a couple who live together without being legally married.

**Cohabitation** refers to the sharing of a household by a couple who live together without being legally married. Attitudes about cohabitation have changed in the last few decades, something that is reflected in Figure 13.1. In Canada, cohabitation (most commonly referred to as a common-law union) has become an increasingly popular alternative to marriage. The growth of common-law families is the strongest of all family structures. Since the early 1980s, the number of persons living common-law has doubled, going from 700,000 in 1981 to 1.4 million in 2006 (Statistics Canada, 2007c). Almost half of these common-law-couple families included children, whether born to the current union or brought to the family from previous unions. The proportion of people in common-law unions varies considerably by province. In Quebec, one in three couples lives common-law, making it the province with the highest rate of common-law families.

Those most likely to cohabit are young adults between the ages of 25 and 29. Based on the Statistics Canada census data, approximately one in four Canadians in this age group lives in a common-law union. However, the largest growth in common-law unions has occurred among couples in their early 60s, reflecting a growing acceptance among older generations of what was previously a living arrangement of young adults. While "living together" is often a prelude to marriage for young adults, common-law unions are also becoming a popular alternative both to marriage and to remarriage following divorce or separation (Milan, Keown, and Robles Urquijo, 2011).

Today, some people view cohabitation as a form of "trial marriage," but for others, cohabitation is not a first step toward marriage. Some people who have cohabited do eventually marry the person with whom they have been living, whereas others do not. And studies over the past decade

**FIGURE 13.1    PROPORTION OF COMMON-LAW FAMILIES GROWS WHILE IT DECLINES FOR MARRIED FAMILIES, CANADA**

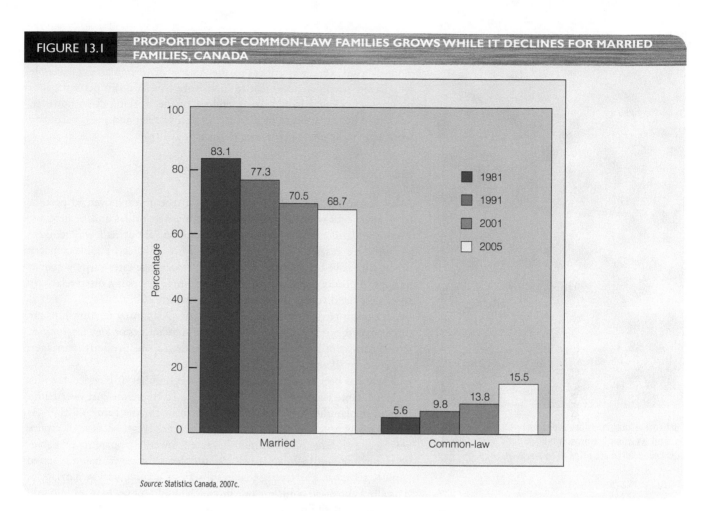

*Source:* Statistics Canada, 2007c.

have supported the proposition that couples who cohabit before marriage do not necessarily have a stable relationship once they are married (Clark and Crompton, 2006).

## Marriage

Despite the prevalence of divorce in our society, marriage continues to be an extremely popular institution. The majority of Canadians will marry at some point in their lives. Furthermore, although marriages today experience many problems, for better or worse the majority of marriages in Canada do last a lifetime (Ward and Belanger, 2011).

Why do people get married? Couples get married for a variety of reasons. Some do so because they are "in love," desire companionship and sex, want to have children, feel social pressure, are attempting to escape from a bad situation in their parents' home, or believe that they will have more money or other resources if married. These factors notwithstanding, the selection of a marital partner is fairly predictable. Most people in Canada tend to choose marriage partners who are similar to themselves. **Homogamy** refers to the pattern of individuals marrying those who have similar characteristics, such as race/ethnicity, religious background, age, education, or social class. However, homogamy provides only the general framework within which people select their partners; people are also influenced by other factors. For example, some researchers claim that people want partners whose personalities match their own in significant ways. As a result, people who are outgoing and friendly may be attracted to people with those same traits. Other researchers, however, claim that people look for partners whose personality traits differ from but complement their own.

Regardless of the individual traits of marriage partners, research indicates that communication and emotional support are crucial to the success of marriages. Common marital problems include

> **homogamy** The pattern of individuals marrying those who have similar characteristics, such as race/ethnicity, religious background, age, education, or social class.

Geostock/Getty Images

Dual-earner marriages are a challenge for many children as well as their parents. While parents are at work, latchkey children are often at home alone.

lack of emotional intimacy, poor communication, and lack of companionship. One study concluded that for many middle- and upper-income couples, women's paid work was critical to the success of their marriages. People who have a strong commitment to their work have two distinct sources of pleasure—work and family. For members of the working class, however, work may not be a source of pleasure. For all women and men, balancing work and family life is a challenge (Marshall, 2011).

## Remarriage

Most people who divorce get remarried. In recent years, over 30 percent of all marriages were between previously married brides and/or grooms. Among individuals who divorce before age 35, about half will remarry within three years of their first divorce. Most divorced people remarry others who have been divorced. However, remarriage rates vary by gender and age. A greater proportion of men than women remarry, often relatively soon after the divorce, regardless of age (Ambert, 2009).

As a result of divorce and remarriage, complex family relationships are often created. Some people become part of stepfamilies or *blended families*, which consist of a husband and wife, children from previous marriages, and children (if any) from the new marriage.

There has been a dramatic increase in the number of blended families in North America over the last 30 years. Today there are just over half a million stepfamilies in Canada (Vanier Institute for the Family, 2010). At least initially, levels of family stress may be fairly high because of rivalry among the children and hostilities directed toward stepparents or babies born into the family. In spite of these problems, however, many blended families succeed. The family that results from divorce and remarriage is typically a complex, binuclear one in which children may have a biological parent and a stepparent, biological siblings and stepsiblings, and an array of other relatives, including aunts, uncles, and cousins.

According to sociologist Andrew Cherlin (1992), the norms governing divorce and remarriage are ambiguous. Because there are no clear-cut guidelines, people must make decisions about family life (such as decisions about Christmas, birthdays, and weddings) based on their own beliefs and feelings about the people involved. Consider the following example of a couple who both brought children to their new marriage:

> The first couple of years after we got married, we had two Christmas trees, one in the living room, and one in the rec room. Once they [Angie's biological children and stepchildren] got older, I could say to them, "It's a really big hassle," but the first couple of years, there was so much decoration and everybody wanted everything: my kids wanted this because we had always had it on our tree, and the other kids wanted that because they had it on their tree. (Church, 2003:66)

Because there are few norms governing these family relationships, it may take years for them to come together, clarify roles and responsibilities, and establish a solid identity as a family unit (Preese, 2004).

### TIME TO REVIEW

- Compare and contrast marriage versus cohabitation. Based on what you have learned about these forms of establishing committed relationships, which do you predict will be most common in your generation?

NEL

## CHILD-RELATED FAMILY ISSUES AND PARENTING  `LO-4`

Not all couples become parents. Those who decide not to have children often consider themselves "child free," whereas those who do not produce children through no choice of their own may consider themselves "childless."

### Deciding to Have Children

Cultural attitudes about having children and the ideal family size began to change in North America in the late 1950s. On average, women are now having 1.5 children. However, rates of fertility differ across racial and ethnic categories. For example, Aboriginal women have a total fertility rate of 2.6 (Statistics Canada, 2007c).

Over the past five decades, advances in birth control techniques—including the birth control pill and contraceptive patches and shots—have made it possible for people to decide whether they want to have children and how many they wish to have, and to determine (at least somewhat) the spacing of their births. Sociologists suggest, however, that fertility is linked not only to reproductive technologies but also to women's beliefs that they do or do not have other opportunities in society that are viable alternatives to childbearing (Lamanna and Riedmann, 2011).

The concept of reproductive freedom includes both the desire *to have* or *not to have* one or more children. Women, more often than men, are the first to choose a child-free lifestyle By age 40, more than 10 percent of Canadian women intend to remain child free (Edmonston, Lee, and Wu, 2008). However, the desire not to have children often comes in conflict with our society's *pronatalist bias,* which assumes that having children is the norm and can be taken for granted, while those who choose not to have children believe they must justify their decision to others (Lamanna and Riedmann, 2011). Many diverse reasons account for why individuals decide not to have children, including never having wanted any, not finding themselves in the right circumstances, and having religious or environmental concerns (Stobert and Kemeny, 2003).

Some couples experience involuntary infertility, whereby they want to have a child but they are physically unable to do so. **Infertility** is defined as an inability to conceive after one year of unprotected sexual relations. Research suggests that fertility problems originate in females in approximately 30 to 40 percent of cases and with males in about 40 percent of cases; in the other approximately 20 percent of cases, the cause is impossible to determine. It is estimated that about half of infertile couples who seek treatments, such as fertility drugs, artificial insemination, and surgery to unblock fallopian tubes, can be helped; however, some are unable to conceive despite expensive treatments such as in vitro fertilization, which costs as much as $15,000 per attempt (IVF.ca, 2012).

People who are involuntarily childless may choose to become parents by adopting a child.

> **infertility** An inability to conceive after one year of unprotected sexual relations.

### Adoption

*Adoption* is a legal process through which the rights and duties of parenting are transferred from a child's biological and/or legal parents to new legal parents. This procedure gives the adopted child all the rights of a biological child. In most adoptions, a new birth certificate is issued and the child has no future contact with the biological parents. In Canada, adoption is regulated provincially. Therefore, adopted persons' access to information regarding their "biological parents" varies, as does their desire to access this information.

Matching children who are available for adoption with prospective adoptive parents can be difficult. The available children have specific needs, and the prospective parents often set specifications on the type of child they want to adopt. There are fewer infants available for adoption today than in the past because better means of contraception exist, abortion is more readily available, and more single parents decide to keep their babies. As a result, many prospective parents pursue international adoptions from countries including China, Haiti, South Korea, and India (Vanier Institute of the Family, 2008).

## Assisted Reproductive Technologies

In recent years, there has been an explosion of research, clinical practice, and experimentation in the area of reproductive technology. For example, in 2007, a Quebec woman froze some of her embryos so that her seven-year-old daughter, who is infertile, could use them. In 2009, a 60-year-old woman gave birth to twin boys in Calgary (she had undergone in vitro fertilization in India) (CBC, 2009). Also in 2009, a woman in California gave birth to eight babies with the use of assisted reproductive technologies. These procedures, in particular, have raised some controversial ethical issues in terms of what role medical science should play in the creation of human life (Marquardt, 2006).

Procedures used in the creation of new life, such as artificial insemination and in vitro fertilization, are referred to as "methods of assisted reproduction" (Achilles, 1996). Artificial insemination is the oldest, simplest, and most common type of assisted reproduction. The most common form of artificial insemination is *intrauterine insemination,* which involves a physician inserting sperm directly into the uterus near the time of ovulation. Inseminations may be performed with donor sperm.

Intrauterine insemination with donor sperm raises several complex issues concerning its moral, legal, and social implications. In most cases, the woman is given no information about the donor and the donor is not told if a pregnancy has occurred. The result of this anonymity is that neither the mother nor the individuals conceived through donor insemination will have access to information regarding the biological father (Achilles, 1996). The term *test-tube baby* is often used incorrectly to describe babies conceived through in vitro fertilization. A real test-tube baby would require conception, gestation, and birth to occur outside of a woman's body. To date, this technology has not been developed (Achilles, 1996). *In vitro* (Latin for "in glass") *fertilization* involves inducing ovulation, removing the egg(s) from a woman, fertilizing the egg(s) with the sperm in a petri dish, and then implanting the fertilized egg(s) (embryos) into the woman.

Another alternative available to couples with fertility problems is the use of a surrogate, or substitute, mother to carry a child for them. There are two types of surrogacy. In *traditional surrogacy,* the surrogate is artificially inseminated with the father's sperm. In this case, the egg is the surrogate's and the child is biologically related to the surrogate and the father. This type of surrogacy is typically used in cases where the woman is infertile or when there is a risk of passing on a serious genetic disorder from mother to child. In the second type of surrogacy, *gestational surrogacy,* the sperm and the eggs from the infertile couple are transferred to the surrogate using an assisted reproductive technology (such as in vitro fertilization). With gestational surrogacy, the surrogate carries the child but is not biologically or genetically related to it. The genetic parents are the man and woman whose eggs and sperm were donated to the surrogate.

The availability of a variety of reproductive technologies is having a dramatic impact on traditional concepts of the family and parenthood. In light of all the assisted reproductive technologies available, what does the term *parent* mean? How many "parents" does the child have? Is *mother* an accurate term for the gestational surrogate mother? Consider the comments of sociologist Christine Overall:

> Thanks to reproductive technology, a baby could, potentially, have five different parents: its genetic mother and genetic father, who supply the ovum and the sperm; its carrying mother, who gestates the embryo produced by the union of the ovum and sperm; and finally, its social mother and father, the individuals who rear the child produced by the carrying mother. (1991:473)

How do the children conceived with assisted reproductive technologies define their families? There are now approximately one million donor-conceived children in the world. Now that they are able to speak for themselves, these children have raised some difficult questions about the rights of the child, biology, identity, and families. Some of these issues are highlighted in the following narrative:

> Is it right to deprive people of knowing who their natural parents are? What happens to your sense of identity when one of your biological parents is missing? Is there a difference when you're raised by "social" rather than biological parents? What if those parents are two women, or two men, or perhaps three people? Are children's understandings of parenthood as flexible as we would like to think? How do kids feel about all this? And do their feelings matter? (Wente, 2006:A21)

In 2004, the federal government enacted legislation to monitor and regulate assisted reproductive technologies. This legislation specifies what practices are forbidden: These include human cloning, sex selection, and buying or selling human embryos and sperm. It also outlines allowed practices, including surrogate mothers, donation of human sperm and embryos, and the use of human embryos and stem cells for scientific research (Department of Justice, 2009a). In 2006, a regulatory agency was established to ensure that these standards are followed.

The issues raised by legislation in this area are complex and emotional, not just scientific and technical (see Box 13.3 for a more detailed discussion). They also have legal, social, moral, and ethical implications. For example, fertility clinics across the country can send cells from embryos conceived through in vitro fertilization to labs in the United States to test them for disorders the new parents want to avoid. As a result of these new technologies, it is possible to screen for a number of life-threatening conditions. However, it is also possible to screen for other conditions that are less severe and may never present themselves until late adulthood if ever. Most disturbing, however, is the suggestion that these new technologies may lead to the creation of what has been described as "unnatural selection," allowing parents to select for traits such as height, weight, hair and eye colour, and athletic ability (Abraham, 2012).

Despite these concerns and unintended consequences, these new reproductive technologies have enabled some infertile couples to become parents. For them, the benefits far outweigh the costs.

---

**BOX 13.3    POINT/COUNTERPOINT**

## Baby by Stealth: Reproduction Law Forcing "Dangerous Alternatives"

At the same time as reproductive technologies stretch the notion of the family beyond the nuclear, and just as Canada bends to accommodate that evolution, a prevailing piece of federal legislation is being accused of inadvertently forcing a slew of prospective parents underground.

At the root of this underworld, some argue, is the 2004 *Assisted Human Reproduction Act*–the Canadian government's most comprehensive attempt to regulate reproductive technologies. Some onlookers fear that the legislation has created a secretive black market, where couples seek sperm and egg donors on Craigslist or in university libraries.

Where those couples quietly compensate donors for their gametes, despite the legislation that criminalizes doing so. Where lesbian couples lie to doctors about their sexual orientation to avoid paying to quarantine a friend's sperm for six months. And where doctors and counsellors sometimes adopt the credo of "Don't ask, don't tell."

The act–which is a result of the Royal Commission on New Reproductive Technologies in 1993–has triggered condemnation from the right and left, and was the focal point of an International Women's Day conference in Toronto last week. There, at the Law Society of Upper Canada, panellists argued that some of the legislation

*(continued)*

does more to imperil and confuse prospective parents and their offspring than it does to protect them.

The act's aftermath has some significant real-world, legal implications, said lawyer Kelly Jordan, who specializes in family law and assisted reproductive technologies at Toronto firm Jordan Battista.

"Right now, we don't have any guidance about the rights of donors, carriers and surrogates, and there has been virtually no case law in Canada to deal with those questions," Ms. Jordan said.

"For example, if an egg donor in Ontario dies without a will, do her genetic children inherit her estate? Can a sperm donor be ordered to pay child support? Those are some of the questions that have yet to be answered."

Ms. Jordan said there is also the lingering issue of jurisdiction: The act is federal, but health falls under provincial purview. In 2008, the Quebec Court of Appeal ruled that large parts of the legislation, including those related to regulating the treatment of infertility, fall under provincial jurisdiction and are therefore unconstitutional. The case made it to the Supreme Court in April 2009 but, nearly a year later, the court has yet to release a decision.

Looking back, Canada has a history of amending its laws to accommodate the evolution of what constitutes a family, and citizens have long fought for the right to create a family no matter their sexual orientation, race, religion, ability or class.

For some, the right to family has gone too far, sacrificing the sanctity of family in the unfounded quest for equity. For others, the concept of the "family" is still too constrained.

What do you think? Where should the government draw the line in terms of a parent's right to use reproductive technologies to establish a family?

*Source:* Kathryn Blaze Carlson, "Baby By Stealth: Reproduction Law Forcing Dangerous Alternatives," *National Post*, March 12 2010. Material reprinted with the express permission of National Post, a division of Postmedia Network Inc.

## TIME TO REVIEW

- What are the some of the legal, social, moral, and ethical implications of assisted reproductive technologies?

## Single-Parent Households

Single parenting is not a new phenomenon in Canada. However, one of the most significant changes in Canadian families is the dramatic increase in single-parent families. Today, there are more than one million single parents in Canada, and more than 80 percent of them are women (Ward and Belanger, 2011). In the past, most single-parent families were created when one parent died. Today, the major causes of single parenthood for women are divorce and separation. Even for a person with a stable income and a network of friends and family to help with child care, raising a child alone can be an emotional and financial burden. Children in mother-only families are more likely than children in two-parent families to have poor academic achievement, higher school absentee and dropout rates, higher early marriage and parenthood, higher divorce rates, and more drug and alcohol abuse (Ambert, 2006b). Does living in a one-parent family cause all of this? Certainly not! Many other factors—including poverty, discrimination, unsafe neighbourhoods, and high crime rates—contribute to these problems.

Currently, men head close to one-fifth of lone-parent families; among many of the men, a pattern of "involved fatherhood" has emerged (Ward and Belanger, 2011). While some single fathers remain actively involved in their children's lives, others may become less involved, spending time with their children around recreational activities and on special occasions. Sometimes this limited role is by choice, but more often it is caused by workplace demands on time and energy, the location of the ex-wife's residence, and the limitations placed on the visitation arrangements. Although the courts continue to award mothers custody in divorces, an increasing number of fathers are attempting to gain sole or joint custody of their children.

As a result, we can expect to see an increase in the number of single fathers in the future (Ward and Belanger, 2011).

## Housework and Child-Care Responsibilities

Thirty years ago, most Canadian families relied on one wage earner. Today, approximately 70 percent of all families in Canada are **dual-earner families**—families in which both partners are in the labour force. More than half of all employed women hold full-time, year-round jobs. Even when their children are very young, most working mothers work full time. Moreover, as discussed in Chapter 11, many married women leave their paid employment at the end of the day and go home to perform hours of housework and child care. Difficulty in balancing work and family is the defining feature of family life today. Parents must make difficult decisions—decisions often driven by economic necessity—between the amount of time they spend at work and the amount of time they can be at home with their children (Barrette, 2009; Marshall, 2011). Sociologist Arlie Hochschild (1989, 2003) refers to this as the **second shift**—the domestic work that employed women perform at home after they complete their workday on the job. Thus, many women today contribute to the economic well-being of their families and also meet many of the domestic needs of family members by cooking, cleaning, shopping, taking care of children, and managing household routines. In households with small children or many children, the amount of housework increases. Hochschild points to the second shift in many families as a sign that the gender revolution has stalled:

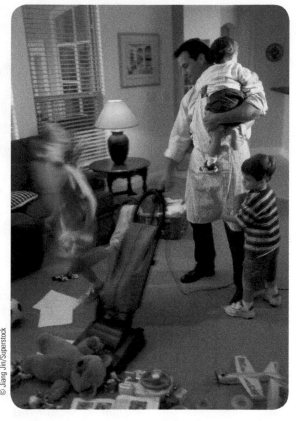

© Jiang Jin/Superstock

In recent years, many more fathers and mothers alike have been confronting the unique challenges of single parenting.

> The move of masses of women into the paid workforce has constituted a revolution. But the slower shift in ideas of "manhood," the resistance of sharing work at home, and the rigid schedules at work make for a "stall" in this gender revolution. It is a stall in the change of institutional arrangement of which men are the principal keepers. (2003:28)

As Hochschild points out, the second shift remains a problem for many women in dual-earner marriages. However, recent time-use surveys of Canadian households indicate that the "stalled" revolution may be picking up the pace. Although a division of labour still exists within families, the hours of paid work, average earnings, and time spent on domestic labour and child care are becoming more similar between spouses in Canada (Marshall, 2011:13). As women's participation in the paid labour market has increased, men's involvement in housework and child care has also risen. In the mid-1980s, only half of men, with or without children, participated in daily housework. Today, approximately seven out of 10 men do so. In recent years, more husbands are sharing more of the household and child-care responsibilities, especially in families in which the wife's earnings are essential to family finances.

Despite the narrowing of the differences, men continue to have an overall greater involvement in paid work and a lesser involvement in housework. An examination of men and women aged 20 to 29 in dual-earner couples confirms the trend that spouses are increasingly sharing economic and domestic responsibilities. For example, in 2010, dual-earner women aged 20 to 29 did 47 percent of couples' total paid work and 53 percent of couples' housework. Also similar to past trends, however, dependent children at home tend to increase the gap between

**dual-earner families** Families in which both partners are in the labour force.

**second shift** Arlie Hochschild's term for the domestic work that employed women perform at home after they complete their workday on the job.

Juggling housework, child care, and a job in the paid workforce are all part of the average day for many women. Why does sociologist Arlie Hochschild believe that many women work a second shift?

paid and unpaid work within young dual-earner couples (Marshall, 2011). Couples with more egalitarian ideas about the roles of women and men tend to share more equally in food preparation, housework, and child care.

Women who are employed full time and who are single parents have the greatest burden of all: complete responsibility for the children and the household, often with little or no help from ex-husbands or relatives. Recent statistics indicate that female single parents with full-time employment work, on average, 11 hours per day when paid and unpaid work are combined (Vanier Institute of the Family, 2009b). See Figure 13.2.

In Canada, millions of parents rely on child care so they can work and their young children can benefit from early educational experiences that will help in their future school endeavours. For millions more parents, after-school care for their school-aged children is an urgent concern because the children need productive and safe activities to engage in while their parents are working. (Children who are in daycare for extended hours often come to think of child-care workers and other caregivers as members of their extended families because they may spend nearly as many hours with them as they do with their own parents.) Obtaining child care for children of divorced parents and other young people living in single-parent households is often an especially pressing concern because of the limited number of available adults and a lack of financial resources (Friendly and Prentice, 2009).

| FIGURE 13.2 | TIME SPENT ON PAID AND UNPAID WORK, MEN AND WOMEN |

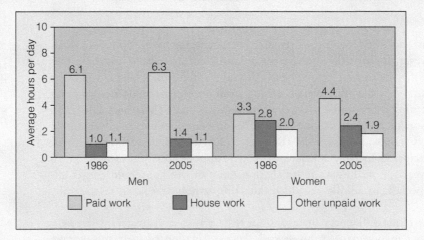

Source: Statistics Canada, "General Social Survey: Paid and Unpaid Work," The Daily, June 19, 2006.

## TRANSITIONS AND PROBLEMS IN FAMILIES  LO-5

Families go through many transitions and experience a wide variety of problems ranging from separation and divorce to unplanned pregnancy to family violence. These all-too-common experiences highlight two important facts about families: (1) For good or ill, families are central to our existence, and (2) the reality of family life is far more complicated than the idealized image found in the media and in many political discussions. Whereas some families provide their members with love, warmth, and satisfying emotional experiences, other families may be hazardous to the individual's physical and mental well-being. Because of this dichotomy in family life, sociologists have described families as both a "haven in a heartless world" (Lasch, 1977) and a "cradle of violence" (Gelles and Straus, 1988).

### Family Violence

Violence between men and women in the home is often referred to as spouse abuse or domestic violence. *Spouse abuse* refers to the violence or mistreatment that a woman or man may experience at the hands of a marital, common-law, or same-sex partner. Forms of spousal abuse include physical abuse, emotional abuse, sexual abuse, and economic/financial abuse. These various forms of violence often occur in combination with one another. As discussed in Chapter 4, *child abuse* refers to physical or sexual abuse and/or neglect by a parent or caregiver.

How much do we know about violence in families? Women, as compared with men, are more likely to be victims of violence perpetrated by intimate partners. Recent statistics indicate that women are five times more likely than men to experience such violence and that many of these women live in households with children witnessing the violence (Ogrodnik, 2008). However, we cannot know the true extent of family violence because much of it is not reported to police. For example, results from the 2009 General Social Survey indicated that just under one-quarter (22 percent) of victims of spousal violence reported the incident to police (Department of Justice, 2011).

Although everyone in a household where family violence occurs is harmed psychologically, children are especially affected by household violence. Children who are raised in an environment of violence suffer profoundly, even if they are not the direct targets. Their own physical and emotional needs are often neglected, and they may learn by example to deal with conflict through violence (Johnson and Dawson, 2011). Not surprisingly, the research indicates that domestic violence and child maltreatment often take place in the same household.

It is estimated that approximately one million Canadian children witness some form of domestic violence in their homes each year (Beattie, 2005b). Long-term effects associated with witnessing violence include aggressive behaviour, emotional problems, and effects on social and academic development (Ross, Scott, and Kelly, 1996). In some situations, family violence can be reduced or eliminated through counselling, the removal of one parent from the household, or other steps that are taken either by the family or by social service agencies or law enforcement officials. However, as noted above, children who witness violence in the home may display certain emotional and behavioural problems that adversely affect their school life and communication with other people. In short, there are no easy solutions to a problem as complex as family violence.

Although differences in power and privilege between women and men do not inevitably result in violence, gender-based inequalities can still produce sustained marital conflicts. In any case, a common consequence of marital strife and unhappiness is divorce.

Although public awareness of domestic violence has increased in recent years, society is far from finding an effective solution for this pressing social problem.

## Divorce

Divorce is the legal process of dissolving a marriage that allows former spouses to remarry if they so choose. Prior to 1968, it was difficult to obtain a divorce in Canada. A divorce was granted only on the grounds of adultery. In 1968, the grounds for divorce were expanded to include marital breakdown—that is, desertion, imprisonment, or separation of three or more years—and marital offences (physical or mental cruelty). As shown in Figure 13.3, the divorce rate increased dramatically as a result of the wider grounds for divorce. In 1985, the *Divorce Act* introduced "no fault" provisions that made marital breakdown the sole ground for divorce. Under no-fault divorce laws, proof of "blameworthiness" is no longer necessary. When children are involved, however, the issue of blame may assume greater importance in the determination of parental custody.

Have you heard statements such as "One out of every two marriages ends in divorce"? Statistics might initially appear to bear out this statement. In 2008, for example, 147,000 Canadian couples married and 70,229 divorces were granted (Vanier Institute for the Family, 2011). However, comparing the number of marriages with the number of divorces from year to year can be misleading. The couples who are divorced in any given year are unlikely to come from the group that married that year. Some people also may go through several marriages and divorces, thus skewing the divorce rate. The likelihood of divorce goes up with each subsequent marriage in the serial monogamy pattern (Ambert, 2009).

To accurately assess the probability of a marriage ending in divorce, it is necessary to use what is referred to as a *cohort approach*. This approach establishes probabilities based on assumptions about how the various age groups (cohorts) in society might behave, given their marriage rate, their age at first marriage, and their responses to various social, cultural, and economic changes. Canadian estimates based on a cohort approach are that 35 to 40 percent of marriages will end in divorce (Ambert, 2009).

**CAUSES OF DIVORCE** Why do divorces occur? As you will recall from Chapter 2, sociologists look for correlations (relationships between two variables) in attempting to answer questions such as this. Existing research has identified a number of factors at both the macro- and microlevels that make some couples more or less likely to divorce. At the macrolevel, societal factors contributing to higher rates of divorce include changes in social institutions such as religion, the family, and the legal system. Some religions have taken a more lenient attitude toward divorce, and the social stigma associated with divorce has lessened. Further, as we have seen in this chapter, the family has undergone a major change that has resulted in less economic and emotional dependency among family members—and thus reduced a barrier to divorce. And, as Figure 13.3 demonstrates, the liberalization of divorce laws in Canada has had a dramatic impact on the divorce rate.

At the microlevel, a number of factors contribute to a couple's "statistical" likelihood of becoming divorced. Anne-Marie Ambert (2009) has identified some of the primary risk factors for divorce:

■ youthful marriage
■ low incomes and poverty, as well as rapid upward social mobility
■ cohabitation prior to marriage
■ remarriage

- parents who are divorced or have unhappy marriages
- low religiosity
- the presence of children (depending on their gender and age at the beginning of the marriage)

The interrelationship of these and other factors is complicated. For example, the effect of age is intertwined with economic resources: Persons from families at the low end of the income scale tend to marry earlier than those at more affluent income levels. Thus, the question becomes whether age is a factor or whether economic resources are more closely associated with divorce.

**CONSEQUENCES OF DIVORCE** Divorce may have a dramatic economic and emotional impact on family members. Few children want their parents to divorce, no matter how unhappy the marriage is. For children, divorce results in the most significant changes they have experienced in their lifetimes—new relationships with each parent, often new residences, changes in schedules to accommodate visitation privileges, and, in some cases, a new parental figure.

The exact number of children affected by divorce in Canada is difficult to determine because no official information is available on out-of-court custody decisions, but approximately 40,000 Canadian children per year are involved in custody disputes. In the majority of these cases, the children reside primarily with their mother, meaning that the mother has *physical* custody of the children. Only about 10 percent of children live with their father despite the fact that joint *legal* custody now represents almost 50 percent of custody orders awarded. Parental joint custody is also an option for some divorcing couples. When joint custody is a voluntary arrangement, and when there is motivation to make it work, it has benefits for both children and parents (Ambert, 2009). However, this arrangement may also create unique problems for children, who must adjust to living in two homes and to the fact that their parents no longer live together. The worst thing that can happen to children after a divorce is that their parents remain in conflict (Buchanan, Maccoby, and Dornbusch, 1996).

The consequences of divorce are not entirely negative. There is no doubt that some children are better off after their parents divorce. For some people, divorce may be an opportunity to

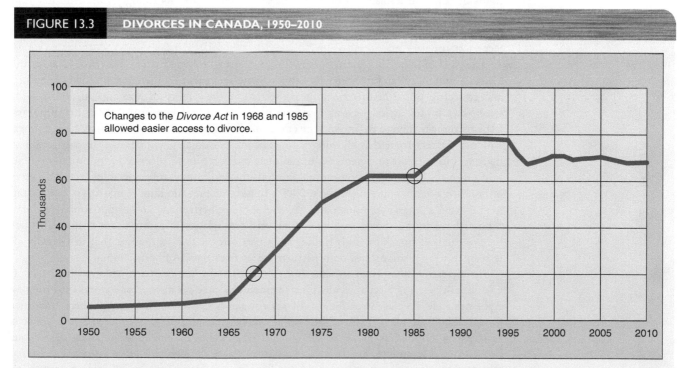

**FIGURE 13.3  DIVORCES IN CANADA, 1950–2010**

Changes to the *Divorce Act* in 1968 and 1985 allowed easier access to divorce.

*Sources:* Statistics Canada, 2005d, 2012c.

terminate destructive relationships. For others, it may represent a way to achieve personal growth by enabling them to manage their lives and social relationships and establish their own identity.

## DIVERSITY IN FAMILIES

### Gay and Lesbian Families

Lesbians and gay men grow up in families, establish long-lasting, committed, emotional relationships, and sometimes become parents. Nevertheless, until recently, discussions of gay and lesbian relationships and families have been excluded from discussions of the family. These relationships were considered by many as threatening to notions of the traditional family. Lesbians and gay men were viewed as existing entirely outside families, and many people felt that recognition of gay and lesbian relationships would result in the demise of "the family." Notions of the family that are limited to unions between members of the opposite sex are examples of **heterosexism**—an attitude in which heterosexuality is considered the only valid form of sexual behaviour, and gay men, lesbians, and bisexuals are considered inferior to heterosexual people.

> **heterosexism** An attitude in which heterosexuality is considered the only valid form of sexual behaviour, and gay men, lesbians, and bisexuals are considered inferior to heterosexual people.

In Canada, the law grants particular rights, benefits, and privileges only to heterosexual relationships, especially legally married partners. Until recently, gays and lesbians have been prohibited from sponsoring the immigration of their partners to Canada, from obtaining custody of their children, from jointly adopting children, or from receiving spousal benefits and survivors' pensions. Until very recently, same-sex couples were prohibited from legally marrying. In 2003, the Ontario Court of Appeal ruled that Canada's legal definition of marriage is unconstitutional and redefined it as "the voluntary union for life of two persons to the exclusion of all others." In her ruling, the judge further explained that "the existing common law rule is inconsistent with the constitutional values in modern Canadian society and offends the equality rights of gays and lesbians" (Kome, 2002:1). In response to this ruling, Prime Minister Jean Chrétien announced that the federal government would rewrite the legal definition of marriage to recognize same-sex marriages. In 2005, Canada became the third country in the world to recognize same-sex marriage.

The issue of same-sex marriages, however, remains a hotly debated and divisive issue for the Canadian public. Even for those who support same-sex marriages there remain many questions and concerns. Some of the concerns are related to the quality of homosexual unions—for example, are they as long-lasting and committed? Many are concerned about the ability of lesbians and gay men to parent and the effect that living in same-sex families may have on their children. Others argue that allowing same-sex couples to marry will devalue the institution of marriage. In contrast to stereotypes of same-sex relationships as short-term, promiscuous, and noncommittal, research on homosexual relationships indicates that partnerships lasting 20 years or more are not uncommon (Ambert, 2009). In fact, the breakup rates of married or cohabiting heterosexual couples and lesbian and gay couples have been found to be approximately equal. Studies have found, however, that lesbian and gay relationships are more egalitarian than heterosexual relationships. This finding is in part attributable to the fact that in virtually all lesbian and gay relationships, both partners are wage earners (Ambert, 2005a).

An increasing number of lesbians and gay males form families with children. In the 2006 Census, just over 45,000 couples identified themselves as same-sex married or common-law couples. Approximately 10 percent of these same-sex couples had children living with them (Statistics Canada, 2008). In many cases, lesbian mothers and gay fathers may have children from a previous marriage or relationship. However, not all children in same-sex families are products of previous heterosexual relationships. Lesbians may become pregnant through *alternative insemination* (sexual relations as a means of getting pregnant or artificial insemination) (Epstein, 2003). Lesbian mothers and gay fathers may also form families through fostering or adoption. Unlike many heterosexual families in which both mother and father have genetic links to their children, gay and lesbian families always have a nonbiological parent. These nonbiological parents are often not regarded as parents either socially or legally. For example, nonbiological parents may not be granted admission to parent–teacher interviews or may be denied permission to make important medical decisions for their children if the biological parent is unavailable.

Many people believe that being parented by same-sex couples is emotionally unhealthy for children and can cause them confusion about their own sexuality. However, the research has shown that the children of lesbians and gay men are as well adjusted as children who grow up in heterosexual households. In addition, these children experience no psychological damage, and they are no more likely to be homosexual than are children raised by heterosexual parents (Ambert, 2005a). According to Rachel Epstein (2003), there

Adoption is a complex legal process for most parents; it can be even more complicated for gay and lesbian couples.

can be positive effects of being raised by lesbian or gay parents, such as a greater appreciation of diversity and increased tolerance, since the children are taught to accept social differences in others.

## TIME TO REVIEW

- What are some of the most significant challenges facing lesbian and gay families today?
- What progress has been made in recent years?

## Diversity Among Singles

While marriage at increasingly younger ages was the trend in Canada during the first half of the 20th century, by the 1960s the trend had reversed and many more adults were remaining single. In 1971, close to half of Canadians aged 20 to 24 were already married. Today, almost 90 percent of Canadians aged 20 to 24 are single (Statistics Canada, 2007c). Currently, approximately 25 percent of households in Canada are one person households. This estimate, however, includes people who are divorced, widowed, or have never married. Given the fact that nine out of 10 Canadians marry at some time in their lives, single status is often temporary. Some never-married singles remain single by choice. Reasons include more opportunity for a career (especially for women), the availability of sexual partners without marriage, the belief that the single lifestyle is full of excitement, and the desire for self-sufficiency and freedom to change and experiment (Stein, 1976, 1981). According to some marriage and family analysts, individuals who prefer to remain single hold more individualistic values and are less family-oriented than those who choose to marry. Friends and personal growth tend to be valued more highly than marriage and children (Alwin, Converse, and Martin, 1985; Crompton, 2005).

Secondary school systems are being pressured to address issues of family diversity in the classroom. In Surrey, British Columbia, in 2002, a battle was fought over the censorship of books about same-sex families.

Other never-married singles remain single out of necessity. For some people, being single is an economic necessity: They cannot afford to marry and set up their own households. Structural changes in the economy have limited the options of many working-class young people. Even some university and college graduates have found that they cannot earn enough money to set up a household separate from that of their parents. Consequently, a growing proportion of young adults are living with one or both parents (Beaupré, Turcotte, and Milan, 2006; Turcotte, 2006).

## Aboriginal Families

It is difficult to discuss Aboriginal families, given the fact that Aboriginal peoples in Canada are by no means a homogeneous group. Aboriginal peoples are composed of many distinct nations with different histories, cultures, economic bases, and languages (Ward and Belanger, 2011 ). In all Aboriginal families, however, the extended family was seen as central to both the individual and the community. The concept of family was defined very broadly. For example, to the Ojibwa, *family* referred to individuals who worked together and were bound together by responsibility and friendship as well as kinship ties. Family size averaged between 20 and 25 persons (Shkilnyk, 1985). A band member describes the economic cooperation and sharing that once existed within the Ojibwa family:

> Trapping kept the family together because everyone in the family had something
> to do; the man had to lay traps and check them; the woman skinned the animals,
> cooked, and looked after the kids. The grandparents helped with the kids; they
> taught them manners, how to behave, and told them stories about our people. The
> kids, if they were old enough, had work to do. (Shkilnyk, 1985:81)

Under this cooperative family system, Aboriginal families were extremely successful in ensuring the survival and well-being of their members.

Four hundred years after contact with the European settlers, the current state of family disruption is evident when you consider the following data. Aboriginal children represent 40 percent of children placed in home care in Canada; the rate of wife abuse among Aboriginal peoples is five times the national average; the rate of spousal homicide is eight times higher among Aboriginal women compared to non-Aboriginal women; and the suicide rate of Aboriginal peoples is double the rate of the general population (Assembly of First Nations, 2008; Ogrodnik, 2008). How did this happen? Aboriginal family life was profoundly changed in the 20th century as a result of the interventionist strategies employed by the Canadian church and state. Families were displaced from their traditional lands, moved to reserves, and denied access to the resources that were central to the economic survival of the extended family unit. An estimated 125,000 Aboriginal children were forcibly removed from their families and placed in residential schools (where they were often sexually and physically abused). This was part of a government "assimilation policy," directed at preventing Aboriginal children from learning their traditional language and culture. The result of this action is the trauma that many Aboriginal families continue to struggle with today. In the 1960s and 1970s, Aboriginal children were once again forcibly removed from their families and adopted by non-Aboriginal families. "In many cases, children were taken from parents whose only crime was poverty and being aboriginal" (Fournier and Crey, 1997:85, cited in Ambert, 2006a). Generations of Aboriginal children were separated from their families and their communities, and this separation also served to sever links with Aboriginal identity, culture, and languages (Frideres, 2007). Consider Chief Cinderina Williams's description of the impact of residential schools on the family:

> Later when these children returned home, they were aliens. They did not speak
> their own language, so they could not communicate with anyone other than
> their own counterparts. Some looked down on their families because of their
> lack of English, their lifestyle, and some were just plain hostile. They had
> formed no bonds with their families, and some couldn't survive without the

regimentation they had become so accustomed to . . . Consequently, when these children became parents, and most did at an early age, they had no parenting skills. They did not have the capability to show affection. (Godin-Beers and Williams, 1994, cited in Castellano, 2002)

After generations of cultural and spiritual destruction, Aboriginal peoples are now reclaiming their culture. They have also united behind the goal of self-government, especially in the areas of social services, education, and child welfare (Castellano, 2002). Aboriginal peoples believe in maintaining the ties between children and their natural parents, as well as caring for children within their Aboriginal communities. This they see as essential to the rebuilding of Aboriginal families in Canada. Many Aboriginal communities are striving to return to the practices and values that traditionally nourished Aboriginal family life: respect for women and children, mutual responsibility, and, above all, the general creed of sharing and caring (Royal Commission of Aboriginal Peoples, 1995:81).

## FAMILY ISSUES IN THE FUTURE

As we have seen, families and intimate relationships have changed dramatically over the last century. Some people believe the family as we know it is doomed. Others believe that a return to traditional values will save this important social institution and create greater stability in society.

Regardless of problems facing families today, the family remains the central institution in the lives of most Canadians. A national opinion poll found that more than three-quarters of Canadians regard the family as the most important thing in their lives—more important than their career or religion—and 92 percent of the respondents with young children at home indicated that the family is becoming *more* important to them. Finally, an overwhelming majority demonstrated their faith in the family by indicating that they want to marry and have children (although fewer than in the past) (Bibby, 2004). Individuals in families are now freer to establish the kinds of family arrangements that best suit them. As Clarence Lochhead, executive director of the Vanier Institute, explains:

> We just have to come to grips with the diversity that actually is within our experience. Then we need to find ways to address and take on the challenges that face families, but do it in an inclusive way that makes sense for the reality and not some ideal notion of what a family is or ought to be (CBC, 2010b).

## KEY TERMS

**bilateral descent** A system of tracing descent through both the mother's and father's sides of the family (p. 375).

**cohabitation** The sharing of a household by a couple who live together without being legally married (p. 380).

**dual-earner families** Families in which both partners are in the labour force (p. 387).

**egalitarian family** A family structure in which both partners share power and authority equally (p. 375).

**extended family** A family unit composed of relatives in addition to parents and children who live in the same household (p. 372).

**families we choose** Social arrangements that include intimate relationships between couples and close familial relationships with other couples, as well as with other adults and children (p. 370).

**family** A relationship in which people live together with commitment, form an economic unit and care for any young, and consider their identity to be significantly attached to the group (p. 371).

**family of orientation** The family into which a person is born and in which early socialization usually takes place (p. 372).

**family of procreation** The family that a person forms by having or adopting children (p. 372).

**heterosexism** An attitude in which heterosexuality is considered the only valid form of sexual behaviour, and gay men, lesbians, and bisexuals are considered inferior to heterosexual people (p. 392).

**homogamy** The pattern of individuals marrying those who have similar characteristics, such as race/ethnicity, religious background, age, education, or social class (p. 381).

**LO-1** Explain why it is difficult to define family.

Families may be defined as relationships in which people live together with commitment, form an economic unit and care for any young, and consider their identity to be significantly attached to the group.

**CONCEPT SNAPSHOT**

| | |
|---|---|
| FUNCTIONALIST PERSPECTIVES Key thinker: Talcott Parsons | In modern societies, families serve the functions of sexual regulation, socialization, economic and psychological support, and provision of social status. |
| CONFLICT PERSPECTIVES Key thinker: Friedrich Engels | Families both mirror and help perpetuate social inequalities based on class and gender. |
| FEMINIST PERSPECTIVES Key thinkers: Nancy Mandell, Ann Duffy | Women's subordination is rooted in patriarchy and men's control over women's labour power. |
| SYMBOLIC INTERACTIONIST PERSPECTIVES Key thinker: Jessie Bernard | Family dynamics, including communication patterns and the subjective meanings that people assign to events, mean that interactions within families create a shared reality. |
| POSTMODERN PERSPECTIVES Key thinkers: David Elkind | In postmodern societies, families are diverse and fragmented. Boundaries between the workplace and home are also blurred. |

**LO-2** Understand the key assumptions of functionalist, conflict, feminist, symbolic interactionist, and postmodernist perspectives on families.

Functionalists emphasize the importance of the family in maintaining the stability of society and the well-being of the individuals. Functions of the family include sexual regulation, socialization, economic and psychological support, and provision of social status. Conflict and feminist perspectives view the family as a source of social inequality and an arena for conflict over values, goals, and access to resources and power. Symbolic interactionists explain family relationships in terms of the subjective meanings and everyday interpretations people give to their lives. Postmodern analysts view families as permeable, reflecting the individualism, particularity, and irregularity of social life in the Information Age.

**LO-3** Understand the various options available to Canadian families in establishing families.

Families are changing dramatically in Canada. Cohabitation has increased significantly in the past two decades. The number of single-parent families has also increased sharply in recent decades. Marriage continues to be an extremely popular institution with the majority of Canadians marrying at some point in their lives. As a result of divorce and remarriage, stepfamilies or *blended families* may be established, which consist of a husband and wife, children from previous marriages, and children (if any) from the new marriage.

**LO-4** Describe the challenges facing families today.

Canadian families are faced with many challenges as a result of the increasing diversity and choice available to individuals establishing intimate relationships. These include choosing among a wide range of reproductive choices and establishing ways to maintain balance between paid work and family responsibilities. With the increase in dual-earner marriages, women increasingly have been burdened by the "second shift"—the domestic work that employed women perform at home after they complete their workday on the job

© Morgan Lane Photography/Shutterstock

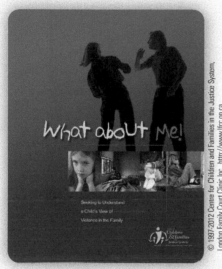
© 1997–2012 Centre for Children and Families in the Justice System, London Family Court Clinic Inc., http://www.lfcc.on.ca

**LO-5** Identify the primary problems facing Canadian families today.

Two of the most significant problems facing families are family violence and divorce. Both *spouse abuse* (violence or mistreatment that a woman or man may experience at the hands of a marital, common-law, or same-sex partner) and *child abuse* (physical or sexual abuse and/or neglect by a parent or caregiver) occur at alarming rates in Canadian families. Divorce is the legal process of dissolving a marriage. At the macrolevel, changes in social institutions may contribute to an increase in divorce rates; at the microlevel, factors contributing to divorce include age at marriage, economic resources, religiosity, and parental marital happiness. Divorce has contributed to greater diversity in family relationships, including stepfamilies or blended families and the complex binuclear family.

## APPLICATION QUESTIONS

1. In your own thinking, what constitutes an ideal family?

2. Based on your understanding of the term *family*, should the following be considered families? Why or why not?

   ▪ Man, woman, no children; married but living apart

   ▪ Woman, woman, and child of one woman living together; women a same-sex couple
   ▪ Man, his biological child, and woman (not his wife) with whom he has a sexual relationship living together
   ▪ Four adults sharing household for many years; none a same-sex couple

**infertility** An inability to conceive after one year of unprotected sexual relations (p. 383).

**kinship** A social network of people based on common ancestry, marriage, or adoption (p. 371).

**marriage** A legally recognized and/or socially approved arrangement between two or more individuals that carries certain rights and obligations and usually involves sexual activity (p. 374).

**matriarchal family** A family structure in which authority is held by the eldest female (usually the mother) (p. 375).

**matrilineal descent** A system of tracing descent through the mother's side of the family (p. 374).

**monogamy** An intimate relationship with one person at a time (p. 374).

**nuclear family** A family made up of one or two parents and their dependent children, all of whom live apart from other relatives (p. 373).

**patriarchal family** A family structure in which authority is held by the eldest male (usually the father) (p. 375).

**patrilineal descent** A system of tracing descent through the father's side of the family (p. 374).

**polyandry** The concurrent marriage of one woman with two or more men (p. 374).

**polygamy** The practice of having more than one spouse at a time (p. 374).

**polygyny** The concurrent marriage of one man with two or more women (p. 374).

**second shift** Arlie Hochschild's term for the domestic work that employed women perform at home after they complete their workday on the job (p. 387).

**sociology of family** The subdiscipline of sociology that attempts to describe and explain patterns of family life and variations in family structure (p. 376).

**CourseMate**

Test your comprehension and assess what you've learned with **CourseMate's** online quizzes.

For other interesting Lived Experiences, watch the video clips on **CourseMate.**

Practise what you've learned with flashcards containing key terms and definitions on **CourseMate.**

# Chapter 17

# The Changing Face of Matrimony

## SAME-SEX CIVIL MARRIAGE IN THE TWENTY-FIRST CENTURY

ADAM ISAIAH GREEN, University of Toronto

## THE RISE OF CIVIL MARRIAGE FOR SAME-SEX COUPLES

As the second decade of the twenty-first century begins, civil marriage for same-sex couples is a legal option in parts of Western Europe, Africa, and North America, including the Netherlands, Belgium, Canada, Spain, South Africa, Norway, and in two states in the United States: Connecticut and Massachusetts. First legalized in the Netherlands in 2001, same-sex civil marriage is a hot-button issue throughout the Western world, vigorously contested in public discourse and policy. In the United States, for instance, a variety of legal measures designed to prevent same-sex marriage have been put into law, including federal Defense of Marriage Act (DOMA) legislation, which prohibits federal recognition of same-sex civil marriage by defining marriage as the explicit union of one man and one woman, and amendments to state constitutions with the same effect. Some countries sidestep the controversy associated with same-sex civil marriage with legal provisions that are roughly comparable with those of civil marriage. A handful of governments, for instance, grant same-sex couples the right to register as a *domestic partnership*, which confers many of the same rights and responsibilities as civil marriage. Parts of the United States and Western Europe offer *civil unions* for same-sex couples in place of civil marriage, although, like domestic partnership, the benefits of this legal arrangement vary widely from place to place.

Advocates of same-sex civil marriage typically reject these alternative, "marriage-like" measures because they regard them as a kind of second-class citizenship for lesbian and gay couples. They argue that state-sanctioned civil marriage is not just a legal status; it is also a symbolic arrangement that provides a vital source of societal legitimization to which same-sex couples are equally entitled (Hausknecht, 2003; Josephson, 2005; Sullivan, 1997). In contrast, opponents of same-sex marriage marshal a wide range of objections, often rooted in religious belief or historical precedent, to preserve the institution of marriage for opposite-sex couples. Legalizing same-sex marriage, they argue, threatens the sanctity of marriage, offends the moral beliefs of people opposed to homosexuality on religious grounds, and threatens the special social status afforded to the reproductive, heterosexual married couple (Baskerville, 2006; Gallagher, 2003). As well, not all lesbian- and gay-identified activists support same-sex marriage. Some of them argue that the institution itself is inextricably tied to the historical subordination of women and the institutionalization of a heterosexual norm founded on reproduction, monogamy, and the nuclear family (otherwise known as *heteronormativity*) (Warner, 1999; Yep, Lovaas, and Elia, 2003). They see civil marriage as an institution that reproduces inequality and an outdated Judeo-Christian model of a moral intimate life.

These arguments aside, the arc of political history in the modern West bends toward the expansion of civil rights. Younger generations in liberal-democratic societies support same-sex marriage much more strongly than their older counterparts do. The lesbian and gay movements continue to mobilize support for same-sex marriage. Accordingly, same-sex civil marriage provisions are likely to become more widespread over time—albeit not without a fight. The twenty-first century has already witnessed dramatic battles over matrimony, and it is likely to continue to do so.

## A BRIEF HISTORY OF CIVIL MARRIAGE AS A SOCIAL CONSTRUCTION

State-sanctioned or *civil* marriage has a thorny past, not least because, throughout history, it restricted *who* could marry, *whom* someone could marry, and the *age* at which a person could marry. In this sense, state-sanctioned marriage has never been a simple entitlement but, rather, one bound to national ideologies concerning class, social status, and citizenship. For instance, Ancient Roman law held that the daughter, granddaughter, or great-granddaughter of a senator could not marry a freedman, an actor, or a man whose father or mother was an actor (Gamsey and Saller, 1987).

Modern civil marriages have been no less restrictive. Besides laws prohibiting same-sex partners to marry, the most common laws restricting marriage involve race, along with gender-specific restrictions on number of spouses and age of marriage. In the early nineteenth century in the United States, for instance, the government prohibited African Americans from civil marriage. Moreover, concern over racial inter-mixing, or *miscegenation*, fuelled a variety of anti-miscegenation laws that made it illegal to marry a person of a different race throughout most of the United States for the greater part of the twentieth century. In fact, a federal decree dissolved the anti-miscegenation only in 1967.

Nazi Germany also institutionalized anti-miscegenation policies to ward off the prospect of "mongrelism." The Nazis first outlawed marriages between Jews and non-Jewish Germans, and then between Germans and Roma ("Gypsies") or blacks. Similarly, under apartheid in South Africa (1948–92), the *Prohibition of Mixed Marriages Act* prohibited marriages between whites and blacks, and between whites and "coloureds" (Asians). Both Nazi Germany and apartheid South Africa even criminalized interracial sexual intercourse. In Nazi Germany, it was punishable by imprisonment or death. In both countries, anti-miscegenation laws were repealed only after enormous political upheaval: the demise of the Nazi regime at the end of World War II and the collapse of apartheid in 1992.

Gender-specific restrictions on the number of spouses and age of marriage have also been common. For instance, in Utah before 1896, marriage was permissible between a man and a woman, or a man and *multiple* women, but never a woman and multiple men. Today, in many parts of the world, women are often encouraged—even coerced—to marry at a younger age than males. For instance, in Ethiopia, it is common for girls under 10 years of age to be married, whereas boys of this age are never married (Haberland, Chong, and Bracken, with Parker, 2005). In Afghanistan, a man must be 18 years old to marry, while a woman can marry at 16, and it is common for girls to be forced into marriage as young as 6 years of age (UNIFEM, 2008). Even in Ohio and Rhode Island, women can marry at 16 years of age, but men must be at least 18 years old.

The history of civil marriage, with its various and changing restrictions, provides sociological clues to the status of the institution of marriage more generally. First, sociologists view marriage as a social construction. The very fact that civil marriage has taken so many historical forms—including, according to some scholars, the inclusion of same-sex couples in early Ancient Rome (Boswell, 1980)—demonstrates the remarkable variety of ways a given society can organize the institution. Civil marriage is constructed out of the norms, values, and political commitments of a given society's policymakers and citizenry. It is not an institution with universal characteristics.

Second, sociologists note that civil marriage helps to institution-alize power relations. People who can marry enjoy advantages over those who cannot marry: certain tax breaks, healthcare benefits, and so on. Moreover, civil marriage serves an implicit legitimating function in that it regards certain two-person arrangements as superior to others and thereby worthy of legal support and protection. For instance, when the United States and Nazi Germany did not recognize interra-cial marriages, the state was making an explicit statement about which relationships were of value to the nation. Similarly, sociologists typi-cally regard the exclusion of same-sex couples from civil marriage as a form of structural disenfranchisement reflecting national sentiments that devalue gay and lesbian relationships.

Historically, marriage has involved an exchange between spouses' families or clans, in which brides were traded for goods or as payment for debts (Levi-Strauss, 1969). Today, marriage typically institution-alizes gender inequality by relegating women to the roles of mother, domestic worker, and sex provider (Friedan, 1963; Hartmann, 1981; Rich, 1980). Thus, civil marriage often has gender-specific conse-quences that tend to disadvantage women. For instance, the fact that women can marry at a younger age than men is less a privileged status than a legal mechanism facilitating the institutionalization of women's roles as mothers and wives. When young women and girls are married off to much older men, often without the girls' consent, a husband typically regards his wife as his property, and she faces a relatively poor quality of life (UNIFEM, 2008). Until the twentieth century, women usually married for economic reasons, and even in postindustrial societies they are socialized to believe that marriage and motherhood are essential for a happy, fulfilling life (Rich, 1980). Thus, although, say, Canadian women are rarely forced to marry, neither are they entirely free to reject marriage. And once married, the institution typically cements a woman's subordination to a man, charging her with the responsibilities of bearing and raising chil-dren, keeping the household clean and orderly, and tending to her husband's emotional and sexual needs—all without remuneration. In this sense, civil marriage is a *patriarchal* institution of social control that establishes the conditions under which women are systematically disadvantaged and men systematically advantaged.

A third and related stream of scholarly analysis, sometimes called *queer theory*, suggests that widespread civil marriage for same-sex married couples may usher in an era of *homonormativity*, involving the consolidation of new lifestyle norms for lesbians and gays centred on domesticity, monogamy, reproduction, and the nuclear family (Duggan, 2002; Valverde, 2006). From this point of view, same-sex marriage may render lesbians and gays indistinguishable from their heterosexual counterparts, with marriages organized by the institutionalization of husband-wife gender roles, an unequal division of labour, and a conservative sexual politics indebted to Judeo-Christian interpretations of what constitutes a moral intimate life. The traditionalization of formerly queer lifestyles is regarded as problematic to the extent that it stigmatizes or renders less valuable lesbian and gay relationships that are not ongoing, monogamous, married, and reproductive (Johnson, 1996). In this sense, homonormativity threatens to dissolve the critical edge of queer culture, which drew attention to the repressive nature of dominant norms around gender roles and sexual sensibilities in the first place.

Some queer theory scholars are also critical of same-sex marriage insofar as the institution may align with broader transformations in political economy, most notably the transition from the era of centralized, governmental concern for the social welfare of its citizenry to neoliberal reforms that place the burden of social welfare on individuals and private entities (Foucault, 1991). From this perspective, same-sex marriage provisions are less an indication of a nation's social inclusiveness than a consequence of neoliberal reform, whereby the state increasingly cedes the care of citizens to the citizens themselves (Whitehead, 2006). Thus, same-sex civil marriage allows lesbian and gay spouses to look to each other, rather than to the welfare state, for care, support, and financial stability (Lessard, 2007).

I now offer a brief analysis of demographic and interview data to provide a statistical and qualitative portrait of same-sex marriage in Canada today.

## A SNAPSHOT OF SAME-SEX MARRIAGE IN CANADA

Popular opinion among Canadians has only recently favoured same-sex marriage. In the first Gallup Canada survey of Canadian attitudes toward same-sex marriage in 1993, 76 percent of those surveyed opposed same-sex marriage. By 2000, that number had fallen to 48 percent.

In 2002, reflecting popular sentiment, the Ontario Supreme Court ruled that the opposite-sex stipulation for common-law marriage was unconstitutional. Similar decisions soon followed throughout Canada, and by 2004, courts in British Columbia, Quebec, Yukon, Manitoba,

Nova Scotia, Saskatchewan, Quebec, and Newfoundland and Labrador fell in line with the Ontario ruling. That same year, the federal government of Canada put forward a request to the Supreme Court of Canada to deliberate on whether the exclusion of same-sex couples from civil marriage was permissible under the Charter guarantees of equality (Nelson, 2008). The Supreme Court ruled that the constitutional definition of marriage did not exclude same-sex couples and that the federal government was within its constitutional rights to redefine marriage to include same-sex couples. Subsequently, Parliament passed Bill C-38, which redefined marriage in line with the Charter. The chief justice of the Supreme Court of Canada signed the Civil Marriage Act into law on July 19, 2005. Same-sex marriage became the law of the land, making Canada only the third country in the world to do so, after the Netherlands and Belgium.

The 2006 census counted 45 345 same-sex couples in Canada, 84 percent of them common law (cohabiting for one year or more) and 16 percent legally married (between July 19, 2005, and the census date) (Statistics Canada, 2008). About 55 percent of same-sex couples were male and 45 percent were female. Eight percent of same-sex couples had children living with them; of these, 82 percent were female couples and 18 percent were male couples. Interestingly, 14 percent of same-sex *married* couples reported having one or more children, compared with just 7 percent of same-sex *common-law* couples. This difference suggests that parenthood may promote civil marriage among same-sex couples—that is, same-sex couples who choose marriage over common-law status may be motivated to do so because they have children or want to have them. Another possibility is that civil marriage promotes parenthood among same-sex couples—marriage may encourage same-sex couples to want to have children. A third possibility is that both circumstances prevail.

The census is mute on such complex questions as whether and to what degree marriage promotes parenthood or vice-versa among same-sex couples. Until sociologists conduct more surveys and interviews of same-sex couples in Canada, we must rely partly on data from other countries to gain insight into many aspects of same-sex marriage. For example, one study found that nearly half of 812 married and registered gay and lesbian individuals in Denmark reported "legal rights" as the chief motivation for having their relationship formally recognized by the state (Eskridge and Spedale, 2006: 134). These legal rights include inheritance rights, tax breaks, and health and employment benefits. The Danish research also found that important intangible benefits derive from marriage, including increased commitment to the relationship, increased legitimacy, and increased social support from family and friends. Taken as a whole, these benefits seem to increase the durability of same-sex relationships.

My study of same-sex marriage in Ontario among 30 spouses, divided evenly by sex, yielded similar results (Green, 2008). Married spouses—men and women—were overwhelmingly surprised about the degree to which civil marriage conferred a sense of legitimacy and permanence to their relationship. In addition, some of these spouses found that the new sense of legitimacy extended beyond their immediate friends and families to the workplace. Co-workers and employers respected the individuals I interviewed—and their intimate relationships—more once they got married. In turn, marriage may produce conditions under which lesbian and gay employees can build better relationships with employers and clients. As one male respondent put it:

> There are honestly work benefits for us being married. When I interact with the partners (of the firm) in general ... it's probably more comfortable if they had us over for dinner. We could get invited as a couple. It's a different comfort aspect to it ... even how people interact and so on, even the signs of stability which is important to them when you get to the next level.... And in contrast to the gay village boys that are at work who might even be at the same career level (but) can't talk about their (partners) at all.... For sure, there's a difference, the whole perception of stability is different between the two. Because even small-talk wise, even if you were gay and kind of semi-in, semi-out at work, you just don't talk about your personal life.... And part of the way you develop rapport with anyone is to talk about your personal life: "Are you married and do you have kids?" It's the standard small-talk question.

Although civil marriage may provide same-sex couples with benefits similar to those enjoyed by heterosexual couples, marriage forms are unlikely to be identical in the two cases. In particular, civil marriage may not produce the same level of monogamy as opposite-sex marriages, especially among male couples. In the United States, nearly all married couples expect sexual exclusivity from their spouses, and the situation is probably not very different in Canada (Laumann, Gagnon, Michael, and Michaels, 1994). In contrast, the Danish study cited earlier found that although some married same-sex male couples embraced monogamy, some did not. In my study, 40 percent of the women and 60 percent of the men reported that they do not believe that marriage must always be monogamous. Some 47 percent of male respondents reported an *explicit* policy of non-monogamous practice, as did a lone female same-sex spouse. However, half of the respondents with explicitly monogamous marriages believed that it is acceptable for marriages to be non-monogamous, while about one in five monogamous males and one in 10 monogamous females remained open to the possibility that their own marriages might one day become non-monogamous. Most interestingly, nearly half of the men with openly non-monogamous marriages decided to have an open marriage *after* getting married. Although my small sample size does not permit generalizing to the broader population of same-sex marriages in Ontario, much less Canada as a whole, the findings are consistent with research on the sexual norms of gay men and gay subcultures (Weeks, Heaphy, and Donovan, 2001; Woolwine and McCarthy, 2005). According to one study, gay men do not articulate a single moral code around sexual fidelity but rather a kind of "morally pragmatic stand" arising in the historical context of anti-homosexual sentiment and associated stigmatization (Woolwine and McCarthy, 2005: 399–400). Put another way, becoming gay is marked by a process of "unlearning" heterosexuality, including the expectation of a heteronormative lifestyle (Herdt and Boxer, 1992). In this light, it is perhaps not surprising that same-sex married couples, historically excluded from the institution of civil marriage, would draw from their prior experience in constructing married life.

If norms and practices around marital fidelity are, on average, different for same-sex couples and their heterosexual counterparts, norms and practices around the domestic division of labour might also represent a departure. In fact, the literature suggests that same-sex couples in general reject "husband-wife" roles in favour of a more egalitarian model of domestic work founded on choice and interest (Blumstein and Schwartz, 1983; Dunne, 1997; Green, 2008; Patterson, 1995). Thus, almost all the same-sex couples in my Ontario study reported sharing equally in housework and child care. On occasion, housework was apportioned according to financial contributions; the partner who earned more money did less housework. However, in these circumstances, it was common for the partners to reverse roles when, for instance, the higher-earning partner lost his job or returned to school. In short, rather than accepting fixed husband-wife roles, the same-sex couples in my study negotiated domestic work on an ongoing basis determined by pragmatic concerns and personal interests. The heavy hand of patriarchy was nowhere to be found. In sum, although more research is needed to explore whether the division of domestic labour among same-sex couples is consistent with their self-reports, preliminary findings suggest that same-sex marriage may differ significantly from heterosexual marriages in this way, too.

## REFERENCES

Baskerville, Stephen. (2006). "The Real Danger of Same-Sex Marriage." *The Family in America* [Online Edition], *20* (5), 6. On the World Wide Web at http://www.profam.org/pub/fia/fia.2005.6.htm (retrieved 13 November 2008).

Blumstein, Philip and Pepper Schwartz. (1983). *American Couples: Money, Work and Sex.* New York: William Morrow.

Boswell, John. (1980). *Christianity, Social Tolerance and Homosexuality: Gay People in Western Europe from the Beginning of the Christian Era.* Chicago: University of Chicago Press.

Duggan, Lisa. (2002). "The New Homonormativity: The Sexual Politics of Neoliberalism." In Russ Castronovo and Dana Nelson, eds., *Materializing Democracy: Toward a Revitalized Cultural Politics* (pp. 175–94). Durham, NC: Duke University Press.

Dunne, Gillian A. (1997). *Lesbian Lifestyles: Women's Work and the Politics of Sexuality.* Toronto: University of Toronto Press.

Eskridge, William Jr. and Darren Spedale. (2006). *Gay Marriage: For Better or for Worse? What We've Learned from the Evidence.* New York: Oxford University Press.

Foucault, Michel. (1991). "Governmentality." In Graham Burchell, Colin Gordon, and Peter Miller, eds., *The Foucault Effect: Studies in Governmentality with Two Lectures by and an Interview with Michel Foucault* (pp. 87–104). Chicago: University of Chicago Press.

Friedan, Betty. (1963). *The Feminine Mystique.* New York: W.W. Norton and Company.

Gallagher, Maggie. (2003). "The Divorce Thing: A Diversion in the Marriage Debate." *National Review Online* (August 13). On the World Wide Web at http://www.dadi.org/divthing.htm (retrieved 13 November 2008).

Gamsey, Peter and Richard Saller. (1987). *The Roman Empire: Economy, Society and Culture.* Los Angeles: University of California Press.

Green, Adam Isaiah. (2008). "Same-Sex Marriage: Lesbian and Gay Spouses Marry Innovation and Change." Paper presented at the Annual Meeting of the American Sociological Association, August 1–4, Boston, Massachusetts.

Haberland, Erica, L. Chong, and Hillary J. Bracken, with Chris Parker. (2005). "Early Marriage and Adolescent Girls." *Youth Lens, 15* (August).

Hartmann, Heidi. (1981). "The Family as the Locus of Gender, Class and Political Struggle: The Example of Housework." *Signs: Journal of Women in Culture and Society, 6*, 366–94.

Hausknecht, Murray. (2003). "Gay Marriage and the Domestication of Sex." *Dissent* (Fall), 8–10.

Herdt, Gilbert and Andrew Boxer. (1992). "Introduction: Culture, History, and Life Course of Gay Men." *Gay Culture in America: Essays from the Field.* Boston: Beacon Press.

Johnson, Fenton. (1996). "Wedded to an Illusion: Do Gays and Lesbians Really Want the Right to Marry?" *Harper's* (November), 41–50.

Josephson, Jyl. (2005). "Citizenship, Same-Sex Marriage, and Feminist Critiques of Marriage." *Perspectives on Politics, 3*, 269–84.

Laumann, E.O., J.H. Gagnon, R.T. Michael, and S. Michaels. (1994). *The Social Organization of Sexuality: Sexual Practices in the United States.* Chicago: University of Chicago Press.

Lessard, Hester. (2007). "Family, Marriage, and Children: Neo-Liberal Choices and Conservative Values." Paper presented at the Annual Meeting of the Law and Society Association, July 25–28, Berlin, Germany.

Levi-Strauss, C. (1969). *The Elementary Structures of Kinship.* London: Eyre and Spottiswoode.

Nelson, Adie. (2008). "What Is a Family? New Challenges in Defining an Everyday Term." In Robert J. Brym, ed., *Society in Question*, 5th ed. (pp. 145–51). Toronto: Nelson.

Patterson, Charlotte, J. (1995). "Families of the Lesbian Baby-Boom: Parents' Division of Labour and Children's Adjustment." *Developmental Psychology, 31,* 115–23.

Rich, A. (1980). "Compulsory Heterosexuality and Lesbian Existence." *Signs, 5* (Summer), 631–60.

Statistics Canada. (2008). "Status of Same-sex Couples (3), Sex (3) and Presence of Other Household Members (5) for the Same sex Couples in Private Households of Canada, Provinces and Territories, 2006 Census—20% Sample Data." On the World Wide

Web at http://www12.statcan.ca/english/census06/data/topics
/RetrieveProductTable.cfm?Temporal=2006&PID=89034&GID=614
135&METH=1&APATH=3&PTYPE=88971&THEME=68&AID=&FREE
=0&FOCUS=&VID=&GC=99&GK=NA&RL=0&TPL=NA&SUB=&d1=0
(retrieved 13 November 2008).

Sullivan, Andrew. (1997). *Same-Sex Marriage. Pro and Con.* New York: Vintage.

UNIFEM. (2008). *United Nations Development Fund for Women: Afghanistan Fact Sheet 2008.* Kabul, Afghanistan: UNIFEM.

Valverde, Mariana. (2006). "A New Entity in the History of Sexuality: The Respectable Same-Sex Couple." *Feminist Studies, 32,* 155–63.

Warner, Michael. (1999). *The Trouble with Normal: Sex, Politics and the Ethics of Queer Life.* New York: Free Press.

Weeks, Jeffrey, Brian Heaphy, and Catherine Donovan. (2001). *Same-Sex Intimacies. Families of Choice and Other Life Experiments.* New York: Routledge.

Whitehead, Jaye. (2006). "Same-Sex Marriage as Risk Management." Paper presented at the Annual Meeting of the American Sociological Association, Montreal Convention Centre, August 11, Montreal, Quebec.

Woolwine, David, and E. Doyle McCarthy. (2005). "Gay Moral Discourse: Talking About Identity, Sex and Commitment." *Studies in Symbolic Interaction, 28,* 379–408.

Yep, Gust A., Karen E. Lovaas, and John P. Elia. (2003). "A Critical Appraisal of Assimilationist and Radical Ideologies Underlying Same-Sex Marriage in LGBT Communities in the United States." *Journal of Homosexuality, 45,* 45–64.

# Research Methods

# CHAPTER 20

# RESEARCH METHODS

**Neil Guppy**
UNIVERSITY OF BRITISH
COLUMBIA

To create this image, the 100 most frequently used words in this chapter were ordered alphabetically from left to right, and the font size for each word was made proportional to the frequency with which each word was used.

SOURCE: © Robert Brym.

- Science is one of several sources of knowledge. Like other sources of knowledge, it can be wrong. However, science uses methods of gathering theoretically relevant evidence that are designed to minimize error.

- Research methods are used by sociologists to gather evidence and test theories about recurring patterns of human activity. Underlying these techniques is a variety of assumptions about the nature of facts, objectivity, and truth.

- In comparison with the evidence available to natural scientists, an added complexity confronts social scientists: humans assign meaning to their actions, and interpreting meaningful action is complicated.

- Sociologists have devised many useful methods of obtaining evidence about the social world, including experiments, interviews, observational techniques, and surveys.

- Good sociological research adds to our knowledge of the social world, expanding opportunities and options by helping to solve social problems.

## INTRODUCTION

Social research involves systematic, purposeful study. The systematic nature of sociological research comes, in part, from the methods sociologists use. Fundamental to methods is the careful, ethical collection of evidence. However, only evidence relevant to theoretical ideas is useful. The purposeful structuring of sociological inquiry comes from asking theoretically informed questions. Systematic sociological study integrates sound theory with careful methods.

This chapter introduces you to the principles of research methods. I begin by outlining some basic assumptions involved in social science research, including assumptions about personal values or bias, the nature of facts, and the sources of knowledge. Next, I explain how the subject matter of the social sciences—people—differs from the objects of inquiry in the natural sciences (e.g., molecules). People studying people adds complexity to social research. This added complexity comes from people interpreting their own behaviour, and the behaviour of others, by trying to understand meanings. Methods of observation and questioning lie at the heart of social research, and I review the strengths and weaknesses of each of these approaches in the final section of the chapter.

## PERSPECTIVE

James Driskell and David Milgaard were convicted of murder. In 2005, 14 years after his conviction, after new DNA tests, James Driskell had his murder charges quashed. David Milgaard had to endure prison longer, but in July 1997, after 23 years in prison, he too was exonerated. Again, DNA testing was instrumental. Judges, juries, and prosecutors had weighed evidence that they believed demonstrated the guilt of these men. Circumstantial evidence, filtered by personal expectations and values, had led justice astray. Subjective judgments had seriously compromised these men's lives.

Gold (1998) claimed that "good science" exonerated Morin, but it was "not science that helped convict him." But what makes for "good science," the kind of science on which we can make serious decisions?

Wrongful convictions are rare. The criminal justice system minimizes such error through rules of evidence and presumptions of innocence. Likewise, science is organized to minimize error. Science is not perfect, however, and it is important not to put

Sociological theories were first proposed in the nineteenth century as secular accounts of rapid social change. By the early twentieth century, systematic methods for empirically testing hypotheses were being introduced.
SOURCE: Carol Wainio, *Untitled* (1985). Acrylic on canvas, 3300 × 5000. Photograph courtesy of the S. L. Simpson Gallery, Toronto. Reproduced with permission of the artist.

scientific practice on a pedestal, somehow immune to human foibles. Like all human activities, the social practice of science is influenced by subjectivity.

## SCIENCE AS A SOCIAL PRACTICE

Science needs subjectivity but it cannot be overwhelmed by it. Subjectivity is important to certain phases in the practice of science but detrimental to other phases. Understanding the complexities of scientific methods requires distinguishing between times when subjectivity is beneficial and times when it is not. But just what is subjectivity? Most people would agree that our personal values and expectations are a core part of subjectivity. Frequently, people separate the world into facts and values; the real and objective versus the personal and subjective.

But what appears to us as reality is filtered or screened. Reality exists, certainly—it is no figment of the imagination. However, our values and expectations filter reality. While the saying "what you see is what you get" has an intuitive appeal, we know the claim is false. It exaggerates. Other things, especially our expectations and values, affect what we see.

Here is an example of filtering. The Sun is real. It is no figment of our imagination. We commonly speak about "sunsets" and "sunrises." But these terms deceive. Although we have all watched a "sunset," the Sun does not set. Our language conditions us to think of a moving Sun, but Earth rotates around the Sun. Earth's spin creates the *illusion* of a moving Sun.

Being skeptical of my claim about a filtered reality is important. Values and expectations influence our perceptions of reality, but they do not completely determine what we see. This is a critical point. The *extent* to which values and expectations influence what we see is debatable, but that is a secondary point. The key point is that *if* our perceptions of reality can be affected by our values, *then* how can scientists ever know for certain that what they "see" is true? Put another way, if observation cannot be a rock-solid foundation of scientific knowledge, then how is the practice of science to be understood?

An important claim of this chapter is that reality does not exist as some neutral scientific judge. Pure observation does not rule supreme. To think of an individual scientist as a detached, arm's-length observer of the physical or social world, making observations to test ideas, is to profoundly misunderstand science. The scientific method is not a mechanical process of collecting facts to prove things. Science is a much more complex social activity, and the methods of scientists are designed in the face of such complexity.

Here is an illustration of how values and expectations may creep into scientific work.

Recall from your high-school biology classes the work of Gregor Mendel. Mendel was the father of genetics. He cross-fertilized varieties of pea plants and noted that inherited traits followed consistent numerical ratios (i.e., the expression of dominant and recessive genes over successive generations). These experiments, demonstrating landmark principles of heredity, remain controversial (see Orel, 1996). R. A. Fisher, while a Cambridge University undergraduate, demonstrated that Mendel's results seemed fabricated. The likelihood that Mendel produced results conforming so closely to his hunches about heredity was, Fisher showed, in the order of 1 in 30 000.

Mendel may have been lucky, producing possible but very unlikely results. Alternatively, Mendel, or his assistant, may have unconsciously misclassified some pea plants. Classifications made by Mendel were not clear-cut, so his experimental results may have been interpreted as favouring his preconceived ideas. In this vein, Fisher (1966 [1936]: 123) claimed that Mendel's results were a "carefully planned demonstration of his conclusion."

"Observer bias" (making unconscious mistakes in classifying or selecting observations) is now commonly discussed as a danger to good methodological procedure. Mendel did not clearly and publicly describe his procedures. His data are no longer available for reexamination. Although it is impossible to know exactly why his results came out as they did, his ideas about genetics have proven invaluable.

Good research methods are designed to minimize the types of errors that have been attributed to Mendel's experimental evidence. These methods do not eliminate the biasing effect that values and expectations have on scientific research. They do, however, seek to minimize their impact.

## MINIMIZING BIAS IN SOCIAL SCIENCE

Sociologists apply scientific practices to the study of human society. These practices incorporate several ways of reducing bias, especially the twin pillars of public (open) scrutiny and skeptical reasoning. Scientific ideas become provisionally accepted only after scrutiny by the scientific community. Individual scientists do not just proclaim a link between family background and children's school success or between HIV and AIDS; these links must be demonstrated by presenting research findings at scientific conferences, subjecting findings to peer review, and ensuring that research results can be replicated. The scientific community is organized to promote critical scrutiny.

Scrutiny is not enough, however. If the scrutiny is not rigorous and probing, then it is of little value. Scientific practice also encourages skeptical reasoning. New ideas are accepted only after others have critically examined them, only after they have withstood a barrage of questions from doubters. Examples of this doubting come from questions like this: Could something other than HIV cause AIDS? If HIV does cause AIDS, exactly how does the causal process work? Does HIV cause AIDS among all people? This process of doubting is built into the way science is conducted.

Scientists are also trained in methods of research designed to minimize the influence of their personal values and expectations on the results of their research work. They work to root out error in reasoning and observation. So, for example, scientists learn to collect and analyze information according to rules that reduce the risk that results will be affected by bias. Much of the latter part of this chapter focuses on these specific research techniques.

Science has prospered because of this healthy skepticism and public scrutiny. Both natural and social sciences have played a pivotal role in making our world a better place in which to live by helping to curtail malaria, improving the life chances of children with disabilities, and reducing gender inequity. Scientists are not infallible saints, however. The scientific community is not some sacred haven where only truth and enlightenment reign. Fraud and deceit are also part of science (Park, 2000).

It is also important to correct a possible misinterpretation about the role of values and expectations. I have portrayed these as "problems." This is too one-sided. Science would be substantially weaker, if not impotent, without values and expectations. Science is soaked through with individual judgments. Mendel's brilliance came from his expectation that dominant and recessive genes played a fundamental role in explaining inheritance. Mendel provided a new way of seeing the world, a new conceptual map for understanding.

Expectations and values are in tension within the scientific enterprise. Without them the spark of creativity and passion would be low, but with them we can be led to false conclusions (as judges and juries are occasionally misled). Put differently, objectivity and subjectivity each play an important role in science, including sociology. **Objectivity,** which is what courtroom judges and jurors strive for, stresses that observations should be free of the distorting effects of a person's values and expectations. Conversely, subjectivity is essential to change and innovation. Without people championing their own visions, we would have little creativity. A hallmark of science is its creativity. Mendel's was a beautiful solution to the mystery of inheritance, even if he may have been too exuberant in his experimental claims.

Science depends on both the creativity of new explanations and the assessment of whether these explanations are plausible. In sociology, this dual character resides in a division between theory (explanations of how the world works) and methods (ways of assessing the veracity of explanations).

This chapter is about assessing evidence. It explores how sociologists work within the rules of the scientific method. First, however, I contrast scientific knowledge with other forms of knowledge. The discussion moves next to the steps involved in the sociological research process. I then describe the main methods of gathering sociological data and the decisions that have to be made during the research process. Finally, I return in the conclusion to the role of subjectivity in research.

## SCIENTIFIC VERSUS NONSCIENTIFIC THINKING

To differentiate good and bad science, consider what characterizes scientific thinking. Before the eighteenth century and the rise of science, our ancestors knew many things about the world. Much of this was custom or common sense—when to plant, what to plant, where to plant. Religious knowledge held centre stage in community life. Stories of creation, of how we came to be on Earth, were powerful tales that gave coherence to peoples' lives. Religious doctrine and common sense remain powerful in many societies, but scientific ways of knowing have increasing authority in industrial nations.

What characterizes this scientific way of knowing? A key contribution came from Scottish philosopher David Hume (1711–76). He disputed the popular argument of his day that science begins with observation. Hume argued that no matter how many observations you make, you cannot infer your next observation. This is the *problem of induction*. Put

more graphically, no matter how many white swans you see, you cannot logically infer that all swans are white. However, observing one black swan is sufficient to refute the claim that all swans are white.[1] Hume was railing against Francis Bacon's claim that observation was the bedrock of science. For Hume, the collection of "facts" is useless unless you understand how to interpret them.

In Charles Dickens's *Hard Times*, Mr. Gradgrind demands facts: "What I want is Facts. ... Facts alone are wanted in life." Contrary to the popular saying, though, facts do not speak for themselves. Blue mould growing on spoiling food is a fact of life. It was only in 1928, however, that Alexander Fleming recognized this blue mould as a potent medical tool. Many people, perhaps even Mr. Gradgrind, had seen blue mould, but only Fleming understood it as penicillin. Science is not a collection of facts. However, among other things, it is a method of collecting facts.

Facts are bits of evidence, information that we can verify by using our senses. Because trillions of bits of human activity might be taken as facts, how do we select what should count as evidence? How do sociologists avoid idiosyncratic fact gathering? Sociological theory provides guidance for the hunting and gathering of facts. Evidence is gathered to test ideas, hunches, or theories. Only selected bits of human activity are used as evidence. Those selected bits are chosen because they relate to a sociologist's theory about how the world works.

In the twentieth century, Sir Karl Popper (1977 [1934]) improved this thinking with his ideas about falsification. As he claimed, observations refuting a well-conceived idea are always more important than evidence supporting or proving a theory (e.g., observing one black swan was more important than observing yet another white swan). For Popper, science does not start by gathering raw facts. It starts with a question or hunch, or in his words, a well-conceived conjecture.

Two core ideas about distinguishing scientific thinking from other ways of thinking have been presented earlier: public scrutiny and skeptical reasoning. Popper added the principles of testability and uncertainty. Testability is easy to understand. For an idea to be scientific it must have testable implications; it must be falsifiable (i.e., *if* an assertion is false, this can be demonstrated by evidence).

The concept of uncertainty may be more difficult to accept. Many people misunderstand science as a doctrine of certainty. As Park (2000: 39) puts it, "many people are uneasy standing on ... loose soil; they seek a certainty that science cannot offer." As Hume argued centuries before, observations cannot be the bedrock of science because of the problem of induction. Equally, however, science cannot proceed, as Popper correctly argued, without the possibility of observations that could refute a scientific claim. Observations based on well-reasoned methods can ferret out error and misunderstanding, although these same observations cannot guarantee universal truth or perfect certainty (see Box 20.1).

## NATURAL VERSUS SOCIAL SCIENCE

The scientific practices of chemists and sociologists share many elements. The research methods of both disciplines help in understanding and explaining why certain patterns emerge. Furthermore, values are important in this process because these values underlie the creative imagination so central to scientific puzzle solving. Values also have the potential to bias or distort observations, and both the natural and the social sciences guard against distortion. If the scientific method is defined as a set of practices or procedures for testing knowledge claims, then both chemists and sociologists are doing science.

There is, however, a profound difference between the subject matter of the natural and the social sciences: Bacteria don't blush. This phrase neatly captures the key distinction. Human beings are conscious and creative; we can think, act, reason, and decide. As sociologists, we study "ourselves"— that is, our contemporaries and our ancestors. Bacteria, having no knowledge of social norms, do not blush when exposed to the beam of an electron microscope. Bacteria cannot think, act, reason, and decide; they cannot consciously control their surroundings or reactions in the same way human beings can.[2]

Perhaps the single most important difference is that, unlike chemists, sociologists study **meaningful action**—that is, activities that are meaningful to the people involved. For example, bacteria may not blush when studied, but people often react self-consciously when they know they are being observed. To study love, friendship, or charisma depends on learning something about the meanings people ascribe to actions. This has advantages and disadvantages. Unlike chemists, sociologists can ask questions of the people whom we study (bacteria don't talk either). But this advantage can also be a disadvantage. Interpreting people's answers is not easy.

---

**BOX 20.1**    **SEEING SCIENCE SOCIOLOGICALLY**

One of the most influential academic books of the twentieth century was Thomas Kuhn's (1962) *The Structure of Scientific Revolutions*. Before Kuhn, many people held a "brick-building" conception of science. They thought that individual scientists contributed to building a structure called scientific knowledge, one brick at a time. As scientific knowledge accumulated, the structure became taller and sturdier.

Kuhn challenged this view on several fronts. First, he held that science developed through contributions from a community of scholars who use "paradigms" as guiding tools about how the world is organized (Mendelian genetics is such a paradigm). Paradigms guide questions and answers. Evidence not fitting a paradigm is ignored. However, if anomalous evidence accumulates, a "scientific revolution" results. Scholars opt for a new guiding paradigm. The transition from Newton's mechanics to Einstein's relativity illustrates a paradigm shift, or a scientific revolution (Kleppner and Jackiw, 2000).

Second, Kuhn proposed a discontinuous view of scientific progress. The community of scholars did not keep building the Newtonian structure but shifted to a new structure defined by the Einsteinian paradigm. This discontinuous view of scientific progress also influenced debates about truth. Earth as the "third rock from the Sun" we now hold as a fundamental truth. But our ancestors were equally convinced that Earth was the universe's central rock. In the future, will our "third rock" conception seem equally odd? Kuhn's view suggests that truth is contextual. A new paradigm establishes a new context, showing us that beliefs we once held to be true were naive or misleading (like a setting Sun).

Finally, the argument about community was sociologically compelling. In Kuhn's hands, the practice of science was not understood as individual scientists ruthlessly questioning all ideas. To the contrary, paradigms provided a set of convictions about how the world was ordered. With faith in a paradigm, a community of scholars searched for what they were convinced existed. Paradigms had a disciplining effect, focusing attention on a delimited set of questions and answers. Notice also that Kuhn emphasized that scientific change was not gradual, but sudden (revolutionary) and that the change was organized or predictable (structured).

Because of this difference in subject matter, sociologists have developed an array of methods to help in understanding and explaining human activity. Since asking questions has advantages and disadvantages, good sociological research either employs a variety of ways to ask questions or relies on observational techniques to aid understanding and explanation.

# METHODS OF SOCIAL RESEARCH

## EXPLANATION

Sociologists have shown repeatedly that the years of schooling people receive is strongly influenced by family background. Children raised in poverty tend not to go as far in school as do children from upper-class families. Although this research demonstrates a link between family background and educational attainment, this link is, as I have reported it, descriptive, not explanatory. I have offered no reason *why* this relationship between family origin and educational destination exists. It is true that I have noted a potential cause (family background) and an effect (years of schooling), but I have failed to provide any mechanisms through which this implied causal process might operate. An **explanation** would be judged adequate only if it could show how family background actually influences educational outcomes.

The mere association or correlation between social origin and educational destination does not prove causality. The relationship between smoking and lung cancer is a good example of the rule that *correlation does not prove causation*. Smoking has long been linked to lung cancer, but only in the past few decades have we learned more about the causal mechanisms underlying this correlation. Cigarette companies, especially, have argued that the presumed connection was a **spurious relationship,** meaning that something other than smoking caused lung cancer (see Box 20.2). Accumulated evidence and more precise understanding and observation of the underlying modes of transmission have established that the original correlation is causal.

We might try to explain the link between family and schooling in several ways (Davies and Guppy, 2010). An obvious factor is money. Although public schooling is free, costs are incurred for field trips, tutoring, international tours, postsecondary education, and a host of other events. Children living in poverty may remain in school for fewer years than their upper-class peers because of these costs (and they may seek employment sooner to help with family income).

Money seems to be a partial explanation for the link, but other factors may be at work as well. Many skills and values taught in school may be more readily grasped by children from upper-class families, not because these children are smarter than are children living in poverty, but because the home environments of the children may expose them to different skills and values. The classroom culture may be more like the culture in upper-class homes (e.g., abstract word games are valued, reading and music are prized) and these children may therefore be advantaged.

The first explanation is largely about money and material resources. The policy implications of this explanation point to eliminating or reducing the costs of schooling. This has been accomplished in large measure in Canada. However, even when the costs of postsecondary education have also been reduced (e.g., in Quebec), social-class disparities in educational attainment remain. The second explanation points to cultural factors in the home (e.g., reading) as a reason for the family–school link. This explanation has influenced policies related to compensatory education, such as Head Start and After Four, educational programs designed to help disadvantaged children by giving them educational enrichment (see also Guppy and Davies, 2009).

The mechanisms by which causes have effects are essential for adequate explanation (Gross, 2009). You might think of these mechanisms as the social "cogs and levers" greasing the wheels that link causes with effects. Furthermore, multiple causes are involved in social-scientific explanations; a single unitary cause rarely provides a sufficient explanation. Sociologists search for the multiple factors that can help explain some particular state of affairs. So, in the family–school example, although only two explanations for the link are mentioned here, other explanations may also be tested and refined as sociologists attempt to see how greater equality of educational opportunity might be attained.

## UNDERSTANDING

Sociologists must not be content merely to offer explanations for why a particular relationship exists. These explanations are often sterile unless they also address the meaningfulness of human activity. People make the social world happen, and in doing so they give meaning to their actions and to the actions of

## BOX 20.2    CORRELATION AND CAUSATION

Where fires cause much damage, many fire trucks gather. This is a correlation; a lot of damage tends to go along with many trucks, while minimal damage tends to draw only a few trucks. But this "truck and damage" correlation does not prove that fire trucks cause fires. Consider Figure 20.1. The curved, double-headed arrow depicts the correlation between the amount of damage and the number of fire trucks. The single-headed, straight arrows show the direction of causation. The size of the fire is a common prior cause of both other variables (number of trucks and amount of damage).

**FIGURE 20.1**    AN EXAMPLE TO ILLUSTRATE THAT CORRELATION DOES NOT PROVE CAUSATION

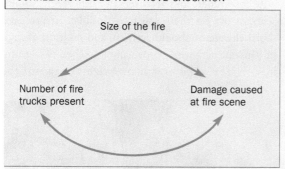

Causality is controversial because it often involves something we cannot observe directly. For example, no one can see lung cancer being caused by smoking. We infer that conclusion from assembled evidence that fits with theoretical conjecture.

Here is another example. Women living in poverty typically eat less nutritious meals and consequently are more likely than better-off women are to have premature babies. But not all women living in poverty have premature babies. There is a correlation between poverty levels and the incidence of premature births, and nutrition level has been identified as a key causal mechanism. Notice, however, that living in poverty does not guarantee premature births. Living in poverty only raises the probability that a mother will have a premature baby.

In a **causal relationship**, a change or variation in one thing produces a change or variation in another. If four basic conditions are met, causality may be established.

First, two variables must be associated or correlated. Consider again our two variables—the likelihood of premature births and poverty. Premature births must be more likely to occur among poor women than among women who are not poor if a causal relationship exists.

Second, the cause, or independent variable (poverty level), must precede the effect, or dependent variable (premature births), in time. (For more on independent and dependent variables, see p. 502.) Establishing that a woman is poor (or not) while she is pregnant confirms the causal ordering or temporal sequencing of the variables.

Third, the original association must not disappear once the effects of other variables on the dependent variable are examined. We need to verify that we have not made a false inference. Does the causal process really go from poverty to poor diet to premature babies?

Could it be that stress, and not poverty, is the causal agent? It may be that poor women are under more stress and that stress, not poverty, increases the likelihood of premature births. The initial causal relation between poverty and premature births would be spurious if stress was determined to be the operative factor (poverty may be correlated with stress, of course, but stress may still be the real causal agent).

Finally, we must offer a theoretical account of how one variable causes another. We must illustrate the social mechanism(s) through which causation operates. This theoretical reasoning also enables us to establish which variables are important to examine when we test to see whether a causal relation might be spurious. In the example, we theorize that poverty affects nutrition, which in turn affects the likelihood of premature birth.

others. A failure to address these meanings would leave sociology underdeveloped.

It is no simple matter, however, to understand what someone or some group means by their actions or utterances. One way to think about **understanding** is as follows. The first time I saw a cricket match, I could not fathom what was happening. To the extent that I have come to understand this complex social activity, I have learned *how to proceed with the activity*. To understand a cricket

match means being able to participate fully in the activity, knowing what others mean by their actions and utterances, and knowing how others will interpret our actions and utterances.

A fundamental social process, called "taking the role of the other," nicely captures this idea of understanding. By imagining yourself in another person's role, you come to appreciate someone else's point of view. You come to understand, to reflect on, that person's ideas and issues. I do not mean that you must become Caesar to understand him; that would be impossible. Instead, sociologists focus on the web of relations in which people interact, paying attention to how people understand and interpret the views of others. They pay attention to "the definition of the situation," to the meanings of the people involved.

Erving Goffman's work in an insane asylum (as it was called then) is a good illustration of sociological understanding (Goffman, 1961). Goffman was interested in how the patterns of social activity in the asylum were organized. He came to see the mental hospital from the patients' point of view. By dispensing with the medical categories and scientific labels assigned to individual patients, Goffman began to understand the ways in which patients worked cooperatively to produce a coherent social structure. He learned to appreciate how the patients defined the routine activities of the asylum and how they coped with institutional procedures that denied them privacy and stripped them of their personal identities (e.g., by issuing institutional clothing and confiscating personal objects).

Goffman (1961: 129) also learned about what he calls the "careers" of patients with mental illnesses: "Persons who become mental-hospital patients vary widely in the kind and degree of illness that a psychiatrist would impute to them. ... But once [in treatment] they are confronted by some importantly similar circumstances and respond to these in some importantly similar ways. Since these similarities do not come from mental illness, they would seem to occur in spite of it." Although social life on the "inside" might seem unique or even bizarre at first, Goffman argues that anyone, patient or researcher, would, in time, come to find it much like many other communities in which he or she has participated, possessing an identifiable social organization and rhythm of activity.

Returning to the education example, explanations of high-school dropout rates that ignore the attitudes and values of the people who drop out are one-sided. An appreciation of the experiences of people who drop out is essential to a more complete account of the schooling process. Especially important here is the resistance of students to authority, often expressed through music and clothing. This resistance is not some idiosyncratic expression of random individuals, but represents part of a youth subculture that must be understood by anyone who wants to alter the schooling process to make it a better environment. How young school resisters define the situation of schooling is important to a full appreciation of dropping out.

Understanding and explanation work together. Although explanations of dropping out that ignore student values are deficient, merely reporting the stories of young resisters would be equally vacuous. A full appreciation of dropping out, or of any other social activity, requires both understanding and explanation. Often, different researchers pursue these two activities and their combined results contribute to fruitful research programs leading to social change.

Is it enough to just understand and explain? Most sociologists are progressive in the sense of wanting to see a better, more just world—a world with less human suffering and misery. Should sociologists be both researchers and activists? Put differently, should scholars act on their research findings to promote social change or should activism and political change be separate activities? Especially for scholars working in such areas as poverty, human rights or racism, the

Explanations of high-school dropout rates that ignore the attitudes and values of those who drop out are one-sided. An appreciation of the experiences of students who drop out is essential to a more complete account of the schooling process.
SOURCE: © iStockphoto.com/Rosmarie Gearhart.

urge to promote social change is pressing. Feminist scholars have been particularly adept at bridging the divide between research and social change advocacy.

Feminist research has done so by engaging in scholarship that disrupts traditional or accepted knowledge. Sociologists often ask questions from the vantage point of those on the margins of society (for example, the poor, the dispossessed, the victim). Feminist research has been pivotal in challenging traditional knowledge that excludes women, ignores discrimination or accepts the status quo as legitimate and proper. Further, feminist methodology has stressed minimizing harm and raising ethical standards. Academic feminism pushed against traditional social science that had helped to sustain the oppression of women by focusing exclusively on men or by examining issues of interest only to men (DeVault, 1996).

## TECHNIQUES OF SOCIAL RESEARCH

Sociologists have developed a variety of techniques for gathering evidence. I will review three of the most important: experiments, survey research, and observational studies. As you read my accounts of research procedures, keep asking yourself these questions: How do sociologists go about developing insights about, or knowledge of, the social world? How do they come to know what they claim to know? What methods do they use and how believable are the results generated by these methods?

### EXPERIMENTS

**Experiments** are the hallmark of scientific research and are commonly, though inaccurately, equated with science itself. Experiments are useful because they enable researchers to isolate causes and measure their effects. By no other method can researchers determine causation so precisely. An example is the best way to illustrate the point.

The shape of families has changed recently. At one time, the family was understood as a married couple—a man and a woman—with children. No longer. Single parent families have become more prevalent recently, as have common-law unions and same-sex couples. Nathan Lauster and Adam Easterbrook (2011) examined how successful people in these new types of families were in securing rental housing and, if they encountered resistance in renting, what the likely source of the resistance was.

A landlord could choose to rent to people in some types of family and not others. Landlords might judge new types of families as morally suspect or as violating the traditional family norms of existing tenants. Landlords also face the risk of damage to their premises and failure to pay rent, and they may judge people in new family types as riskier, less stable, or more likely to miss rent payments. These perceptions might vary with a landlord's previous experience with similar types of families, so there may be neighbourhood effects. That is, in neighbourhoods where people in new family forms are already renting, there might be less discrimination than in neighbourhoods where the traditional family form still dominates.

To explore these questions, Lauster and Easterbrook (2011) chose to conduct a field experiment. They wanted to compare the ability of people in different family configurations to find rental accommodation. They also wanted to know if their ability varied by neighbourhood.

The field experiment worked as follows. In Vancouver, such websites as craigslist.org and kijiji.com carry the largest volume of rental advertisements. The researchers wrote an email inquiry in which the only information they varied was the type of family that was inquiring and the size of the unit required. The family types were as follows: male-female couple; male-male couple; female-female couple; female adult, male son; male adult, male son. Five versions of the scripted email, with appropriate variations, read as follows:

> Hi, my name is [Matt/Melissa/Kate/Kevin], and [appropriate form; e.g., my son and I] saw your listing for a [#] bedroom [apartment/ suite] on [website]. We are non-smokers and don't have any pets [or kids, if appropriate]. I'm a teacher and [she's/he's enrolled in a professional program; or he's enrolled in third grade]. Please let us know if the [apartment/ suite] is still available and if we can view it. Thanks, [names of two people].

The scripted emails were sent to landlords who had advertised a one- or two- bedroom unit for less than $1700/month. Because the family forms existing in a neighbourhood might influence responses, they targeted nine different neighbourhoods. For example, they reasoned that in neighbourhoods with higher concentrations of same-sex couples, discrimination against same-sex couples would likely be lower than in neighbourhoods where traditional male-female couples predominated. By including nine neighbour-hoods, the researchers were also able to see whether such neighbourhood factors as percentage of gay couples or lone-parent families, population under 15, and average monthly rent affected their findings.

The scripted emails ensured that all landlords received identical inquiries, save for the change in type of family. Sending emails asking about every one- or two- bedroom rental property advertised on a given day was ruled out because that would lead to a possible duplication of requests to the same landlord. Also, the experimenters wanted to code details of each advertisement, such as location, rent, and size, so they used a randomly selected set of advertisements. They also wanted to stagger their requests over two weeks to ensure no bias crept in from differences in the day of the week they inquired.

The results showed that heterosexual couples and female couples received the most positive responses (about 62 percent each), while male couples received positive responses only about 50 percent of the time. Single parents, either mother or father, received positive responses about 54 percent of the time.

Lauster and Easterbrook (2011) were interested in one other thing. They wanted to know if the likeli-hood of a positive response to the email sent for each family type varied by neighbourhood. For example, did male couples also receive significantly lower positive responses to their inquiries when the rental units were in traditionally gay neighbourhoods? The answer was no. As expected, male couples were more likely to receive positive responses when the email was directed to rental units in an area where male couples lived. While, overall, male couples experienced the greatest rental discrimination, it was lessened in neighbourhoods where many gay men already lived (although even in those neighbourhoods gay men were disadvantaged relative to heterosexual couples).

Female couples did not experience rental dis-crimination. Why not? Lauster and Easterbrook (2011) suggest two possible explanations. First, land-lords could prefer women tenants, and this prefer-ence may override any negative views about family type. Second, perhaps landlords could accept female couples as an acceptable family form. The authors note that lesbian women experience other forms of discrimination and, in that light, it is surprising that they don't experience rental discrimination.

By dissecting the Lauster and Easterbrook (2011) experiment, we can examine more carefully several key research design features. The researchers began with a **hypothesis**—an unverified but testable knowledge claim. They hypothesized that "type of family" would affect "rental discrimination," with heterosexual cou-ples more likely to receive favourable responses than the other family types.

To test this hypothesis, Lauster and Easterbrook (2011) examined the relationship between two **variables.** A variable is a measurable concept that can have more than one value. Age is a concept we use in referring to how long someone has lived. For new-borns, we measure age in weeks or months, but for everyone else it is measured in years. In the language of research, Lauster and Easterbrook were interested in how type of family, their **independent variable** (the hypothesized cause), influenced rental discrimi-nation, their **dependent variable** (the hypothesized effect). Lauster and Easterbrook used five different conditions or "treatments" for their independent vari-able: heterosexual couple, male couple, female couple, single mother, and single father. They reasoned that the likelihood of a positive response to the email about renting depended on which type of family the email was from. The dependent variable had three values: a positive response (yes, please come and see the unit), no response, or a negative response (rented already).

How did Lauster and Easterbrook (2011) know that only type of family and not another factor, such as a household size or social class, influenced rental dis-crimination? They were confident in their conclusion because, by design, they know that landlords received fictitious emails where only the type of family differed. By randomly sending the email to different landlords and referencing one of the five family conditions, they could compare how landlords responded, knowing that family type was the only factor that could have affected landlord responses. Household size was identical in each email. Social class was also constant since the ref-erence was always to a teacher. It is true that rental units differed in price, and they could have been one- or two-bedroom units, but the researchers accounted for differences of this sort in their statistical analysis.

Random assignment or **randomization** lies at the heart of experimental design. Using a random procedure, such as flipping a coin or rolling a die, researchers assign people in an experiment to an experimental condition based on chance. If the coin comes up heads, a person is placed in experimental condition one; if the coin comes up tails, the person is assigned to condition two. Although in Lauster and Easterbrook's (2011) case, landlords differed by sex, age, income, and so on, the emails went to an approximately equal number of women and men, people with different annual incomes, and so on. The experiment was designed to ensure that the landlords receiving each type of email constituted a randomized group. Lauster and Easterbrook used this random assignment process to ensure that the only difference among the five conditions was family type.

Sociology experiments of the type conducted by Lauster and Easterbrook (2011) are relatively rare, largely because many social processes that interest sociologists are not amenable to experimentation. Ethical and practical problems also limit the use of experiments (see Box 20.3).

Laboratory experiments have been used in sociology although they have become less common in recent decades. A good example of a recent lab experiment is one undertaken by Martha Foschi and Jerilee Valenzuela (2008). They investigated the extent to which hiring decisions for junior engineering positions were influenced by the sex of the applicant and the sex of the decision maker. To do this, they had university students rate application files in which the applications were said to be from a short list (and

hence very similar). The files contained a standard application form, a résumé, and an academic transcript. Precise details in the files differed but were nearly identical in terms of average grades across all courses, level of work experience, type of education, and so forth. The key difference was the sex of the applicant. Each person received two applications and were asked to choose the best candidate.

Foschi and Valenzuela (2008) found no difference between female and male applicants, nor any difference in outcomes whether the rater was male or female. That is, no bias toward male applicants being preferred occurred and indeed women raters tended to favour the female applicant. They conclude that (2008: 1034) "the social climate has been changing towards equality regarding views of men's and women's competence. This is particularly the case in experiments with university students as subjects, where recent work reveals that decisions do not always favor men."

As they note, using university students likely influences the results because people who are more educated tend to be more liberal in orientation. Also, university students might have been suspicious of the

---

**BOX 20.3 ETHICS IN SOCIAL RESEARCH**

Three groups share an interest in the conduct of sociological research: the sociological investigator, the people being observed or questioned, and the members of the larger society who enable such research to occur. Sociologists have a self-interest in their own research, but it is imperative that proper weight also be given to the interests of research participants and the public. Although primary responsibility for the rights and welfare of both participants and the public must reside with the sociologist as researcher, the self-interest of the sociologist requires that some arm's-length body review research designs and procedures to ensure the protection of all.

What are the typical risks involved in social research? These are of two broad types: risks to individuals and risks to communities or social groups. Understanding the first type—individual harm—is fairly straightforward. Social research can cause harm by asking people threatening questions that cause individual trauma (e.g., asking Aboriginal peoples about their memories of residential schools). Appreciating the second type—collective harm—may be less obvious. The results of social research can harm communities or groups by, for example, reinforcing stigmas and stereotypes (e.g., people living in poverty smoke more) or supporting

policies that help some groups at the expense of others. Who sponsors the sociologist's research is an important issue, especially in this latter context. Here, too, relations between political advocacy and scientific research come to the fore.

Ethically responsible research must minimize threats or risks. Informed consent is key. Researchers must ensure that people not only consent but that they also consent after knowing what the research entails. Very occasionally in sociological research, deception is involved. This occurs in cases where the research requires that people not know exactly what is being studied (on the grounds that such knowledge may lead them to change their behaviour or lead them to respond in certain ways). For example, if you tell respondents your research is about the environment and then ask them what the most important problem is facing their region, many more will respond "environment" than if you did not provide this initial cue (Urmetzer, Blake, and Guppy, 1999).

In discussing a range of research projects in the remainder of the chapter, I will comment further on issues of ethics. An insightful sociological analysis of ethics is also provided by Kevin Haggerty (2004), who discusses "ethics creep" as a form of surveillance.

experiment and tried hard not to show any gender bias. They might have thought that this was a "study" and therefore they might not have acted naturally (but similar experiments in earlier decades did reveal male preference). As with any research, we must be cautious in generalizing the results. The latter problem is expressed technically as the issue of **external validity,** or the degree to which experimental findings remain valid in different contexts. External validity is often low; relationships discovered in experiments, especially lab experiments, do not always hold in more "real-life" settings. There is therefore good reason to be cautious about generalization. The field experiment, conducted in a natural as opposed to a laboratory setting, reduces the problem of artificiality. However, Lauster and Easterbrook (2011), in their field experiment could explore only a limited range of family types and family size, which was a complicating factor. They chose to keep family size constant at two, and so an alternative explanation for some of their findings might be the presence of childern as opposed to it being a single parent that influenced their results.

One field experiment that investigated the extent of job discrimination faced by people of different ethnic backgrounds found that whites had a 3-to-1 advantage over blacks in job offers.
SOURCE: © iStockphoto.com/DWlabs Inc.

As mentioned earlier, when people know they are being studied, they often become self-conscious. The very fact of being studied may influence their behaviour. This was demonstrated in productivity experiments conducted by Roethlisberger and Dickson (1939) at the Western Electric Company's Hawthorne factory. They found that productivity (the dependent variable) increased when they brightened the lighting but also when they dimmed the lighting. The researchers realized that people worked harder whenever the research team was studying them. Productivity increased in response to the researchers' presence, not because of changes they introduced. Social scientists have subsequently used the term **Hawthorne effect** when referring to changes in people's behaviour caused by their awareness of being studied. Sociologists have had to develop other techniques for collecting sociological evidence to avoid some of the problems associated with experiments.

## SURVEY RESEARCH

The social survey is the primary means of collecting social science evidence. Researchers collect information through surveys by asking a sample of people identical questions. Political pollsters, market researchers, labour unions, governments, and university researchers all rely heavily on survey-based knowledge. Survey research is useful because it provides a method of systematically comparing answers to identical questions from a large sample of people, and it allows researchers to generalize the results to the larger population from which the sample was chosen. Questions can be posed either on a **self-administered questionnaire** or through a personal **interview.** Increasingly, the Internet is used as a way to conduct surveys (Brym and Lenton, 2001).

Rhonda Lenton (1990) used survey research to investigate parents' aggression toward their children. Because of strong taboos against child abuse, getting honest answers to questions about abusive behaviour is very difficult. The privacy surrounding child discipline makes observation or experiments inappropriate. Furthermore, asking blunt questions about "smacking your child" is unacceptable. Many alcoholics deny they have a drinking problem, just like many child abusers think of themselves as "strict disciplinarians." Parents use different strategies to influence their children, and Lenton wanted to examine the full range of this behaviour. Therefore, she chose to field a survey in which parents could be questioned by experienced and trained interviewers. She included questions covering an array of child–parent interactions, from praising and positive modelling through withholding privileges and love to spanking, slapping, and hitting.

A key problem facing Lenton was whether her questions about aggression and discipline would really measure child abuse. Child abuse is a theoretical concept. You and I may use the same term to mean different things. What types of maltreatment ought to be considered child abuse? Lenton (1990: 159) defines child abuse as "any act, excluding sexual mistreatment [which she separated as sexual abuse], carried out by a parent ... that has the intention of, or is perceived as having the intention of, hurting a child." Lenton wanted to include as "abuse" any act that a parent understands may hurt the child. To measure abuse, she asked parents whether they had done any of the following, ever, and in the past year: yell at a child, ridicule a child, withdraw emotionally from a child, hit a child with an object, withhold food from a child, and 24 other actions. Do these items provide an indication of what Lenton defines as child abuse? That is, are these valid indicators? **Validity** refers to accuracy or relevancy. Lenton's measurement of child abuse is valid to the degree that the items she uses as measures of abuse actually measure abuse as she defines it theoretically.

Lenton (1990) interviewed each parent and child separately. Each family member was asked to complete a child-discipline questionnaire, on which each of the 29 abuse items was listed. This sheet was completed privately and handed to the interviewer in a sealed envelope. By comparing the responses of all family members, Lenton could determine the consistency with which abuse was reported by different family members. This gave her confidence in the **reliability** of her measure. **Measurements** are reliable if they are consistent or repeatable. If different measures or indicators of the same concept give similar results, the measurements are reliable or, in other words, internally consistent.

Lenton (1990) faced another problem. She needed to find families with children. No publicly available list of such families exists. Lenton selected a random sample of Toronto families from the telephone directory. After first phoning to ensure that children lived in the household, members of the research team visited each eligible address to ask for permission to interview parents and children.

Surveys always involve **sampling.** Lenton's research team could never have interviewed all Toronto families (a complete enumeration of all families would be a *census*), nor would the expenditure of time and money have been efficient. Although the entire population could not be interviewed, it is this larger population about which Lenton wanted to draw conclusions. To use a different example, in doing research on urban household waste, interviewing all city dwellers is both unnecessary and impractical, even though the intention might be to use survey results to help design city policy. Information obtained from a subset of the population, the *sample*, is used to represent the views and characteristics of everyone. Samples selected by using rules of chance or probability provide random samples. Samples must represent the larger population from which they are drawn. For example, one or even a few kindergarten classes cannot be taken to represent all kindergarten classes, because not all kindergarten classes are alike. Therefore, if we want to generalize about social processes common to all kindergarten classes, we need to select a number of classes for study and we must know the probability of selecting each class.

Exactly how many kindergarten classes or, more generally, how many units must be included in a sample is a complex question. How many families should Lenton (1990) have selected? The precise answer depends mainly on the amount of variation or heterogeneity in the population and the degree of accuracy required in the study's conclusions. If you need very accurate results, you need a larger sample. Likewise, if the population is very variable, you need a larger sample to reflect that heterogeneity adequately. In studies of the Canadian electorate, very accurate forecasts of voting can be achieved with a random sample of about 1200 voters.

Selecting samples is not as easy as it might seem. How would you go about selecting a random sample of students in your faculty or program? Distributing questionnaires in classes would be one method, but many students do not attend every class. Students who attend regularly are, by definition, different from those who attend infrequently. A sample of students present in classes would therefore be biased. Using email addresses might seem practical, but many students do not let schools know their working addresses or filter Internet surveys out as junk mail. Registration lists give an approximation of the student population, but these lists are never perfect. Students drop out as the term progresses, while others change their address and phone number. If you were studying student retention or student financial needs, the people who might be hardest to find might be the very people to whom it would be most important to speak. Even with this severe limitation, however, student lists maintained by the registrar might be the best alternative available. The list from which a sample is selected is called the sampling frame. This frame must come as close as possible to including everyone in the population.

As noted, surveys that use the Internet have become popular. The same basic principles of design hold, and for targeted populations, such as university students or members of an organization, this can be an effective way of collecting data. However, for general populations, sampling issues are frequently a problem since sampling frames are next to impossible to establish. The result, then, is survey respondents who are volunteers, and these volunteers are not necessarily representative of the larger population. This creates the problems of external validity noted earlier.

Market-research firms use mainly telephone interviews in conducting their surveys. These firms usually rely on *random-digit-dialling* procedures to establish random samples. They select "banks" (i.e., lists) of working telephone numbers (e.g., 902-424-79xx), and let the computer randomly dial the last, or the last two, numbers. This method, used by Statistics Canada in some of its surveys, provides a random sample of households, including households with unlisted telephone numbers. Two important refinements are used. First, some households have more than one telephone number, increasing their chances of inclusion. Statistics Canada asks respondents how many working telephone numbers there are in a house so that it can correct for this small bias. Second, the person who is interviewed in the house must also be randomly selected (because, for example, women are more likely than men are to answer the phone even when both are at home). One popular strategy for obtaining a random sample of

Researchers collect information through surveys by asking people in a representative sample a set of identical questions. People interviewed on a downtown street corner do not constitute a representative sample of a country's adults. That is because the sample does not include people who live outside the urban core, underestimates the number of seniors and people with disabilities, does not take into account regional diversity, and so on.

SOURCE: © Janine Wiedel Photolibrary/Alamy.

household members is to interview the person who had the most recent birthday.

Telephone surveys require that people be interviewed. An alternative to interviewing is the use of self-administered questionnaires, which can be either mailed or delivered to members of the sample. Mailing questionnaires to people and handing them out to groups (e.g., students in a classroom, patients in a clinic) are less expensive than interviewing.

However, questionnaires lack the personal touch of interviewing. In an interview, misunderstandings can be clarified and responses can be expanded on. This cannot be done with self-administered questionnaires. Questionnaires work best with what are called close-ended questions, like those on multiple-choice exams, to which there are a limited number of set answers. Interviews, especially face-to-face as opposed to telephone interviews, allow for more open-ended questions, in which respondents can be encouraged to elaborate to ensure that they are properly understood. Lenton (1990), for example, chose to use personal interviews because she thought that the subject matter was best handled with face-to-face interaction. Notice, however, that she incorporated a short questionnaire on disciplinary techniques because she thought the questionnaire would be less threatening to people in that it was more anonymous. Once Lenton had established her sample and pretested her research strategy to ensure that she would obtain usable information, she set out to gather evidence that would allow her to evaluate the merits of three different hypotheses. A "cycle of violence" hypothesis holds that practices of child abuse are handed down from generation to generation. A "social-situational" hypothesis maintains that abusive parents may be reacting to stress and that stress itself may be linked to a family's socioeconomic status. Finally, a "cultural" hypothesis suggests that the attitudes of the family toward corporal punishment best differentiate the use of aggressive and nonaggressive behaviour in child discipline. Her research was designed to yield evidence that would help her decide which hypotheses were wrong. After analyzing the data, Lenton (1990: 176) concluded that "parents are inclined to use the disciplinary repertoires they learned when they were children—but only as long as certain current structural conditions are consonant with these repertoires." In particular, she pointed to structural conditions, such as unemployment in the family and low family income. To the extent that these structural conditions can be eliminated or reduced, the "cycle of family violence" can be arrested.

I mentioned earlier that the ability of sociologists to ask questions of people has both advantages and disadvantages. Lenton's (1990) work illustrates this. The physical punishment of children in the privacy of the home represents social activity that is not easily studied by any sociological method. Yet, as Lenton argues, child abuse is a public issue, not a private matter. By asking questions of people, she was able, first, to describe the extent of physical aggression used to discipline children and, second, to explain why some families were more likely than others were to use physical discipline. The disadvantage of asking questions of people, especially questions that people may find threatening, is that people may distort their responses. For example, Lenton found that in more than 75 percent of all families, children had been spanked or slapped in the previous year. Given current social norms about child abuse, this estimate of physical discipline is more likely to be an underestimate than an overestimate of such activity. If, however, different social classes subscribe to these norms to different degrees, people's responses to the 29 disciplinary measures might have altered. Lenton herself anticipated this criticism and asked people not just about their behaviour but also about their attitudes. She was therefore able to examine whether people from different social classes held different norms about child discipline.

This distinction between attitudes and behaviours, or words and deeds, is important. I always intend to give more money to charity than I do. Most people believe that littering is irresponsible, but most people still litter sometimes. When you read research focusing on people's attitudes, remember that thought is not easily translated into action. Interpreting the answers that people give to researchers' questions is complicated by more than this behaviour–attitude distinction. In asking people questions, either in interviews or on questionnaires, we must be careful about making assumptions (Guppy and Gray, 2008):

- *Do not assume that people understand what you are asking.* Language is notoriously ambiguous. How many friends did you see yesterday? This question may look simple at first, but people will differ in their understanding of "friends" and others will take "see" in the most literal way. The same words may mean different things to different people and in different contexts.

- *Do not assume that people know the answer to questions.* Most people do not want to appear ignorant when asked a question. This was illustrated nicely in a study of the prestige of occupations by Peter Pineo and John Porter (1967). They asked people to rate the prestige of two fictitious jobs: archaeopotrist and biologer. Most respondents cooperated and assigned these nonexistent jobs a prestige rating. When asked about their attitude on some issue, many people feel they must respond, even if they have no opinion on the topic or only a weakly formulated view.

- *Do not assume that people will admit the answer to themselves.* Alcoholics frequently claim that they can "quit any time." They refuse to admit that they are addicted. Similarly, child abusers may define themselves as strict disciplinarians. People routinely deceive themselves, sometimes only in minor ways, but "admitting the truth to ourselves" is a problem.

- *Do not assume that people will give valid answers to others.* People feel better about themselves when they are seen in a favourable light. In asking questions of people, researchers face the potential problem of "social desirability," because respondents may only give answers that reflect well on them. "What type of work do you do?" "Oh, I'm in public relations." Such a response could come from people working as telephone receptionists, tour guides, or corporate representatives.

Sociologists use many techniques in asking questions to gather valid and reliable evidence. For example, they will ask several questions rather than relying on a single question, use supplementary questions to expand on or clarify answers, and test questions before using them to improve any wording that is unclear or misleading (see Houtkoop, 2000).

Survey researchers do not focus only on individuals, although it is individuals who respond to survey questions. For example, it is possible to survey organizations, groups, corporations, electoral ridings, or job vacancies. Although people answer survey questions, the questions may apply to a unit or group of which someone is a member. For example, Janice Aruni (2004) studied private tutoring businesses by using a semi-structured interview survey to gather information about businesses that provide for-profit, supplementary instruction in academic subjects (e.g., K–12 school subjects).

I am making two points here. First, surveys can focus on different units of observation (individuals, businesses, workplaces, and so on). Second, individuals can act as informants to report information that pertains not to themselves but to some group or unit about which they have information. People can, for example, report on individual events (e.g., job vacancies), family composition, or corporate policy. Although each of these represents different units of observation, individuals are still answering the questions.

## OBSERVATIONAL STUDIES

Another method commonly used by sociologists to gather information is observation. Sometimes sociologists act as outside observers; at other times they act as insiders and engage in **participant observation.** The obvious advantage of observation is that sociologists can see what people actually do, rather than relying on reports of what people say they do. One disadvantage is that gaining access to private actions or events can be difficult. For example, Lenton might have tried to observe parents disciplining their children rather than relying on what parents told her they did. But entering people's homes to make such observations would have been difficult. Furthermore, her presence may have influenced the type of discipline parents used (the Hawthorne effect).

In observation studies, examining the intentionality of social action is especially important. Max Weber (1949 [1904]) was one of the first sociologists to address the issue of intention as a focus of social research. Weber argued that in interacting with other people, we draw on meanings. For example, the clothing we choose to wear speaks to others. We attribute meaning to bow ties, jack boots, Laura Ashley scarves, and baseball caps. None of this is done naively, because what we wear helps define who we are. Skateboarders, for example, dress in a particular style; they wear a uniform of sorts. Making social life intelligible is part of what Weber thought sociologists must address. To understand skateboarding, it is essential to see how skateboarders "define the situation." It is important to learn about their culture and to understand their systems of meaning. The aim of such research is not to explain the behaviour of skateboarders from an outside point of view, but to investigate their shared values and beliefs—their "worldview."

Weber maintained that causal logic can be used to accomplish some of what sociologists want to explain. He thought, however, that sociology also had to make intelligible the subjective basis of social action. Weber used the German word *Verstehen*, or understanding, to refer to this mode of sociological analysis. To understand the meaning of social action requires being able, at least in principle, to fully engage in the social activity. An example is the best way to illustrate such understanding.

Youth subculture in Canada seems less influential and less prominent than in such countries as the United Kingdom or the United States. Sometimes this observation is expressed in the claim that youth culture in Canada is derivative of trends south of the border or across the Atlantic. However, as skateboarders and squeegee kids have risen in profile, as youth unemployment has grown, and as the plight of young criminal offenders has been debated, understanding Canadian youth subcultures has become increasingly important. For that reason, Brian Wilson (2002) undertook a study of the rave subculture in Southern Ontario.

Banishing squeegee kids or skateboarders to some less visible place, be it jail, another neighbourhood, or "just off the streets," is one reaction to youth considered deviant. Denouncing ravers as for amphetamine drug use and social disturbance is another. What these suggestions mainly reflect is a misunderstanding of youth culture and its social context. Gaining an appreciation of the rave subculture was Wilson's intent. Among the issues he pursued were the reasons for people participating in this activity—put simply, was it the lure of adventure and excitement in the rave scene or was it a push from family or school that led to involvement with the rave subculture?

To gain an understanding of this process, he chose participant observation as one of his methodological strategies. He attended more than a dozen raves, hung out in rave record stores, sat in on rave radio sessions, and attended public meetings focused on raves. He observed the rave subculture by participating in it, by being a part of the party. By participating with ravers in rave parties and in rave settings, he was able to learn, first-hand, about their lifestyles, values, and aspirations.

However, Wilson did more than just participate. He also interviewed 37 ravers. He used what he calls "in-depth, open-ended, semi-formal interviews" (Wilson, 2002: 301). An in-depth interview means that he explored specific topics in great detail, often pursuing nuances and tangents. They were open-ended in the sense that he allowed respondents to range widely

In participant observation, it is often necessary to "look" the part. Brian Wilson participated in rave parties to study first-hand the rave subculture of Southern Ontario.
SOURCE: © Alexandru/Shutterstock.

in their replies. Finally, they were semi-structured in that he had a set of general issues he wanted to discuss, but he did not ask every person he interviewed exactly the same questions in exactly the same order. His goal was to have a meaningful conversation with each person, guided by his interest in the subject but also by their knowledge, willingness, and interest in pursuing specific details.

He also did not interview a representative sample of rave participants. Such a sample would be difficult to define since no one has a list of regular rave members. Instead, Wilson (2002) sought to talk with a variety of people and he was careful not to draw all the people he interviewed from the same place. Diversity was more important to him than was representativeness.

Finally, Wilson (2002) paid particular attention to written materials that form part of the rave scene, including magazines (hard copy and ezines), flyers promoting specific raves, and rave recordings (complete with commentary by the DJ).

These materials provided another window into how ravers communicate with one another, what they stress and emphasize.

In essence, Wilson used a cluster of methods, with observation being his primary source of data. Participant observation was critical in giving him personal access to the subculture. He supplemented this by reading material and listening to rave productions. Finally, he also interviewed people to test out his interpretations of the rave subculture. In particular, he used the interviews to assess his own impressions of the rave scene.

Ethnographers study people in their own environment or their own natural setting. Although **ethnography** includes the researcher being immersed in a group or a subculture, it also typically involves a cluster of methods, including both in-depth, unstructured interviewing and the analysis of documents. Speaking with key informants who are central to the group or the subculture is crucial (Cresswell, 1998).

In part, Wilson (2002) came to understand the rave subculture in generational terms. Youth rebellion against perceived autocratic organizations (school, family, the justice system) leads to a lifestyle of resistance—to escaping authority, flaunting convention, and disregarding conservative norms. But it is a resistance that is not about political change or efforts to alter organizational forms. It is a resistance focused mainly on creating an autonomous space in which social identity can be fostered, nourished, and supported. In this sense the subculture has a "magical" quality where the reality of other worlds can be transcended or bracketed. Contrast this with, for example, the student-led demonstrations in many countries pushing for stronger democratic governance—China, Indonesia, Iran, Korea—or the resistance to globalization seen at World Trade Organization meetings (Tanner, 2001).

Wilson (2002) was able to gain an understanding of the rave lifestyle by participating in the life of the group. By hanging out with them, he gained an in-depth appreciation of their activity. As a participant observer, he was able to ask many questions of many different group members, gradually drawing a sociological portrait of the rave scene. In particular, he was able to contrast various interpretations of the rave scene—was it about resistance, pleasure-seeking, or escapism? As his work progressed, Wilson was able to refine his understanding. He could cross-reference his observations by seeing how other group members

reacted to each new insight he gained, thereby increasing both the reliability and the validity of his conclusions. In short, he came to "define the situation" as rave participants themselves define it.

As with experiments, the external validity of ethnography can be problematic. How confident can Wilson be that his conclusions are not dependent on the impressions he formed from a single group of ravers? The intensive, in-depth nature of ethnography makes generalizability problematic. The key tradeoff is between the richly textured, "thick description" of ethnography and the insularity of detailed study of one or a few settings. Unlike survey researchers, ethnographers do not select different sets of random individuals or groups. The groups or settings they investigate are purposively chosen, sometimes because of easy access. For example, Wilson (2002) did not randomly choose rave subcultures; he made arrangements to participate with some rave scenes in Southern Ontario, and even then it was only one form of youth subculture. Imagine also, the ethical issues Wilson confronted (see also Haggerty, 2004).

Wilson's (2002) research portrays a subculture from its members' points of view. There are potential pitfalls of which Wilson had to be aware. First, how much did his presence influence his findings? Did people act differently when he was not around? In principle, there is no way to answer these questions, although ethnographers have tried to account for the effect of their presence in various ways. Some researchers conceal their research role; in effect, they try to be known to the other participants as one of them, rather than as a researcher (the ethics of this are dicey). Other researchers report that, with time, participants' awareness of their presence fades and they are treated as a member. Notice that this problem of presence is the Hawthorne effect in another guise. Whether in survey research, experiments, or observation studies, the researcher's presence can distort the domain of investigation. Researcher presence may undermine validity.

Beyond the potential pitfall of mere presence is the second problem: the findings of researchers may be ethnocentric. That is, researchers may impose their own values—their own worldviews—on the subject matter of their study. How do we know, for example, that Wilson (2002) depicted the ravers' point of view and not his own? One method of reducing personal bias is known as the "member test of validity" (Douglas, 1970: 21). For example, if the rave participants Wilson spoke with did not recognize themselves in his account—that is, if they saw Wilson's account as inauthentic—then we would worry about bias or distortion. Wilson was careful to "test" his tentative observations and insights on his informants by asking them questions and checking for observations that would falsify his impressions. Again, this is a research problem that extends well beyond ethnography. In fact, ethnography can be seen as the method that takes most seriously the task of understanding the members of a group from the members' point of view, stressing in particular their definition of the situation.

A third problem beyond presence and ethnocentrism is this: How do researchers know that the "tools" of their inquiry (e.g., questions, instructions, requests) did not in fact "create" or "generate" the resulting "findings"? For example, did Wilson (2002) create a finding by focusing attention on the ravers' resistance to dominant culture? Alternatively, did Lenton (1990) invent a relationship between social class and child discipline by asking questions that might be interpreted in different ways by the members of different classes? Again, this involves issues of reliability and validity. Lenton can be confident that she did not construct or create a pseudo-relationship between class and discipline to the extent that she shows that the basic pattern of findings is repeated across different questions about the disciplining of children. Wilson distinguished between (1) ravers' comments made in response to his questions and (2) statements his informants volunteered or that he overheard during his fieldwork. In addition, he used information provided to him by others on the margins of the rave scene: DJs, security guards, and radio station personnel. These alternative sources of information helped him avoid the problem of "creating" meaning. If ravers volunteered information that corroborated Wilson's impressions, and if these impressions were further reinforced by other knowledgeable observers, his faith in the authenticity of his account increased.

Not all observation can involve participation. Rik Scarce (2000) was interested in nature, and especially human domination of nature. His interest was in whether we could still speak of "wild salmon" or whether, like the cow and the dog, salmon were now domesticated. He argued that the very concept of "resource management" speaks to the idea of humans improving on nature, of scientists enhancing nature.

In studying the "domestication of salmon," Scarce (2000) used ethnographic methods. He could not participate as a scientist, but he could observe what scientists did, interview them, read their papers, and listen to their testimony at public inquiries. After doing all these things, he wrote an ethnographic account called *Fishy Business: Salmon, Biology, and the Social Construction of Nature*.

He was especially interested in how salmon had been manipulated to serve human ends. In the modern fishery, such phrases as *fish farming, aquaculture, genetic engineering, fish stocking*, and *fish hatcheries* are commonplace. We have engineered a new breed of salmon, mixing wild stocks and creating farmed salmon.

Scarce (2000) learned about this by hanging around fish hatcheries and asking questions, by visiting fishery research centres and watching what scientists were doing in their experiments, and by talking with scientists at their conventions and at public inquiries. He came to see the fish hatchery as a biological factory and to understand how salmon were increasingly "tooled" and "engineered." Observation was his staple method.

The believability of Scarce's (2000) research is enhanced by the fact that he observed events in their natural settings. He did not create a situation to see how people reacted (e.g., laboratory experiments) nor did he rely on people reporting on their own attitudes or behaviours (as in survey research). He was not a participant in the activity and so his involvement could not have distorted events (as may occur in participant observation). His presence as an observer may have influenced people, but he was often one of many observers (e.g., at scientific conferences and public inquiries).

## OTHER METHODS OF RESEARCH

### Historical Sociology

Many sociologists study social change. Max Weber, for example, attempted to explain the rise of capitalism by showing how Protestantism invigorated capitalist growth. Émile Durkheim was interested in how moral education helped to socially integrate a rapidly changing society. Both writers sought to answer sociological questions by examining historical change as evidence of significant social processes. Sociologists are more likely than historians are to use historical evidence to test theories of social change. Sociologists place less emphasis on history for history's sake.

Liliana Riga's (2008) work shows how sociologists make effective use of historical methods (see also Brym, 1978). Riga reexamined the nature of revolutionary Bolshevism among the leadership of the 1917–23 Russian Revolution. She wanted to understand the roots of the socialist ethic that inspired the revolution. This critical juncture in world history has often been contextualized within a framework stressing the class basis and "Russian" ethnicity of the revolutionary leadership. Riga argued that, in large measure, it was social inequalities made most visible by diverse ethnicities, and not so much by social class, that lay behind the radical mobilization. She arrived at this conclusion after systematically comparing the experiences of class and ethnicity among the revolutionary elite leaders.

Of course, these leaders have long since died, and so Riga (2008) could not interview or observe them. What she could do, however, was reconstruct their biographies. She used autobiographies, biographies, and memoirs, supplemented by police arrest records where ethnic backgrounds were often noted. She used sources predominantly constructed before the late 1920s. This latter refinement was essential when you recall that revolutionary leaders first had to mask their true identities in Tsarist Russia but even more importantly had to maintain social identities consistent with the *Soviet* revolutionary movement (especially problematic in the Stalinist era from 1922 to 1953).

The logic of Riga's (2008) analysis is not unlike that of other sociological research. Her key dependent variable is the revolutionary identity and politics of the Bolshevik elite. She wanted to know how important social class, ethnicity, and their intersection was to formation of this radical group. She therefore needed to measure social class and did so by examining such indicators as landholding, occupation, education, and relations to capital of individual members of the elite (and their parents). She also needed to measure ethnicity, and this too is complicated. In the end she used a mixture of birthplace, religion, and nationality. She concluded by noting that "ethnocultural identities were often more salient dimensions to many of their social experiences—and therefore to identities and politics—than was class."

## Documentary Analysis

Sociologists have also made useful contributions to knowledge through the examination of official documents. Scott Davies (2002) examined how education reformers consciously designed their recommendations about policy change to fit with historically current political priorities and cultural settings. He showed how three successive education commissions

in Ontario (1950, 1968, and 1995) each designed messages based on "progressive education," while simultaneously making policy recommendations that were diametrically opposed (e.g., some supported and some rejected standardized testing). Most change agents want to do "progressive" things. By carefully analyzing commission reports, Davies showed how the language of progressive education was reshaped by successive commissions to sell their brand of education reform.

Renisa Mawani (2003) examined archival documents, including colonial maps, to demonstrate a social process whereby geographical spaces were rendered "vacant" and therefore accessible to settlement and development. By showing how Aboriginal land use was made to vanish at some points, only to have later colonial authorities redraw the maps to show their presence, Mawani demonstrates the contested nature of landscape, both then and now. She also draws on legal documents, such as cases and statutes, to understand how the rule of law was also used to displace Aboriginal peoples and, again reflecting contestation, how it was used by Aboriginal peoples in resistance. As a third methodological strategy, she examined the ways in which an Aboriginal presence has been commemorated (e.g., via totem poles). By a careful comparison of the evidence offered through these documented sources, she argued that Vancouver's civic identity has shifted from a settler society to a postcolonial, multicultural city.

## Use of Official Statistics

Governments have a long history of collecting statistical data (Box 20.4). Government bureaucracies first began to collect statistics to help rulers determine both the size of their taxation base and the number of men they could put on the battlefield. Since then, the scope of government or official statistics has expanded and now includes information on births and deaths, unemployment rates, imports and exports, and so on. Sociologists have made good use of official statistics (see especially Haggerty, 2001).

Wortley and Tanner (2003) used official arrest records from Toronto to examine the extent of racial profiling in patterns of search and arrests practices. Detecting racial profiling requires determining that law enforcement officers use race as a significant factor in their decisions. That might sound easy, but it is incredibly complex because higher search or arrest rates among certain groups might be due to reasonable assumptions based on existing crime patterns, surveillance, or neighbourhood requests

Governments routinely use a survey of the entire population, called a census, to monitor key indicators of a country, such as the distribution of age cohorts, marital statuses, and so on. In June 2010, the federal government decided to change a critical component of the Canadian census. It decided to make the long-form census non-mandatory, keeping only a small number of questions on a short-form census, on the grounds that in previous censuses, a few Canadians had objected to being required to answer questions about ancestry, income, or housing characteristics.

The questions previously asked on the long-form census are now included in a *voluntary* survey to which Canadians are urged, but not required, to respond. This change might seem like allowing free choice to flourish by keeping the state out of the private business of individual citizens. However, a closer look reveals that the long-form census played a pivotal role in understanding a wide array of critical issues, from housing policy, to immigrant adaptation, to unemployment. A significant proportion of Canadians chose not to answer the long-form

census in 2011. This means that the validity of the voluntary responses are suspect.

The government uses a host of other surveys, such as the *Labour Force Survey* (LFS), to measure key social and economic indicators, such as the male–female wage rate differences and the unemployment rate. The validity of these other surveys was always measured in relation to the long-form census, for which the response rate was close to 100 percent because it was mandatory. Now, however, not only is the validity of the long-form census in question but so too is the validity of the LFS and every other survey that previously relied on the long-form census as a measurement standard (Green and Milligan, 2010). Furthermore, the long-form census contained questions about education, occupation, and income, along with questions about sex, ethnicity, and region. These and related questions allowed for a careful assessment of issues related to the Charter of Rights and Freedoms and other issues pertaining to social justice and fairness. Such assessments are now more difficult to achieve.

for greater police presence. Ruling out these latter factors, and other possible explanations for racial differentials in police decision making must occur before conclusions about racial bias in decision-making can be claimed.

Wortley and Tanner (2003) were following up on an investigative report published in the *Toronto Star* in October 2002. The *Star* analysis alleged that racial profiling did occur in Toronto, an accusation that police officials disputed. Wortley and Tanner, two sociologists at the University of Toronto, examined both the *Star's* original claims and the subsequent findings put forward by the Toronto Police Service. Wortley and Tanner cautiously claimed that their analyses of both official statistics and survey research were consistent with the findings of other international studies that racial profiling is a practice used by law enforcement officers (Wortley and Tanner, 2003, 2005).

The racial profiling example illustrates a central problem with official statistics. These statistics are not objective facts on which everyone agrees. The very definition of racial profiling makes it difficult to prove. Furthermore, different interest groups have much at stake over whether such practices occur (Gabor, 2004). The police are charged with the difficult task of upholding the law fairly and without

prejudice. Certain groups may request more police presence than do other groups and so what might appear to be racial profiling might actually reflect community requests. Official statistics require interpretation and such interpretation can be complex.

# THE ANALYSIS OF NUMERICAL DATA

Sociological evidence frequently comes in numerical form—that is, as quantifiable evidence (e.g., number of disciplinarians, arsons, or voters). Finding and interpreting patterns in numerical data is complex. To help in summarizing numerical information, social scientists routinely rely on statistical techniques. In this section, I briefly illustrate some key aspects of the process. I explore the following simple question: Do women and men earn the same income as a result of having the same levels of education? Men and women have, on average, similar levels of schooling. However, as a group, men have higher incomes than do women.

Notice the causal logic here. Education is hypothesized to affect income. However, since women and men earn different wages in the labour market, yet have similar levels of schooling, maybe the causal link between education and income differs by sex. Although I can present only an elementary analysis here, issues of a wage gap between the sexes are part of the continuing debate over pay equity, comparable worth, and employment equity, all important policy questions (Fortin, 2005).

To begin, we need to examine the link between education and income. I do this by using data from the *General Social Survey* (Statistics Canada, 2004), a survey conducted by Statistics Canada of a nationally representative sample of Canadians (24 951 randomly chosen Canadians, to be precise). Does education have a big effect on income? Table 20.1, called a contingency table or a cross-tabulation, gives us an answer. Education, the independent variable displayed across the top of the table, has three categories (low: high school or less; medium: some postsecondary education; and high: university degree or higher). For ease of presentation, annual personal income, the dependent variable, has two categories (low: personal income below $30 000 annually; and high: annual income at or above $30 000).

Notice first the table's arrangement. The title describes the two variables being related. The independent variable (education) is placed on the top of the table and its values are clearly delineated. Below each value for education is a column of numbers. The dependent variable (income) is arrayed on the side of the table, again with the value labels clearly shown. Beside each value of the dependent variable is a row of numbers. To illustrate, Table 20.1 shows

---

**TABLE 20.1**   THE RELATIONSHIP BETWEEN LEVEL OF EDUCATION AND INDIVIDUAL INCOME FOR PEOPLE AGED 25–34

**LEVEL OF EDUCATION**

| Income | Low | Medium | High | Row Totals |
|--------|-----|--------|------|------------|
| Low | 53% (333) | 45% (783) | 31% (358) | 42% (1473) |
| High | 47% (296) | 55% (939) | 69% (814) | 58% (2049) |
| Column Totals | 100% (629) | 100% (1722) | 100% (1172) | 100% (3522) |

SOURCE: Data is adapted from Statistics Canada, "SCF Public Use Microdata File: Income of Census Family Units," Catalogue no. 13M0001XDB, 19 August 1999.

---

that there are 333 people in the top left cell, the cell defined by a low level of education and a low income. At the intersection of each column and row is a table cell (there are six cells in Table 20.1 because row and column totals are ignored in counting the number of cells in a table).

The concept of a contingency table comes from the idea that the category into which a person falls on the dependent variable may be contingent on, or depends on, the category that a person occupies on the independent variable. If the hypothesis were true in this case, we would expect that, as we move across the education categories from low to high, the number of people receiving high incomes ought to rise. Do the data reveal this pattern? For people with low education, 296 had high incomes. For people with a high level of education, 814 had high incomes. These figures seem, at first glance, to support our expectation. Notice, however, that because of how education was categorized, 629 people had what I defined as low education, while 1172 had high education. Comparing the actual number of people in each cell is therefore misleading, because there are different numbers of people in each column.

Rather than focusing on the raw numbers, a better understanding of the patterns comes when we standardize the data. We need to ask what *percentage* of people in each education category had high incomes. By expressing the numbers as percentages—that is, by standardizing the data—it is much easier to see the patterns. So, 296 of 629 people in the low-education column had high incomes, or 47 percent (296 divided by 629 and then multiplied by 100). This tells us that for every 100 people with low education, 47 had high incomes. Making the same calculation for the high education column—(814/1172) × 100—we find that 69 percent of highly educated people earned high incomes (or 69 of every 100 people).

If you examine Table 20.1, you will see that the percentages are entered in the table. The actual number of people in each cell appears in parentheses. Notice that the percentages are calculated separately for each column, summing to 100 percent at the bottom of each column.

So, do relatively more people with high education receive high income in comparison with people with low education? Yes. Of every 100 people in the high-education column, 69 receive high income (69 percent), compared with only 47 of every 100 in the low-education column (47 percent). The difference between these two percentages (22 percent) is one measure of the strength of the relationship between education and income; the higher the percentage difference, the stronger the relationship.

In studying this table, some readers may have taken exception to my definitions of high and low incomes. Why should earning more than $30 000 be considered a high income? What is defined as low and high income is arbitrary. However, when I define the lows and highs of income and education differently and produce several different tables, the basic patterns in the tables do not change. This replication gives me confidence that my decisions about how to categorize the variables do not affect the results.

The evidence in Table 20.1 corroborates the first part of the question about the relationship between education and income. But how does gender figure into the pattern? Table 20.2 contains two contingency tables separated by a dotted vertical line. Here the question is how the link between education and income varies for women in comparison with men. Table 20.2 can be usefully thought of as Table 20.1 but with women and men separated into their own subtables.

For women, the basic pattern of Table 20.1 is repeated in Table 20.2, although the relationship between income and education is stronger: 66 percent of women with a high level of education are likely to have high income, whereas only 23 percent of women with a low level of education are likely to have a high income. The difference between these two cell percentages is 43 percent.

For men, although the pattern is similar, the percentage difference is smaller (and therefore the relationship between income and education is weaker). Of men with a high level of education, 73 percent have a high income, whereas for men with a low level of education, 64 percent have a high income. The percentage difference is only 9 percent. This suggests that for men, education level is not as important as it is for women in earning a high income. Contrasting the percentage differences between the two subtables in Table 20.2 gives us a way of comparing the strength of the link between income and education for women versus men. A more complex method of investigating the causal linkages among gender, education, and income relies on multiple regression (see Box 20.5).

So what do we learn from this analysis? We learn first, from Table 20.1, that people with more education are likely to earn higher incomes. Second, from Table 20.2 we learn that this is especially true for women, in that for men education level has less of an impact on earning high incomes than is the case for women (remember only people between 25 and 34 are included in the tables).

Why is the link between education and income different for women and men? First, men without university education may still earn high pay in resource and manufacturing jobs. That could account for the difference. Second, the labour force is still at least partially differentiated into "male" and "female" jobs, and education level may be more important for finding work in traditional female jobs than in certain

**TABLE 20.2**  THE RELATIONSHIP BETWEEN LEVEL OF EDUCATION, INDIVIDUAL INCOME, AND GENDER FOR PEOPLE AGED 25–34

| | WOMEN LEVEL OF EDUCATION | | | | MEN LEVEL OF EDUCATION | | | |
| --- | --- | --- | --- | --- | --- | --- | --- | --- |
| **Income** | Low | Medium | High | **Total** | Low | Medium | High | **Total** |
| Low | 78% | 60% | 34% | (893) | 37% | 32% | 27% | (580) |
| High | 23% | 40% | 66% | (778) | 64% | 68% | 73% | (1270) |
| Totals | 100% | 100% | 100% | | | 100% | 100% | 100% |
| | (252) | (822) | (599) | (1671) | (377) | (900) | (573) | (1851) |

NOTE: Column and row totals are not equal for women because of rounding.

SOURCE: Data from Statistics Canada (2004), *General Social Survey*.

## BOX 20.5    INTRODUCING STATISTICAL IDEAS ABOUT REGRESSION ANALYSIS

In further exploring the linkage among gender, education, and income, I would want to introduce a series of alternative explanations. Testing each of these ideas by using contingency tables would be difficult because, with so many possible confounding variables, the tables would quickly become huge and unwieldy. An alternative to contingency-table analysis is regression analysis. The basic idea of regression can be explained most easily in graphic form.

Figure 20.2 is a graph with years of schooling arrayed along the horizontal axis (x-axis) and annual income displayed along the vertical axis (y-axis). On this graph, I can plot where each person in the sample falls. In other words, I can choose someone from the sample and move along the x-axis until I come to the level of education attained by the selected person. I can then proceed up from there, now using the y-axis as a guide, until I reach the level of the same person's annual income. The point that I reach is the intersection of two perpendicular lines, one drawn vertically from the x-axis (at the person's level of education) and the other drawn horizontally from the y-axis (at that person's annual income). For each person in the sample, I can locate exactly where these two lines fall in the graph and place a mark at the appropriate spot. The result, similar to what I have depicted, is a scatter plot.

A scatter plot can be summarized statistically using regression techniques. To summarize the relationship between education and income, a straight line can be drawn through the data points in such a way that the distance from each point to the line is minimized. If all points lie exactly on the line, the fit of the line to the data will be perfect. The farther the points are from the best-fitting line, the poorer is the ability to use a straight line to summarize the information and the weaker is the association between the two variables. The strength of association between two variables in a scatter plot is given by the correlation coefficient ($r$). The value of $r$ can vary from $-1$ (a perfectly inverse relationship or negative association) to 0 (no association) to $+1$ (a perfectly proportionate relationship or positive association). The farther $r$ is from 0, the stronger the association. The correlation coefficient is, then, analogous to the percentage difference in tables.

With the education and income scatter plot, I can capture the central characteristics of the best-fitting line with two numbers. One number captures the slope of the line and tells how much vertical increase (or decrease) occurs in the line for every unit of horizontal change along the x-axis. Using my example, for every additional year of schooling, how much does annual income increase? An easy way to remember this is to think of this number as the rise (income increase) over the run (change in years of schooling). A second number tells at what point the line intersects the y-axis. If I have a perfectly fitting line, the equation for a straight line can be expressed as $y = a + bx$, where $x$ and $y$ are values on the two axes of the graph, $a$ is the point at which the line crosses the y-axis, and $b$ is the slope of the line.

What I have described here is a statistical technique known as simple linear regression, for one independent and one dependent variable. To explore the alternative interpretations for the link among gender, education, and income that I offered earlier, you would need to use multiple regression, where one dependent variable can be linked to a series of independent variables. This data analysis approach has been instrumental in shaping social policy and refining sociological knowledge.

### FIGURE 20.2    HYPOTHETICAL RELATIONSHIP BETWEEN EMPLOYMENT INCOME AND YEARS OF SCHOOLING

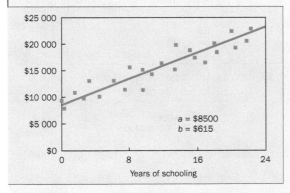

$a = \$8500$
$b = \$615$

Years of schooling

male jobs (e.g., nursing versus oil rigging). Third, women and men could be working different numbers of hours per week, or weeks per year, and these differences could be related to both education and income. Many other possible explanations exist, and further research is essential to sort them out (Drolet, 2011; Fortin, 2005; Guppy and Davies, 1998).

## THE FUTURE OF SOCIAL RESEARCH

Social research involves systematically studying the social world. The aim of such research activity is to develop explanations and understandings of social patterns beneficial to improving the human condition.

Today, it is becoming increasingly obvious that we need to find innovative ways of organizing and running human affairs. Starvation, environmental degradation, terrorism, and social injustice are among the many social problems we must confront. Solutions require adequate explanations for, and understandings of, how these problems arise and persist.

Earlier in the chapter, I outlined several sources of knowledge: common sense, religious faith, and science. Although these forms of knowledge share certain features (e.g., they are all imperfect), scientific reason encourages a set of practices, open review and critical skepticism, which together work to reduce error.

Another way of emphasizing what is distinctive about the scientific method is to compare how social research differs from the work of other professionals who concentrate on similar social issues (e.g., the environment, gender relations). For example, what differentiates the work of documentary filmmakers, novelists, or journalists from that of social researchers? I have emphasized three features of scientific research that, in combination, separate it from the work of these other professionals:

1. Research results are subjected to the critical skepticism of other scientists.
2. Social theory guides, either directly or indirectly, the evidence gathered.
3. Evidence is systematically collected and analyzed.

Although some of these features are found in the work of other professionals, such as journalists, all three features are found in good social research. Replication and reproducibility have high currency in science as ways of encouraging skepticism. Good research contributes new ideas or evidence to our common stock of social theory. Finally, good research publicly displays the careful collection and analysis of evidence.

These principles are a feature of all good research, but the methods that sociologists use to pursue their goal of explaining and understanding the social world take many forms. This diverse array of methods, including observing, questioning, and experimenting, offers sociologists many ways of inquiring responsibly and ethically about the social world. Each method has different strengths and weaknesses, which makes the choice of research strategy dependent on the sociological question being asked.

Social science research will continue to contribute to knowledge of the world around us. Research on the environment, reproductive technology, multiculturalism, violence, and social-support networks all point to practical ways in which human problems can be influenced by research findings. Effective policy solutions that benefit all people require sound social research.

## SUMMARY

1. Research methods are ways of gathering evidence to test suppositions about the world. Behind the various techniques we use (e.g., experiments, interviews) lie important assumptions about facts, objectivity, and truth.

2. Science is one of several sources of knowledge. Like other kinds of knowledge, scientific knowledge can be wrong. However, unlike other ways of knowing, science incorporates explicit methods designed to reduce error in what is currently accepted as scientific knowledge. Evidence must be systematically collected, and rigorously and publicly evaluated.

3. Good science integrates strong theory and robust research. Theories are ideas about how

the world works or claims about how to explain or understand the recurring, patterned nature of human activity.

4. Evidence is crucial to developing, revising, or discarding theoretical claims. In comparison with the evidence available in the natural sciences, the evidence available to social scientists presents added complexity because of the meaningful character of human social action. People, unlike molecules, assign meaning to their actions and to the actions of others.

5. Sociologists have devised many useful methods for obtaining evidence about the social world. Observing and questioning people are the two principal techniques, although each of them

is conducted by using a variety of formats, including experiments, surveys, participant observation, and interviews.

6. Good research adds to our knowledge of the world. Such knowledge expands our opportuni-

ties and options. Sociological knowledge helps either in solving social problems or, by sensitizing us to the human condition, expanding our social horizons.

## QUESTIONS TO CONSIDER

1. The teaching effectiveness of faculty members in university and college departments could be evaluated in various ways. Suggest different sociological methods of doing such an evaluation and comment on the strengths and weaknesses of each approach.

2. Lenton (1990) chose to examine issues of child abuse by focusing on child discipline and surveying parents about their disciplinary techniques. Suggest alternative designs for her study, commenting on the strengths and weaknesses of the various approaches, including important ethical considerations.

3. Policymakers frequently debate raising or lowering age restrictions on activities, such as driving a car, drinking alcoholic beverages, or voting. Suggest how you might design a study that could provide evidence about the possible consequences of either raising or lowering one of these age restrictions.

4. Immigration levels remain a contentious issue in Canada. Construct a short series of interview questions designed to assess people's knowledge of current immigration practices. Ask these questions of your friends or family. Ask how many immigrants enter Canada and from which countries they originate. Compare your findings with official statistics that are available in government

publications at your college or university or on the Internet. How might you explain the patterns you discovered?

5. Discuss the claim that "facts speak for themselves." What problems exist in making this claim? Conversely, what problems exist in claiming that facts do not speak for themselves? Consider especially the claim that we need firm standards against which to evaluate ideas or theoretical claims. Is it possible to establish such standards?

6. At parties, people are expected to be relaxed. Parties are times for having fun, for stepping outside the routines of school or work. However, phrases like "party pooper" or "killjoy" suggest that parties have rules and that violators of such rules can be ostracized. Others are glorified as "party animals," implying that some people take to partying better than others. How might you engage in a participant observation study to investigate these hunches systematically? Do such categories as "party animal" or "party pooper" exist, and, if so, how are they understood? Do "rules" exist at a party even though parties are in very important ways "escapist"? How might a sociologist seek to understand party life at your college or university?

## GLOSSARY

A **causal relationship** (p. 499) involves a relationship between two variables in which change or variation in one variable produces change or variation in a second variable. Four criteria are essential to establishing a causal relation between two variables: association, time ordering, nonspuriousness, and theoretical rationale.

The **dependent variable** (p. 502) is a variable that is assumed to depend on or be caused by one or more other variables (independent variables); it is the variable that is the effect, or outcome, in a cause–effect relationship.

**Ethnography** (p. 510) is the detailed description of a particular culture or way of life, or the written results of a participant-observation study.

An **experiment** (p. 501) is a controlled test of the causal effects of a particular variable or set of variables on a dependent or outcome variable.

An **explanation** (p. 498) is an account of the causal logic that shows how and why variables influence one another.

**External validity** (p. 504) is the generalizability of a particular finding from the study group to a larger population; the relevance of conclusions for a larger population; or the ability to infer that the results of a study are representative of processes operating in a broader population.

In the **Hawthorne effect** (p. 504), people involved in a study may be influenced by the very process of being studied; the study has an impact on the subjects of the study.

A **hypothesis** (p. 502) is a knowledge claim or hunch about how the world works; it is a testable statement, derived from a theory, about the relationship between two variables.

The **independent variable** (p. 502) is a variable that is presumed to affect or influence other variables; it is the causal variable.

An **interview** (p. 504) is a method of collecting information by asking people questions, either in person or over the telephone. Interviews range from highly structured (preset questions in a fixed order) to loosely structured (topic guidelines, but no prescribed question wording).

In **meaningful action** (p. 497), human action, as distinct from physical behaviour, occurs with specific intentions or reasons in mind. The uncontrollable tic in a person's eye is physical behaviour, which differs from that of a person who is winking at someone, where intention or purpose is central to understanding what is happening. Most human activity is meaningful action, or social action.

**Measurement** (p. 505) comprises procedures for assigning numbers to observations according to preset rules; it is the act of finding data or information relevant to theoretical concepts.

**Objectivity** (p. 496) is the attempt to minimize the effect of personal bias on research results or the idea of impartiality, of "fair hearings." Objectivity is an ideal enhanced by the work of any single researcher being open to the critical scrutiny of others. Objectivity as complete impartiality is a myth.

In **participant observation** (p. 508), the study of social life involves the participation of the researcher, to varying degrees, in the activities of the group under investigation; it attempts to give an "insider's" account of a particular way of life or cultural system.

**Randomization** (p. 502) is a procedure used in experiments to assign test subjects to experimental conditions on the basis of chance.

**Reliability** (p. 505) is the consistency of measurements and the ability to reproduce the same measurements on repeated occasions.

**Sampling** (p. 505) is the process of selecting units from a larger population. Random sampling involves the selection of representative units (e.g., people, organizations) from a population (e.g., all Canadians, voluntary organizations in a city). Samples can be selected by probability (where every unit has a non-zero chance of selection) or nonprobability (where chance does not enter into the selection of sample units).

A **self-administered questionnaire** (p. 504) is a method of collecting information by having people record their own answers to preset questions.

**Spurious relationships** (p. 498) involve an incorrect inference about the causal relations between variables.

**Understanding** (p. 499) is the ability to provide a definition of a situation that members of a culture find authentic and valid.

**Validity** (p. 505) is the relevance or accuracy of measurement in relation to the theoretical concept that it is supposed to measure.

A **variable** (p. 502) is something that varies or an attribute or event that can take on more than one value (e.g., unemployment rates, age, sex).

## SUGGESTED READING

Babbie, Earl and Lucia Benaquisto. (2009). *Fundamentals of Social Research,* 2nd ed. Toronto: Thomson Nelson. Babbie and Benaquisto provide the best general account of research methods available in sociology.

Becker, Howard. (1998). *Tricks of the Trade: How to Think about Your Research While You're Doing It.* Chicago: University of Chicago Press. Written by one of sociology's best qualitative researchers, Becker's book discusses how to think about research and is valuable to both qualitative and quantitative researchers.

Cresswell, John. (2009). *Research Design: Qualitative, Quantitative, and Mixed Methods Approaches,* 3rd ed. Thousand Oaks, CA: Sage Publications.

This text offers an excellent, balanced view of the strengths and weaknesses of various research designs and is a useful guide to conducting good research by using multiple methods.

Denzin, Norman. (1997). *Interpretative Ethnography: Ethnographic Practices for the 21st Century.* Thousand Oaks, CA: Sage. Denzin provides a good general introduction to the practices and debates of qualitative research.

Guppy, Neil and George Gray. (2008). *Successful Surveys: Research Methods and Practice,* 4th ed. Toronto: Thomson Nelson. This is a practical guidebook to developing research designs and using effective survey research techniques. The authors cover questionnaires and interviews.

## NOTES

1. Black swans, native to Australia, were unknown to Europeans before exploration. The idea that all swans are white is thus similar to the idea that Earth is the central body in the solar system—a claim once understood to be true but now thought to be false.

2. Please do not overinterpret this claim. As a community, we have frequently treated humans as exceptional. We have distanced ourselves from nature. Our theories and actions often evince a "control of nature" paradigm. Highlighting differences between the subject matter of the natural and the social sciences is complicated. For example, monkeys make friends with zoologists and, when studied, may react in similar ways as humans. It is important to consider in what ways the study of people by people may add complexity to research, and how this in turn may stimulate us to think differently about how people study non-humans. For example, issues of animal rights and environmental ethics raise questions about our traditionally human-centric view of the world. Perhaps bacteria do blush and we are just too ignorant to notice!

# Committing
# Sociology

# 1

# The Sociological Eye

## RANDALL COLLINS

*This short essay outlines the essence of sociology's core as a discipline. Collins, one of sociology's leading contemporary theorists, generates excitement about sociology by focusing attention on the lens, or eye, of sociology. He discusses the way it concentrates its particular attention on reality, from analyses of basic social interaction to larger social institutions and social structure, which can all be dynamically captured by the everyday life observer. Hopefully, after taking this course, you, too, will share in his excitement about the unique perspective that sociology offers. How is the sociological eye different from the commonsensical eye? What makes the sociological perspective unique?*

Does sociology have a core? Yes, but it is not an eternal essence; not a set of texts or ideas, but an activity.

This is not the same as saying the discipline of sociology will always exist. Sociology became a self-conscious community only in the mid-1800s, about five generations ago, and has been an academic discipline for four generations or less. Disciplines go in and out of existence. The very concept of disciplinary specialization as we know it was created in the Napoleonic period at the time of reorganization of the French Academies, as Johan Heilbron has shown in *The Rise of Social Theory* (1995). There is no guarantee that any particular discipline will remain fixed. Biology, a discipline first recognized by Auguste Comte, has repeatedly shifted its boundaries, combining with physics and chemistry, or spinning off genetics and ecology, making up a shifting array of new fields. Discoveries do not respect administrative boundary lines. Major advances in research or theory tend to pull followers after them, who institutionalize themselves in turn for a while in some organizational form, if only until the next big round of discovery.

SOURCE: Randall Collins, "The Sociological Eye," *Contemporary Sociology* 27(1), 1998. Reprinted by permission of the American Sociological Association and the author.

7

In much the same way, sociologists keep forming hybrid communities on their borders, for example, with economics, literary theory, or computer science. In recent decades, hybrid disciplines have split off from, overlapped with, or encroached upon sociology as criminal justice, ethnic studies, gender studies, management, science and technology studies (i.e., what was once "sociology of science"), and no doubt more to come. There is nothing to lament in this. A glance at the history of long-term intellectual networks, and of academic organizations, shows that branching and recombining are central to what drives intellectual innovation. (The pattern of such long-term networks is documented in my book, *The Sociology of Philosophies* [1998].)

Sociology, like everything else, is a product of particular historical conditions. But I also believe we have hit upon a distinctive intellectual activity. Its appeal is strong enough to keep it alive, whatever its name will be in the future and whatever happens to the surrounding institutional forms. The lure of this activity is what drew many of us into sociology. One becomes hooked on being a sociologist. The activity is this: It is looking at the world around us, the immediate world you and I live in, through the sociological eye.

There is a sociology of everything. You can turn on your sociological eye no matter where you are or what you are doing. Stuck in a boring committee meeting (for that matter, a sociology department meeting), you can check the pattern of who is sitting next to whom, who gets the floor, who makes eye contact, and what is the rhythm of laughter (forced or spontaneous) or of pompous speechmaking. Walking down the street, or out for a run, you can scan the class and ethnic pattern of the neighborhood, look for lines of age segregation, or for little pockets of solidarity. Waiting for a medical appointment, you can read the professions and the bureaucracy instead of old copies of *National Geographic*. Caught in a traffic jam, you can study the correlation of car models with bumper stickers or with the types of music blaring from radios. There is literally nothing you can't see in a fresh way if you turn your sociological eye to it. Being a sociologist means never having to be bored.

But doesn't every discipline have its special angle on all of reality? Couldn't a physicist see the laws of motion everywhere, or an economist think of supply curves of whatever happens in everyday life? I still think sociology is uniquely appealing in this respect. What physicists or chemists can see in everyday life is no doubt rather banal for them, and most of their discoveries in recent centuries have been made by esoteric laboratory equipment. Fields like economics, it is true, could probably impose an application of some of their theories upon a great many things. But for virtually all disciplines, the immediate world is a sideshow. For sociologists, it is our arena of discovery, and the source at which we renew our energies and our enthusiasm....

All of us who are turned on by sociology, who love doing what we do, have the sociological eye. It is this that gives us new theoretical ideas and makes alive the theories that we carry from the past. The world a sociologist can see is not bounded by the immediate microsituation. Reading the newspaper, whether the business section or the personal ads, is for us like an astronomer training his or her telescope on the sky. Where the ordinary reader is pulled into the journalistic mode, reading the news through one or another political bias or schema of popular melodrama, the sociological eye sees suggestions of social movements mobilizing or winding down, indications of class domination or conflict, or perhaps the organizational process whereby just this kind of story ended up in print, defined as news. For us, novels depict the boundaries of status groups and the saga of social mobility, just as detective stories show us about backstages. Whatever we read with the sociological eye becomes a clue to the larger patterns of society, here or in the past. The same goes for the future: Today's sociologists are not just caught up in the fad of the Internet; they are already beginning to look at it as another frontier for sociological discovery.

I want to claim, in short, that all kinds of sociologists, microethnographers and statisticians, historical comparativists and theorists alike, have the sociological eye. I think that virtually all of the most productive sociologists among us do. We all went through a gestalt switch in our way of looking at the world, sometime early in our careers, that was the key moment in our initiation into sociology. Turn on the sociological eye and go look at something. Don't take someone else's word for what there is to see, or some common cliché (even a current trendy one), above all not a media-hype version of what is there; go and see it yourself. Make it observationally strange, as if you'd never seen it before. The energy comes back. In that way, I suspect, sociologists are probably more energized by their subject matter than practitioners of virtually any other discipline.

## REFERENCES

Collins, Randall. 1998. *The Sociology of Philosophies*. Cambridge, MA: Harvard University Press.

Heilbron, Johan. 1995. *The Rise of Social Theory*. Minneapolis: University of Minnesota Press.

# CREDITS FOR VOLUME 1 and VOLUME 2 of COMMIT SOCIOLOGY